Corporate Citizen?

Corporate Citizen?

An Argument for the Separation of Corporation and State

Ciara Torres-Spelliscy

Associate Professor of Law
Stetson University College of Law

Carolina Academic Press
Durham, North Carolina

LCCN: 2016940496
Print ISBN: 978-1-6328-4726-3
e-Book ISBN: 978-1-6328-4727-0

CAROLINA ACADEMIC PRESS, LLC
700 Kent Street
Durham, North Carolina 27701
Telephone (919) 489-7486
Fax (919) 493-5668
www.cap-press.com

Printed in the United States of America

Contents

Acknowledgments

Thank you to Stetson University College of Law, which provided me with the time and the resources to write this book, including a scholarship grant. Thank you to all of my interviewees for taking time out of your extraordinarily busy lives to talk to me. Portions of this book first appeared as pieces on the Brennan Center's Blog. Thank you to the Brennan Center for giving these pieces a first home and an audience.

This book would not have been possible without my research assistants at Stetson Law School including Max Holzbaur, Andrew Graf, Jordan Sager, Raphael Rashkin, Alex Farris, Courtney Chaipel, Kevin Crews, Adam LaBonte, Christian Moriarty, and Carolina Suazo. But most especially I must thank Elizabeth Harbaugh, Cherylin Blitch, and Meagan Salisbury who helped me finish this book. I would also like to thank Librarian Sally Waters for pulling citations long after business hours were over. Thank you to Professors Elizabeth Pollman, Atiba Ellis, Tamara Piety, Jordan Singer, Ellen Podgor, Glynn Torres-Spelliscy, as well as attorneys Shane Spelliscy, Jeffrey D. Clements, Ron Fein, Heather McCready, Elizabeth Kennedy, and Jack Ucciferri for reading chapters and giving me invaluable feedback on earlier drafts. And finally, I would not have been able to dedicate the time to traveling to interviews, writing, and research and hours of editing without the loving support of my husband and my son to whom this book is dedicated.

About the Author

Ciara Torres-Spelliscy is an Associate Professor of Law at Stetson University College of Law and a Fellow at the Brennan Center for Justice at NYU School of Law. She is a former member of the Board of Directors of the National Institute on Money in State Politics and a member of the Board of Directors of the Mertz Gilmore Foundation.

Corporate Citizen?

Prologue

"Money to get power, power to protect money" was the motto of the Medici family. It seems sadly relevant to American politics today. Those powerful elites ruled Florence for centuries. We can't wait that long.
—Jacob S. Hacker & Nathaniel Loewentheil[1]

The change started early in the year—on Thursday, January 21, 2010.

On that fateful day, campaign finance lawyers around the country were, as the Supreme Court watchers say, "waiting for Lyle." Lyle is Lyle Denniston, the venerable reporter for *SCOTUS Blog*, a webpage that keeps meticulous track of what is happening at the U.S. Supreme Court. Because the high court does not allow cameras inside, getting information from Lyle is often the fastest way to find out if the Supreme Court has ruled.

Like other lawyers in the field, I hit refresh on my computer again. And again. And again. The case we were waiting for was *Citizens United v. Federal Election Commission*. What hung in the balance was the power of corporations to spend in politics.

This caused pangs of déjà vu. Six months before, in June 2009, the election law world was also "waiting for Lyle" to report on *Citizens United*. But the Court, in a surprise move, ordered the case to be re-argued.[2] Ordering re-argument is rare, but often signals that the Justices realize the case presents a particularly weighty issue. *Brown v. Board of Education* (which ended segre-

---

1. Jacob S. Hacker & Nathaniel Loewentheil, *How Big Money Corrupts the Economy*, 27 Democracy (2013), http://www.democracyjournal.org/27/how-big-money-corrupts-the-economy.php?page=all.

2. Citizens United v. FEC, 558 U.S. 310 (2010) (Argued Mar. 24, 2009—Reargued Sept. 9, 2009).

gation in public schools)[3] and *Roe v. Wade* (which granted U.S. women the right to an abortion) were both argued twice.[4]

During the summer of 2009, a baker's dozen of amici briefs, including one I signed, were filed at the Supreme Court in favor of keeping the campaign finance restrictions on corporations. I was in the Supreme Court when *Citizens United* was reargued on September 9, 2009. I watched as U.S. Solicitor General Elena Kagan argued the case on behalf of the United States. (A year later she would become a Supreme Court Justice herself.) In her brief, she argued that if Citizens United won, this could present a problem of corporate managers using "other people's money."[5] As Solicitor General Kagan drily noted in her brief, founding father "John Hancock pledged his own fortune; when the CEO of John Hancock Financial uses corporate-treasury funds for electoral advertising, he pledges someone else's."[6]

For months we waited, until January 21, 2010, when *SCOTUS Blog* finally linked to the text of the *Citizens United* opinion. I sat in my office reading as quickly as I could. The full opinion with dissenting and concurring opinions is 183 pages. The worst I feared had happened. The *Citizens United* opinion made me sick to my stomach. Hairs on my temple that had been dark brown, turned grey.

Corporations had just won the First Amendment right to spend as much money as they wished on political ads in American elections. Laws dating back more than 60 years at the federal level, and more than a century in some states, were all invalidated. As corporate governance expert Robert A.G. Monks articulated, "[w]e need a new language after *Citizens United*. It's not a continuation of the past. We have something quite new. The Supreme Court made it impossible for any state to limit corporate involvement in politics."[7]

I cared about this case not just because I was an election lawyer at the time. I also cared because I had started my legal career as a corporate lawyer. For years, I had pondered about the proper role of corporate money in America's democracy. And two weeks after the Supreme Court ruled, I put out a policy paper from the Brennan Center for Justice at NYU School of Law about how the rul-

---

3. Brown v. Board of Education, 347 U.S. 483 (1954) (Argued Dec. 9–11, 1952—Reargued Dec. 7–9, 1953).

4. Roe v. Wade, 410 US 113 (1973) (Argued Dec.13, 1971—Reargued Oct. 11, 1972).

5. LOUIS BRANDEIS, OTHER PEOPLE'S MONEY, AND HOW THE BANKERS USE IT (1914).

6. Supplemental Reply Brief for Appellee, Citizens United v. FEC, No. 08-205 at 7 (2009).

7. Interview with Robert A.G. Monks (Aug. 17, 2015).

ing could impact corporate shareholders.[8] (I had been working on the topic for two years as the case worked its way through the judiciary, which was why it was ready to go so soon after *Citizens United* was handed down from the bench.)

The months that followed were a whirlwind of activity as I was invited to testify before Congress and state legislatures. I also spoke at universities across the land. One thing became crystal clear as I traveled from capitol to capitol and one lecture hall to the next: for the ubiquity of corporations in Americans' daily lives, there was widespread confusion in the audiences I met (including some lawmakers) about what corporations were and how the Supreme Court had changed their role. That is one motivation for writing this book. I want more people to understand what corporations are and how their role in our democracy is evolving. And I also wanted to share the knowledge that I have learned from the many people I have met along the way in my journeys across America—from Trevor Potter (better known as Stephen Colbert's lawyer) to Justice James Nelson, a retired member of the Montana Supreme Court, to Dr. Gretchen Goldman, a brilliant young scientist who works at the Center for Science and Democracy at the Union of Concerned Scientists.

I hope that this book will be a way for readers to get out of their respective silos and to look at what corporations *writ large* are up to. Most of us are stuck in a narrow part of the world—we see only the walls of our cubicle, or if we're a little luckier, the walls of our office. We work in sub-specialties, a type of accounting, a branch of law, a field of medicine, a particular language of computer coding, an artistic discipline, a sport.

But all the while, as we toil away at our day jobs, even if our day job is the law, the legal landscape continues to evolve in courts across the United States, whether we notice it or not. This is particularly true of the law that applies to corporations. Any small piece of this story may not even be covered by the press—until there is a crisis—and then the change in the status of corporations, newly endowed with more rights, is reported as if it came out of nowhere. When all along, lawyers pushing for more rights for corporations have been racking up quiet wins, slightly out of view of busy citizens. The lawyers expanding corporate rights have a clearer view of the big picture. The average citizen may only get a glimpse of what is happening in an article here, a *NPR* piece there, or a sardonic comedy bit on late night TV.

The bigger picture is this: over the past decade, building on previous legal precedent from centuries before, corporations—especially large, wealthy,

8. Ciara Torres-Spelliscy, *Corporate Campaign Spending: Giving Shareholders a Voice* (Brennan Ctr. 2010).

multinational corporations—are getting more legal rights and fewer legal responsibilities. Indeed, many corporations seem to treat the rights and responsibilities that usually attach as a package to ordinary citizens, as a buffet. While an average American citizen (the human variety) expects to abide by America's laws, pay taxes, and register for the selective service (for men), many corporations seem to have no compunction with cherry-picking the choicest rights and trying mightily to shirk as many responsibilities as possible from human rights liabilities, to environmental responsibilities, to taxes.

Corporations have long held a panoply of rights from contract rights, to property rights, to due process rights. But the rights that I will focus on in this book are of a narrow variety: American First Amendment rights, including commercial speech, political speech, and religious rights. Over the past 40 years, courts have methodically been expanding First Amendment rights for all corporations from a one-person sole proprietorship to the largest multinational.

The explanation of how corporations have fewer responsibilities is a more complex story. For one, not all corporations are in the business of avoiding responsibilities. Rather, the corporations doing this and making arguments in court allowing them to do this tend to be the largest firms on the planet (think big oil companies, big tobacco companies, and the largest food companies). At times, courts are excusing multinational corporations from responsibilities—like refusing to require particular corporations to stand trial for human rights abuses committed abroad. In other cases, certain large corporations are legally evading the responsibility to pay taxes in the United States through elaborate tax schemes. In still other instances, some corporations are avoiding criminal liability because of the reluctance of prosecutors to hold them accountable. And in the field of environmental stewardship, certain corporations are capturing regulators and exploiting exemptions from federal laws they lobbied for and got.

In many cases dealing with human citizens, the Supreme Court couples rights and responsibilities, such as in *Nebraska Press Association,* where Chief Justice Warren Burger noted, "[t]he extraordinary protections afforded by the First Amendment carry with them something in the nature of a fiduciary duty to exercise the protected rights responsibly[.]"[9] More recently, Justice Anthony Kennedy said "[r]esponsibilities, as well as rights, enhance the dignity and integrity of the person."[10] But this is not the Supreme Court's approach when it

---

9. Nebraska Press Ass'n v. Stuart, 427 U.S. 539, 560 (1976) (Burger, C.J.).
10. United States v. Windsor, 133 S. Ct. 2675, 2694 (2013) (Kennedy, J.).

comes to corporations. For corporations, rights are becoming decoupled from responsibilities.

For those who are concerned about these events, you are not alone. There have been strong reactions from investors, customers, entrepreneurs and lawmakers, which I will discuss in the following chapters. This book will also offer solutions from courts realizing they are treading down the wrong path, to customers flexing their buying power, to investors using their voice on corporate proxies, to lawmakers improving rules to create more transparency, to entrepreneurs abandoning older corporate models that privilege profits over all else.

In Part I, this book will explore the question of whether corporations are citizens at all, looking at the history of the expansion of corporations in American history; the story of corporations' gaining political influence, including some episodes of venal illegality; as well as the U.S. Supreme Court's uneven record of granting corporations rights. In Part II, the book will discuss the expansion of corporate rights in the hands of the Roberts Supreme Court and the D.C. Circuit, including *Citizens United, R.J. Reynolds, NAM v. SEC, Sorrell v. IMS Health,* and *Hobby Lobby.* In Part III, the book will consider the ways in which certain corporations avoid responsibilities, from avoiding taxes while receiving taxpayer subsidies; avoiding environmental responsibilities; avoiding human rights responsibilities; to avoiding criminal prosecution. When corporations are criticized for being poor citizens often the critique is centered on their negative environmental impacts. But they are also criticized for enabling human rights violations, skating past prosecutors without criminal liability, and not paying their fair share of taxes. In Part IV, the book surveys various reactions to these developments in corporate power, including the response of investors, who have filed a record number of shareholder proposals on the proxies of publicly traded companies, as well as shareholder suits to get more transparency from firms. This section also covers the rejoinders from customers who have new technologies to help them boycott firms that they believe are not acting appropriately. Then the book explores a new corporate form called the benefit corporation, which allows entrepreneurs, including entrepreneurs who wish to avail themselves of Delaware law, to embrace social missions in the articles of incorporation of their firms. And finally the book will end with a discussion of how lawmakers are reacting through proposed legislation, new rules and laws, as well as critiques of the Supreme Court's approach from other jurists.

Part I

Are Corporations Citizens?

The year 2010 was a momentous year in the evolution of corporate rights. The Supreme Court issued its precedent altering *Citizens United* decision, which was a culmination of over 200 years of the Court recognizing and expanding corporate citizen-style rights. Over the years, many corporations have been eager to participate in America's privately financed elections. The most politically active have been eager to spend on electing candidates as well as eager to spend on lobbying those who are elected. Historically, this has inspired laws at the federal and state level to get corporations to get back to business and out of politics. In the twentieth century, the Supreme Court typically upheld restrictions on corporate spending. But in the new millennium, a new Supreme Court would look askance on the efforts of the federal government and states to limit corporate speech.

Chapter 1

The Year the World Changed

Citizens United v. FEC gave corporations the ability to influence the political process more directly, which has in turn made elected officials more responsive to moneyed interests, and therefore as a matter of logic, less responsive to less-wealthy citizens.
    —Chief Justice of Delaware Supreme Court Leo Strine[1]

The year 2010 was an inflection point for the role of corporations in our democracy. Biologist Stephen Jay Gould, who taught at Harvard, had a theory of evolution called "punctuated equilibrium."[2] According to Professor Gould, evolution isn't always a slow and gradual process. Rather, evolution can take huge, fast, punctuated leaps forward. *Citizens United v. Federal Election Commission* was such a punctuated moment in the evolution of corporate citizenship. Before *Citizens United* was decided, corporate funded political ads were illegal in federal elections. But at the moment the Supreme Court issued the opinion in *Citizens United*, suddenly corporations could fund an unlimited supply of political ads right out of the corporate treasury. And while the Supreme Court ruled that the disclosure of funders of organizations, like Citizens United, was perfectly constitutional, existing law provides many loopholes that allow groups to spend political money, but maintain anonymity. Despite losing in the Supreme Court on this point, Citizens United went on to avoid federal disclosure requirements by claiming that it was a press entity. In an advisory opinion, the FEC agreed, thereby granting it a media exemption from disclosure.[3]

---

1. Leo E. Strine, Jr., *Corporate Power Ratchet: The Courts' Role in Eroding "We the People's" Ability to Constrain Our Corporate Creations*, 51 HARV. CIVIL RIGHTS-CIVIL LIBERTIES L. REV. (Forthcoming 2016) (manuscript at 15).
2. STEPHEN JAY GOULD, PUNCTUATED EQUILIBRIUM (2007).
3. *See* Federal Election Comm., A.O. 2010-08, Citizens United (2010).

Citizens United shifted the landscape, but it wasn't the only thing going on in the evolution of corporate citizenship in 2010. The Supreme Court wasn't the only part of the government to do something portentous that would affect the place of corporations in our democracy. During 2010, the world financial system, including in the United States, was still reeling from the financial collapse that had taken place in 2008. Congress issued two landmark pieces of legislation in 2010, both of which propelled litigation that had a profound impact on how the courts conceptualized the relationship among corporations, individuals, and the state. The first piece of legislation was the Dodd-Frank Wall Street Reform and Consumer Protection Act (or just Dodd-Frank for short).[4] This law was primarily a response to the 2008 financial crisis, but it also contained revisions to corporate governance regulation, including disclosure of select raw materials in supply chains. The second piece of legislation was the Patient Protection and Affordable Care Act (also known as ACA), which expanded access to health insurance for millions of Americans, and required employers to provide coverage, which included birth control for women.[5]

While both laws were epic in scope, they had been watered down by corporate lobbying during the legislative process.[6] While these laws imposed new responsibilities on corporations, corporate lawyers would spend the next five years trying to resist and punch holes in these laws. Both laws would be weakened by lobbying in the administrative rulemaking process, and through targeted litigation by trade associations.[7] Parts of the ACA were challenged as

---

4. Dodd-Frank Wall Street Reform & Consumer Protection Act (Pub. L. 111–203, H.R. 4173).

5. The Patient Protection & Affordable Care Act (Pub. L. 111–148, H.R. 3590).

6. Interview with Nell Minow, Vice Chair, ValueEdge Advisors (Aug. 19, 2015) ("By definition, the reforms that got included in Dodd-Frank are the ones that corporations shrug their shoulders over. Majority vote was dropped from the bill."); interview with Robert A.G. Monks (Aug. 17, 2015). ("Basically Dodd-Frank is pathetic."); HELAINE OLEN, POUND FOOLISH EXPOSING THE DARK SIDE OF THE PERSONAL FINANCE INDUSTRY 218 (2012) ("When Elizabeth Warren ... proposed that credit cards, mortgages, and other financial products come with a so-called 'plain vanilla' documentation, an easy-to understand write-up of the terms, as part of Dodd-Frank, the language was dropped from the bill before it passed Congress. That happened because the financial services industry ... opposed it.").

7. Patrick Caldwell, *Did You Know That Antonin Scalia's Son Is Sabotaging Wall Street Reform?*, MOTHER JONES (July/August 2014), http://www.motherjones.com/politics/2014/07/eugene-scalia-court-antonin-financial-reform-dodd-frank; JENNIFER TAUB, OTHER PEOPLE'S HOUSES 291 (2014) ("since Dodd-Frank was enacted in 2010, the financial services lobby devoted considerable resources to delay implementation of the strongest parts ...").

being beyond Congress' Commerce Clause and Spending Powers.[8] Some of Dodd-Frank's rules were challenged as violating the First Amendment.[9]

Back in the courtroom in 2010, human rights lawyers were busy trying to enforce claims against Royal Dutch Petroleum (better known as Shell) for its alleged participation in the execution of environmental activists in Nigeria. The U.S. Court of Appeals for the Second Circuit, in a case called *Kiobel*, rejected the claim, holding that Shell could not be sued for these alleged human rights abuses in the American federal courts.[10] This case would be appealed to the Supreme Court where it—like *Citizens United*—would be argued twice.[11] The Court would side with Shell, albeit on different grounds of extraterritoriality, thereby closing the federal courthouse door against these, and potentially future human rights victims, who were harmed by multinational corporations abroad.

Meanwhile, as the courts debated the legal rights and responsibilities of corporations, a different conversation was occurring in state capitals throughout the country about the purpose of corporations and the positive role they could play in American society. Many negative effects of business corporations are traceable to their requirement to focus relentlessly on making profits. But at the prodding of innovative entrepreneurs, state lawmakers finally asked the question: what if corporations had a broader mission that took account of societal needs? In 2010, Maryland became the first state in America to allow for a new form of incorporation called benefit corporations.[12] Since then, 30 other states, including Delaware, a state that contains more corporations than human beings, have adopted benefit corporation laws. This structure allows benefit

---

8. National Federation of Independent Business v. Sebelius, 132 S. Ct. 2566 (2012) (upholding the individual mandate); King v. Burwell, 576 U.S. _ (2015) (upholding federal health care exchanges).

9. Nat'l Ass'n of Mfrs. v. S.E.C., 748 F.3d 359, 363 (D.C. Cir. 2014) *adhered to on reh'g sub nom.* Nat'l Ass'n of Mfrs. v. S.E.C., 800 F.3d 518 (D.C. Cir. 2015) *overruled by* Am. Meat Inst. v. U.S. Dep't of Agric., 760 F.3d 18 (D.C. Cir. 2014); Am. Petroleum Inst. v. S.E.C., 953 F. Supp. 2d 5, 11 (D.D.C. 2013) ("Plaintiffs argue that section 13(q) and the Rule compel speech in violation of the First Amendment.... The Court will not reach plaintiffs' First Amendment challenge ..."); Consumer Fin. Prot. Bureau v. ITT Educ. Servs., Inc., No. 1:14-CV-00292-SEB, 2015 WL 1013508, at *16 (S.D. Ind. Mar. 6, 2015) ("ITT urges that ... the regulation of its communications to its students chills its First Amendment speech rights ...").

10. Joel Slawotsky, *ATS Liability for Rogue Banking in a Post-Kiobel World*, 37 HASTINGS INT'L & COMP. L. REV. 121, 132–136 (2014).

11. Kiobel v. Royal Dutch Petroleum, 133 S. Ct. 1659 (2013) (Argued Feb. 28, 2012—Reargued Oct. 1, 2012).

12. Maryland S.B. 690 (2010), http://mlis.state.md.us/2010rs/chapters_noln/Ch_97_sb0690T.pdf.

corporations (also colloquially known as "B corps") to build social values into their foundational corporate documents (including articles of incorporation and by-laws), instead of merely being focused on profit maximization.[13]

Near the end of this momentous year, the midterm Congressional election also took place. The impact of *Citizens United* was immediately clear. Roughly $450 million in outside money was spent in this federal election,[14] and $131 million of that spending was from dark money sources.[15] "Dark money," means political spending where the original source is impossible for the public to discover. As the Chair of the Federal Election Commission (FEC) Ann Ravel noted, "[t]here are circuitous ways to spend. We have the nesting doll problem with dark money."[16] Because much of that dark money was funneled through trade associations like the U.S. Chamber of Commerce, there is a deep suspicion that much of this dark money came from corporations exercising their new *Citizens United* rights to spend.[17] But because the money is dark, the public may never know for sure. As prominent political lawyer Trevor Potter explained, "[w]e only know corporate funding of most political ads when it is inadvertently disclosed."[18]

Corporate political spending, to the extent it is uncovered, is revealed piecemeal and haphazardly.[19] On occasion, the truth about the corporate source of dark money comes out because of litigation. For example, after two dark money groups hid the source of spending for two California ballot initiatives in 2012 and were sued, they settled with California for a $1 million fine and disclosed where the money came from.[20] A similar story happened in Mon-

13. Benefit Corp. Info. Ctr., *State by State Legislative Status* (2015), http://benefit-corp.net/state-by-state-legislative-status (listing 30 states plus D.C. with benefit corporation laws).

14. Paul Blumenthal, *The* Citizens United *Effect: 40 Percent of Outside Money Made Possible by Supreme Court Ruling*, SUNLIGHT FOUNDATION (Nov. 4, 2010), http://sunlight-foundation.com/blog/2010/11/04/the-citizens-united-effect-40-percent-of-outside-money-ma de-possible-by-supreme-court-ruling/.

15. Robert Maguire, *How 2014 Is Shaping Up to Be the Darkest Money Election to Date*, CTR. FOR RESPONSIVE POLITICS (Apr. 30, 2014), https://www.opensecrets.org/news/2014/04/how-2014-is-shaping-up-to-be-the-darkest-money-election-to-date/.

16. Interview with Ann Ravel, Chair, Federal Election Commission (Nov. 3, 2015).

17. Interview with Frederick A.O. Schwarz, Chief Counsel Brennan Center for Justice at NYU School of Law (July 21, 2015) ("After *Citizens United*, investors don't know if companies are spending in politics.").

18. Interview with Trevor Potter, President Campaign Legal Ctr. (July 27, 2015).

19. Ciara Torres-Spelliscy, *Courts Shine Light on Dark Money*, BRENNAN CTR. BLOG (May 26, 2015), https://www.brennancenter.org/blog/courts-shine-light-dark-money.

20. Kim Barker, *Dark Money Groups Pay $1 Million in Fines in California Case*, PRO PUBLICA (Oct. 24, 2013), http://www.propublica.org/article/dark-money-groups-pay-1-

tana when a judge ordered a dark money group called Western Tradition Partnership (which later changed its name to American Tradition Partnership) to release its bank records.[21] Among the documents in that case was "a PowerPoint presentation, in which the leader of Western Tradition was telling donors that they could anonymously donate huge sums to influence the election results in Montana, and that no one would know that they had given the money that had won the candidate his or her seat in office. The anonymous donors could sit back on Election Day and watch results roll in and no one would know. No one in the public would know that they had basically distorted that election."[22] Bankruptcy court is another place where the truth can slip out. The bankruptcy court filings of Corinthian Colleges, which had been a publicly traded for-profit education company, showed in the 1,753-page creditors' list the political lobbying group American Legislative Exchange Council (also known as ALEC) and Crossroads GPS, a dark money political nonprofit.[23]

The years since 2010 have revealed a pitched battle about what types of citizens corporations can or should be. One aspect of this fight is deep disagreement about the scope of "corporate personhood." For example, when Jonathan Frieman was pulled over in California for driving alone in the HOV lane in October 2012, he claimed that far from being alone he was accompanied by another "person" since he had the corporate papers of his family's foundation in the passenger seat. He had been hoping to be pulled over for 10 years so that he would have a chance to prove a point about the absurdity of corporate personhood.

---

million-dollars-in-fines-in-california-case ("the Center to Protect Patient Rights conceded it was responsible for funneling $11 million through Americans for Responsible Leadership to a political committee ... The Center to Protect Patient Rights also gave an additional $4 million to another dark money group, the American Future Fund ...").

21. Kim Barker, Rick Young & Emma Schwartz, *Dark Money Group's Donors Revealed*, FRONTLINE (Nov. 5, 2012, 10:18 am ET), http://www.pbs.org/wgbh/pages/frontline/government-elections-politics/big-sky-big-money/dark-money-groups-donors-revealed/ ("The WTP bank records ... show that the group raised almost $1.1 million from other social welfare nonprofits, corporations, a political committee and individuals. It received $650,000 from the nonprofits, $70,000 from an Oklahoma businessman and his company and $50,000 from a Colorado homebuilder.").

22. Interview with Lisa Graves, Executive Director Center for Media & Democracy (July 17, 2015).

23. In re Corinthian Colleges, Inc., No. 15-10952 (KJC) (Bankr. Ct DDE May 4, 2015), http://www.republicreport.org/wp-content/uploads/2015/05/corinthian-creditormatrix.pdf (Creditor Matrix).

When contesting the traffic ticket for driving alone in the HOV lane, Mr. Frieman invoked the long legal tradition of recognizing corporate personhood as the reason why there really were two people in his car. The judge in traffic court ruled against him. He appealed to California Superior Court, where again he lost. The Superior Court Judge held, "[n]otwithstanding some recent appellate decisions which might be viewed as anthropomorphizing corporations [like *Citizens United*], a corporation is a mere creature of statute[.]"[24] And moreover, "the statute requires at least two human beings in the HOV lane."[25] Corporations may be legal persons for many purposes—but not for the HOV lane. So, just as drivers with mannequins and blow up dolls have learned before, the HOV lane requires multiple actual human beings with a pulse. A corporate person isn't good enough.[26]

But why did Jonathan Frieman lose? How could a corporation be a legal person in one context (spending money in elections) and not in another (the HOV lane in California)?

The short answer is the law is inconsistent and is in near-constant flux. The longer answer is this book. The Supreme Court has not granted identical rights to humans and corporations. And the rights that have been recognized for corporations have been granted slowly and piecemeal, case by arduous case, until recently when the pro-corporate rulings started flowing rapidly from the Court. The past few years has been a tumultuous time for corporations as different constituencies from voters, to shareholders, judges, human rights lawyers, environmentalists, and entrepreneurs have contested the dimensions of corporate "citizenship" within our democracy.

Reporter William Greider argued in his book WHO WILL TELL THE PEOPLE?:

> The great project of corporate lawyers, extending over generations, has been to establish full citizenship for their business organizations. They argue that their companies are entitled to the same political rights, save voting, that the Constitution guarantees to people.... [Corporate lawyers] are invoking the Bill of Rights to protect their organizations from federal laws ... Corporations, in other words, claim to be 'citizens' of the Republic, not simply for propaganda or good pub-

---

24. People of California v. Frieman, No. SC 184051A (Ref. Traffic Case No. CT12035109) (Marin Co. Cal. Sup. Ct. Aug. 15. 2013) (citing *Citizens United*).

25. *Id.*

26. Justin Berton, *Corporation not Person in Carpool Lanes*, SAN FRANCISCO CHRONICLE (Jan. 8, 2013), http://www.sfgate.com/bayarea/article/Corporation-not-person-in-carpool-lanes-4173366.php.

lic relations, but in the actual legal sense of claiming constitutional rights and protections.[27]

This effort to expand corporate "citizenship," continues to this day. The scope of the rights corporations want shows no sign of abating.

Now whether it is useful or accurate to call corporations "citizens" at all is a matter of rich debate. Fordham Law Professor Zephyr Teachout considered the phrase nonsensical. "Saying 'a corporation is a citizen' doesn't make any sense. It is like saying 'a liability is a citizen.'"[28] As Counsel at the nonprofit Demos, Elizabeth Kennedy stated, "'corporate rights' is a problematic phrase."[29] And Executive Director of the Center for Media and Democracy, Lisa Graves, indicated, "[o]nly human beings can be citizens."[30] Yet many firms have co-opted the language of "good corporate citizenship" in response to external and internal pressures to be more socially responsible. And corporations are often described as being "citizens" of the state where they were incorporated. But both of these types of "corporate citizenship" are different from the way citizenship for a human being is typically conceived.

"Citizenship" for Americans has a very long and complicated history given the historical context of racism, sexism, immigration, naturalization, and classism. Depending on the historical period under consideration, who was deemed to be a full American citizen with the ability to vote, sit on a jury, own property, travel freely, and pursue a chosen profession, ranged from a very tiny sliver of the population of property-owning white men aged 21 and over, to nearly everyone who was either born in America or naturalized.[31] If the ability to marry the person of your own choosing is considered a component of citizenship, then LGBT Americans just became full citizens when the Supreme Court recognized marriage equality in 2015.[32]

A Supreme Court Justice once argued that, "[t]hose who won our independence believed that ... the greatest menace to freedom is an inert people;

27. WILLIAM GREIDER, WHO WILL TELL THE PEOPLE? THE BETRAYAL OF AMERICAN DEMOCRACY 348–49 (1992).

28. Interview with Fordham Law Professor Zephyr Teachout (Aug. 10, 2015).

29. Interview with Elizabeth Kennedy, Counsel Demos (Aug. 12, 2015).

30. Interview with Lisa Graves, Executive Director Center for Media & Democracy (July 17, 2015).

31. HOWARD FINEMAN, THE THIRTEEN AMERICAN ARGUMENTS 24 (2009) ("it took nearly a century and a half for women to win a constitutional right to vote ...).

32. Obergefell v. Hodges, 135 S. Ct. 2584 (2015) (recognizing the right of marriage equality of same-sex couples); see also United States v. Windsor, 133 S. Ct. 2675, 2694 (2013) (invalidating Defense of Marriage Act (DOMA)).

[and] that public discussion is a political duty[.]"[33] Many would disagree about the *sine qua non* of true (human) citizenship. It could be any number of aspects of modern civic engagement. Is it voting on a regular basis? Is it registering members of your community to vote? Is it volunteering in political campaigns, places of worship, or in your neighborhood? Is it being engaged with the lawmaking process through lobbying? Is it dutifully paying taxes? Is it running for office? Is it joining the army?

Granting corporations citizen-style rights is peculiar given that they are just piles of paper. Even Chief Justice Leo Strine of the Delaware Supreme Court, which is widely regarded as pro-business, is worried that the U.S. Supreme Court is losing grasp of the key distinctions between people and corporations. As Chief Justice Strine wrote in a 2015 law review article, the Supreme Court "ignores the reality that nonhuman corporations are fundamentally distinct from their ultimate human investors."[34]

But one thing is certain, corporations are gaining more rights that previously were only reserved or recognized as components of human citizenship. In particular, this book will focus on three areas where corporate rights are expanding: (1) in commercial speech, (2) in politics, and (3) in religion. With a few notable exceptions, the judiciary is the source of these expanded corporate rights. Expanding corporate citizenship rights outside of the normal democratic process of legislatures and elections is particularly problematic as unelected judges slowly grant more privileges to inanimate legal fictions. Although the judiciary is often referred to as Alexander Hamilton once put it, as "the least dangerous branch," nonetheless the judiciary, utilizing its power of judicial review to invalidate laws created by legislatures, including Congress and by the people themselves through the referendum and initiative process. To get certain changes in the law, you do not need to convince hundreds of legislators or millions of voters; all you really need to convince are five Justices on the Supreme Court. This presents what is known as the judiciary's "counter-majoritarian difficulty."[35] Just a few men (and until very recently it was all men) could change the course of American legal destiny. As Justice Frankfurter once warned:

> Courts are not representative bodies. They are not designed to be a good reflex of a democratic society.... Their essential quality is de-

---

33. Whitney v. California, 274 U.S. 357, 375 (1927) (Brandeis, J. concurring).
34. Leo E. Strine, Jr. & Nicholas Walter, *Conservative Collision Course?: The Tension Between Conservative Corporate Law Theory and* Citizens United, 100 CORNELL L. REV. 335, 386 (2015).
35. ALEXANDER BICKEL, THE LEAST DANGEROUS BRANCH (1962).

tachment, founded on independence. History teaches that the independence of the judiciary is jeopardized when courts become embroiled in the passions of the day and assume primary responsibility in choosing between competing political, economic and social pressures.[36]

Not every case makes it to the Supreme Court. The Justices largely have control over their docket, and thus, they can pick and choose which cases to hear.[37] So in the majority of legal disputes in America, the final decision is rendered in one of the lower federal courts like the D.C. Circuit, which hears the bulk of appeals about federal agency rules,[38] the Second Circuit, which hears many business cases arising out of New York City and its environs,[39] and the Ninth Circuit, which has authority over the most populous state of California, with a population the size of Canada,[40] or in state courts. Consequently, frequently the expansion of corporate rights is the result of lower court cases that never reached the Supreme Court. In some of these lower court decisions, only two of three judges are needed to change the course of legal history.

"The chief business of the American people," said Republican President Calvin Coolidge, "is business."[41] Coolidge's instincts have deep American roots. Founding father Alexander Hamilton concluded that "social stability rested on firm alliance of government and business."[42] But even if Coolidge and Hamilton are right, this never meant that business interests should trump the interests of the American people. Concern over the impact of large corporations

---

36. *Dennis v. United States*, 341 U.S. 494, 525 (1951) (Frankfurter, J., concurring).

37. *Federal Courts and What They Do*, FED'L JUDICIAL CTR, http://www.fjc.gov/ public/pdf.nsf/lookup/FCtsWhat.pdf/$file/FCtsWhat.pdf (last visited Aug. 16, 2014) ("Unlike the U.S. courts of appeals … the Supreme Court does not have to hear every case that it is asked to review.").

38. Brad Plumer, *The D.C. Circuit is the Court at the Center of the Filibuster Fight. Here's Why it Matters.*, WASH. POST (Nov. 21, 2013), http://www.washingtonpost.com/ blogs/wonkblog/wp/2013/11/21/the-d-c-circuit-court-was-at-the-center-of-the-filibuster-fight-hereswhy-it-matters/ ("The D.C. Circuit is surprisingly powerful—not least because it rules on decisions made by federal administrative agencies. If people want to challenge various federal regulations in court, the cases often end up here.").

39. About the Court, Second Circuit Court of Appeals, http://www.ca2.uscourts.gov/ about_the_court.html (last visited July 25, 2015).

40. About the Court, Ninth Circuit Court of Appeals, http://www.ca9.uscourts.gov/in-formation/ (last visited July 25, 2015).

41. HEATHER COX RICHARDSON, TO MAKE MEN FREE: A HISTORY OF THE REPUBLICAN PARTY, xvii (2014).

42. ARTHUR M. SCHLESINGER JR., THE AGE OF JACKSON 9 (1953) (quoting Alexander Hamilton).

on American democracy is not a new worry.[43] One of the leading thinkers on this issue was a man who would end up on the U.S. Supreme Court, Louis D. Brandeis.[44] Before he was a jurist, he spoke publicly about his concerns with concentrated wealth and its potential deleterious effect on American democracy.[45] He testified before Congress in 1912 stating of the monopolist trust U.S. Steel: "we cannot maintain democratic conditions in America if we allow organizations to arise in our midst with the power of the [U.S.] Steel Corporation. Liberty of the American citizen cannot endure against such organizations."[46] A hundred years later in 2012, according to one poll, more than half of Americans do not think corporations and people should have the same rights.[47] Indeed, another poll found, "69% of respondents agreed that 'new rules that let corporations, unions and people give unlimited money to Super PACs will lead to corruption.' Only 15% disagreed."[48] In yet another poll from October 2012, nearly 9 in 10 Americans agree that there is too much cor-

---

43. Victor Brudney, *Business Corporations and Stockholders' Rights under the First Amendment*, 91 YALE L. J. 235, 237 (1981) (stating "[t]he use of that wealth and power by corporate management to move government toward goals that management favors—with little or no formal consultation with investors—is also a phenomenon that is generally undeniable").

44. Louis D. Brandeis, *Cutthroat Prices—The Competition That Kills*, HARPER'S WEEKLY, 12 (Nov. 15, 1913) reprinted in BRANDEIS, BUSINESS—A PROFESSION 242, 260 (1933 ed.) ("[T]he displacement of the small independent business man by the huge corporation with its myriad of employees, its absentee ownership, and its financier control, presents a grave danger to our democracy.").

45. Statement of Brandeis, *Final Report and Testimony of the Commission on Industrial Relations*, S. Doc. No. 415, 64th Cong., 1st Sess., vol. VIII, at 7663 (1915) ("Concentration of power has been shown to be dangerous in a democracy, even though that power may be used beneficently.").

46. Statement of Brandeis, *Hearings Before the House Committee on Investigation of United States Steel Corporation*, 62d Cong., 2d Sess. 2862 (1912).

47. Andrew Joseph, *Poll: Most Voters Oppose* Citizens United *Decision*, NAT. J. BLOG (Jan. 20, 2012), http://www.nationaljournal.com/blogs/influencealley/2012/01/poll-most-voters-oppose-citizens-united-decision-20 ("The poll found that 62 percent of all voters oppose the Supreme Court's *Citizens United* decision ... and 46 percent of voters strongly oppose it. Meanwhile, 55 percent of voters do not believe that corporations should have the same rights as people.").

48. Ian Millhiser, *More Americans Believe in Witchcraft than Agree with* Citizens United, THINK PROGRESS (Apr. 24, 2012), http://thinkprogress.org/justice/2012/04/24/470450/more-americans-believe-in-witchcraft-than-agree-with-citizens-united/.

porate money in politics.[49] But as the cases in this book show, the courts are getting out of step with what the majority of Americans desire about the role of corporate power in their democracy.

Interestingly, the unexpected death of Justice Scalia in early 2016, and the possibility of his replacement taking different stances on corporate rights than he did during his long tenure on the Supreme Court, could place the Supreme Court on an entirely new trajectory. But until that change happens, the Supreme Court has built up decades of precedents that recognize more and more corporate rights, which once only applied to human beings.

---

49. Press Release, *New Poll: Americans Condemn High Levels of Corporate Political Spending, Overwhelmingly Support Strong Transparency and Accountability Reforms*, PUBLIC CITIZEN (Oct. 25, 2012), http://www.citizen.org/pressroom/pressroomredirect.cfm?ID=3748.

Chapter 2

Yes, Virginia, Corporations Are People, But Not Citizens

Governance is really about self-governance. It's about 'We, the people.'
—Dr. Marcy Murninghan[1]

Around the time that *Citizens United* was decided, bumper stickers started showing up saying "I'll believe a corporation is a person when Texas executes one." What this clever, but macabre, phrase captures is the fact that corporations are not corporeal. Contemporary corporations, unlike their human counterparts, can exist in perpetuity, thus why they are sometimes referred to as being "immortal."[2] Without a body, corporations cannot feel pain, experience joy, or really die. Cryogenics aside, although Walt Disney the man died, the Walt Disney Company shows no signs of going anywhere anytime soon. Or as University of Virginia Law professor Brandon Garrett framed the matter, "[c]ompanies are slippery creatures. They cannot serve jail time, but they can have immortal life[.]"[3]

Understanding how corporations have evolved over 225 years in the United States is necessary to appreciate why the largest corporations are so powerful now. Part of this evolution is the product of competition among states for corporate charters. Every state in America would like to collect corporate filing fees from as many corporations as possible. Consequently, states have created corporate laws that are more lenient and permissive so that corporations will

---

1. Interview with Dr. Marcy Murninghan, corporate governance expert (July 24, 2015).
2. Interview with Robert A.G. Monks (Aug. 17, 2015) ("The problem of corporations and human beings clashing is humans have finite life and smaller size.").
3. BRANDON L. GARRETT, TOO BIG TO JAIL: HOW PROSECUTORS COMPROMISE WITH CORPORATIONS 169 (2014).

be enticed to incorporate there. Another catalyst is the Supreme Court's choice to recognize or not recognize new rights for corporations. In the end, states have given corporations the ability to exist for any lawful purpose and the Supreme Court has been willing (with a few notable exceptions) to grant corporations grander rights decade after decade.

Take almost any topic that the Supreme Court has considered from 1791 to today and the Court is likely to have changed its position. Over that time span, the Court has ruled in favor of[4] and against racial segregation,[5] in favor of[6] and against gay marriage,[7] and in favor of[8] and against equality for women.[9] This schizophrenia over social issues might be expected as the Court adapts to the changes in the country. What might be surprising is how much the Court has equivocated on issues about corporate rights as well.

The Roberts Supreme Court—which started in 2005 and will continue until Chief Justice Roberts retires, dies, or is impeached (which could be decades from now as he is only 61 years old) has been particularly pro-business and has expanded the scope of the rights of corporations in several dimensions.[10] According to Judge Richard Posner and his co-authors, five of the most pro-business Justices, since the mid-twentieth century, are serving on the Roberts Supreme Court presently, and Justices Roberts and Alito are the two most pro-business Justices since 1946.[11] This why the Roberts Court has earned the nickname "the corporate court."[12]

---

4. Plessy v. Ferguson, 163 U.S. 537 (1896).
5. Brown v. Board of Education of Topeka, 347 U.S. 483 (1954).
6. Obergefell v. Hodges, 135 S. Ct. 2584 (2015).
7. Baker v. Nelson, 291 Minn. 310 (1971), *summarily affirmed* 409 U.S. 810 (1972).
8. United States v. Virginia, 518 U.S. 515 (1996).
9. Bradwell v. State of Illinois, 83 U.S. 130 (1873).
10. Jedediah Purdy, *The Roberts Court v. America*, 23 DEMOCRACY (2012), http://www.democracyjournal.org/23/the-roberts-court-v-america.php?page=all ("What's missing from the criticism is a picture of what these cases add up to: an identity for the Roberts Court as the judicial voice of the idea that nearly everything works best on market logic, that economic models of behavior capture most of what matters ..."); Lee Epstein, William M. Landes & Richard A. Posner, *How Business Fares in the Supreme Court*, 97 MINN. L. REV. 1431, 1472 (2013) ("Whether measured by decisions or Justices' votes, a plunge in warmth toward business during the 1960s (the heyday of the Warren Court) was quickly reversed; and the Roberts Court is much friendlier to business than either the Burger or Rehnquist Courts, which preceded it, were."); Erwin Chemerinsky, *The Roberts Court at Age Three*, 54 WAYNE L. REV. 947, 956 (2008) ("Also, it is a Court that, overall, is very pro-business.").
11. 97 MINN. L. REV. at 1450–51; *Id.* at 1471–72. Note: this book was written before Justice Scalia died in 2016. He was one of the five Judge Posner counted as pro-corporate.
12. Nan Aron, AT&T Mobility v. Concepcion: *The Corporate Court Does it Again*, HUFF.

But the period from 2005 to the present is just a sliver of judicial time if the Court's entire history is examined going back to its beginning in 1791. When it comes to the expansion of rights for corporations, students of history should remember that it wasn't always like this. First, corporations were not as numerous or powerful, and second, courts and lawmakers had not conceded that corporations deserved as many rights as modern courts have granted.

A. How Corporations Have Evolved

A for-profit corporation is particular legal structure of organizing a business entity. The basic structure is: the corporation has a board of directors that makes major decisions for the firm. The members of the board are elected by the shareholders, who have investment money in the firm. Directors are re-elected on an annual basis. The management of the company is conducted by corporate officers, including the CEO. In smaller firms, individuals within the corporate structure can wear many hats, such as investor, officer, and board member. But in most publicly traded corporations, these roles are held by different people. To incentivize investment, investors cannot be sued for the corporation's wrongdoing. The board of directors owes fiduciary duties to investors to run the firm prudently.

Corporations date back to the Middle Ages in Europe.[13] But corporations were a bit of rarity in early America, because creating a corporation required an act of a state legislature. Indeed, "originally in the U.S., every corporate charter had to be voted on separately by the legislature to make sure its purpose was legitimate."[14] According to Professors Margaret Blair and Elizabeth Pollman, "[b]etween 1781 and 1791, American states chartered only thirty-two business corporations. Most of these were created to provide transportation infrastructure such as canals and bridges, and the rest included banks, insurance companies, and manufacturing companies."[15] But change

---

POST (Apr. 29, 2011).

13. Maximilian Koessler, *The Person in Imagination or Persona Ficta of the Corporation*, 9 LOUISIANA L. REV. 435, 435 (1949).

14. ROBERT A.G. MONKS & NELL MINOW, CORPORATE GOVERNANCE 14 (Fifth ed. 2011); Murninghan Interview, *supra* note 1 ("After the Revolutionary War, corporate charters were granted by local governing bodies, rather than the Crown. In the chartering process, you had to demonstrate some public sense of value in exchange for 'standing' or 'status.'").

15. Margaret M. Blair & Elizabeth Pollman, *The Derivative Nature of Corporate Constitutional Rights*, 56 WM. & MARY L. REV. 1673, 1698 (2015), http://scholarship.law.wm.edu/wmlr/vol56/iss5/2 (internal citations omitted).

occurred rapidly as the number and size of corporations in America expanded markedly through the nineteenth century. Historian Arthur Schlesinger Jr. picked up the story a few decades later, "[f]rom the start of the [nineteenth] century, ... the corporation was gradually becoming the dominant form of economic organization ... But those on the outside had a feeling of deep misgiving which was less an economic or political than a moral protest: it was basically a sense of shock."[16] The "shock" was a reaction to the loss of interpersonal relationships in business.[17] According to Schlesinger, "the corporation had one outstanding characteristic: its moral irresponsibility ... Beyond good and evil, insensible to argument or appeal, they symbolized the mounting independence of the new economy from the restraints and scruples of personal life."[18]

Justice Brandeis, in his famous dissent in *Liggett* in 1933, explained the historical path of the expansion of corporations from single-purpose entities with limited terms of existence into the multi-purpose, immortal behemoths we have today. As Justice Brandeis wrote:

> The prevalence of the corporation in America has led men of this generation to act, at times, as if the privilege of doing business in corporate form were inherent in the citizen; and has led them to accept the evils attendant upon the free and unrestricted use of the corporate mechanism as if these evils were the inescapable price of civilized life, and, hence, to be borne with resignation. Throughout the greater part of our history a different view prevailed.... There was a sense of some insidious menace inherent in large aggregations of capital, particularly when held by corporations. So at first the corporate privilege was granted sparingly; and only when the grant seemed necessary in order to procure for the community some specific benefit otherwise unattainable. The later enactment of general incorporation laws does not signify that the apprehension of corporate domination had been overcome.[19]

Justice Brandeis went on to expound upon the history of the development of corporate laws in the American context, including the fact that statutes in many states originally limited the amount of capital a corporation could raise,

---

16. ARTHUR M. SCHLESINGER JR., THE AGE OF JACKSON 334 (1953).

17. *Id.* at 335.

18. *Id.* at 335.

19. Louis K. Liggett Co. v. Lee, 288 U.S. 517, 548–49 (1933) (Brandeis, J., dissenting in part) (internal citations omitted).

but that these capital limits were eventually ended.[20] Justice Brandeis also noted that the purposes of corporations were once narrow and are now incredibly broad.

> Limitations upon the scope of a business corporation's powers and activity were also long universal. At first, corporations could be formed under the general laws only for a limited number of purposes—usually those which required a relatively large fixed capital, like transportation, banking, and insurance, and mechanical, mining, and manufacturing enterprises. Permission to incorporate for 'any lawful purpose was not common until 1875; ... All, or a majority, of the incorporators or directors, or both, were required to be residents of the incorporating state. The powers which the corporation might exercise in carrying out its purposes were sparingly conferred and strictly construed.[21]

The ability of corporations to exist at the start of the United States was typically limited by law to a term of years. Until 1875, "the duration of corporate franchises was generally limited to a period of 20, 30, or 50 years."[22] But eventually, as states competed in a race to the bottom for corporate charters, they all eventually allowed corporations to continue in perpetuity. So now, anyone can incorporate a corporation, and those corporations do not have to be for a limited purpose, or for a limited time. This, of course, could be changed if state laws, like laws in Delaware, were changed to require corporations only for limited terms.[23]

But today, immortality is a feature of modern corporations, not a bug. This can be a good thing because "[c]orporations give individuals a greater and more lasting sphere of action. Corporations have no boundaries in time or space. A corporation continues despite the death or retirement of its founder or highest officers ... [And] the purpose of the corporate structure [is] to transcend the ability and the lifespan of any individual."[24] But this may be why

---

20. *Liggett*, 288 U.S. at 550–54 (Brandeis, J., dissenting in part).

21. *Liggett*, 288 U.S. at 554–56 (Brandeis, J., dissenting in part) (internal citations omitted).

22. *Liggett*, 288 U.S. at 554–56 (Brandeis, J., dissenting in part) (internal citations omitted).

23. Jeffrey D. Clements, Corporations Are Not People 66 (2012) ("If a majority of the Delaware legislature wanted to ... simply declare that corporations may exist for a period of twenty years, they could do so.").

24. Monks & Minow, *supra* note 12, at 4.

granting corporations the same rights as individuals doesn't always make sense. As the Supreme Court once concluded, "[s]ometimes the grossest discrimination can lie in treating things that are different as though they were exactly alike[.]"[25] And this seems particularly apt, when corporations and humans are being balanced on the scales of justice.

The rise of large corporations happened at the turn of the twentieth century. By 1910 the U.S. economy was dominated by large corporations, thousands of which had at least $1 million in capital. Professors Blair and Pollman noted, "[m]ost of these corporations had been formed through the industry-by-industry combinations of dozens of smaller corporations during the great merger movement, so these corporations were not just large, they also had near monopoly control, or at least oligopoly control, over their industries."[26] Fears over the power of monopoly in the marketplace were intertwined with fears of monopoly power in the democratic process as well. "These huge pools of capital [in corporations and trusts] raised the frightening prospect that candidates and elections might actually be bought in systematic fashion."[27]

One of the big changes from the founding to today is that, at the founding, only a special legislative act could create a corporation.[28] By contrast, now, under general incorporation statutes, incorporators can file a few administrative papers, pay a few fees, and be the proud owner of their very own corporation. And many take advantage of this ease and convenience. Approximately two million corporations are incorporated annually in the U.S.[29] Delaware has clearly won the race for corporate charters as the majority of U.S. corporations are incorporated in Delaware, America's second smallest state.[30]

Additionally, at the founding, corporations were created for a limited purpose, like building a road from point A to point B. Now, while incorporators could limit the purpose of a corporation in its articles of incorporation, few do. Rather, the norm presently is for entrepreneurs to establish corporations

---

25. Buckley v. Valeo, 424 U.S. 1, 97–98 (1976).

26. Blair & Pollman, *supra* note 13, at 1709 (internal citations omitted).

27. Marc Hager, *Bodies Politic: The Progressive History of Organizational "Real Entity" Theory*, 50 U. Pitt L. Rev. 575, 639 (1989).

28. Jonathan R. Macey, *Crony Capitalism: Right Here, Right Now*, 37 Harv. J.L. & Pub. Pol'y 5, 7–8 (2014) ("[At] the end of the nineteenth century … the States had none of the current rules for obtaining a corporate charter. It was, rather, the era of special charters. To get a corporate charter, a group of individuals had to go to its state legislature and get it to pass a special statute for the group to, say, put in this turnpike or build that bridge.").

29. Garrett, *supra* note 21, at 22.

30. Monks & Minow, *supra* note 12, at 45.

for "any lawful purpose." This allows modern firms to do multiple lines of business as well as assert the ability to act in non-business fora.

Finally, the diffusion of stock ownership has grown dramatically over time. At the founding, the owners of a corporation would typically be a small circle of people. As Justice Brandeis illuminated, "[t]he typical business corporation of the last century, [was] owned by a small group of individuals, managed by their owners, and limited in size by their personal wealth[.]"[31] As such, a small group of investors could easily keep an eye on how their investments were being managed. But with the modern publicly traded corporation, millions of people may own stock in a single firm. Justice Brandeis noted that the traditional smaller firm was "being supplanted by huge concerns in which the lives of tens or hundreds of thousands of employees and the property of tens or hundreds of thousands of investors are subjected, through the corporate mechanism, to the control of a few men. Ownership has been separated from control; and this separation has removed many of the checks which formerly operated to curb the misuse of wealth and power."[32] Now shareholders are geographically dispersed, and because each one typically owns only a fraction of a percent of the firm, the incentive to keep a watchful eye over management is diminished.

Back in the 1930s, Professors Berle and Means worried that this separation of management from control would prove troublesome. And time has shown that Berle's and Means' instincts were correct. Whether the issue is executive compensation or other aspects of corporate governance, shareholders have collective action problems coordinating large numbers of investors, and they also have a rational disinterest in not monitoring corporate insiders on a regular basis. Corporate managers, thus, may act in undisciplined and self-serving ways at the expense of shareholders, like helping themselves to generous retirement packages or the use of perks like corporate jets. As Nobel Prize-winning economist Joseph Stiglitz explained, "basically we have a system in which corporate executives, the CEOs, are trying to makes sure the legal system works not for the companies, not for the shareholders, not for the bondholders—but for themselves. So it's like theft. These corporations are basically now working for the CEOs and the executives and not for any of the other stakeholders in the corporation, let alone for our broader society."[33]

---

31. *Liggett*, 288 U.S. at 564–65 (Brandeis, J., dissenting in part) (internal citations omitted).

32. *Id.*

33. MONKS & MINOW, *supra* note 12, at 476 (quoting Stiglitz).

This is known as an agency problem — corporate managers are the share-holders' agent's within the firm, and the managers have a fiduciary duty to act in the shareholders' best interest, but because the shareholders are not con-tinually monitoring the behavior of mangers, the managers may produce sub-optimal returns for investors because of self-serving behaviors like enjoying expensive perks on the company's dime.[34] And "[i]nvestors do not self-organ-ize. Most investors have their money in passively managed index funds or let their brokerage vote their shares."[35] This could be why editorialist Ambrose Bierce once jibed that a corporation is "[a]n ingenious device for obtaining in-dividual profit without individual responsibility."[36] The worries raised by agency theory become more acute as firms become larger and the temptation to tap corporate resources for personal reasons — like backing a favorite political cause at shareholder expense — grows.

At the same time that statutory powers of corporations expanded, the Supreme Court also decided which constitutional rights could attach to the corporate form. The Supreme Court's approach to the rights for corporations can be divided into two distinct strains of case law. When the Supreme Court uses the Fourteenth Amendment and the First Amendment, the court has been on trajectory of increasing corporate rights. (Though until the 1970s, the Supreme Court did not use the First Amendment to empower corporations, but there will be more on that in Chapter 5). But when the Supreme Court uses Article IV's Privileges and Immunities Clause, the Court has severely lim-ited the rights of corporations.[37] One of the key differences is that, in the for-mer cases, the Court embraces a strong version of corporate personhood, while in the latter cases, the Court finds a meaningful distinction between humans and corporations. Interestingly, while the Court has concluded that corpora-tions are "persons" within the meaning of the Equal Protection Clause of the

---

34. ROBERT A.G. MONKS & NELL MINOW, WATCHING THE WATCHERS: CORPORATE GOV-ERNANCE FOR THE 21ST CENTURY xix (1996) ("The price we pay for the benefits of the cor-porate structure is our loss of control. Investors lose control over the use of their capital. Managers lose control over their sources of funding.").

35. Interview with Warren Langley, Former President of the Pacific Stock Exchange (July 14, 2015).

36. MONKS & MINOW, *supra* note 12, at 5–6 (quoting Bierce).

37. There are other limits on corporate rights, for example, they do not enjoy the right to privacy. 3 Restatement (Second), Torts §652I, comment c (1977) ("A corporation ... has no personal right of privacy"); FCC v. AT&T Inc., 562 U.S. 397, 409–10 (2011) ("The pro-tection in FOIA against disclosure of law enforcement information on the ground that it would constitute an unwarranted invasion of personal privacy does not extend to corpora-tions. We trust that AT&T will not take it personally.").

Fourteenth Amendment, the Court has been quite reticent to concede that corporations are "citizens" for the purpose of the Privileges and Immunities Clause.

To understand this two-pronged evolution of the law takes a little history about the Constitution. The Constitution was first ratified in 1789. Shortly thereafter in 1791, 10 amendments, known as the Bill of Rights, were added to the document. The First Amendment and the Fifth Amendment are both part of the Bill of Rights. The Constitution was last amended in 1992 when the Twenty-Seventh Amendment was added. After the Bill of Rights, the most significant set of Amendments to the Constitution are known as the Civil War Amendments (or the Reconstruction Amendments): these are the Thirteenth (abolishing slavery), the Fourteenth (establishing birthright citizenship, due process and equal protection, among other items), and the Fifteenth (granting African Americans the right to vote).[38] There are two Due Process Clauses in the Constitution—one in the Fifth Amendment, which applies to the federal government, and one in the Fourteenth Amendment, which applies to the states. The Supreme Court treats the Equal Protection Clause as if it appears in both the Fourteenth and Fifth Amendments, even though it really only appears in the text of the Fourteenth Amendment. There are also two Privileges and Immunities Clauses—one in Article IV, which applies to state citizenship, and one in the Fourteenth Amendment, which applies to national citizenship, but because of Supreme Court precedent, the latter is generally thought of as being a dead letter.[39]

Here are your rules of thumb: (1) The U.S. Constitution has changed over time between 1791 and 1992, through the Article V amendment process, and (2) the Supreme Court has asserted since the seminal case of *Marbury v. Madison,* that the Court has the right to "say what the law is."[40]

---

38. Thurgood Marshall, *Reflections on the Bicentennial of the United States Constitution,* 101 Harv. L. Rev. 1, 4 (1987) ("While the Union survived the civil war, the Constitution did not. In its place arose a new, more promising basis for justice and equality, the fourteenth amendment, ensuring protection of the life, liberty, and property of *all* persons against deprivations without due process, and guaranteeing equal protection of the laws.").

39. John Hart Ely, Democracy and Distrust: A Theory of Judicial Review 22 (1980) ("there is not a bit of legislative history that supports the view that the Privileges or Immunities Clause was intended to be meaningless. Yet the *Slaughter-House* interpretation persists to the present day."); Howard Jay Graham, Everyman's Constitution, Historical Essay on the Fourteenth Amendment, the "Conspiracy Theory," and American Constitutionalism 11 (2013) ("In the *Slaughter-Houses* the freedmen weren't even in Court. But their rights and the 14th Amendment were. Everybody got half slaughtered at the start[.]").

40. Marbury v. Madison, 5 U.S. 137 (1803).

B. Equal Protection for Corporations

There is a widely held misconception that *Citizens United* was the first case to create corporate personhood. This claim lands quite wide of the mark. First, the phrase "corporate personhood" does not appear in the opinion at all. Second, *Citizens United* did not grant corporations personhood. Corporations already had it. As lawyers David Gans and Douglas Kendall have documented, despite the fact that the U.S. Constitution never mentions the word "corporation,"[41] and given that corporations are creatures of state law,[42] the legal concept of corporate personhood has been slithering around American constitutional law for a very long time.[43] The idea of anthropomorphizing corporations through "corporate personhood" dates back to a medieval pope who was also a lawyer.[44] But now, "personifying separate legal entities other than human individuals [ ] conquered the legal world, the term 'person,' originally the exclusive designation of man, came in addition to mean any rights and duties bearing unit[,]" including corporations.[45]

Throughout American legal history, corporations have been litigious. Often corporations have been near the first in line to claim various constitutional rights. This was true when it came to corporations' claiming rights protecting private property and rights protecting the right to contract. For example, the Supreme Court in very early cases decided that corporations were covered by the Contract Clause of the Constitution. This part of the Constitution says, "[n]o State shall … pass any … Law impairing the Obligation of Contracts.…"[46] This means that a state, like New Hampshire, could not pass a law that interfered with a pre-existing contract between two parties.

---

41. Interview with Nicole Gordon, Former Executive Director, New York City Campaign Finance Board (Aug. 10, 2015) ("The Constitution is about the structure of government and individual rights.").

42. Cort v. Ash, 422 U.S. 66, 84 (1975) ("Corporations are creatures of state law, and investors commit their funds to corporate directors on the understanding that, except where federal law expressly requires certain responsibilities of directors with respect to stockholders, state law will govern the internal affairs of the corporation.").

43. David H. Gans & Douglas T. Kendall, *A Capitalist Joker, The Strange Origins, Disturbing Past and Uncertain Future of Corporate Personhood in American Law*, CONSTITUTIONAL ACCOUNTABILITY CTR (2010), http://theusconstitution.org/sites/default/files/briefs/A%20Capitalist%20Joker.pdf.

44. Koessler, *supra* note 13, at 437 ("the imaginative personality of a corporation or juristic person appeared for the first time in the writings of [Pope Innocent IV (1243–1254)].").

45. *Id.* at 435.

46. U.S. Constitution, Art. I, Sec. 10, Cl. 1.

In the *Dartmouth College* case in 1819, the college (a corporation) claimed protection under the Constitution's Contract Clause. The Supreme Court agreed that it applied, ruling that even the Revolutionary War had not changed contractual rights for educational corporations like the college: "[i]t is too clear ... that all contracts and rights respecting property, remained unchanged by the [American] revolution."[47] In this case, the early Supreme Court drew some distinctions between corporations and citizens. In *Dartmouth College*, the Court held, "this being [the corporation] does not share in the civil government of the country, unless that be the purpose for which it was created. Its immortality no more confers on it political power, or a political character, than immortality would confer such power or character on a natural person."[48] Yet despite recognizing differences between corporations and actual citizens, the Supreme Court held that New Hampshire had violated the Contracts Clause when the state essentially tried to take over the private college.

Just a few years prior, the Supreme Court had considered the property rights of corporations. In *Terrett v. Taylor* in 1815, the Episcopal Church (a corporation) asserted property rights over certain land. The Supreme Court stated that the property rights were not disturbed by the Revolutionary War: "[s]uch were some of the rights and powers of the Episcopal church at the time of the American revolution; and under the authority thereof the purchase of the lands stated in the bill before the Court, was undoubtedly made. And the property so acquired by the church remained unimpaired, notwithstanding the revolution[.]"[49] And as the Supreme Court stated: "[t]he dissolution of the regal government no more destroyed the right to possess or enjoy this property than it did the right of any other corporation or individual to his or its own property[.]"[50] The *Terrett* case also made clear that religious corporations did not have to be abolished because of the First Amendment finding, "that [n]either public [n]or constitutional principles required the abolition of all religious corporations."[51] The Supreme Court held in *Terrett* that religious corporations, like other corporations, have rights to their property.

The early American cases *Dartmouth College* and *Terrett* follow the approach of the British Common Law in the famous case of *Sutton's Hospital* from 1612.[52]

---

47. Trustees of Dartmouth College v. Woodward, 17 U.S. 518, 651 (1819).
48. *Dartmouth,* 17 U.S. at 636.
49. Terrett v. Taylor, 13 U.S. 43, 47 (1815).
50. *Terrett,* 13 U.S. at 50.
51. *Terrett,* 13 U.S. at 49.
52. *Dartmouth,* 17 U.S. at 670–71 (citing *Sutton's Hospital*). *Terrett* does not explicitly cite to *Sutton's Hospital,* but the legal approach is remarkably similar.

In that case, Mr. Sutton asked for a corporate charter to set up a hospital. The King of England granted the charter and Mr. Sutton conveyed land to the corporation for the hospital. Then Mr. Sutton died. His heirs wanted the land back so they argued both that the corporation did not exist and that the conveyance of the land to the corporation was void. The British court (the Court of the King's Bench) ruled against the heirs, finding the corporation was valid and the corporation (not the heirs) was the true owner of the property.[53] Even in *Sutton's Hospital,* the early British court grappled with the conceptual difficulties of corporate personhood when it stated,

> a corporation aggregate of many is invisible, immortal, and rests only in intendment and consideration of the law.... They cannot commit treason, nor be outlawed, nor excommunicate, for they have no souls, neither can they appear in person, but by attorney.... A corporation aggregate of many cannot do fealty, for an invisible body can neither be in person nor swear.[54]

In certain early American cases, the Supreme Court was reluctant to grant corporations diversity jurisdiction in the federal courts, which requires that the plaintiff and defendant be citizens from different states. The reasoning that Chief Justice John Marshall deployed was that corporations were legal fictions, consequently they did not deserve all the rights of men and women. As Justice Marshall wrote in *Bank of the United States v. Deveaux,* with echoes of *Sutton's Hospital,*

> [a] corporation aggregate is an *artificial, invisible* body, existing only in *contemplation of law.* It has no analogy to a natural person. It has no organ but its *seal.* It cannot sue, or be sued, for any personal injury. It cannot be outlawed. It is not subject to an attachment of contempt. It never dies. It cannot be a citizen of any state, because it cannot owe allegiance. It cannot commit treason nor felony. It can have no residence, because it is an artificial, invisible, intangible body. It cannot appear in person, but must appear by attorney. For all these reasons it cannot come within the description of those who are enti-

---

53. Edward H. Warren, *Collateral Attack on Incorporation,* 21 HARV. L. REV. 305, 306 (1908).

54. *Id.* at 306–07 (quoting *Sutton's Hospital* case from 1612); *see also* Sierra Club v. Morton, 405 U.S. 727, 743 n.4 (1972) ("Early jurists considered the conventional corporation to be a highly artificial entity. Lord Coke opined that a corporation's creation 'rests only in intendment and consideration of the law.' Case of Sutton's Hospital, 77 Eng. Rep. 937, 973 (K.B.1612).").

2 · YES, VIRGINIA, CORPORATIONS ARE PEOPLE, NOT CITIZENS   35

tled to sue in the circuit courts of the United States. Neither residence nor inhabitancy is sufficient to give jurisdiction. It must be a *citizen*, possessing political rights, and owing allegiance to some state.[55]

The Court evolved from this position in *Deveaux* allowing corporations to sue and be sued and be subject to criminal liability as well.[56] But it is worth noting where the Supreme Court started. Its original stance was that corporations were not citizens at all, even for jurisdictional purposes.[57]

The first big leap in corporate personhood from holding mere property and contract rights to possessing more expansive rights was a claim that the Equal Protection Clause applied to corporations. One of the strangest twists in American constitutional law was the moment that corporations gained personhood under the Equal Protection Clause of the Fourteenth Amendment. It occurred in a case called *Santa Clara County*, and what was odd was the Supreme Court did not really even decide the matter in the actual opinion.

The Fourteenth Amendment to the U.S. Constitution, adopted after the Civil War in 1868 to grant emancipated slaves full citizenship, says, "[n]o state shall ... deprive any person of life, liberty, or property without due process of law, nor deny to any person ... the equal protection of the laws."[58] This latter phrase is known as the Equal Protection Clause. "Originating as the constitutional embodiment of abolitionist ideology, the [Fourteenth] amendment was primarily meant to secure the rights of man without distinctions based on race; nevertheless, for many decades the principal beneficiary of the amendment was corporate capitalism."[59]

Corporations were very aggressive in asserting Fourteenth Amendment rights after the Civil War. We have the likes of former U.S. Senator Roscoe Conkling to thank for the extension of Equal Protection to corporations.[60]

---

55. Bank of the United States v. Deveaux, 9 U.S. 61, 73 (1809) (italics in the original).

56. Blair & Pollman, *supra* note 13, at 1685 ("In *Louisville, Cincinnati & Charleston Railroad v. Letson*, the Court overruled *Deveaux* ...").

57. The Court in *Deveaux* found diversity jurisdiction by looking at the citizenship of the shareholders, even though it did not find citizenship for the corporation itself.

58. U.S. Constitution, Am. XIV.

59. Leonard W. Levy, *Foreword* to HOWARD JAY GRAHAM, EVERYMAN'S CONSTITUTION, HISTORICAL ESSAY ON THE FOURTEENTH AMENDMENT, THE "CONSPIRACY THEORY," AND AMERICAN CONSTITUTIONALISM vii (2013).

60. HEATHER COX RICHARDSON, TO MAKE MEN FREE: A HISTORY OF THE REPUBLICAN PARTY, 120–121 (2014). ("In the mid 1880s, Republicans enshrined their argument against government action on behalf of workers in the nation's fundamental law.... Roscoe Conkling ... turned to litigating for big business. In the 1882 case *San Mateo County v. Southern Pacific Railroad*, he insisted, based on his role as a congressman who had helped frame

Conkling helped draft the Fourteenth Amendment. He then left the Senate to become a lawyer. His Gilded Age law practice was going so swimmingly that Conkling turned down a seat on the Supreme Court not once, but twice.[61] Conkling argued as an expert witness in 1882 in *San Mateo County v. Southern Pacific Rail Road* that the Fourteenth Amendment is not limited to natural persons.[62] He produced a journal that seemed to show that the Joint Congressional Committee that drafted the Fourteenth Amendment vacillated between using "citizen" and "person" and the drafters chose "person" specifically to include corporations. According to historian Howard Jay Graham, Conkling was simply lying.[63]

Nonetheless, the Supreme Court embraced Conkling's reading of the Fourteenth Amendment, not in the *San Mateo County* case, but rather in a headnote four years later in 1886 in *Santa Clara County v. Southern Pacific Rail Road,* which stated: "[b]efore argument, Mr. Chief Justice Waite said: 'The Court does not wish to hear argument on the question whether the provision in the Fourteenth Amendment to the Constitution which forbids a state to deny to any person within its jurisdiction the equal protection of the laws applies to these corporations. We are all of opinion that it does.'"[64] This was not part of the formal opinion. But the damage was done. Later cases uncritically cited the headnote as if it had been part of the case. Once the Supreme Court concluded that the Fourteenth Amendment did apply to corporations, the Supreme reaffirmed this proposition repeatedly. In 1897 the Supreme Court asserted that "[i]t is well settled that corporations are persons within the provisions of the fourteenth amendment of the constitution of the United States."[65] The

---

the Fourteenth Amendment, that Congress had intended the due process clause of that amendment to protect corporations as well as individuals.... The principle that corporations were protected by the Fourteenth Amendment dramatically limited potential government regulation of business.").

61. Howard Jay Graham, *The "Conspiracy Theory" of the Fourteenth Amendment*, 47 Yale L. J. 371, 371 (1938).

62. County of San Mateo v. Southern Pac. R. Co., 116 U.S. 138 (1885).

63. GRAHAM, *supra* note 39, at 17 ("Conkling resorted to fraud and misquotations — reared an edifice that has taken eighty years to unlock and to level."); *see also* Charles A. Miller, *The Forest of Due Process of Law* in DUE PROCESS: NOMOS XVIII at 23 (Ronald Pennock & John W. Chapman eds) (1977).

64. Santa Clara County v. Southern Pacific R. Co., 118 U.S. 394 (1886); THOM HARTMANN, UNEQUAL PROTECTION: THE RISE OF CORPORATE DOMINANCE AND THEFT OF HUMAN RIGHTS (2010).

65. Gulf, C. & S.F. Ry. Co. v. Ellis, 165 U.S. 150, 154 (1897) (citing previous cases on corporate personhood including Santa Clara Co. v. Southern Pac. R. Co., 118 U. S. 394; Pembina Consol. Silver Min., etc., Co. v. Pennsylvania, 125 U. S. 181; Railway Co. v.

Court explained in the same case, "[a] state has no more power to deny to corporations the equal protection of the law than it has to individual citizens."[66]

The *Santa Clara* approach is controversial. Chief Counsel of the Brennan Center, Fritz Schwarz said, "I can't imagine that when they wrote the Fourteenth Amendment that they intended corporations to have all the rights of persons. I don't think anyone could have conceived that they were granting them the right of free speech."[67] Historically, even sitting Supreme Court Justices objected to the *Santa Clara* argument that corporations were "persons" covered by the Fourteenth Amendment. For instance, Justice Hugo Black stated in a dissenting opinion in 1938, "I do not believe the word 'person' in the Fourteenth Amendment includes corporations.... [and] I believe this Court should now overrule previous decisions which interpreted the Fourteenth Amendment to include corporations."[68] Justice Black argued, "[t]he history of the [Fourteenth] amendment proves that the people were told that its purpose was to protect weak and helpless human beings [e.g. ex-slaves] and were not told that it was intended to remove corporations in any fashion from the control of state governments."[69] He also wrote that corporations were elbowing in on rights that were meant for African Americans, noting "of the cases in this Court in which the Fourteenth Amendment was applied during the first fifty years after its adoption, less than one-half of 1 per cent. invoked it in protection of the [black] race, and more than 50 per cent. asked that its benefits be extended to corporations."[70]

Dissenting in *Wheeling Steel Corp.* in 1949, Justices William O. Douglas and Hugo Black, again, noted that the corporate personhood issue was not such an open and shut case: "[in *Santa Clara*] [t]here was no history, logic, or reason given to support that view.... [T]he purpose of the [Fourteenth] Amendment was to protect human rights—primarily the rights of a race which had just won its freedom."[71] Justices Douglas and Black thought the question of corporate personhood should be decided by the people, not the unelected

---

Mackey, 127 U. S. 205; Railway Co. v. Herrick, 127 U. S. 210; Railway Co. v. Beckwith, 129 U. S. 26; Railroad Co. v. Gibbes, 142 U. S. 386; Road Co. v. Sandford, 164 U. S. 578).

66. Gulf, C. & S.F. Ry. Co. v. Ellis, 165 U.S. 150, 154 (1897).

67. Interview with Frederick A.O. Schwarz, Chief Counsel Brennan Center for Justice at NYU School of Law (July 21, 2015).

68. Connecticut General Life Ins. Co. v. Johnson, 303 U.S. 77, 85 (1938) (Black, J., dissenting).

69. *Connecticut General Life Ins. Co.*, 303 U.S. at 87 (Black, J., dissenting).

70. *Connecticut General Life Ins. Co.*, 303 U.S. at 90 (Black, J., dissenting).

71. Wheeling Steel Corp. v. Glander, 337 U.S. 562, 577 (1949) (Douglas, J. & Black. J., dissenting).

Supreme Court. But they could not convince their fellow Justices. It is really too bad that Douglas, who had been the Chair of the Securities and Exchange Commission (SEC) before he became a Supreme Court Justice, didn't have more sway over this matter of corporate law.[72]

In the 1970s, *Santa Clara* was used to justify granting corporations the First Amendment right to spend unlimited corporate funds on ballot initiatives in a case called *Bellotti*. (There will be more on that case below in Chapter 5.) The Supreme Court in *Bellotti* relied on *Santa Clara* when it stated that "[i]t has been settled for almost a century that corporations are persons within the meaning of the Fourteenth Amendment."[73]

In *Citizens United* in 2010, when the Supreme Court held that political speech is "indispensable to decision making in a democracy, and this is no less true because the speech comes from a corporation," they cited *Bellotti*. Thus, it's only a hop, skip, and a jump from *Santa Clara* to *Citizens United*. So *Citizens United* was more of a culmination, and not the beginning, of the Supreme Court's granting ever more expansive rights to corporate "persons."

C. Not Citizens under the Comity Clause

Article IV's Privileges and Immunities Clause cases are one of the few areas of law where the Supreme Court has refused to extend the rights of humans to corporations. This clause of the Constitution reads: "[t]he Citizens of each State shall be entitled to all Privileges and Immunities of Citizens in the several States."[74] The point of the Privileges and Immunities Clause, also known as the Comity Clause, is to stop a given state from treating out-of-staters worse than it treats its own citizens.

Article IV of the U.S. Constitution was based on Article IV of the Articles of Confederation, which preceded it. However, there are key differences. In the Articles of Confederation, there was an exception in the Comity Clause for "paupers, vagabonds and fugitives from justice" from the Clause's coverage, which in any case, only applied to "free" inhabitants.[75] The language in the Constitution, by contrast, has no such carve outs and applies broadly to pro-

---

72. Kent Greenfield, *The Stakeholder Strategy*, 26 DEMOCRACY (2012), http://www.democracyjournal.org/26/the-stakeholder-strategy.php?page=all.

73. First Nat'l Bank of Boston v. Bellotti, 435 U.S. 765, 780 n.15 (1978).

74. U.S. Constitution Art IV, Section 2, Clause 1.

75. Articles of Confederation, Art. 4 (Mar. 1, 1781), http://press-pubs.uchicago.edu/founders/documents/a4_2_1s5.html.

tect *all* citizens of the several states. The language was changed to its current inclusive form in the drafting process of the Constitutional Convention. At various times, the draft of the Comity Clause had included the words "free citizens," which would have excluded slaves from its application. But eventually the drafters of the Constitution settled on just "citizens" which is far more inclusive.[76] As Joseph F. Zimmerman wrote in his book UNIFYING THE NATION about the Privileges and Immunities Clause, "[s]tate governments are subject to centripetal forces and provincial centrifugal forces. The latter forces must be controlled effectively by the Constitution in order to avoid fragmentation of the Union, and to ensure that citizens of each state generally are treated as citizens of one nation when traveling in sister states."[77]

The Comity Clause helps safeguard the principle that Americans have the same rights no matter where they are within the United States. As Yale Professor John Hart Ely explained, "[t]his was an equality provision, intended to keep states from treating outsiders worse than their own citizens."[78] Professor Ely continued, "the reason inequalities against nonresidents and not others were singled out for prohibition in the original document is obvious: nonresidents are a paradigmatically powerless class politically. And their protection proceeds by what amounts to a system of virtual representation: by constitutionally tying the fate of outsiders to the fate of those possessing political power, the framers insured that their interests would be well looked after."[79]

Founding father Alexander Hamilton, in Federalist No. 80, argued that the Comity Clause was "the basis of the union."[80] The Supreme Court also articulated a similar reason for the clause: "[t]he primary purpose of [the Comity] clause ... was to help fuse into one Nation a collection of independent, sovereign States.... Indeed, without ... [it], the Republic would have constituted little more than a league of States; it would not have constituted the Union

---

76. Records of the Federal Convention, Article 4, Section 2, Clause 1, *available at* http://press-pubs.uchicago.edu/founders/documents/a4_2_1s6.html.

77. JOSEPH F. ZIMMERMAN, UNIFYING THE NATION, ARTICLE IV OF THE UNITED STATES CONSTITUTION 157 (2015).

78. ELY, *supra* note 39 at 23.

79. *Id.* at 83.

80. Alexander Hamilton, *Federalist Paper No. 80* in THE FEDERALIST PAPERS 476 (Clinton Rossiter ed.) (2003); *see also* BENJAMIN FRANKLIN, EMBLEMATICAL REPRESENTATIONS (circa 1774) in THE COMPLETE WORKS OF BENJAMIN FRANKLIN Vol. 5, p. 417 (1887) ("The ordaining of laws in favor of one part of the nation, to the prejudice and oppression of another, is certainly the most erroneous and mistaken policy. An equal dispensation of protection, rights, privileges, and advantages, is what every part is entitled to, and ought to enjoy ...").

which now exists."[81] In the same case, the Supreme Court clarified that the Comity Clause protects the right to do business in another state as well, noting "it was long ago decided that one of the privileges which the clause guarantees to citizens of State A is that of doing business in State B on terms of substantial equality with the citizens of that State."[82]

In 1832, Justice Washington, riding Circuit in Pennsylvania, wrote in the case of *Corfield v. Coryell* one of the longest articulations of what the phrase "Privileges and Immunities" actually means:

> Protection by the government; the enjoyment of life and liberty, with the right to acquire and possess property of every kind, and to pursue and obtain happiness and safety; subject nevertheless to such restraints as the government may justly prescribe for the general good of the whole. The right of a citizen of one state to pass through, or to reside in any other state, for purposes of trade, agriculture, professional pursuits, or otherwise; to claim the benefit of the writ of habeas corpus; to institute and maintain actions of any kind in the courts of the state; to take, hold and dispose of property, either real or personal; and an exemption from higher taxes or impositions than are paid by the other citizens of the state; may be mentioned as some of the particular privileges and immunities of citizens, which are clearly embraced by the general description of privileges deemed to be fundamental: to which may be added, the elective franchise, as regulated and established by the laws or constitution of the state in which it is to be exercised.[83]

Given that this list includes *habeas corpus*, voting, and the enjoyment of life, a fair reading of this case would cabin the application of the Comity Clause to human beings.

The Privileges and Immunities Clause, like many parts of the Constitution, has been dragged through the mud on occasion, in particularly badly reasoned cases by the Supreme Court. For example, the Court drew entirely the wrong conclusions when it applied the Comity Clause to African American slaves in the *Dred Scott* decision. Chief Justice Taney wrote in *Dred Scott*, one of the Court's most reviled cases, "it [is] absolutely certain that the African race were

---

81. Toomer v. Witsell, 334 U.S. 385, 395–96 (1948) (internal citations omitted).
82. *Id.* at 396.
83. Corfield v. Coryell, 6 F. Cas. 546, 551–52 (C.C. Pa. 1823).

not included under the name of citizens of a States, and were not in contemplation of the framers of the Constitution when these privileges and immunities were provided for the protection of the citizens in other States."[84] This reading of the Comity Clause was overruled when the Constitution was amended after the Civil War by the Thirteenth and Fourteenth Amendments.

On the other hand, the Comity Clause has also been used in positive ways, including to ensure the freedom of Americans to travel among the 50 states and the right of Americans to move to a new state. This was clarified in a Supreme Court case called *Saenz v. Roe* in 1999. Justice John Paul Stevens, writing for the majority in *Saenz*, stated, "[a] component of the right to travel is, however, expressly protected by the text of the Constitution [in the Comity Clause]."[85] Justice Stevens writing in *Saenz* explained, "by virtue of a person's state citizenship, a citizen of one State who travels in other States, intending to return home at the end of his journey, is entitled to enjoy the 'Privileges and Immunities of Citizens in the several States' that he visits.... It provides important protections for nonresidents who enter a State whether to obtain employment, [or] to procure medical services ..." But the Clause protects more than just travelers; it also protects individuals who want to move from one state to another permanently. According to *Saenz*, "[p]ermissible justifications for discrimination between residents and nonresidents are simply inapplicable to a nonresident's exercise of the right to move into another State and become a resident of that State."[86] Or as the Supreme Court put it in another case, the Comity Clause protects against "discrimination against nonresidents seeking to ply their trade, practice their occupation, or pursue a common calling within the State."[87]

In contradistinction to the Supreme Court's approach under the Fourteenth Amendment of treating humans and corporations as functional equivalents, under the Comity Cause the Court has not extended corporations "citizenship." The Supreme Court's holding that corporations are not covered by the Comity Clause traces back to 1839 in *Bank of Augusta v. Earle*, where the Court concluded that "[t]he only rights [a corporation] can claim are the rights which are given to it in that character, and not the rights which belong to its members as citizens of a state."[88]

---

84. Scott v. Sandford, 60 U.S. 393 (1856).
85. Saenz v. Roe, 526 U.S. 489, 501–02 (1999) (internal citations omitted).
86. *Saenz*, 526 U.S. at 501–02 (internal citations omitted).
87. Hicklin v. Orbeck, 437 U.S. 518, 524 (1978).
88. Bank of Augusta v. Earle, 38 U.S. 519, 587 (1839); *see also id.* at 578–79 ("Corporations are neither persons nor partners, but artificial bodies politic, created by act of state,

In 1869, the Supreme Court decided in *Paul v. Virginia,* just months after
the Fourteenth Amendment was ratified, that "in no case which has come
under our observation, either in the State or Federal courts, has a corporation
been considered a citizen within the meaning of [the Comity Clause] of the
Constitution ..."[89] The Supreme Court in the *Paul* case was clear that giving
corporations the protection of the Privileges and Immunities Clause could give
them too much power:

> There is scarcely a business pursued requiring the expenditure of large
> capital.... that is not carried on by corporations. It is not too much
> to say that the wealth and business of the country are to a great ex-
> tent controlled by them. And if, when composed of citizens of one
> State, their corporate powers and franchises could be exercised in other
> States without restriction, it is easy to see that, with the advantages
> thus possessed, the most important business of those States would
> soon pass into their hands. The principal business of every State
> would, in fact, be controlled by corporations created by other States.[90]

The next year, the Court reaffirmed the *Paul* holding. The lawyer arguing the
new case tried to make an argument that corporations were "quasi citizens." The
Court rejected this argument stating tartly, "the Constitution does not recognize
quasi citizens, or their rights."[91] The Supreme Court reaffirmed this approach to
corporations not being citizens in 1888 in *Pembina Mining.*[92] This position was
again reaffirmed in 1890.[93] By 1898, the Supreme Court referred to it as settled
law that corporations were not covered by the Privileges and Immunities Clause.[94]

---

always ad hoc, and their franchises are granted for public good, of which they are the supposed instruments.").

89. Paul v. State of Virginia, 75 U.S. 168, 178 (1869); *see also* Ducat v. Chicago, 77 U.S.
410 (1870) (accord).

90. *Paul,* 75 U.S. at 181–182 (emphasis added).

91. *Ducat,* 77 U.S. at 413.

92. Pembina Consol. Silver Mining & Milling Co. v. Pennsylvania, 125 U.S. 181, 187–88
(1888) (indicating "[c]orporations are not citizens within the meaning of [Art. IV, §2,
which] 'applies only to natural persons.'").

93. Norfolk & W.R. Co. v. Com. of Pennsylvania, 136 U.S. 114, 118 (1890) ("In [*Pembina*] we held ... that corporations are not citizens within the meaning of clause, 1, sec. 2,
of art. IV of the Constitution of the United States declaring that 'the citizens of each State
shall be entitled to all privileges and immunities of citizens in the several States.'").

94. Blake v. McClung, 172 U.S. 239, 259 (1898) ("[I]t is equally well settled ... a corporation is not a citizen within the meaning of the constitutional provision that 'the citizens of each state shall be entitled to all privileges and immunities of citizens in the several
states.'"); *see also* Orient Ins. Co. v. Daggs, 172 U.S. 557, 561 (1899) ("A corporation is not

And the Supreme Court held this view distinguishing corporations from citizens throughout the twentieth century,[95] holding for example that "[o]f still less merit is the suggestion that the statute abridges the rights and privileges of citizens; for a corporation cannot be deemed a citizen within the meaning of the clause of the Constitution of the United States which protects the privileges and immunities of citizens of the United States against being abridged or impaired by the law of a state."[96] In 1921, the Supreme Court allowed Mississippi to exclude out-of-state corporations and the Court distinguished corporations and individuals.[97] The Court also concurred in *Grosjean* in 1936: "A corporation, we have held, is not a 'citizen' within the meaning of the privileges and immunities clause. But a corporation is a 'person' within the meaning of the equal protection and due process of law clauses[.]"[98]

As discussed above, corporations have changed radically over time in their scope, purpose, and duration, and courts have been willing to grant expansive rights to corporations, but they have not granted corporations and people identical rights. To this day, the Supreme Court has been of at least two minds when it comes to corporations—they are treated as "persons" who are covered by the Equal Protection Clause (and Contracts Clause among others),

a citizen ... and hence has not 'privileges and immunities' secured to 'citizen' against state legislation.").

95. Waters-Pierce Oil Co. v. State of Texas, 177 U.S. 28, 45 (1900) ("a corporation did not have the rights of its personal members, and could not invoke that provision of §2, article 4, of the Constitution of the United States, which gave to the citizens of each state the privileges and immunities of citizens of the several states."); Hemphill v. Orloff, 277 U.S. 537, 548 (1928) ("A corporation is not a mere collection of individuals capable of claiming all benefits assured them by section 2, article 4, of the Constitution."); Asbury Hospital v. Cass County, N.D., 326 U.S. 207, 210–211 (1945) ("Appellant, [a Minnesota non-profit corporation] does not invoke the commerce clause, and is neither a citizen of a state nor of the United States within the protection of the privileges and immunities clauses of Article IV, §2 of the Constitution and the Fourteenth Amendment."); Western & Southern Life Ins. Co. v. State Bd. of Equalization of California, 451 U.S. 648, 656 (1981) ("[T]he Privileges and Immunities Clause is inapplicable to corporations.").

96. Western Turf Association v. Greenberg, 204 U.S. 359, 363 (1907).

97. Crescent Cotton Oil Co. v. State of Mississippi, 257 U.S. 129, 137 (1921) (Citing Hammond Packing Co. v. Arkansas, 212 U. S. 322, 343, 344; Baltic Mining Co. v. Massachusetts, 231 U.S. 68, 83; And see Ft. Smith Lumber Co. v. Arkansas, 251 U.S. 532, 533; Am. Sugar Refining Co. v. Louisiana, 179 U.S. 89; Williams v. Fears, 179 U.S. 270, 276; W. W. Cargill Co. v. Minnesota, 180 U. S. 452).

98. Grosjean v. Am. Press Co., 297 U.S. 233, 244 (1936) (citing Covington & L. Turnpike Road Co. v. Sandford, 164 U.S. 578, 592; Smyth v. Ames, 169 U.S. 466, 522).

but they are excluded from the definition of "citizens" under the Comity Clause.[99]

This is why the Supreme Court's inconsistent approaches matter. America is a common law country. Accordingly, when cases are litigated, lawyers need to point to precedent from prior cases to argue why their client should win their present case. When the Supreme Court has been consistent on a particular point of law for centuries, lawyers typically won't waste their breath arguing to the contrary. But where the Court has a history of waffling on a particular point, this opens the door for lawyers to argue that a new case could go either way and still be consistent with precedent. Consequently, one of the reasons the anti-corporate citizenship Comity Clause cases are so important is they serve as a legal basis to challenge the direction of a pro-business court. A newly reconstituted Supreme Court, post-Justice Scalia, should consider the wisdom of the Comity Clause cases when considering the appropriate scope of corporate rights in the future.

---

99. Stewart Jay, *The Curious Exclusion of Corporations from the Privileges and Immunities Clause of Article IV*, 44 HOFSTRA L. REV. (Fall 2015) ("If states were obliged to treat foreign corporations like individual citizens for purposes of the [Comity] clause, rather than domestic corporations, their police powers would be seriously undermined.").

Chapter 3

The Price of the Ticket

> Commerce is entitled to a complete and efficient protection in all its legal rights, but the moment it presumes to control ... it should be frowned on, and rebuked.
>
> —James Fenimore Cooper[1]

Corporate rights appear to snowball as they roll forward though time. As soon as the Supreme Court grants a new right to corporations, corporate lawyers are back in court arguing for additional rights in a seemingly insatiable quest for more. Given America's privately funded elections, corporations have tried to expand their rights in parallel tracks. First, they influenced who sat in government through spending money in elections. Second, they have sought to influence elected officials by spending much more on lobbyists. The fact that more money is spent by corporations on lobbying instead of elections makes sense, because election day is once every two years (for House Members), to four years (for Presidents), to six years (for Senators). But governing happens every day. Nonetheless, the two types of spending are linked, as corporate campaign spending greases the skids and the corporate lobbying attempts to steer the ship of state.

When laws were crafted to regulate either campaign spending or lobbying, corporations have complained in court that regulations of any kind, including plain vanilla disclosures, are unconstitutional. For most of the twentieth century, the Supreme Court rejected these arguments and upheld most limits and regulations that Congress and the states passed to protect the integrity of elections and the trustworthiness of the democratic process. But as later chap-

---

1. ARTHUR M. SCHLESINGER JR., THE AGE OF JACKSON 339 (1953) (quoting Fenimore Cooper).

ters will show, the Supreme Court in the early twenty-first century is reversing course. The story is a complicated one, because even when there were criminal penalties for corporate spending in politics, many corporations were willing to bend or break the law to move their political agendas forward.

A. Privately Financed Democracy

America's privately financed democratic elections have been a source of consternation for more than a century as citizens worry that candidates in the general election are two political elites that have arrived on the ballot through support by financial elites during the primary season. For some thinkers, private money in politics poses an existential threat to the democratic process.[2] The Brennan Center's Fritz Schwarz states, "[w]e surely have a scandal in this country now of too much money in politics."[3] And polls show that a super majority of the American public agrees with Mr. Schwarz. In 2015, a *New York Times/CBS* Poll found 84% thought money in American political campaigns had too much influence.[4] Another poll in 2015 from Pew found 84% of Democrats and 72% of Republicans favored limiting the amount of money in politics.[5] One of the reasons for campaign contribution limits in the first place is to democratize the funding of candidates. Contribution limits "constrain the inegalitarian bias of a system dominated by private giving. To be sure, any system of private finance gives the upper hand to the upper classes[.]"[6]

In 2015, Former President Jimmy Carter, who has worked extensively monitoring the integrity of democratic elections around the world, expressed his

---

2. Interview with Nell Minow, Vice Chair, ValueEdge Advisors (Aug. 19, 2015) ("I'm not given to hyperbole, but if the Republican candidate for president out of 17 people that are running is chosen not through the primary system, but through 18 billionaires, then we can just give up on the idea of democracy.").

3. Interview with Frederick A.O. Schwarz, Chief Counsel Brennan Center for Justice at NYU School of Law (July 21, 2015).

4. N.Y. Times/CBS News Poll, *Americans' Views on Money in Politics: Most Americans Say that Money Has Too Much of an Influence on Politicians and that Campaign Finance Changes Are Needed*, N.Y. TIMES (June 2, 2015), http://www.nytimes.com/interactive/2015/06/02/us/politics/money-in-politics-poll.html?_r=0.

5. *Beyond Distrust: How Americans View Their Government 6. Perceptions of Elected Officials and the Role of Money in Politics*, PEW RESEARCH CTR. (Nov. 23, 2015).

6. BRUCE ACKERMAN & IAN AYRES, VOTING WITH DOLLARS: A NEW PARADIGM FOR CAMPAIGN FINANCE 50 (2002).

deep worry about the American campaign finance system perpetuating incumbency: "we've just seen a complete subversion of our political system as a payoff to major contributors, who want and expect and sometimes get favors for themselves after the election's over…. The incumbents, Democrats and Republicans, look upon this unlimited money as a great benefit to themselves. Somebody's who's already in Congress has a lot more to sell to an avid contributor than somebody who's just a challenger."[7] President Carter is right to worry about incumbency as rates of reelection seem to defy both gravity and opinion polling—hovering in the 90% range for Congress, despite average congressional approval rating of less than 25% in the last decade.[8]

In recent election cycles, only a tiny sliver of the American electorate donated to political campaigns, and an even tinier sliver gave the maximum.[9] What may discourage the small donor at the federal level is the perception that bigger spenders will overwhelm the impact of any modest donation. The President of Demos, Heather McGhee, argued: "[t]he voices of those with money are structurally amplified by weak campaign finance rules. The more this is true, the less powerful ordinary voters feel that they are with their one vote and their $30 donation. And, the less powerful they actually are."[10]

For some thinkers, money in politics is the causal explanation of a panoply of poor policies. Businessman Ben Cohen, who is deeply concerned about campaign finance,[11] argues:

---

7. Jon Schwarz, *Jimmy Carter: The U.S. Is an "Oligarchy With Unlimited Political Bribery,"* THE INTERCEPT (July 30, 2015); JOHN NICHOLS & ROBERT W. MCCHESNEY, DOLLAROCRACY HOW THE MONEY AND MEDIA ELECTION COMPLEX IS DESTROYING AMERICA xiv (quoting President Carter) ("we have one of the worst election processes in the world right in United States of America, and it's almost entirely because of the excessive influx of money.").

8. Louis Jacobson, *Congress has 11% Approval Ratings but 96% Incumbent Reelection Rate, Meme Says*, POLITIFACT (Nov. 11, 2014), http://www.politifact.com/truth-o-meter/statements/2014/nov/11/facebook-posts/congress-has-11-approval-ratings-96-incumbent-re-e/ ("Congress had roughly a 14 percent approval rate, and the incumbent re-election rate may be as low as 95 percent.").

9. Lee Drutman, *The Political 1% of the 1% in 2012*, SUNLIGHT FOUNDATION (June 24, 2013), http://sunlightfoundation.com/blog/2013/06/24/1pct_of_the_1pct/; *Constructing a New Paradigm 2013 Annual Report*, National Institute on Money in State Politics, 9 (Sept. 2013) (In the 2012 election 1% gave $3.4 billion in contributions while 99% gave $3.3 billion in contributions).

10. Interview with Heather McGhee, President Demos (Aug. 11, 2015).

11. Ben Cohen is the organizer of the Stamp Stampede, which urges campaign finance reforms, including amending the constitution to reverse *Citizens United v. FEC* by stamping political messages on U.S. currency. *About Us*, STAMP STAMPEDE, http://www.stamp-stampede.org/pages/about-us.

> Money in politics is why weapons manufacturers are able to get Congress to be over-militaristic. It's the reason why the health insurance industry has prevented national healthcare from happening. It's the reason why the fossil fuel industry has prevented environmental regulations and a reasonable energy policy. It's the reason why the financial industry … is involved in usurious credit card rates and absurd student loan policy.[12]

Whether any of these are causally linked is an empirical question. But many share Mr. Cohen's intuition that money in politics is driving policy outcomes.[13] Many worry that corporate financial power is deployed in the political arena in self-serving ways. As the book CORPORATE GOVERNANCE argues:

> The corporate 'citizen,' with the right to political speech (and political contributions) has had a powerful impact on the laws that affect it. In theory, corporations support the free market, with as little interference from government as possible. In reality, whenever corporations can persuade the government to protect them from the free market, by legislating barriers to competition or limiting liability, they do so.[14]

From a democratic point of view, having corporations elbow in on politics may ruin political debate because an average citizen simply can't keep up with the volume of expression that a sizeable corporation can generate. And the influence of big private money can seem at times to overwhelm the power of the individual voter. As author Eric Alterman explained, "[c]onsider the absurdity: Wealthy donors who cannot legally vote on the outcome of a local representative election because the winner will not represent them can wield far more influence at the ATM than at the ballot box."[15] If big spending hasn't already appeared, it may be coming to a local election near you soon. As Lisa Graves noted, "[t]here is a move by corporations like Chevron … to spend their money in local elections instead of working in federal or state wide elections. To win a local race might only take $50,000. Now corporations are injecting millions

---

12. B Corporation, *B Inspired @ Burlington, VT: Ben Cohen*, YOUTUBE (Feb. 24, 2015), https://www.youtube.com/watch?v=Wa3VpDVfSC8.

13. Alex Seitz-Wald, *Everyone Hates* Citizens United*: A New Poll Shows the Vast Majority of Americans Think There's Too Much Money in Politics*, SALON.COM (Oct 25, 2012), http://www.salon.com/2012/10/25/people_really_hate_citizens_united/.

14. ROBERT A.G. MONKS & NELL MINOW, CORPORATE GOVERNANCE 19 (Fifth ed. 2011).

15. ERIC ALTERMAN, KABUKI DEMOCRACY: THE SYSTEM VS. BARACK OBAMA 123 (2011) ("In Democrat John Kerry's 2008 Massachusetts Senate race, for example, two-thirds of both candidates' contributions were from out-of-state.").

in state races and they are overwhelming the local fundraising base."[16] A corporation can spend in elections all 50 states simultaneously. Yet the voter only gets one vote, in one election, in one county, in one state. While the voter is landlocked, corporate money flows across city, county, and state lines.

Though the impact of money in politics is bad enough in the political branches (the executive and legislative), the impact can be particularly troubling when it comes to the judiciary.[17] In 39 states, at least some judicial offices are elected. And too frequently the contributors to judicial campaigns are attorneys and their corporate clients, who will have cases pending before these elected judges.[18] Studies have shown that the money spent in judicial elections is on the rise and that it often has an impact on judicial decision making.[19] Professors Michael Kang and Joanna Shepard found, "using a dataset of every state supreme court case in all fifty states over a four-year period, ... elected judges are more likely to decide in favor of business interests as the amount of campaign contributions received from those interests increases. In other words, every dollar of direct contributions from business groups is associated with an increase in the probability that the judge in question will vote for business litigants."[20]

Not surprisingly, political spending in judicial elections affects the way the public perceives the impartiality of the judiciary.[21] As retired Justice Sandra

---

16. Interview with Lisa Graves, Executive Director Center for Media & Democracy (July 17, 2015).

17. Brief of Amici Curiae Public Citizen, Inc. & Democracy 21 in Support of Respondent at 13–14, Williams-Yulee v. The Florida Bar, No. 13-1499 (U.S. brief filed Dec. 23, 2014) ("An elected judge who receives half of her donations from business groups would be expected to vote pro-business almost two-thirds of the time, and the correlation has grown stronger over time.").

18. Brief of Professors of Law, Economics, and Political Science as Amici Curiae in Support of Respondent at 8–9, Williams-Yulee v. The Florida Bar, No. 13-1499 (U.S. brief filed Dec. 23, 2014) ("That business interests, lawyers, and lobbyists together account for nearly 60 percent of campaign contributions to candidates for judicial office is problematic because of the fear that campaign contributions affect judicial decision-making.").

19. *Id.* at 9–10 ("studies have shown that campaign contributions from business interests, lawyers, and lobbyists can be correlated with favorable decisions in cases before recipient judges.... Because approximately one-third of cases before state supreme courts involve business litigants, there is much at stake.").

20. Michael S. Kang & Joanna M. Shepherd, *The Partisan Price of Justice: An Empirical Analysis of Campaign Contributions and Judicial Decisions*, 86 N.Y.U. L. Rev. 69 (2011).

21. Brief for Amici Curiae of Brennan Ctr. for Justice at NYU School of Law et al. in Support of Respondent at 19, Williams-Yulee v. The Florida Bar, No. 13-1499 (U.S. brief filed Dec. 23, 2014) ("Survey data demonstrates that these contributions impact the public's confidence in the judiciary. In a 2013 poll, 95% of respondents indicated that they be-

Day O'Connor stated, "[t]his rise in judicial campaigning ... [is] a problem for an independent judiciary." She continued, "[n]o state can possibly benefit from having that much money injected into a political campaign."[22] Since retiring, Justice O'Connor has advocated for states to stop electing judges altogether and to adopt merit selection of judges—sometimes known as the Missouri Plan. Retired Montana Supreme Court Justice Nelson has reached the same conclusion even after being an elected Justice himself. "I've always been a proponent of judicial elections. But ... I now think that Montana should go to a merit selection process to get money out of judicial elections to the extent humanly possible."[23] Ex-State Supreme Court Justices are similarly dismayed at the impact of money in politics on judicial elections, as two recently wrote in a bipartisan op-ed: "the surge in interest group spending to influence state judicial elections ... has helped fuel a perception that justice is for sale, which undermines the public's trust in impartial courts."[24]

B. Scandal and Reform

Campaign finance restrictions of corporations' spending in elections are typically the result of political scandals. Throughout American history, the pattern is first scandal, then reform. Then rinse and repeat. First scandal, then reform. This pattern has repeated itself for the past 100 years.

The problem of veiled corporate political expenditures dominated the national consciousness in 1905[25] when the public discovered that the biggest insurance companies in the country had given vast sums of money to the

---

lieve contributions to judicial elections have at least a little impact on judicial decisions. 2013 National Poll, at 3. In the same survey, 70% of respondents indicated that it is a 'very serious' problem when a judicial candidate receives campaign contributions from an individual, lawyer, business or interest group with a case on which the judicial candidate may have to rule, while an additional 20% thought it was a 'somewhat serious' problem. *Id.* Only 1% of respondents thought it was 'no problem.'").

22. Matthew Mosk, *O'Connor Calls* Citizens United *Ruling 'A Problem'*, ABC News, (Jan. 26, 2010), http://abcnews.go.com/Blotter/oconnor-citizens-united-ruling-problem/story?id=9668044.

23. Interview with Retired Montana Supreme Court Justice James Nelson (Aug. 4, 2015).

24. Wallace Jefferson & Barbara Pariente, *The 'Citizens United' Anniversary Is a Regrettable Date for State Courts*, DALLAS MORNING NEWS (Jan. 20, 2015).

25. Adam Winkler, *'Other People's Money': Corporations, Agency Costs, and Campaign Finance Law*, 92 GEORGETOWN L. J. 871, 893–94 (June 2004); *see also id.* at 914–15 (one insurance executive involved in the 1905 scandal was charged with grand larceny, but the criminal charges were thrown out by the New York courts).

Republican Party using policyholder money, including for the 1904 re-election of President Theodore Roosevelt. This wasn't the only corporate money spent for Roosevelt's election. The industrialist Henry Clay Frick later complained about Roosevelt that "[w]e bought the son of a bitch, and then he didn't stay bought."[26] Besides the problem of using other people's money in politics, the public was outraged when they learned that this corporate spending had been done covertly as a series of secret backroom deals. After President Roosevelt was embroiled in the New York Life Insurance Scandal, he told Congress, "[a]ll contributions by corporations to any political committee or for any political purpose should be forbidden by law; directors should not be permitted to use stockholders' money for such purposes; and, moreover, a prohibition of this kind would be … an effective method of stopping [corrupt] evils[.]"[27] Congress' response was twofold. First, it passed the Tillman Act in 1907, prohibiting corporations from making contributions to candidates for federal office.[28] As Justice Frankfurter explained of the Tillman Act: "its aim was not merely to prevent the subversion of the integrity of the electoral process. Its underlying philosophy was to sustain the active, alert responsibility of the individual citizen in a democracy for the wise conduct of government."[29] Second, Congress passed the Publicity Act of 1910, the first federal law to require public disclosure of financial spending by political parties.[30]

Meanwhile in Montana, the pattern of scandal and reform repeated because of the actions of W.A. Clark, one of the richest men in America at the time. He has the ignoble distinction of being one of few U.S. Senators to resign in indignity in 1900 because it was clear that he had bribed the Montana legislature to get his seat in 1899.[31] Though Clark complained that, "I never bought

---

26. David E. Sanger, *The Nation: Big Time; From Trustbusters to Trust Trusters*, N.Y. TIMES (Dec. 6, 1998), http://www.nytimes.com/1998/12/06/weekinreview/the-nation-big-time-from-trustbusters-to-trust-trusters.html?pagewanted=all (quoting Henry Clay Frick).

27. Theodore Roosevelt, *Fifth Annual Message*, Dec. 5, 1905, http://www.presidency.ucsb.edu/ws/?pid=29546.

28. *See* United States v. U.S. Brewers Ass'n, 239 F. 163 (W.D. Pa. 1916) (upholding the Tillman Act and finding "[t]hese artificial creatures [e.g., corporations] are not citizens of the United States, and, so far as the franchise is concerned, must at all times be held subservient and subordinate to the government and the citizenship of which it is composed.").

29. United States v. Int'l Union United Auto., Aircraft & Agr. Implement Workers of Am. (UAW-CIO), 352 U.S. 567, 575 (1957) (Frankfurter, J.).

30. Act of June 25, 1910, c. 392, 36 Stat. 822.

31. *The Election Case of William A. Clark of Montana (1900)*, U.S. SENATE, http://www.senate.gov/artandhistory/history/common/contested_elections/089William_Clark.htm (last visited Nov. 23, 2015).

a man who wasn't for sale,"[32] His unsavory actions were part of a bigger trend of increasing corporate power at the time. As corporations grew in strength, and courts granted them more rights in the post-Civil War period through the Fourteenth Amendment, political corruption from corporate sources festered. Politics in the Gilded Age was notoriously crooked as "the political life of the people [was] dominated and exploited for private ends by rich working corporations in alliance with professional party politicians."[33] *The Chicago Tribune* noted at the time, " '[b]ehind every one of half the portly and well-dressed members of the Senate can be seen the outlines of some corporation interested in getting or preventing legislation.' "[34] Whether it was the railroads sending representatives onto the floor of the Pennsylvania legislature, or the "Copper Kings' " influence over Montana,[35] corporate incursions into the government processes were legend during the Gilded Age.[36]

U.S. Senator Max Baucus of Montana once explained in congressional testimony the particular influence that copper companies had in his state. The copper dome on the state capitol was "a symbol of the copper barons and their ultimate power to decide who represented the people of Montana. While miners risked their lives working thousands of feet below the earth, the copper kings lived high on the hog. Corporations were literally buying elections."[37] As a sitting governor of Montana wrote in the *New York Times* in 2012, W.A. Clark

---

32. Brian Schweitzer, *Mining for Influence in Montana*, N.Y. TIMES, June 3, 2012, http://www.nytimes.com/2012/06/04/opinion/an-invitation-to-keep-money-out-of-politics.html?_r=0 (quoting Clark).

33. ROBERT C. POST, CITIZENS DIVIDED CAMPAIGN FINANCE REFORM AND THE CONSTITUTION 28 (2014) (quoting Edward A. Ross, *Political Decay—An Interpretation*, 61 INDEPENDENT 123, 124 (1906)).

34. HEATHER COX RICHARDSON, TO MAKE MEN FREE: A HISTORY OF THE REPUBLICAN PARTY, 121 (2014).

35. *The Copper Kings*, GREAT FALLS TRIBUNE, http://archive.greatfallstribune.com/multimedia/125newsmakers6/copperkings.html (last visited July 17, 2015).

36. *Quay and the Democrats: The Boss and the Pennsylvania Railroad at Work*, N.Y. TIMES (June 14, 1890) (Reporting that "[William Latta then General Agent of the Pennsylvania Railroad,] for many years worked openly and aboveboard as the recognized representative of the Pennsylvania Road and has a seat in the select council chamber at its regular meetings every Thursday, and uses his privilege with so much freedom that he calls the pages, sends notes to the members, and simply indicates to them what he wants done and directs what they shall do.").

37. Testimony of U.S. Senator Max Baucus, Montana Senate Judiciary Committee Subcommittee on the Constitution, Civil Rights and Human Rights Hearing on Taking Back Our Democracy: Responding to *Citizens United* and the Rise of Super PACs (July 24, 2012),

"bought up half the state of Montana, and if he needed favors from politicians, he bought those as well."[38] A contemporaneous editorial from Clark's time in Montana wrote, "[i]f the copper trust must rule Montana, why not cut out all pretense of representative government and haul down the flag of a free state?"[39]

The U.S. Senate's investigation into Clark turned up "a dazzling list of bribes ranging from $240 to $100,000. In a high-pressure, well-organized scheme coordinated by Clark's son, Clark's agents had paid mortgages, purchased ranches, paid debts, financed banks, and blatantly presented envelopes of cash to legislators."[40] This whole Clark episode encouraged the adoption of the Seventeenth Amendment to the U.S. Constitution, which allows for the direct election of Senators by the people instead of through state legislatures.[41] This history of corporate abuse also led to the passage of Montana's Corrupt Practices Act in 1912, which banned corporations from spending in Montana elections.[42]

Back at the federal level, following the Teapot Dome scandal, a pay-to-play scheme where oil companies gave payoffs to federal officials in exchange for oil leases, federal disclosures were expanded in the Federal Corrupt Practices Act of 1925.[43] That Act required political committees to report total contributions and expenditures.[44] The 1925 Act was largely a dead letter because of lack of enforcement.[45] In the 1960s, President Johnson said that this campaign finance law was "more loophole than law."[46] But it would take the epic Watergate scandal from the next President for the country to tackle its money in politics rules again.

---

38. Schweitzer, *supra* note 32.

39. Jeff Wiltse, *The Origins of Montana's Corrupt Practices Act: A More Complete History*, 72 MONT. L. REV 299, 319 (2012) (quoting *Haul Down the Flag!*, WESTERN NEWS 4 (Feb. 17, 1911)).

40. *The Election Case of William A. Clark of Montana (1900)*, *supra* note 31.

41. JOHN PAUL STEVENS, SIX AMENDMENTS HOW AND WHY WE SHOULD CHANGE THE CONSTITUTION 9 (2014).

42. Testimony of Montana Attorney General Steve Bullock before the United States Senate Committee on Rules and Administration, Feb. 2, 2010, http://classic.followthemoney.org/press/Reports/02022010_Bullock_Testimony.pdf.

43. 43 Stat. 1070.

44. *Id.* at §305(a), 43 Stat. 1071; *see also* Burroughs v. United States, 290 U.S. 534 (1934) (upholding the 1925 Act).

45. Frank Pasquale, *Reclaiming Egalitarianism in the Political Theory of Campaign Finance Reform*, 2008 U. ILL. L. REV. 599, 607 (2008).

46. Lyndon B. Johnson, *Statement by the President Upon Signing the Foreign Investors Tax Act and the Presidential Election Fund Act*, AM. PRESIDENCY PROJECT (Nov. 13, 1966), http://www.presidency.ucsb.edu/ws/?pid=28030.

In the 1970s, after the Watergate scandal, Congress passed several reforms, including corporate reforms. The Senate Watergate hearing had revealed that Gulf Oil, and many other corporations, had given President Nixon's campaign illegal contributions. This prompted a parallel investigation at the SEC because Stanley Sporkin, then-Director of SEC Enforcement, wanted to know how corporate payments from publicly traded corporations could make their way into a presidential campaign when such donations violated the Tillman Act's prohibition on corporation contributions.[47] Mr. Sporkin remarked:

> How does Gulf Oil record a transaction of a $50,000 cash payment? I wanted to know, what account did they charge? Do they have an account called "Bribery"? And so I decided to ask one of my investigators to go out and find out how they did it.... When we looked into these funds, we found out they were not only being used domestically in the United States for illegal campaign contributions, but we found that the same monies were being used to bribe officials overseas in connection with the companies' business.[48]

When the SEC asked publicly traded corporations for voluntary disclosures of political payments,[49] they were flummoxed to find that the payments to Nixon's campaign were just the tip of the iceberg.[50] As the SEC reported to Congress in 1976: "Millions of dollars ... have been inaccurately

---

47. *Black Money: Transcript*, Frontline (Apr. 7, 2009), http://www.pbs.org/wgbh/pages/frontline/blackmoney/etc/script.html; Report of the Securities and Exchange Commission on Questionable and Illegal Corporate Payments and Practices Submitted to the Senate Banking, Housing and Urban Affairs Committee 2 (May 12, 1976), http://c0403731.cdn.cloudfiles.rackspacecloud.com/collection/papers/1970/1976_0512_SEC-Questionable.pdf ("In 1973, as a result of the work of the Office of the Special Prosecutor, several corporations and executive officers were charged with using corporate funds for illegal domestic political contributions. The Commission recognized that these activities involved matters of possible significance to public investors, the nondisclosure of which might entail violations of the federal securities laws.... The Commission's inquiry into the circumstances surrounding alleged illegal political campaign contributions revealed that violations of the federal securities laws had indeed occurred.").

48. *Black Money: Transcript*, Frontline.

49. SEC Report on Illegal Corporate Payments, *supra* note 47, at 3–5 (describing the SEC's voluntary disclosure program).

50. *Id.* at 36. At nearly the same time, the Chair of United Brands Corporation, Eli Black, committed suicide by jumping off the Pan Am building in New York City on Feb. 3, 1975 prompting the SEC to investigate. It found that $1,250,000 had been paid to Honduras to lessen a tax on bananas. *See* John T. Noonan, Jr., Bribes 656 (1984).

recorded in corporate books and records to facilitate the making of questionable payments."[51]

Corporate violations of campaign finance laws during Watergate shocked the conscience of certain regulators at the time. Consider for a moment this reaction by then-sitting SEC Commissioner A.A. Sommer, Jr. who painted a gruesome picture of the corporate political spending:

> [W]e have indeed lost our innocence; we have in a sense known sin and been repelled by its face.... [T]he pattern of illegal political contributions extended back many years.... [T]hese contributions were carefully planned, artfully concealed and in no sense the fruit of illicit pressures. The means of tucking the money away for future distribution were often carefully developed, with clear assignments of responsibilities and well developed techniques for the bestowal of the favors.... [S]ubstantial pools of money [ ] had been sucked out of the corporate accountability process and squirreled away in the accounts of overseas agents, Swiss bank accounts, Bahamian subsidiaries, and in various other places where the use of the money would be free of the questions of nosey auditors, responsible directors, and scrupulous underlings. These systems were characterized by such interesting phenomena as the transportation in suitcases of vast sums of money in one hundred dollar bills by top executives.... [I]t was the executive suite itself which was engaged in deceit, cunning and deviousness worthy of the most fabled political boss or fixer.[52]

The scope of the questionable and illegal payments was quite sizable, occurring in nearly 500 American firms.[53]

Bribing a foreign official was not a crime at the time, but the SEC lobbied Congress to make it a crime.[54] Congress obliged by creating the Foreign Cor-

---

51. SEC Report on Illegal Corporate Payments, *supra* note 47, at 2.

52. A. A. Sommer, Jr., *Crisis and the Corporate Community*, Midwest Securities Commissioners Association Conference, Aspen, CO (July 21, 1975), http://c0403731.cdn.cloud-files.rackspacecloud.com/collection/papers/1970/1975_0721_Sommer_CrisisT.pdf.

53. SEC Report on Illegal Corporate Payments, *supra* note 47, at 16–35 (listing firms involved).

54. H. Lowell Brown, *Parent-Subsidiary Liability Under the Foreign Corrupt Practices Act*, 50 BAYLOR L. REV. 1, 3–4 (1998) (arguing that the Watergate scandal sparked an SEC investigation which ultimately led Congress to enact the Foreign Corrupt Practices Act).

rupt Practices Act of 1977 (FCPA)[55] to restore public confidence in the integrity of the American capital markets.[56] The FCPA requires registered issuers to keep detailed books, records, and accounts that accurately record corporate payments and transactions.[57] And the FCPA prohibits domestic corporations from bribing a foreign official, a foreign political party, party official, or candidate for the purpose of obtaining or maintaining business.[58] The FCPA applies to political contributions abroad from American companies, or foreign companies registered on a U.S. exchange, if they are made with corrupt motives.[59] Watergate also inspired Congress to pass the Federal Election Campaign Act (FECA), which will be discussed in more detail in Chapter 5.

Similarly, decades later, after Enron collapsed in a massive accounting fraud, following years of giving lavishly to both sides of the political spectrum, Congress acted by passing both (1) the Bipartisan Campaign Reform Act of 2002 (BCRA, which is also known as McCain-Feingold), and (2) Public Company Accounting Reform and Investor Protection Act of 2002 (which is also known as Sarbanes-Oxley or SOX). McCain-Feingold tried to keep corporate money out of political ads, as well as away from political parties.[60] SOX (not unlike

---

55. Noonan, *supra* note 50, at 680 ("One aspect of the FCPA was absolutely unique. Its prohibitions applied only to payments intended to influence a country other than the United States ... For the first time, a country made it criminal to corrupt officials of another country.").

56. Statement on Signing S. 305 into Law, 2 Pub. Papers 2157 (Dec. 20, 1977) (Statement by President Jimmy Carter) ("Corrupt practices between corporations and public officials overseas undermine the integrity and stability of governments...."); *see also* H.R. Rep. No. 95-640, at 7 (1977), *available at* http://www.justice.gov/criminal/fraud/fcpa/history/1977/houseprt-95-640.pdf ("The payment of bribes to influence the acts or decisions of foreign officials ... is unethical.... But not only is it unethical, it is bad business as well.... In short, it rewards corruption instead of efficiency and puts pressure on ethical enterprises to lower their standards or risk losing business.").

57. *Id.*

58. 15 U.S.C. §§ 78dd-1 & Dd-2 (2010).

59. ROBERT W. TARUN, THE FOREIGN CORRUPT PRACTICES ACT HANDBOOK, A PRACTICAL GUIDE FOR MULTINATIONAL GENERAL COUNSEL, TRANSACTIONAL LAWYERS AND WHITE COLLAR CRIMINAL PRACTITIONERS 146 (2d Ed. 2012).

60. Al Hunt, *Enron's One Good Return: Political Investments*, WALL ST. J., Jan. 31, 2002 (arguing Enron "played with funny money. But their political investment helped prolong the Ponzi scheme."); Anthony Corrado, *The Legislative Odyssey of BCRA* in LIFE AFTER REFORM 37 (Michael Malbin, ed., 2003), http://www.cfinst.org/pdf/books-reports/LAR/LAR_ch2.pdf ("the bankruptcy of the Enron Corporation and other corporate scandals were matters of national attention, and raised alarming questions about the role political contributions played in policy decisions favorable to Enron and other corporations.").

the FCPA) tried to ensure that the financials given to investors were actually accurate.

C. The Court and Corporate Political Activity

For much of the twentieth century, the Supreme Court stood as a bulwark between corporation and state. For example, take this passage from Justice Frankfurter writing the opinion for the Supreme Court: "[w]e all know ... that one of the great political evils of the time is the apparent hold on political parties which business interests ... seek and sometimes obtain by reason of liberal campaign contributions."[61] In the same case, the Supreme Court discussed the need for legislation to "avoid the deleterious influences on federal elections resulting from the use of money by those who exercise control over large aggregations of capital."[62] Furthermore, the Supreme Court once held that one of the reasons keeping corporations out of politics is that their wealth is not connected with the public's support of their political affinities:

> The resources in the treasury of a business corporation, however, are not an indication of popular support for the corporation's political ideas. They reflect instead the economically motivated decisions of investors and customers. The availability of these resources may make a corporation a formidable political presence, even though the power of the corporation may be no reflection of the power of its ideas.[63]

And as Justice William Brennan wrote, laws requiring corporations to pay for political expenditures through corporate PACs instead of dipping into the corporation's general bank account, "[protect] dissenting shareholders of business corporations."[64] The issue of the lack of consent led the Supreme Court to reason, in a case from 1972 called *Pipefitters Local Union No. 562*, that corporate managers should not be able to spend in politics without assent from investors: "[w]e are of the opinion that Congress intended to insure against [corporate] officers proceeding in such matters without obtaining the consent

---

61. United States v. Int'l Union United Auto., Aircraft & Agric. Implement Workers, 352 U.S. 567, 576 (1957) (Frankfurter, J.) (quoting 65 Cong. Rec. 9507–08 (1924)).

62. Int'l Union United Auto., 352 U.S. at 585.

63. FEC v. Massachusetts Citizens for Life, Inc. (MCFL), 479 U.S. 238, 257–58 (1986) (citations omitted).

64. Austin v. Mich. Chamber of Commerce, 494 U.S. 652, 673 (1990) (Brennan, J., concurring).

of shareholders by forbidding all such [political] expenditures."[65] Furthermore, the Supreme Court explained that Taft-Hartley's prohibition of corporate funded political advertisements was motivated by "the feeling that corporate officials had no moral right to use corporate funds for contribution to political parties without the consent of the stockholders."[66]

In *Austin* from 1990 and *McConnell* from 2003, two cases that were overturned by *Citizens United*, the Supreme Court again held that corporations could be restricted from spending corporate resources on election ads and giving contributions to political parties.[67] Even as recently as 2003, the Supreme Court recognized in a case called *Beaumont,* which is still good law, that, "the [corporate treasury spending] ban has always done further duty in protecting 'the individuals who have paid money into a corporation … for purposes other than the support of candidates from having that money used to support political candidates to whom they may be opposed[.]'"[68]

Interestingly, one of the proponents of keeping the federal corporate contribution ban is none other than the Sage of Omaha, Warren Buffet, CEO of Berkshire Hathaway. Mr. Buffet once wrote in a *New York Times* Op-Ed: "[o]nly individuals vote—and then just once per election. Let only individuals contribute—with sensible limits per election. Otherwise, we are well on our way to ensuring that a government of the moneyed, by the moneyed, and for the moneyed shall not perish from the earth."[69]

One could question whether it really matters whether corporations can spend in elections or not. If corporate spending behavior were akin to ordinary citizens' spending behavior, then perhaps this argument would hold greater sway. But there is evidence that corporate spending is different from spending by real citizens. For one, corporate spending can be quite large in comparison to citizen spending. Consider, for example, a municipal election

---

65. Pipefitters Local Union No. 562 v. United States, 407 U.S. 385, 415 n.28 (1972) (quoting United States v. Lewis Food Co., 366 F.2d 710, 713 (9th Cir. 1966)).

66. United States v. Cong. of Indus. Orgs., 335 U.S. 106, 113 (1948).

67. McConnell v. FEC, 540 U.S. 93 (2003) (upholding BCRA's "soft-money" ban); *Austin,* 494 U.S. 652 (upholding the constitutionality of a ban on corporate expenditures from general corporate treasury funds in support of or in opposition to candidates in state elections).

68. FEC v. Beaumont, 539 U.S. 146, 154 (2003) ("In barring corporate earnings from conversion into political 'war chests,' the ban was and is intended to 'preven[t] corruption or the appearance of corruption.'" (quoting FEC v. Nat'l Conservative PAC, 470 U.S. 480, 496–97 (1985)).

69. Warren Buffet, *The Billionaire's Buyout Plan,* N.Y. TIMES (Sept. 10, 2000), http://www.nytimes.com/2000/09/10/opinion/the-billionaire-s-buyout-plan.html.

in California in 2014 where Chevron spent $3 million. The candidates they opposed only had raised only $50,000.[70]

Another behavior that corporations display, which is comparatively rare among human campaign donors, is giving to both major political parties at the same time. As political scientist Donald Green concluded, this isn't about fostering a stronger democratic process. "[D]onors seem to throw ideological affinity to the wind, ensuring instead that whichever party wins remains in their debt.... The tactic of two-party donations has become commonplace ... [And] it strains credulity to think that their evenhanded distribution of shareholders' money to both parties grows out of their desire to foster democratic discourse."[71]

Both historically and presently, many states and the federal government have treated corporate campaign spenders differently from human campaign spenders. This was true for more than a century. In 1891, Kentucky prohibited corporate campaign spending in its Constitution.[72] By 1897, Nebraska and Tennessee had enacted statutes to ban corporate campaigning.[73] Since then, states, both red and blue, have barred corporations from giving money to candidates for state office.[74] As mentioned above, in 1907, Congress banned cor-

---

70. Richard Gonzales, *Chevron Spends Big, and Loses Big, in a City Council Race*, NPR (Nov. 5, 2014), http://www.npr.org/sections/thetwo-way/2014/11/05/361875792/chevron-spends-big-and-loses-big-in-a-city-council-race.

71. Donald Green, *The Need for Federal Regulation of State Party Activity*, in INSIDE THE CAMPAIGN FINANCE BATTLE: COURT TESTIMONY ON THE NEW REFORMS 97, 106 (Corrado et al., eds., 2003).

72. Ky. Const. § 150.

73. See Act of Apr. 3, 1897, ch. 19, 1897 Neb. Election Laws 42; see also Acts of Apr. 29, 1897, ch. 18, 1897 Tenn. Pub. & Priv. Acts 143.

74. Ark. Ballot Issue 3 (2014) ("prohibiting certain contributions, including contributions by corporations, to candidates for public office"); Ariz. Rev. Stat. Ann. § 16-919 (2011) (barring corporations and unions from making "any contribution of money or anything of value for the purpose of influencing an election"); Iowa Code § 68A.503(1) (2003) ("It is unlawful for ... [a] corporation ... to contribute any money, property, labor, or thing of value, directly or indirectly, to a committee, or to expressly advocate that the vote of an elector be used to nominate, elect, or defeat a candidate for public office, except that such resources may be so expended in connection with a ... ballot issue."); Mich. Comp. Laws § 169.254(1) (2009) ("[A] corporation ... or labor organization shall not make a contribution or expenditure...."); N.D. Cent. Code § 16.1-08.1-03.3(1) ("A corporation, cooperative corporation, limited liability company, or association may not make a direct contribution: [ ]To aid any political party, political committee, or organization...."); Ohio Rev. Code Ann. § 3599.03 (West 2011) (Corporations and unions are barred from spending "for or in aid of or opposition to a political party, a candidate for election or nomination to public office, a political action committee...."); 25 Pa. Cons. Stat. § 3253(a) (West 2011) (Corporations are barred from "mak[ing] a contribution or expenditure in connec-

porations from giving campaign contributions to federal candidates under the
Tillman Act.[75] The Tillman Act (as of 2016) is still good statutory law because
Beaumont is still good case law.[76]

---

tion with the election of any candidate or for any political purpose...."); S.D. Codified Laws
§ 12-27-18 (2011) (barring organizations from donating to a candidate committee or political party); Tex. Elec. Code Ann. § 253.094 (West 2011) (barring corporate and union
contributions and expenditures); Alaska Stat. § 15.13.074(f) (2012) (Corporations and
unions "may not make a contribution to a candidate, group, or nongroup entity...."); Mass.
Gen. Laws ch. 55 § 8 (2011) ("No corporation ... shall directly or indirectly give, pay, ex-
pend or contribute ... any money or other valuable thing for the purpose of aiding, promoting or preventing the nomination or election of any person to public office, or aiding
or promoting or antagonizing the interest of any political party."); Minn. Stat. § 211B.15
subdiv. 2 (2011) ("A corporation may not make an expenditure or offer or agree to make
an expenditure to promote or defeat the candidacy of an individual for nomination, election, or appointment to a political office, unless the expenditure is an independent expenditure."); Mont. Code Ann. § 13-35-227 (2011) ("A corporation may not make a
contribution or an expenditure in connection with a candidate or a political committee that
supports or opposes a candidate or a political party."); N.C. Gen. Stat. § 163-278.19(a)
(2012) ("[I]t shall be unlawful for any corporation, business entity, labor union, professional association or insurance company directly or indirectly do [sic] any of the following:
[]To make any contribution to a candidate or political committee...."); Okl. Stat. Ann. Tit.
21, § 187.2(A) (2011) ("No corporation shall contribute to any campaign fund of any party
committee of this state or to any other person for the benefit of such party committee or
its candidates...."); R.I. Gen. Laws § 17-25-10.1(h)(1) (2012) ("It shall be unlawful for any
corporation, whether profit or non-profit, domestic corporation or foreign corporation ...
or other business entity to make any campaign contribution or expenditure ... to or for any
candidate, political action committee, or political party committee...."); W. Va. Code § 3-
8-8(a) (2011) ("An officer, agent or person acting on behalf of any corporation, whether
incorporated under the laws of this or any other state or of a foreign country, may not pay,
give, lend or authorize to be paid, any money or other thing of value belonging to the corporation to any candidate or candidate's campaign for nomination or election to any
statewide office or any other elective office in the state or any of its subdivisions."); Wis.
Stat. § 11.38(1)(a)(1) (2012) ("No foreign or domestic corporation ... may make any contribution or disbursement, directly or indirectly, either independently or through any political party, committee, group, candidate or individual for any purpose other than to
promote or defeat a referendum."); Wyo. Stat. Ann. § 22-25-102(a) (2012) (No corporation or union "shall contribute funds, other items of value or election assistance directly to
any candidate or group of candidates.").

75. Robert E. Mutch, *Three Centuries of Campaign Finance Law*, in A USER'S GUIDE TO
CAMPAIGN FINANCE REFORM 23 (Gerald C. Lubenow ed., 2001) (noting that in 1907 Congress banned corporate contributions to federal candidates).

76. Jeremy G. Mallory, *Still Other People's Money: Reconciling* Citizens United *with* Abood
and Beck, 47 CAL. W. L. REV. 1, 34 (2010) ("[H]iding in plain sight, is the fact that the Tillman Act has not yet been struck down: corporations cannot make campaign contributions
directly to [federal] candidates.").

On occasion, the Supreme Court has acknowledged that money in politics can undermine the democratic process. For example, in the *McConnell v. FEC* case decided by the Rehnquist Court in 2003, the Supreme Court established that "[o]f 'almost equal' importance has been the Government's interest in combating the appearance or perception of corruption engendered by large campaign contributions. Take away Congress' authority to regulate the appearance of undue influence and 'the cynical assumption that large donors call the tune could jeopardize the willingness of voters to take part in democratic governance.'"[77] But more recently the Roberts Supreme Court has largely reversed course. In *McCutcheon v. FEC* in 2014, Chief Justice Roberts, writing for the majority, drew a disconcerting moral equivalence between voting and donating campaign contributions.[78] This case invalidated aggregate contribution limits for individuals. Realistically, some of the individuals who are most deeply affected are federal lobbyists who are easy targets for political fundraisers. Norman Ornstein, who has been tracking the issue of money in politics for years, sounded a very pessimistic note: "I can tell you, from being inside the belly of the beast, that it is thoroughly … corrupting in both directions.… [L]awmakers … shake down donors and donors have no protection. You cannot say, 'I maxed out.' There is no maximum anymore."[79] A lobbyist told the press after *McCutcheon*, "I'm horrified, planning to de-list my phone number and destroy my email address … What I was really hoping for is a ban on lobbyists making contributions entirely."[80]

Another aspect of this problem is that donors may have outsized influence on the policy positions of the politicians that they fund. Professor Zephyr Teachout, who ran for Governor of New York, provided this concrete example from her experience in that race:

> Corporate spending … created my opponent. My opponent, Andrew Cuomo, had an incoherent ideology. It was an ideology that was cob-

---

77. McConnell v. FEC, 540 U.S. 93, 143–44 (2003).

78. McCutcheon v. FEC, 134 S. Ct. 1434, 1440–41 (2014) ("Citizens can exercise that right [to participate in electing our political leaders] in a variety of ways: They can run for office themselves, vote, urge others to vote for a particular candidate, volunteer to work on a campaign, and contribute to a candidate's campaign."); *see also* Ciara Torres-Spelliscy, *The Democracy We Left Behind in* Greece *and* McCutcheon, 89 N.Y.U. L. Rev. On. 112 (2014).

79. Norman J. Ornstein, *J. Byron McCormick Society for Law and Public Affairs Lecture*, 54 Ariz. L. Rev. 481, 491 (2012).

80. Anna Palmer & Tarini Parti, *Big Donors Fear Shakedown*, Politico (Apr. 2, 2014), http://www.politico.com/story/2014/04/supreme-court-campaign-finance-donations-mc-cutcheon-105320#ixzz3seZZ9o8X.

bled together by his donors like big real estate and big hedge funders. [One donor] figured out a hundred different entities to give him money. You can hear [the donor] in Andrew Cuomo's rhetoric. And it doesn't make sense when you hear him say we need tax breaks for big real estate. It doesn't make for down state votes or upstate votes. It only makes sense for his donors.[81]

Professor Teachout also related that corporations cast a disturbing pall over politics and what politicians are even willing to say against corporate interests: "[t]here is a shadow of corporate power hanging over races. There is a plague of silence in politics … [Politicians] have to think, is it really worth it to take on Comcast—because we don't know how many votes that will get us. But if Comcast notices, if the great beast turns around, I could be killed."[82]

Politicians may change their legislative actions to placate the whims of big political spenders so that they retain their backing in future elections. Norman Ornstein agreed with this view, noting: "[a]fter spending a long time with lawmakers and their staffs on Capitol Hill, I can say the corruption is insidious." He added, "frankly, it doesn't even take the spending of money. All a lobbyist has to say is a group that has more money than God wants this amendment and they will spend $20 million against you if you vote against this. The lawmaker thinks, if I do this little amendment, I can head off a $20 million attack on myself."[83] And many of these small legislative moves, an amendment here, a cloture vote there, will fly under the radar of most observers.

D. Legal versus Illegal Money in Politics

Just because the Tillman Act has been on the books since 1907 banning corporations from giving to federal candidates does not mean that the law has been followed by corporations. The most complete public record of violations of this part of federal campaign finance law comes from the Watergate investigations by federal prosecutors, the U.S. Senate, and the SEC.[84]

Indeed, Watergate prosecutors had their hands full with Tillman Act violations. During the Watergate prosecutions, 21 companies pleaded guilty to

---

81. Interview with Fordham Law Professor Zephyr Teachout (Aug. 10, 2015).

82. *Id.*

83. Interview with Norman Ornstein, Fellow Am. Enterprise Instit. (July 24, 2015).

84. Noonan, *supra* note 50, at 674 ("Approximately 500 corporations came forward to confess to the canonical offense of making unreported, questionable payments overseas.").

charges of making illegal corporate contributions totaling $968,000.[85] Among the companies that ran afoul of the corporate campaign finance laws in Nixon's reelection campaign were several companies that are still around today, including American Airlines, Goodyear, Philips, Greyhound, 3M, Carnation, Hertz, and Northrop.[86]

Prominent industrialists were also caught up in the scandal. For example, George Steinbrenner ran into criminal legal trouble for his role in allowing corporate contributions to be given to the Nixon campaign, among others. In the scheme, Mr. Steinbrenner's firm, the American Ship Building Company, gave fake bonuses to disguise campaign contributions that were coming from the company itself. A digital copy of Mr. Steinbrenner's indictment is available online as part of his FBI file, which was released to the public under a Freedom of Information Act (FOIA) request. The indictment explains the conspiracy to violate the law banning corporate contributions:

> It was part of the conspiracy that, among other means, contributions by the defendant, THE AMERICAN SHIPBUILDING COMPANY, to candidates in said elections would be made in the following manner: the defendant, GEORGE M. STEINBRENNER III, together with Robert E. Bartlomo and Stanley J. Lepkowski, would select a group of trusted employees, who were to receive what appeared to be bonuses from THE AMERICAN SHIPBUILDING COMPANY and would be directed to contribute the net proceeds after taxes from these bonuses to candidates in said elections; STEINBRENNER would authorize the payment of such bonuses to the employees who had been selected; STEINBRENNER would also direct the submission of fictitious expense vouchers by employees of The AMERICAN SHIPBUILDING COMPANY to create a cash fund in order to reimburse employees for contributions; STEINBRENNER would instruct Bartlomo what candidates were to receive contributions and STEINBRENNER would specify the amount of the contributions; Bartlomo would direct the

---

85. Herbert E. Alexander, Financing Politics: Money, Elections, & Political Reform 18 (4th Ed. 1992).

86. See S. Rep. No. 93—981, at 507–10 (1974), http://www.maryferrell.org/mffweb/archive/viewer/showDoc.do?mode=searchResult&absPageId= 1477617. (listing corporate contributions solicited by the Nixon campaign); id. at 446–92 (detailing illegal corporate contributions from 13 companies); Stanley I. Kutler, The Wars of Watergate 435 (1990) (listing corporations breaking campaign finance laws); Trevor Potter's Keynote Address at Conference Board's Symposium on Corporate Political Spending, Campaign Legal Ctr. Blog (Oct. 21, 2011) (same).

employees who had received the bonuses and those who were to be reimbursed from the cash fund to make out personal checks for the contributions specified by STEINBRENNER; the employees would write out their personal checks for the contributions[.][87]

Mr. Steinbrenner pled guilty to violating federal campaign finance law for his role in disguising illegal corporate contributions as if they had been given by individuals.[88] Other executives in his company also pled guilty to participating in the illegal scheme.[89] However, by pleading guilty, Steinbrenner avoided going to jail and was only fined $15,000.[90] Mr. Steinbrenner was eventually pardoned for this crime by President Ronald Reagan.[91]

In contrast to George Steinbrenner's illegal donations to the Nixon campaign, there were also perfectly legal donations from CEOs, which also raised eyebrows and its own appearance of corruption as this political spending frequently appears to have been done to help the donor's business and not the public weal. Take, for example, the story of McDonald's CEO Ray Kroc during the Nixon administration.[92] Mr. Kroc had a few problems that the federal government could help fix if it were so inclined. Problem one was he wanted

87. Federal Bureau of Investigation, George Steinbrenner (2010) *available at* FBI Records, The Vault, Part 3, 44 (last viewed Oct. 23, 2015), https://vault.fbi.gov/george-steinbrenner/george-steinbrenner-part-03-of-12/view (capitalizations in the original).

88. *Guilty Pleas in Campaign Gift Case*, San Francisco Chronicle (Aug. 24, 1974), http://jfk.hood.edu/Collection/White%20%20Files/Watergate/Watergate%20Items%2018095%20to%2018285/Watergate%2018174.pdf ("Shipbuilding executive George M. Steinbrenner III, a co-owner of the New York Yankees, pleaded guilty to conspiracy in a scheme to funnel corporate funds to both Republican and Democratic campaigns.").

89. *Id.* ("American Shipbuilding's executive vice president and general counsel pleaded guilty to aiding and abetting Steinbrenner in a complex plot to pour corporate funds into the campaigns of former President Nixon and various candidates for Congress.").

90. Julie Johnson, *Steinbrenner Pardons by Reagan for '72 Election Law Violations*, N.Y. Times (Jan. 20, 1989), http://www.nytimes.com/1989/01/20/us/steinbrenner-pardoned-by-reagan-for-72-election-law-violations.html ("Mr. Steinbrenner, ... was convicted in the election law case in 1974. He was fined $15,000 but did not go to jail.").

91. *Former Yankees owner George Steinbrenner Blamed Illegal Nixon Campaign Contribution on Bad Advice*, NJ.com (May 9, 2011), http://www.nj.com/yankees/index.ssf/2011/05/former_yankees_owner_george_st.html ("Reagan pardoned Steinbrenner for his convictions in a case involving campaign donations to President Richard Nixon and other politicians.").

92. Daniel Gross, *Ray Kroc, McDonald's, and the Fast-Food Industry* in Forbes Greatest Business Stories of All Time (1996), http://www.wiley.com/legacy/products/subject/business/forbes/kroc.pdf.

the minimum wage dropped for his then-largely teenage workforce. Problem two was he wanted to raise the price of his hamburgers when the Nixon administration had imposed price controls on many consumer goods, including food, in a vain attempt to stave off inflation. In either case, the benefit of these changes in policy would redound to Mr. Kroc and McDonald's.

Mr. Kroc decided to donate more than $250,000 in 1972 (roughly $1.4 million today) to the Nixon's Committee to Reelect the President (derisively known as "CREEP") by routing the money through multiple committees. What happened after this generous gift of campaign cash from CEO Kroc? No one who knows is telling. One theory about what the $250,000 bought for McDonald's was the chance to get a "subminimum" wage for teenagers. According to Eric Schlosser in FAST FOOD NATION, the minimum wage, which was then $1.60/hour, would have been slashed to $1.28 for teenagers under what became known as the "McDonald's bill."[93] But Congress refused to put the subminimum wage into the final bill presented to President Nixon for signature. According to contemporaneous reporting by *Congressional Quarterly*, President Nixon vetoed the bill because it lacked the subminimum wage.[94] That's why *People Magazine* called it the "McDonald's Veto."[95]

Next there was Kroc's problem number two. Under President Nixon, price controls were administered by a Cost of Living Council chaired by Treasury Secretary John B. Connolly and a Price Commission.[96] The basic idea was to freeze the price of consumer goods in America. The timing of what happened to the price of the Quarter Pounder was certainly suspicious. In November 1971, during the period when the general price freeze was in effect, McDonald's raised the price of its Quarter Pounder with Cheese from 59 cents to 65 cents without authorization from the Price Commission.[97] In May 1972, the Commission ordered McDonald's to drop the price back to the original cost in compliance with the general price freeze. Between May and September 1972, Ray Kroc con-

---

93. ERIC SCHLOSSER, FAST FOOD NATION: THE DARK SIDE OF THE ALL-AMERICAN MEAL 37 (2005).

94. *Nixon Signs Minimum Wage Increase* in 1974 CQ ALMANAC 239 (1974), http://digitalcollections.library.cmu.edu/awweb/awarchive?type=file&item=558873.

95. Ralph Novak, *The McDonald's Man: What Ray Kroc Hath Wrought Around the World*, PEOPLE Vol. 3 No. 19 (May 19, 1975), http://www.people.com/people/archive/article/0,,20065264,00.html.

96. Richard Nixon, *Statement About the Cost of Living Council's Quarterly Report on the Economic Stabilization Program*, Feb. 12, 1972, http://www.presidency.ucsb.edu/ws/?pid=3742.

97. *Nixon McDonald's Hamburger Helper*, THE YUMA DAILY SUN 4 (Mar. 27, 1974), http://www.newspapers.com/newspage/47171787/.

tributed the $250,000 to CREEP. And in September 1972, the Price Commission reversed its decision and granted McDonald's its desired price increase.[98] The relief was for McDonald's alone. From the outside it looked like a *quid pro quo* and critics like Senator Harrison Williams called out the corruption.[99] Mr. Kroc called Senator Williams names that can't be repeated here.

E. Corporate Lobbying

What Ray Kroc was doing was lobbying at a very high level. Corporations do this all the time and it is perfectly legal. In fact, one of the ways corporations have gained power is not just through the courts, but also through lobbying the political branches. Former Chair of the FEC Trevor Potter posited that to appreciate corporate power in America's democracy, "[y]ou need to look at the whole system. Not just the money spent on political ads. But consider as well the lobbying and lobbyists acting as bundlers for campaigns, and the revolving door between government and industry. Those are all part and parcel of how corporations wield influence."[100]

As corporate governance expert Heidi Welsh explained, campaign spending and lobbying are "two sides of the coin. If you are talking about corporate influence on the political system, then you have to look at election spending and who gets elected. And then you have to look at lobbying, which is what happens after the elections, and what decisions are made."[101] Most of the corporate money spent on political activity is actually spent on lobbying who is in power after elections are long over. Data from Opensecrets.org and Followthemoney.org show that 87% of $1.1 billion spent on corporate political activity by the S&P 500 went to federal lobbying.[102]

---

98. *Price Board Hit on Burger Ruling*, Sarasota Herald-Tribune (Nov. 3, 1972), https://news.google.com/newspapers?nid=1755&dat=19721103&id=RrEvAAAAIBAJ&sjid=jmYEAAAAIBAJ&pg=5955,903656&hl=en.

99. *McDonald's Ray Kroc Dies of Heart Failure*, Lakeland Ledger (Jan. 15, 1984), https://news.google.com/newspapers?nid=1346&dat=19840115&id=fNwvAAAAIBAJ&sjid=bfsDAAAAIBAJ&pg=2473,4684848&hl=en.

100. Interview with Trevor Potter, President Campaign Legal Ctr. (July 27, 2015).

101. Interview with Heidi Welsh, Executive Director Sustainable Investment Institute (July 8, 2015).

102. Heidi Welsh & Robin Young, *Corporate Governance of Political Expenditures: 2011 Benchmark Report on S&P 500 Companies*, Sustainable Invest. Instit. 47 (Nov. 2011) (emphasis added).

Lobbying by corporations has built up over time. According Harvard Professor Theda Skocpol, in the 1970s and 1980s, "segments of the business world formed more specialized associations, ... to do battle with citizen groups. What is more, many corporations and preexisting business associations opened offices for the first time in Washington, D.C., the better to monitor government and counter the newly mobilized rights groups and citizen associations."[103] Consequently, it is difficult for ordinary citizens to match even a fraction of corporate lobbying power. Election law expert Professor Richard Hasen asserted, "[c]itizen groups use resources besides finances, such as mobilizing voters, to attempt to fight business lobbying interests, but it is often a losing battle."[104] Some of this disparity between citizens and corporations may be explained by the resources dedicated to lobbying.[105]

The trouble with lobbying is that it may bring lawmakers further from, instead of closer to, the truth of the matter at hand because "[l]obbying is biased information flow."[106] Part of why elected officials may be persuaded by lobbying is their own self-interest in landing a lucrative lobbying job. This is known as the revolving door problem. AEI Fellow Norman Ornstein argued that unscrupulous D.C. lobbyists dangle the prospect of future private sector jobs to get elected officials and staffers to bend to their will.

> The fact that lobbyists make three to ten times as much or more as elected officials and their staffs has an impact. Remember Jack Abramoff. He would say to a Congressional staffer 'you know I really like you. I've got my eye on you.' With that statement, he had that person because he knew their salary was $40,000 or $50,000 but Jack could

---

103. Theda Skocpol, Diminished Democracy, From Membership to Management in American Civic Life 144–45 (2003).

104. Richard L. Hasen, *Lobbying, Rent-Seeking, and the Constitution*, 64 Stan. L. Rev. 191, 228 (2012) (citing Kay Lehman Schlozman & John T. Tierney, Organized Interests and American Democracy 28 (1986)).

105. Christopher P. Skroupa, *Investors Want Disclosure of Corporate Political Contributions and Lobbying Expenditures*, Forbes (Apr. 20, 2012), http://www.forbes.com/sites/christopherskroupa/2012/04/20/investors-want-disclosure-of-corporate-political-contributionsand-lobbying-expenditures-2/ ("A 2011 Si2 study found that S&P 500 companies spent a total of $1.1 billion on 2010 political contributions. Of this figure, 87% or $973 million went to federal lobbying expenditure. Note this figure does not include corporate lobbying expenditures for state and local governments....").

106. Interview with Warren Langley, Former President of the Pacific Stock Exchange (July 14, 2015).

pay $400,000 or $500,000. The staffers didn't want to alienate him because they wanted to work for him.[107]

In the 1990s and 2000s, lobbyists' power continued to expand and salaries matched this power. As Robert Kaiser explained in his book So Damn Much Money, "in earlier generations enterprising young men came to Washington looking for power and political adventure, often with ambition to save or reform the country or the world. In the last fourth of the twentieth century such aspirations were supplanted by another American yearning: to get rich."[108] Being a lobbyist became a career path not just for Hill staffers, but also for elected Members of Congress.[109]

The Supreme Court did not always hold the view of the five-person majority from 2005 to early 2016 about the contours of First Amendment rights for corporations, or lobbying, for that matter.[110] In particular, the Court was once quite concerned about giving corporations too much power in the political sphere to shape the very laws and rules that apply to business through the power of hired lobbyists. For example, the Court expressed in *dicta* in 1874 that there could be corrupt lobbying by corporations:

> If any of the great corporations of the country were to hire adventurers who make market of themselves in this way, to procure the passage of a general law with a view to the promotion of their private interests, the moral sense of every right-minded man would instinctively denounce the employer and employed as steeped in corruption and the employment as infamous.[111]

In another case the Supreme Court was equally concerned about the impact of lobbying on the federal legislative process. The Court heard a challenge

---

107. Ornstein interview *supra* note 83.

108. Robert Kaiser, So Damn Much Money: The Triumph of Lobbying and the Corrosion of American Government 21 (2009).

109. Interview with Robert A.G. Monks (Aug. 17, 2015) (stating "of members of Congress who retire, 50% stay in Washington as lobbyists. What that means is what was a clear line between government and business is getting blurred.").

110. Tony Mauro, *Campaign Finance Overview*, First Amendment Ctr. (Jan. 30, 2010), http://www.firstamendmentcenter.org/campaign-finance-overview ("For more than 30 years after the Watergate scandal…, Congress and the Supreme Court were mostly on the same page concerning campaign-finance regulation.… Most campaign-finance measures passed by Congress, even though they touched on core political speech, were upheld by the Supreme Court. That seeming consensus began unraveling in 2007[.]"). Justice Scalia who died in early 2016 was part of the five Justice majority referrenced here.

111. Trist v. Child, 88 U.S. 441, 451 (1874).

to a 1946 law called the Lobbying Act, which required disclosure of who was lobbying Congress. A corporation and two individuals (one named Harriss) were criminally charged with not reporting their respective congressional lobbying expenditures. They appealed their convictions, arguing that the law itself was unconstitutional.[112] In *Harriss* in 1954, the Supreme Court upheld disclosure for congressional lobbying, reasoning:

> Present-day legislative complexities are such that individual members of Congress cannot be expected to explore the myriad pressures to which they are regularly subjected. Yet full realization of the American ideal of government by elected representatives depends to no small extent on their ability to properly evaluate such pressures. Otherwise, the voice of the people may all too easily be drowned out by the voice of special interest groups seeking favored treatment while masquerading as proponents of the public weal. This is the evil which the Lobbying Act was designed to help prevent.[113]

In 2009, the D.C. Circuit upheld a modern revision of the congressional lobbying laws by citing to *Harriss*: "[m]ore than fifty years ago, the Supreme Court held that the public disclosure of 'who is being hired, who is putting up the money, and how much' they are spending to influence legislation is 'a vital national interest.' Today, we consider a constitutional challenge to ... the Honest Leadership and Open Government Act of 2007. Because nothing has transpired in the last half century to suggest that the national interest in public disclosure of lobbying information is any less vital..., we reject that challenge."[114] The legislative history of the Honest Leadership and Open Government Act of 2007 indicated some of the problems that still happen when lobbyists cross the legal and ethical lines trying to influence Congress:

> Federal lobbying is a multi-billion dollar industry, and spending to influence Members of Congress and Executive Branch officials has continued to increase over the last decade.... [D]uring the 109th Congress [there were] the conviction of a high-profile lobbyist, as well as a number of highly publicized incidents involving and the provision

---

112. United States v. Harriss, 347 U.S. 612, 614–15 (1954) ("One such count charges the National Farm Committee, a Texas corporation, with failure to report the solicitation and receipt of contributions to influence the passage of legislation which would cause a rise in the price of agricultural commodities and commodity futures and the defeat of legislation which would cause a decline in those prices.").

113. *Id.* at 625.

114. National Association of Manufacturers v. Taylor, 582 F.3d 1 (D.C. Cir. 2009).

of privately funded travel, free meals, and lavish entertainment by lobbyists to Members of Congress, congressional staff, and some Executive Branch officials in exchange for favorable treatment for clients with specific interests before the Government.[115]

In 2015, another D.C. Circuit case called *Wagner v. FEC* considered and upheld the constitutionality of the Hatch Act's ban on political contributions from federal contractors. In explaining why the Hatch Act's anti-pay-to-play restrictions were still necessary, the *Wagner* Court highlighted lobbying scandals including "[i]n 2006, Representative Bob Ney [ ] pled guilty to a series of *quid pro quos* with the lobbyist Jack Abramoff, including steering a 'multi-million dollar' contract for a House of Representatives infrastructure project to one of Abramoff's clients."[116]

No matter what the underlying topic is, industry can typically lap their public interest counterparts in terms of lobbying dollars and the number of hired lobbyists. Take the example of telecommunication industry, which has recently been resisting net neutrality rules, among other public interest policies. The fact that the public actually won this debate on net neutrality at the FCC was an unexpected David v. Goliath outcome, because as the President of Free Press Craig Aaron noted, "the cable industry has a personal registered lobbyist for every member of Congress. Our [public interest] shop has one registered lobbyist."[117] Craig Aaron illustrated the power differential with this anecdote: "AT&T was trying to get all of its lobbyists together and no one's office was big enough, so they had to rent a movie theater to get all their lobbyists in one place. Their opponents, who work for the public interest, could share a cab."[118]

The full result of corporate lobbying is difficult to quantify, but one impact is agenda setting. As Craig Aaron noted, "Washington's definition of what is possible is so narrow and is so skewed towards the corporate interests. That is the result of money in politics … This is not reflective of what the public wants based on polling and surveys."[119] Different studies have conflicted about how much impact corporate lobbying has on legislative outcomes. One of the more recent studies from Princeton comes to a very troubling conclusion for any-

---

115. Honest Leadership and Open Government Act of 2007—House Report No. 110–161.
116. *Id.*
117. Interview with Craig Aaron, President Free Press (July 27, 2015).
118. *Id.*
119. *Id.*

one who wants human voters to be at the center of our policy making apparatus.[120] The Princeton study found, "economic elites and organized groups representing business interests have substantial independent impacts on U.S. government policy, while average citizens and mass-based interest groups have little or no independent influence."[121]

Without laws to fence corporations out, privately financed elections turn into corporate playgrounds. Corporations have used the twin powers of spending in elections to influence who is a viable candidate and who wins. Then after the election, corporations use even more money to lobby to get the legislative outcomes they want, frequently from Members they just helped elect. As the Watergate records demonstrated, at times certain corporations have jumped the fence and spent in elections even when it was illegal. If the progress of campaign finance law has followed the pattern of scandal, reform, scandal, reform, then speaking in 2015, the Chair of the FEC Ann Ravel left us with this sobering thought that "[w]e're never going to have the kind of scandal that occurred in the Nixon administration because the press is not well funded and the FEC is not looking out. And if the FEC saw a scandal, we would not do anything about it."[122]

---

120. Martin Gilens & Benjamin I. Page, *Testing Theories of American Politics: Elites, Interest Groups, and Average Citizens*, 12(3) PERSP. ON POL. 564, 564 (2014), https://scholar.princeton.edu/sites/default/files/mgilens/files/gilens_and_page_2014_-testing_theories_of_american_politics.doc.pdf.

121. *Id.*

122. Interview with Ann Ravel, Chair, Federal Election Commission (Nov. 3, 2015).

Part II

The Expansion of Corporate Rights

> I think the framers would be rolling in their graves over what corporate rights look like now.
>
> —Nicole Gordon[1]

Corporations have laid claim to various First Amendment rights over time from commercial speech rights, to political rights, to religious rights. To appreciate this part of the law requires a little background about how the Supreme Court interprets the First Amendment. The First Amendment has been dissected into its constituent clauses by the Supreme Court. Thus, there are whole lines of cases that only deal with the petition clause, and whole lines of cases that deal with the establishment of religion, which are distinct from the free exercise of religion cases, the freedom of expression cases and the right to assemble cases. As Dean of Yale Law School Robert Post put it, "First Amendment jurisprudence contains distinct doctrinal regimes that apply to distinct forms of speech. First Amendment doctrine is plural, not singular."[2] And the Supreme Court has made further distinctions within its First Amendment jurisprudence: political speech cases are treated as largely distinct from commercial speech cases (though those distinctions are coming under increasing strain).[3] Many corporate litigants appear to seek absolute First Amendment

---

1. Interview with Nicole Gordon, Former Executive Director, New York City Campaign Finance Board (Aug. 10, 2015).

2. Robert Post, *Compelled Commercial Speech*, 117 W. Va. L. Rev. 867, 871 (2015).

3. Darrel C. Menthe, *The Marketplace Metaphor and Commercial Speech Doctrine: Or How I Learned to Stop Worrying About and Love* Citizens United, 38 Hastings Const. L.Q. 131, 132 (2010) ("*Citizens United* has broad implications for commercial speech doctrine.

rights for corporations. And as American courts have adopted broader and broader notions of corporate personhood, consequently those litigants have gotten exactly what they wanted: an unprecedented expansion of First Amendment rights for corporations.

Before corporate lawyers were bold enough to assert First Amendment rights, they started with asserting more modest economic constitutional rights. If *Dartmouth College* and *Terrett v. Taylor* are considered, the Supreme Court has since the early 1800s shown incredible respect of contract and property rights of corporations—holding that even the Revolutionary War did not disturb these corporate rights. So perhaps it is not surprising that eventually, the Court would recognize commercial speech rights for corporations as well. What's slightly more puzzling is how the Court stretches to give corporations political and religious rights, which could be viewed as two bridges too far.

It means that the basis for treating commercial speech differently must be its content, not its corporate authorship.").

Chapter 4

Now a Word from
Our Sponsors

Ordinary commercial corporations are not vehicles of self-governance.
—Robert Post, Dean of Yale Law School[4]

In our democracy, members of Congress and state legislatures are elected to
write laws that further the public interest. To ensure they do so, the Constitution grants individuals the right to free speech in the First Amendment, allowing individuals to participate in the political dialogue. A legislature could not
tell individuals that they must be silent on Saturdays. Such an absurd law would
violate the First Amendment. The Supreme Court's First Amendment case law
was originally based on respect for individual autonomy. Democratically elected
governments have since passed laws and regulations to prevent infringement of
the individual's right to participate in political dialogue and to encourage
broader political participation among citizens. These laws further democratic
values, but lately corporate plaintiffs have been using First Amendment cases
to gut them. The scary thing is many corporations are winning these arguments
in court. Commercial speech rights, which had no protection until the 1970s,
continue to grow monumental in scope—displacing rules, regulations, and
laws meant to rein in corporate power.

Just as lawyers for corporations have been aggressive in asserting political
rights for corporations, they have also been litigating for greater commercial
speech rights for corporations. Frequently, the tactic is to assert the "compelled
speech" doctrine as an excuse why a given law or regulation cannot be applied

---

4. Robert C. Post, Citizens Divided: Campaign Finance Reform and the Constitution 73 (2014).

to corporate commercial speech. For example, as will be discussed below, tobacco companies have successfully thwarted attempts to include more graphic warnings on cigarette labels using the compelled speech doctrine.

Political speech rights are only a subset of the First Amendment rights asserted by corporations and recognized by the Supreme Court. There is a whole universe of commercial speech rights that corporations enjoy in America.[5] As Duke Professor Jedediah Purdy once explained, the First Amendment "has become a linchpin in the Supreme Court's anti-regulatory cases."[6] Commercial speech, which used to get less First Amendment protection than political speech, is receiving more solicitude from U.S. courts post-*Citizens United*.[7] And Yale Dean Robert Post asserted, "[c]onscripting the First Amendment to an anti-regulatory agenda would be a grave constitutional abuse."[8]

Harvard Law Professor John C. Coates IV recently wrote an empirical analysis of the use of the First Amendment by businesses. He concluded, "[n]early half of First Amendment legal challenges now benefit business corporations and trade groups, rather than other kinds of organizations or individuals."[9] There are more of these cases in the pipeline. As Elizabeth Kennedy of Demos reported: "[w]hat we see is a larger number of corporate challenges bubbling up from the lower courts to rules and regulations of corporate activity. Whether it is the corporate challenge to the Seattle minimum wage law where corporations were making a corporate equal protection argument or whether it is GMO labeling in Vermont that is in front of the Second Circuit, corporate actors are

5. Saru M. Matambanadzo, *The Body, Incorporated*, 87 Tul. L. Rev. 457, 472 (2013) ("Corporate persons also enjoy extensive free speech protections, including the right to political speech, commercial speech, and negative speech (that is, the right not to be associated with the speech of others)."); United States v. Phillip Morris USA, Inc., 566 F.3d 1095, 1142 (D.C. Cir. 2009) ("The First Amendment protects against government infringement on the right to speak freely and the right to refrain from speaking at all. This holds true whether applied to individuals or to companies."); Int'l Dairy Foods Ass'n v. Amestoy, 92 F.3d 67, 71 (2d Cir. 1996) ("The right not to speak inheres in political and commercial speech alike.").

6. Jedediah Purdy, *The Roberts Court v. America*, 23 Democracy (2012), http://www.democracyjournal.org/23/the-roberts-court-v-america.php?page=all.

7. Robert Sprague & Mary Ellen Wells, *The Supreme Court as Prometheus: Breathing Life into the Corporate Supercitizen*, 49 Am. Bus. L.J. 507, 549 (2012) ("It is possible that, post-*Citizens United*, any corporate speech—assuming, as we argue, that any speech by a commercial entity must be, to some degree, commercial—is an inextricably intertwined combination of commercial and political speech and therefore cannot be regulated.").

8. Post, *supra* note 2, at 874.

9. John C. Coates IV, *Corporate Speech & The First Amendment: History, Data, and Implications*, 30 Const. Comment. 223, 224 (Summer 2015).

using the First Amendment as a sword to fight democratic oversight of their conduct."[10]

Each time the Supreme Court confronts the issue of whether the government has authority to regulate commercial speech, the result hinges on whether the Court considers a given case under the commercial speech doctrine, which gives the government more room to maneuver, or whether the Court considers the case using the compelled speech doctrine, which leaves the government very little capacity to regulate.[11] This unpredictability is at least partly to blame for the doctrinal upheaval in this area of the law.

A. Commercial Speech

Commercial speech received no protection at all from the Supreme Court before 1976.[12] But since then, the Supreme Court has been clear that just because speech is commercial, that does not mean it is unprotected by the First Amendment.[13] As the Court concluded: "it is clear ... that speech does not lose its First Amendment protection because money is spent to project it, as in a paid advertisement ... [or] that is 'sold' for-profit."[14] The commercial speech doctrine applies to advertisements, statements, and other means of communication meant to make a company a profit.[15] Since expanding its First Amend-

---

10. Interview with Elizabeth Kennedy, Counsel, Demos (Aug. 12, 2015).

11. Much turns on how broadly or narrowly the Court reads a case called *Zauderer*, which allowed for governmental regulations of an attorney's advertisements. Justice White, writing for the majority in *Zauderer*, held "that an advertiser's [First Amendment] rights are adequately protected as long as disclosure requirements are reasonably related to the State's interest in preventing deception of consumers." *Zauderer v. Office of Disciplinary Counsel*, 471 U.S. 626, 651 (1985). Thus *Zauderer* applied rational basis analysis to the regulation of commercial speech.

12. Post, *Compelled Commercial Speech, supra* note 2, at 872.

13. United States v. United Foods, Inc., 533 U.S. 405, 410–11 (2001) ("Just as the First Amendment may prevent the government from prohibiting speech, the Amendment may prevent the government from compelling individuals to express certain views ... The fact that the speech is in aid of a commercial purpose does not deprive respondent of all First Amendment protection ...").

14. Virginia State Board of Pharmacy v. Virginia Citizens Council, 425 U.S. 748 (1976) (internal citation omitted).

15. Post, *Compelled Commercial Speech, supra* note 2, at 874 ("Persons do not engage in commercial speech in order to influence the content of public opinion, but to facilitate transactions in the marketplace.").

ment jurisprudence to cover commercial speech, the Court has heard a number of cases challenging government action. However, the Court has consistently stated that regulation to prevent advertising that is false, deceptive, or misleading is permissible. The cases challenging regulations limiting commercial speech are common in two categories: (1) attorneys and other professionals, and (2) vice (gambling and alcohol regulations). Generally, commercial speech is subject to "intermediate scrutiny," though this law is in a state of flux, which means that courts have been known to apply anything from rational basis scrutiny to strict scrutiny.

The Supreme Court's original approach to commercial speech was not to give it constitutional protection. In the 1942 case of *Valentine v. Chrestensen*,[16] a submarine owner hoping to attract customers challenged a New York City ordinance prohibiting distribution of commercial advertisement handbills. The ordinance allowed information regarding general public information or public protests, but not other commercial speech. After being told his advertisement did not comport with the ordinance, Christensen placed a notice of a protest on the other side of the handbill to skirt the restriction. While a lower court issued a decree barring enforcement of the ordinance, the Supreme Court reversed. The Court stated, "[w]e are ... clear that the Constitution imposes no such restraint on the government as respects purely commercial advertising."[17]

The Supreme Court first extended First Amendment protection to purely commercial speech in 1976 in *Virginia State Board of Pharmacy v. Virginia Citizens Consumer Council, Inc.*[18] This case was brought by consumers challenging a Virginia statute that prohibited licensed pharmacists from advertising the prices of prescription drugs. The Court addressed the case law that had previously rendered commercial speech unprotected under the First Amendment. The Court framed the issue as: "[o]ur question is whether speech which does 'no more than propose a commercial transaction' is so removed from any 'exposition of ideas' and from 'truth, science, morality, and arts in general, in its diffusion of liberal sentiments on the administration of Government,' that it lacks all protection. Our answer is that it is not."[19] Though the Court added the caveat that, "[i]n concluding that commercial speech, like other varieties, is protected, we of course do not hold that it can never

---

16. *Valentine v. Chrestensen*, 316 U.S. 52 (1942).
17. *Id.* at 54.
18. 425 U.S. 748 (1976).
19. *Id.* at 762.

be regulated in any way. Some forms of commercial speech regulation are surely permissible."[20]

Moreover, Justice Blackmun wrote for the Court in *Virginia Pharmacy* that consumers are regularly more interested in hearing commercial information instead of political speech: "[a]s to the particular consumer's interest in the free flow of commercial information, that interest may be as keen, if not keener by far, than his interest in the day's most urgent political debate."[21] Furthermore, the Court presumed that the poor would benefit from more advertisements of drug prices, so that they could shop for the lowest cost prescriptions.[22] In another passage from *Virginia Pharmacy*, the Supreme Court noted that capitalism required the free flow of information on price in particular: "[a]dvertising, however tasteless and excessive it sometimes may seem, is nonetheless dissemination of information as to who is ... selling what product ... and at what price. So long as we preserve a predominantly free enterprise economy ... the free flow of commercial information is indispensable."[23]

Dissenting in *Virginia Pharmacy*, Justice Rehnquist seemed disgusted with the Supreme Court's giving commercial speech so much First Amendment protection. He wrote,

> "[i]t is undoubtedly arguable that many people in the country regard the choice of shampoo as just as important as who may be elected to local, state, or national political office, but that does not automatically bring information about competing shampoos within the protection of the First Amendment."[24]
>
> Justice Rehnquist thought of the First Amendment as primarily protecting the political process of self-governance and not the commercial marketplace. Justice Rehnquist, with a not-so-subtle nod to the much-despised *Lochner* argued, "there is certainly nothing in the United States Constitution which requires the Virginia Legislature to hew to the teachings of Adam Smith in its legislative decisions regulating the pharmacy profession."[25]

This case was a turning point. As Professor Coates recently found in his empirical study of the Supreme Court's approach to business

---

20. *Id.* at 770.
21. *Id.* at 764–65.
22. *Id.* at 764–65.
23. *Id.* at 748.
24. *Id.* at 787 (Rehnquist, J., dissenting).
25. *Id.* at 784 (Rehnquist, J., dissenting).

cases that invoked the First Amendment, "before *Virginia Pharmacy*, businesses won 20 percent of the First Amendment cases, and 55 percent after it."[26]

After extending commercial speech protection under the First Amendment, the Court heard a number of challenges to governmental restrictions on commercial speech.[27] But the next shift in the Court's commercial speech doctrine jurisprudence came in *Central Hudson Gas & Electric Corp. v. Public Service Commission of New York*.[28] In this case, a utility company challenged a New York regulation that precluded utility companies from advertising.[29] *Central Hudson* created a four-part analysis for commercial speech cases:

> [1] we must determine whether the expression is protected by the First Amendment. For commercial speech to come within that provision, it at least must concern lawful activity and not be misleading. [2] Next, we ask whether the asserted governmental interest is substantial. If both inquiries yield positive answers, [3] we must determine whether the regulation directly advances the governmental interest asserted, and [4] whether it is not more extensive than is necessary to serve that interest.[30]

In *Central Hudson*, like in *Virginia Pharmacy*, the Supreme Court privileged the interest of the free flow of commercial information in a free market economy. The Supreme Court held: "[t]he First Amendment ... protects commercial speech from unwarranted governmental regulation. Commercial expression not only serves the economic interest of the speaker, but also assists consumers and furthers the societal interest in the fullest possible dissemination of information."[31] And the Supreme Court acknowledged that advertisements for prod-

---

26. Elliot Zaret, *Commercial Speech and the Evolution of the First Amendment*, Wash. Lawyer 25 (Sept. 2015), https://www.dcbar.org/bar-resources/publications/washington-lawyer/articles/september-2015-commercial-speech.cfm.

27. Linmark Associates, Inc. v. Willingboro Township, 431 U.S. 85 (1977); Bates v. State Bar of Arizona 433 U.S. 350 (1977); Ohralik v. Ohio State Bar Ass'n, 436 U.S. 447, 449 (1978); Friedman v. Rogers, 440 U.S. 1 (1979).

28. 447 U.S. 557 (1980).

29. *Id.* at 561.

30. *Id.* at 566.

31. Cent. Hudson Gas & Elec. Corp. v. Pub. Serv. Comm'n of New York, 447 U.S. 557, 561–62 (1980) (internal citations omitted).

ucts and services can be less than completely accurate, but "[e]ven when advertising communicates only an incomplete version of the relevant facts, the First Amendment presumes that some accurate information is better than no information at all."[32]

Justice Rehnquist dissenting in *Central Hudson* raised objections that have yet to be fully addressed by the Supreme Court. Justice Rehnquist warned:

> I remain of the view that the Court unlocked a Pandora's Box when it "elevated" commercial speech to the level of traditional political speech by according it First Amendment protection ... [I]n a democracy, the economic is subordinate to the political, a lesson that our ancestors learned long ago, and that our descendants will undoubtedly have to relearn many years hence.[33]

Central Hudson has been criticized for being so terribly imprecise that it empowers lower courts to come to any conclusion they wish with respect to a challenged law or rule. As Robert Post stated, "*Central Hudson*'s fourth prong is in fact so vague that it has sometimes functioned chiefly to provide a hunting license for judges who dislike market regulations."[34] Accordingly, under the commercial speech doctrine, U.S. courts frequently use intermediate scrutiny, which allows them to rule for or against governmental regulations of commercial speech under the pliable *Central Hudson* standards.

First Amendment scholar Professor Tamara Piety shares some of Justice Rehnquist's concerns raised in his *Central Hudson* dissent.

> it seems clear that much advertising, rather than respecting consumers' autonomy instead treats consumers as prey, so regulation is appropriate. In advertising and marketing consumers are a resource to be mined and strong First Amendment protection for all these activities limits consumers' ability to seek redress or protection through collective action, that is, government. That result does not seem consistent with democratic principles.[35]

---

32. *Id.* at 562 (internal citations omitted).

33. *Id.* at 598–99.

34. Post, *Compelled Commercial Speech*, *supra* note 2, at 885.

35. Tamara R. Piety, *The Corporate First Amendment, Why Protection for Commercial and Corporate Speech Does Not Advance First Amendment Values*, Corporate Reform Coalition, 37–40 (July 20, 2015), http://www.citizen.org/documents/crc-corporate-free-speech-report.pdf.

As the *Sorrell* case addressed below shows, advertisers of all types, whether political or commercial, seem to be gaining more First Amendment rights.

B. Compelled Speech

The compelled-speech doctrine is an application of the First Amendment, and it means that the government cannot force individuals to endorse statements they do not espouse. The compelled speech doctrine is being used to object to a host of government regulations, which require disclosures to the public of various kinds. As First Amendment scholar Robert Post recently wrote, there have been a "growing number of circuit court decisions that have used the specific doctrine of 'compelled commercial speech' to strike down mandatory commercial disclosures."[36] This legal result is not inevitable. Professor Post suggests, "[r]egulations that force a speaker to disgorge *more* information to an audience do not contradict the constitutional purpose of commercial speech doctrine. They may even enhance it."[37]

In the iconic *Wooley* case, a New Hampshire man won the right in 1977 to cover up his state's motto "Live Free or Die" on his license plate, because the state could not constitutionally compel him to have the government's speech on his private car. The Court found that the statute in question effectively required individuals to "use their private property as a 'mobile billboard' for the State's ideological message."[38]

This line of compelled speech cases has also empowered newspaper editors to edit their papers as they see fit.[39] For example, a Florida law had required newspapers to allow political candidates a right of reply when the newspaper published items that were critical of the politician. As a unanimous Supreme

---

36. Post, *Compelled Commercial Speech, supra* note 2, at 868 (citing Nat'l Ass'n of Mfrs. v. SEC, 748 F.3d 359 (D.C. Cir. 2014); Nat'l Ass'n of Mfrs. v. NLRB, 717 F.3d 947 (D.C. Cir. 2013); R.J. Reynolds Tobacco Co. v. FDA, 696 F.3d 1205 (D.C. Cir. 2012); Authentic Beverages Co. v. Tex. Alcoholic Beverage Comm'n, 835 F. Supp. 2d 227 (W.D. Tex. 2011)).

37. Post, *Compelled Commercial Speech, supra* note 2, at 877.

38. Wooley v. Maynard, 430 U.S. 705, 714–15 (1977) ("Here, as in *Barnette*, we are faced with a state measure which forces an individual, as part of his daily life indeed constantly while his automobile is in public view to be an instrument for fostering public adherence to an ideological point of view he finds unacceptable. In doing so, the State 'invades the sphere of intellect and spirit which it is the purpose of the First Amendment to our Constitution to reserve from all official control.'").

39. *Miami Herald Publishing Co. v. Tornillo,* 418 U.S. 241, 258 (1974) (right-of-reply statute violates editors' right to determine the content of their newspapers).

Court noted in *Miami Herald*, "[c]ompelling editors or publishers to publish that which 'reason' tells them should not be published is what is at issue in this case."[40] The Supreme Court held "[t]he Florida statute [unconstitutionally] exacts a penalty on the basis of the content of a newspaper."[41]

In addition to compelled speech, the Supreme Court has been equally concerned with compelled silence.[42] And the case that started it all, *Barnette*, which was written in the middle of World War II about the right of a Jehovah's Witness who did not want to pledge allegiance to the flag in a public school, was clear what the risks of forced governmental conformity could mean for the individual:

> Struggles to coerce uniformity of sentiment in support of some end thought essential to their time and country have been waged by many good as well as by evil men.... Ultimate futility of [ ] attempts to compel coherence is the lesson of every such effort from the Roman drive to stamp out Christianity as a disturber of its pagan unity, the Inquisition, as a means to religious and dynastic unity, the Siberian exiles as a means to Russian unity, down to the fast failing efforts of our present totalitarian enemies. Those who begin coercive elimination of dissent soon find themselves exterminating dissenters. Compulsory unification of opinion achieves only the unanimity of the graveyard.[43]

The Supreme Court thereby recognized the right to be free of government compelled speech extended to students when such a pledge violated the students' religious beliefs.[44] The Supreme Court held government compelled speech was unconstitutional because it "require[d] the individual to communicate by word and sign his acceptance" of government-dictated political ideas, whether or not he subscribed to them.[45]

In other words, the origin of the compelled speech doctrine was the autonomy of the human individual to resist being forced to parrot the government's views. More recently, the Court applied the doctrine to nonprofits fighting HIV abroad, who were required to make anti-prostitution pledges as

---

40. *Id.*

41. *Id.*

42. Riley v. Nat'l Fed'n of the Blind of N. Carolina, Inc., 487 U.S. 781, 795–98 (1988) ("There is certainly some difference between compelled speech and compelled silence, but in the context of protected speech, the difference is without constitutional significance...").

43. W. Virginia State Bd. of Educ. v. Barnette, 319 U.S. 624, 640–41 (1943).

44. *Id.* at 642.

45. *Id.* at 633.

a condition of receiving government funds. The Supreme Court made clear that it is "a basic First Amendment principle that 'freedom of speech prohibits the government from telling people what they must say.'"[46] The Court also noted, "'[a]t the heart of the First Amendment lies the principle that each person should decide for himself or herself the ideas and beliefs deserving of expression, consideration, and adherence.'"[47] The Court harkened back to *Barnette* that, "'[i]f there is any fixed star in our constitutional constellation, it is that no official, high or petty, can prescribe what shall be orthodox in politics, nationalism, religion, or other matters of opinion or force citizens to confess by word or act their faith therein.'"[48]

1. Graphic Cigarette Warnings

But there are less benign applications of this First Amendment right to be free of government compelled speech, especially when applied to for-profit corporations.[49] In 2012 the D.C. Circuit, which has jurisdiction over most administrative agency rules that are created by the federal government, heard a challenge to FDA regulations that required cigarette companies to place graphic warnings on their cigarette packaging.[50] The tobacco companies argued that this was unconstitutionally compelled speech. Such graphic warnings are used in several countries, and the U.S. previously required text health warning on cigarette packages for years. As the D.C. Circuit explained the context of the challenged rule:

> FDA asserted the government's 'substantial interest in reducing the number of Americans, particularly children and adolescents, who use cigarettes ... in order to prevent the life-threatening health consequences associated with tobacco use.' ... FDA proposed a dramatic expansion of the existing health warnings, which it justified based on

---

46. Agency for Intern. Development v. Alliance for Open Society Intern., Inc., 133 S. Ct. 2321, 2327 (2013).

47. *Id.*; *see also* Rumsfeld v. Forum for Academic & Institutional Rights, Inc., 547 U.S. 47, 61–62, 126 S. Ct. 1297, 1308, 164 L. Ed. 2d 156 (2006). ("Some of this Court's leading First Amendment precedents have established the principle that freedom of speech prohibits the government from telling people what they must say.").

48. *Agency for Intern. Development*, 133 S. Ct. at 2332.

49. Pacific Gas & Elec. Co. v. Public Util. Comm'n of Cal., 475 U.S. 1, 20–21 (1986) (plurality opinion); *id.* at 25 (Marshall, J., concurring in judgment) (state cannot require a utility company to include a third-party newsletter in its billing envelope).

50. *Post, supra* note 2, at 907 ("*R.J. Reynolds Tobacco Co. v. FDA* ... involved nine graphic warnings which the FDA required to be affixed to cigarette packages and advertisements. The warnings were challenged under the First Amendment.").

scientific literature and a "strong worldwide consensus" regarding the relative effectiveness of graphic warnings compared to the text-only warnings the United States currently requires.[51]

The new warnings included, among other images, pictures of a smoker smoking through a stoma in his neck, and a seeming cadaver with a toe tag. These images were created by the FDA, but would have been required labels on packages of cigarettes. As the D.C. Circuit framed the issue in the case: "this case raises novel questions about the scope of the government's authority to force the manufacturer ... [to] mak[e] 'every single pack of cigarettes in the country [a] mini billboard' for the government's anti-smoking message."[52] The FDA argued that graphic warnings were needed because the agency's "previous efforts to combat the tobacco companies' advertising campaigns have been like bringing a butter knife to a gun fight.... tobacco companies spent approximately $12.49 billion on advertising and promotion in 2006 alone ... The graphic warnings represent FDA's attempt to level the playing field[.]"[53]

The D.C. Circuit Court held it against the FDA that they could not prove that the graphic warnings were having an impact on lessening tobacco addiction, a product with notoriously inelastic demand.[54] The D.C. Circuit agreed with the tobacco companies that requiring graphic pictures on cigarette packages infringed on the free speech rights of the corporations involved.[55] Professor Rebecca Tushnet quarreled with the D.C. Circuit's conclusion in *R.J. Reynolds.* She argued, "the image accompanying the text '[c]igarettes are addictive' depicted a man smoking through a tracheotomy opening in his throat.... In fact, fifty percent of neck and head cancer patients continue to smoke—this image didn't depict an extreme or unusual situation."[56]

---

51. R.J. Reynolds Tobacco Co. v. Food and Drug Admin., 696 F.3d 1205, 1209 (D.C. Cir. 2012).

52. *Id.* at 1212 (D.C. Cir. 2012).

53. *Id.* at 1221.

54. *Id.* at 1219.

55. *Constitutional Law—First Amendment—Compelled Commercial Speech—D.C. Circuit Holds That FDA Rule Mandating Graphic Warning Images on Cigarette Packaging and Advertisements Violates First Amendment.—R.J.* Reynolds Tobacco Co. v. Food & Drug Administration, *696 F.3d 1205 (D.C. Cir. 2012)*, 126 Harv. L. Rev. 818, 822 (2013) ("Accordingly, restrictions on commercial speech are generally subjected to intermediate scrutiny while mandated disclosures are generally subjected to *Zauderer's* more lenient 'reasonable relationship' test.").

56. Rebecca Tushnet, *More Than A Feeling: Emotion and the First Amendment,* 127 Harv. L. Rev. 2392, 2409-12 (2014).

R.J. Reynolds runs counter to a long history of the FDA requiring drugs to provide adequate warning to consumers. As Professor Tamara Piety recounted the history of regulating drugs:

> Much of the early political impetus to regulate commerce as it related to consumer products arose from the patent medicine trade.... [where] [t]he active ingredient in most was alcohol, but many also contained cocaine, opiates, and other psychotropic ingredients. Most troubling of all, some contained arsenic, and other substances which were unambiguously poisonous.[57]

Circuit Judge Rogers in her dissent in *R.J. Reynolds* argued simply that this holding was outrageous given the tobacco industry's history of lying to the public about the dangers of their products.[58] Judge Rogers stated, "the court applies the wrong level of scrutiny, disregarding the tobacco companies' history of deceptive advertising and the government's stated 'primary goal, which is to effectively convey the negative health consequences of smoking on cigarette packages and in advertisements[.]'"[59] Judge Rogers would have applied rational basis scrutiny under a Supreme Court case called *Zauderer*, while the majority applied *Central Hudson*'s intermediate scrutiny.[60] Judge Rogers continued, "this court has 'recognize[d] that the government's interest in preventing consumer fraud/confusion may well take on added importance in the context of a product ... that can affect the public's health.' Tobacco products necessarily affect the public health, and to a significant degree. Unlike other

57. Tamara R. Piety, *The Corporate First Amendment, supra* note 35, at 37–40.

58. The D.C. Circuit itself had come to similar conclusions in a 2009 case about fraud by tobacco companies. U.S. v. Philip Morris USA Inc., 566 F.3d 1095, 1116 (D.C. Cir. 2009) ("The district court found—permissibly in our view—that the enterprise had the common purpose of obtaining cigarette proceeds by defrauding existing and potential smokers[.]").

59. R.J. Reynolds Tobacco Co. v. Food and Drug Admin., 696 F.3d 1205, 1222 (D.C. Cir. 2012) (Rogers, J., dissenting).

60. *Id.* at 1222 (Rogers, J., dissenting) ("Because the warning labels present factually accurate information and address misleading commercial speech, as defined in Supreme Court precedent, *Zauderer* scrutiny applies[.]"); The D.C. Circuit en banc overrules R.J. Reynolds on its reading of *Zauderer*. Am. Meat Institute v. U.S. Dept. of Agriculture, 760 F.3d 18, 22–23 (D.C. Cir. 2014) ("To the extent that other cases in this circuit may be read as holding to the contrary and limiting *Zauderer* to cases in which the government points to an interest in correcting deception, we now overrule them. See, e.g., Nat'l Ass'n of Mfrs. v. SEC, 748 F.3d 359, 370–71 (D.C. Cir. 2014); *Nat'l Ass'n of Mfrs. v. NLRB,* 717 F.3d 947, 959 n. 18 (D.C.Cir.2013); R.J. Reynolds Tobacco Co. v. FDA, 696 F.3d 1205, 1214 (D.C. Cir. 2012)").

consumer products, 'tobacco products are "dangerous to health" when used in the manner prescribed.'"[61] The deleterious health impacts listed by Judge Rogers included,

> Tobacco use is the leading preventable cause of death in the United States. It causes or contributes to at least sixteen kinds of cancer, as well as heart and cerebrovascular disease, chronic bronchitis, and emphysema, thereby 'kill[ing] more than 400,000 Americans every year— more deaths than from AIDS, alcohol, car accidents, murders, suicides, drugs, and fires, combined.' President's Cancer Panel, *Promoting Healthy Lifestyles* 61 (2007). The nicotine contained in tobacco is 'one of the most addictive substances used by humans.' Institute of Medicine, *Ending the Tobacco Problem* (2007).[62]

And Judge Rogers noted in her dissent, "it is also beyond dispute that the tobacco companies have engaged in a decades-long campaign to deceive consumers about these facts. Despite knowledge of 'the negative health consequences of smoking, the addictiveness and manipulation of nicotine, [and] the harmfulness of secondhand smoke,' tobacco company executives ... 'publicly denied and distorted the truth about the addictive nature of their products, suppressed research revealing the addictiveness of nicotine, and denied their efforts to control nicotine levels and delivery,' all while 'engineer[ing] their products around creating and sustaining [nicotine] addiction.'"[63] Or as Professor Richard J. Bonnie argued, the result in *R.J. Reynolds* is peculiar because the government regulates the content of commercial packaging all the time, especially for dangerous substances. Professor Bonnie points out:

> The company has no constitutionally protected interest in selling the product in the first place.... Package regulation is a well-established component of product regulation. Just as the government can regulate the packaging of poisons to curtail dangerous use..., so too can it regulate tobacco packaging as a means for curtailing dangerous use of tobacco products.[64]

---

61. *Id.* at 1222 (Rogers, J., dissenting).

62. *Id.* at 1223–24 (Rogers, J., dissenting).

63. *Id.* at 1224 (Rogers, J., dissenting).

64. Richard J. Bonnie, *The Impending Collision Between First Amendment Protection for Commercial Speech and the Public Health: The Case of Tobacco Control*, 29 J.L. & POL. 599, 613–17 (2014).

And yet, tobacco companies won their battle to keep graphic warnings off of cigarettes because the court agreed that corporations could object to governmental compelled speech under the First Amendment.

2. Disclosing Conflict Minerals

Other industries have also been able to avoid certain regulations under the guise of the compelled speech doctrine. Section 1502 of the Dodd-Frank Wall Street Reform and Consumer Protection Act ("Dodd-Frank") required companies to investigate their supply chains and disclose annually where the minerals used in their products originate and to certify whether they are "conflict-free." Here "conflict minerals" are defined by the statute as tin, gold, tungsten, and tantalum if they were mined in the Democratic Republic of the Congo (DRC) or its neighboring countries, including Rwanda. Under Dodd-Frank, the investigation into their supply chains must include an independent private-sector audit. The law mandates that these firms notify both the Securities and Exchange Commission (SEC) and the public via their Web pages about whether their products are "conflict free" or not. Or at least it did before corporate trade associations challenged the law in court.

Congress included regulations of conflict minerals in Dodd-Frank out of concern for what is known as the "resource curse"—the phenomenon wherein poor countries with the greatest natural resources end up with the most corrupt and repressive governments.[65] The money earned from selling the natural resources props up these harsh regimes and funds violence against their citizens and neighbors. According to the *New York Times*, Rep. Jim McDermott, who championed the disclosure of conflict minerals, visited a group of rape victims in Congo and traced much of the suffering in the country "to rebel soldiers who sold tantalum and other minerals to finance their war."[66] As Dodd-Frank states, "the exploitation and trade of conflict minerals originating in the Democratic Republic of the Congo is helping to finance conflict characterized by extreme levels of violence in the eastern Democratic Repub-

65. Andrew Holland, *Alleviating the Resource Curse*, Am. Security Project 2 (Nov. 2015), https://www.americansecurityproject.org/wp-content/uploads/2015/11/Ref-0196-Alleviating-the-Resource-Curse.pdf ("Many of world's most corrupt nations are both rich in natural resources and home to some of the world's poorest.").

66. Ben Protess, *Unearthing Exotic Provisions Buried in Dodd-Frank*, N.Y. Times (July 13, 2011), http://dealbook.nytimes.com/2011/07/13/unearthing-exotic-provisions-buried-in-dodd-frank/?_r=1.

lic of the Congo, particularly sexual- and gender-based violence, and contributing to an emergency humanitarian situation therein."[67]

Dodd-Frank directed the SEC to implement the law through new rules. Shortly after the rule was finalized, in October 2012, three trade associations, the National Association of Manufacturers (NAM), the Business Roundtable and the U.S. Chamber of Commerce, filed a federal lawsuit to stop the conflict mineral disclosure rules, which were scheduled to take effect May 31, 2014. The case is *NAM v. SEC*. The SEC won at the district court level in 2013 when Judge Wilkins upheld the SEC's conflict mineral rule. He concluded that Congress could pass the disclosure rule as "a reasonable step to shed some light on this literally life-and-death issue," and to "encourage companies using these minerals to source them responsibly."[68] Judge Wilkins rejected the claim that the disclosure rule compels speech.

But the SEC lost the First Amendment argument in the D.C. Circuit on appeal.[69] The D.C. Circuit let much of the rule go forward, but the court agreed with the trade associations litigating the case that requiring corporations to call tin, tungsten, tantalum, and gold from the Democratic Republic of Congo (DRC) and its neighboring nations, "conflict minerals" was unconstitutional compelled speech, because as lawyers for the trade associations had argued, the minerals themselves aren't "conflicted."[70] The D.C. Circuit court agreed that this was a value judgment, and that the government could not force corporations to characterize their raw materials as "not [having] been found to be 'DRC conflict free'" under the First Amendment.

This case was reheard by the D.C. Circuit in 2015 because intervening Circuit case law overruled the original ruling.[71] The intervening case was *Ameri-*

---

67. Dodd-Frank Wall Street Reform and Consumer Protection Act, Conference Report to Accompany H.R. 4173, June 29, 2010, http://www.gpo.gov/fdsys/pkg/CRPT-111hrpt517/pdf/CRPT-111hrpt517.pdf.

68. *Nat'l Ass'n of Mfrs. v. S.E.C.*, 956 F. Supp. 2d 43, 80 (D.D.C. 2013).

69. *Nat'l Ass'n of Mfrs. v. S.E.C.*, 748 F.3d 359, 373 (D.C. Cir. 2014) (holding "we still cannot say that the restriction here is narrowly tailored.").

70. *Nat'l Ass'n of Mfrs.*, 748 F.3d at 371.

71. Nat'l Ass'n of Mfrs. v. S.E.C., 2015 WL 5089667, at *1 (D.C. Cir. 2015) ("we granted the petitions of the Securities and Exchange Commission and intervenor Amnesty International for rehearing to consider what effect, if any, *AMI* had on our judgment that the conflict minerals disclosure requirement … violated the First Amendment to the Constitution."); The D.C. Circuit en banc overruled *Nat'l Ass'n of Mfrs. v. SEC* on its reading of *Zauderer*. Am. Meat Institute v. U.S. Dept. of Agriculture, 760 F.3d 18, 22–23 (D.C. Cir. 2014) ("To the extent that other cases in this circuit may be read as holding to the contrary and limiting *Zauderer* to cases in which the government points to an interest in correcting deception, we now overrule them. See, e.g., Nat'l Ass'n of Mfrs. v. SEC, 748 F.3d 359, 370–71 (D.C. Cir. 2014)[.]").

can Meat Institute (AMI) v. U.S. Department of Agriculture, which upheld country of origin labeling on food *en banc.*[72] Despite *AMI*, the D.C. Circuit in *NAM v. SEC II* reaffirmed its earlier approach, concluding that calling the four elements at issue "conflict minerals" was unconstitutional compelled speech.[73] As the D.C. Circuit concluded, "we continue to agree with NAM [National Association of Manufacturers] that [r]equiring a company to publicly condemn itself is undoubtedly a more 'effective' way for the government to stigmatize and shape behavior than for the government to have to convey its views itself, but that makes the requirement more constitutionally offensive, not less so."[74]

First Amendment objections are being asserted in other cases challenging other Dodd-Frank rules as well. In *American Petroleum Institute (API) v. SEC*, the U.S. Chamber of Commerce and other plaintiffs sued over the SEC rule implementing Dodd-Frank section 1504, arguing the rule was arbitrary and capricious, had a flawed cost-benefit analysis, and violated the First Amendment.[75] This rule would have required extractive industries to report payments to foreign governments.[76] The district court invalidated the extractive industries reporting rule, though on cost-benefit analysis reasons and not on First Amendment grounds.[77]

---

72. Am. Meat Institute v. U.S. Dept. of Agriculture, 760 F.3d 18, 27 (D.C. Cir. 2014) ("Nor does the mandate run afoul of the Court's warning that *Zauderer* does not leave the state 'free to require corporations to carry the messages of third parties, where the messages themselves are biased against or are expressly contrary to the corporation's views' ").

73. *Nat'l Ass'n of Mfrs.*, 2015 WL 5089667, at *8 ("we adhere to our original judgment "that 15 U.S.C. §78m(p)(1)(A)(ii) & (E), and the Commission's final rule, 77 Fed. Reg. at 56,362– 65, violate the First Amendment to the extent the statute and rule require regulated entities to report to the Commission and to state on their website that any of their products have 'not been found to be 'DRC conflict free.' ").

74. *Id.* at *8 (internal citation omitted).

75. 953 F. Supp. 2d 5, 11 (D.D.C. 2013) (failing to reach the cost-benefit argument and invalidating the SEC's rule on other grounds); *id.* at 24–25 (finding that a vacatur of the rule was the appropriate remedy because the rule was invalid; no disruption would occur because of a vacatur as issuers had not been required to disclose yet under the rule; and the SEC has not proffered an argument against a vacatur remedy).

76. Press Release, U.S. Sec. & Exch. Comm'n., SEC Adopts Rules Requiring Payment Disclosures by Resource Extraction Issuers Disclosing Payments by Issuers Engaged in Resource Extraction (Aug. 22, 2012), http://www.sec.gov/News/PressRelease/Detail/PressRelease/1365171484028#.UsL75_Mo7cs ("The Securities and Exchange Commission today adopted rules mandated by the Dodd-Frank Wall Street Reform and Consumer Protection Act requiring resource extraction issuers to disclose certain payments made to the U.S. government or foreign governments.").

77. *Id.* The SEC decided not to appeal the decision. Sarah N. Lynch, *SEC Won't Appeal Ruling vs Disclosing Payments Abroad*, REUTERS (Sept. 3, 2013), http://www.reuters.com/

The conflict mineral case, *NAM v. SEC*, could portend deeper deregulation. As Nell Minow opined, "[t]he D.C. Circuit in the conflict mineral ruling suggested that any requirement of disclosure by the federal government whether it is IPO statements, or proxy statements, or the calorie and fat content of food on the shelf, might be thrown out as a violation of First Amendment rights. That's just insane."[78] The impact of this case for other plain vanilla disclosures that are required to help customers and investors could be quite strikingly broad. As Harvard Professor Cass Sunstein asked, "[d]oes the [D.C. Circuit] court really want to transform the free speech principle into a kind of all-purpose weapon against disclosure requirements imposed on American companies, authorizing unelected judges to make their own independent judgments about tough empirical questions?"[79] This case on conflict mineral disclosures was appealed.[80] But the appeal failed and the trade associations won their compelled speech argument.

C. Data Collection as Speech

In a sleepy little case about data sales, the Supreme Court used the First Amendment to strike down a Vermont law prohibiting the sale of doctors' prescription records to data mining companies. Consequently, the Supreme Court crushed a Vermont law that was intended to protect doctors.[81] Why did doctors need protecting? Because of the barrage of advertising and other aggressive marketing techniques directed at them from pharmaceutical companies.

---

article/2013/09/03/us-sec-resource-extraction-dUSBRE9820Z820130903.

78. Interview with Nell Minow, Vice Chair, ValueEdge Advisors (Aug. 19, 2015).

79. Cass R. Sunstein, *How to Fight Conflict Minerals? Mandatory Disclosure*, BLOOMBERG (Oct. 26, 2015), http://www.bloombergview.com/articles/2015-10-26/how-to-fight-blood-diamonds-mandatory-disclosure-; *see also* TAMARA R. PIETY, BRANDISHING THE FIRST AMENDMENT COMMERCIAL EXPRESSION IN AMERICA (2013) (accord).

80. Nat'l Ass'n of Mfrs. v. S.E.C., petition by Amnesty International for hearing en banc (Oct. 2, 2015), http://www.citizen.org/documents/Filed%20Petition%20for%20Rehearing%20En%20Banc.pdf; Nat'l Ass'n of Mfrs. v. S.E.C., No. 13-5252 (D.C. Cir. Nov. 9, 2015) (hearing en banc denied), http://freespeechforpeople.org/cms/assets/uploads/2015/11/NAM-v-SEC-Petition-for-rehg-en-banc-denied.pdf; Letter from Attorney General Loretta E. Lynch to Speaker Paul Ryan (Mar. 4, 2016) (explaining why cert. petition was not filed).

81. Vt. Stat. 18 §4631 ("It is the intent of the general assembly to advance the state's interest in protecting the public health of Vermonters, protecting the privacy of prescribers and prescribing information, and to ensure costs are contained in the private health care sector, as well as for state purchasers of prescription drugs, through the promotion of less costly drugs and ensuring prescribers receive unbiased information.").

"Pharmaceutical firms [back in the 1990s alone] spen[t] as much as one-fifth of their huge budgets on advertising directed at doctors and pharmacists. The pharmaceutical companies subtly convert doctors into 'pushers' of their drug products."[82] Because pharmaceutical reps typically get commissions and bonuses based on sales, they have the incentive to sell, sell, sell, even by using doctors' own prescribing habits against them.[83] Data mining to sell to information to pharmaceutical reps and other businesses is itself a huge business. As Professor Frank Pasquale explained, "[d]ata brokers have sprung up out of relatively humble soil, like direct marketing and shoppers' lists, and become a multibillion dollar industry that (in the aggregate) has the goal of psychologically, medically, politically, profiling everyone in the world. People don't fully appreciate the extent to which data brokers can trade information amongst themselves to create ever more detailed profiles of individuals."[84]

The case was *Sorrell v. IMS Health*.[85] The issue surrounded a Vermont law that "restricts the sale, disclosure, and use of pharmacy records that reveal the prescribing practices of individual doctors."[86] The part of the law that was at issue in the case stated, among other items: "[p]harmaceutical manufacturers and pharmaceutical marketers shall not use prescriber-identifiable information for marketing or promoting a prescription drug unless the prescriber consents [.]"[87]

"Detailing," as the drug industry euphemistically calls it, is the practice of tailoring drug sales pitches to doctors using data on their past prescribing habits. The legislative history of this law indicated that the Vermont legislature found that "detailing increases the cost of health care and health insurance, § 1(15); encourages hasty and excessive reliance on brand-name drugs, before the profession has observed their effectiveness as compared with older

---

82. Marshall Clinard, Corporate Corruption 58 (1990).

83. Tamara R. Piety, *'A Necessary Cost of Freedom'? The Incoherence of* Sorrell v. IMS, 64 Ala. L. Rev. (Forthcoming 2016), http://ssrn.com/abstract=2042157 ("Data mining gives the detailer insight into the physician's practice that he might prefer the detailer not have, not to mention that it permits the rep to manipulate the doctor's response through the tactics of the 'hard sell.' Data mining creates an asymmetry of information between the rep and the doctor that makes many doctors feel uncomfortable.") (manuscript at 10).

84. Evan Selinger, *Frank Pasquale Unravels the New Machine Age of Algorithms and Bots in His Book "The Black Box Society,"* C.S. Monitor (undated), http://passcode.csmonitor.com/frankpasquale (quoting Pasquale).

85. Ernest A. Young, Sorrell v. IMS Health *and the End of the Constitutional Double Standard*, 36 Vt. L. Rev. 903, 922 (2012) ("Once the regulated activity is speech, then heightened scrutiny follows almost as night follows the day.").

86. Sorrell v. IMS Health Inc., 131 S. Ct. 2653, 2659 (2011).

87. *Id.* at 2660 (quoting the Vermont statute).

and less expensive generic alternatives, § 1(7); and fosters disruptive and re-peated marketing visits tantamount to harassment[.]"[88]

Mr. Sorrell is the Attorney General of Vermont, and is charged with de-fending his state's law. For most people, this law would not be particularly con-troversial. To many, it would be a welcome change to protect physicians and by extension their patients from well-marketed expensive drugs.[89] Who could object to such an admirable law? Those who help market expensive drugs to doctors. The plaintiffs in the case were three corporations—IMS Health, Verispan, and Source Healthcare Analytics, a unit of Dutch publisher Wolters Kluwer.[90] These companies are in the business of aggregating data on the drug prescribing habits of doctors and selling it to drug companies, so that the drug companies can tailor their drug sales pitches (a.k.a. "detailing") to doctors. The corporations challenged the Vermont law as a content-based restriction of their First Amendment rights because under the law "pharmacies may sell the information to private or academic researchers, but not, for example, to pharmaceutical marketers."[91]

The Supreme Court agreed by a vote of 6 to 3 with the corporations in *Sorrell v. IMS Health Inc.* Justice Kennedy, writing for the majority, noted that the Vermont law was unconstitutional under the First Amendment:

> On its face, Vermont's law enacts content-and speaker-based restric-tions on the sale, disclosure, and use of prescriber-identifying infor-mation.... The measure then bars any disclosure when recipient speakers will use the information for marketing. Finally, the provi-sion's second sentence prohibits pharmaceutical manufacturers from using the information for marketing. The statute thus disfavors mar-keting, that is, speech with a particular content. More than that, the statute disfavors specific speakers, namely pharmaceutical manufac-turers. As a result of these content- and speaker-based rules, detailers cannot obtain prescriber-identifying information, even though the

---

88. *Id.* at 2661 (quoting Vermont's legislative history).

89. John M. Greabe, *Foreword: Constitutional Constraints on State Health Care & Privacy Regulations after* Sorrell v. IMS Health, 36 Vᴛ. L. Rᴇᴠ. 809, 809–814 (2012) ("the [*Sorrell*] majority rejected Vermont's attempts to justify the statute in terms of its interests in medical privacy, physician confidentiality, avoidance of harassment, the integrity of the doctor-patient relationship, improving public health, or reducing health care costs.").

90. Sorrell v. IMS Health, The Oyez Project at IIT Chicago-Kent College of Law, http://www.oyez.org/cases/2010-2019/2010/2010_10_779.

91. Sorrell v. IMS Health Inc., 131 S. Ct. 2653, 2662 (2011) (internal citations omitted).

information may be purchased or acquired by other speakers with di-
verse purposes and viewpoints.... The law on its face burdens disfavored speech by disfavored speakers.[92]

In other words, the Justices in the majority thought of the law not as a protection of the privacy of patients or the integrity of the medical profession, but
rather as a form of targeted government censorship.

The Supreme Court found that Vermont was impermissibly picking fa-
vorites. As Justice Kennedy wrote, "Vermont's law thus has the effect of preventing detailers — and only detailers — from communicating with physicians
in an effective and informative manner."[93] The Court went on to say even if
the Vermont law was just burdening the speech of the corporations, "[l]aw-
makers may no more silence unwanted speech by burdening its utterance than
by censoring its content."[94] In response to the argument that drug representatives were harassing doctors using the data at issue in this lawsuit, Justice
Kennedy responded, "[m]any are those who must endure speech they do not
like, but that is a necessary cost of freedom."[95]

Previous cases had given commercial speech less robust protections than
political speech. But in *Sorrell v. IMS Health Inc.*, the Court seemed to reduce
the saliency of this previously important distinction.[96] Picking up on the logic
the Court used in *Virginia Pharmacy*, Justice Kennedy concluded in *Sorrell*:
"[c]ommercial speech is no exception. A consumer's concern for the free flow
of commercial speech often may be far keener than his concern for urgent political dialogue. That reality has great relevance in the fields of medicine and
public health, where information can save lives."[97]

Vermont had argued that data mining (which is what the plaintiff companies do) was merely conduct and not speech and thus lower scrutiny should
apply. An appeals court below accepted this argument. "Consistent with that

---

92. *Id.* at 2663.

93. *Id.*

94. *Id.* at 2664.

95. *Id.* at 2669.

96. Marcia M. Boumilal, *Pharmaceutical Gift Laws and Commercial Speech Under the
First Amendment in the Wake of* Sorrell v. IMS Health, Inc., 8 J. HEALTH & BIOMEDICAL L.
133, 159–169 (2012) ("*Sorrell* then declined to impose the intermediate standard of First
Amendment analysis set forth in *Central Hudson*, determining instead that a heightened
level of constitutional scrutiny was appropriate because the regulation imposed direct (not
incidental) speaker-based and content-based burdens on protected speech (as opposed to
conduct) to suppress a disfavored message contrary to public policy.).

97. Sorrell v. IMS Health Inc., 131 S. Ct. 2653, 2664 (2011) (internal citations and quo-
tation omitted).

submission, the United States Court of Appeals for the First Circuit has characterized prescriber-identifying information as a mere 'commodity' with no greater entitlement to First Amendment protection than 'beef jerky.'[98] The majority of the Supreme Court rejected this argument noting: "[t]his Court has held that the creation and dissemination of information are speech within the meaning of the First Amendment. Facts, after all, are the beginning point for much of the speech ... There is thus a strong argument that prescriber-identifying information is speech for First Amendment purposes."[99] Vermont had also argued that the law protected patient and doctor privacy, but these arguments were brushed aside.[100]

In the end, the Supreme Court concluded that the persuasiveness of commercial speech was not a good enough reason for Vermont to regulate it.[101] And furthermore, that the First Amendment "directs us [the Court] to be especially skeptical of regulations that seek to keep people in the dark for what the government perceives to be their own good. These precepts apply with full force when the audience, in this case prescribing physicians, consists of sophisticated and experienced consumers."[102]

Justices Kagan, Breyer, and Ginsburg in dissent in *Sorrell v. IMS Health Inc.*, argued that this was merely a commercial regulation, and as such, it should not have received the heightened scrutiny that the majority applied. The dissenting Justices reasoned:

> The Vermont statute before us adversely affects expression in one, and only one, way. It deprives pharmaceutical and data-mining companies of data, collected pursuant to the government's regulatory mandate, that could help pharmaceutical companies create better sales messages.... The First Amendment does not require courts to apply a special "heightened" standard of review when reviewing such an effort.[103]

Justice Breyer worried in his *Sorrell* dissent that the logic of the case could undo all sorts of governmental regulations, including long-standing drug regula-

---

98. *Id.* at 2666.

99. *Id.* at 2667 (internal citations omitted).

100. *Id.* at 2670 (*Watchtower Bible* states "[p]ersonal privacy even in one's own home receives 'ample protection' from the 'resident's unquestioned right to refuse to engage in conversation with unwelcome visitors,'" and that "[a] physician's office is no more private and is entitled to no greater protection").

101. *Id.* at 2670.

102. *Id.* at 2670–71 (internal quotations marks omitted).

103. Sorrell v. IMS Health Inc., 131 S. Ct. 2653, 2673 (2011) (Breyer, J., dissenting).

tions. As Breyer explained, "the same First Amendment standards that apply to Vermont here would apply to similar regulatory actions taken by other States or by the Federal Government acting, for example, through Food and Drug Administration (FDA) regulation."[104] Professor Jedediah Purdy also finds *Sorrell* to be a step down a dangerous road of protecting data mining as free speech. As he noted, "what the Vermont decision protects is not verbal expression or even political spending but simply the sale of data. *Sorrell* moves toward constitutionalizing an open market in information … So there is now a constitutionally protected interest in exchanging information on the same terms as everyone else in the market."[105] Professor Purdy asserted, "decisions [like *Sorrell*] don't just trim around the edges of regulation: They go to the heart of whether government can act to balance out private economic power in an era of growing economic inequality and insecurity."[106]

Because *Sorrell* was about one of the most personal and private facts, which types of medicines a doctor was prescribing, the potential impact of the case could be quite large for eroding personal privacy as Professor Ashutosh Bhagwat warned, "all sales or disclosures of information in the possession of the speaker constitute fully protected speech under the First Amendment."[107] He explains the possible reach of the holding in *Sorrell* could include data of all types including:

> personal medical information in the possession of health care providers; financial information in the possession of financial institutions; purchasing histories in the possession of retailers, including online retailers such as Amazon.com; search information in the possession of search engines such as Google; viewing information in the possession of firms such as Comcast and Netflix; and any number of other forms of personal data that individuals voluntarily share with private-sector firms. All of these forms of data…, and

---

104. *Id.* at 2675–76 (Breyer, J., dissenting).

105. Jedediah Purdy, *The Roberts Court v. America*, 23 DEMOCRACY (2012), http://www.democracyjournal.org/23/the-roberts-court-v-america.php?page=all.

106. *Id.*

107. Ashutosh Bhagwat, Sorrell v. IMS Health: *Details, Detailing, and the Death of Privacy*, 36 VT. L. REV. 855, 869 (2011); *see also* LAURENCE TRIBE & JOSHUA MATZ, UNCERTAIN JUSTICE THE ROBERTS COURT AND THE CONSTITUTION 84 (2014) ("*Sorrell* is part of a line of Roberts Court cases suggesting an appetite for a more active judicial role in overseeing economic affairs. Individually they may not say much, but viewed together they point the way toward more assertive use of constitutional law by a majority of the Court to advance deregulatory economic beliefs.").

therefore sales and disclosures of such data by their possessors, constitute protected speech.[108]

Sorrell is particularly troubling as formerly paper records are digitized, downloadable and searchable, at a time when the average person spends three hours a day on social media. From the end user's perspective, she is connected with friends and family and staying up to date on the news of the day. From the data miners' perspective, each click and keystroke is just more information that can be monetized and sold. Professor Neil M. Richards argues that in a digital age the government must be able to regulate data flows. "As we enter the Information Age, in which the trade in information is a multibillion-dollar industry, the government should be able to regulate the huge flows of personal information, as well as the permissible uses of such information. If our lives become digital, but data is speech, regulation of many kinds of social problems will become impossible."[109]

While lower courts have largely not taken up *Sorrell*'s invitation, the Supreme Court itself is building on the foundation it laid down in *Sorrell*.[110] For example, in a case called *Reed v. Town of Gilbert*, the Supreme Court cited to *Sorrell* for the proposition, "[g]overnment regulation of speech is content based if a law applies to particular speech because of the topic discussed or the idea or message expressed."[111] This case wasn't remarkable because it applied strict scrutiny to content based restrictions. That wasn't novel. What was novel in *Reed* was that content based restrictions were redefined to include governmental regulation of a topic. This turn of events has worried Adam Liptak, an attorney and a reporter, who covers the Supreme Court for the *New York Times*. Mr. Liptak noted under the logic of *Reed*, "[a]ny law that singles out a topic for regulation ... discriminates based on content and is therefore presumptively unconstitutional. Securities regulation is a topic. Drug labeling is a topic. Consumer protection is a topic."[112] So we may yet be treated to a new round of deregulation based on *Sorrell* after all. Justice Breyer was sympathetic to

---

108. Bhagwat, 36 Vt. L. Rev. at 869–874; for a contrary view *see* Neil M. Richards, *Why Data Privacy Law is (Mostly) Constitutional*, 56 Wm. & Mary L. Rev. 1501, 1521–1524 (2015) ("*Sorrell* invalidated one particularly clumsy attempt to regulate marketing, but it does not follow from this that data privacy law is largely unconstitutional.").

109. Richards, 56 Wm. & Mary L. Rev. at 1531.

110. Piety, *The Corporate First Amendment supra* note 35, at 51.

111. Reed v. Town of Gilbert, 135 S. Ct. 2218, 2227 (2015).

112. Adam Liptak, *Court's Free-Speech Expansion Has Far-Reaching Consequences*, N.Y. Times (Aug. 17, 2015), http://www.nytimes.com/2015/08/18/us/politics/courts-free-speech-expansion-has-far-reaching-consequences.html?_r=0.

these concerns. He warned in his *Sorrell* dissent that "[a]t best the Court opens a Pandora's Box of First Amendment challenges to many ordinary regulatory practices that may only incidentally affect a commercial message. At worst, it reawakens *Lochner*'s pre-New Deal threat of substituting judicial for democratic decisionmaking where ordinary economic regulation is at issue."[113]

Professor Coates at Harvard is concerned, like Dean Post at Yale, that the overuse of the First Amendment in the hands of corporations puts the rule of law at risk. He summed up the situation in a recent law review article: "[p]recedents are overturned; *stare decisis* becomes a joke; constitutional entrepreneurialism runs amok. Radicals in pinstriped suits rewrite whole elements of long-established legal order. Under First Amendment threat, laws become quantum objects—partly there, partly not there. As a system, they cease to have several of the key indicia of the 'rule of law,' including consistency, predictability, and publicity."[114]

The impact, if these legal arguments are taken to their logical conclusions, could be devastating to future efforts to regulate in the public's interest, as author Elliot Zaret noted in a discussion with First Amendment scholar Professor Frederick Schauer:

> "They are objecting to government regulation, and because they are objecting to a form of government regulation that happens to be about words or signs, all of a sudden the First Amendment gives them an argument," Schauer says. "We operate in a world in which a huge amount of what we do involves words, and therefore involves speech." He says a huge amount of regulation by government agencies such as the FTC, the FDA, the Occupational Safety and Health Administration of the U.S. Department of Labor, the National Labor Relations Board, and the SEC involves the regulation of speech.[115]

The fallout from the abuse of the compelled speech doctrine in commercial context could be, as Professor Tamara Piety warned, that consumer protection laws will be harder to pass in legislatures because "the First Amendment is like a game-ender[.]"[116]

The commercial speech doctrine and the compelled speech doctrine are combining to give corporations powerful tools to argue that government rules

---

113. Sorrell v. IMS Health Inc., 131 S. Ct. 2653, 2685 (2011) (Breyer, J., dissenting) (internal cross references omitted).

114. 30 CONST. COMMENT. at 269–70 (internal citations omitted).

115. Zaret, *supra* note 26 (quoting Schauer).

116. *Id.* (quoting Piety).

that are meant to protect or inform the public are unconstitutional. This has led to corporate victories utilizing the First Amendment invalidating the FDA's graphic warnings on tobacco products, invalidating the SEC's reporting of conflict minerals in products, and invalidating Vermont's regulations against data mining doctors' prescriptions.

MARRIOTT

Chapter 5

This Politician Was
Brought to You By ...

> On the Hill, anybody that moves is seen as a source of food for the
> campaign—that is, they can be turned into contributors.
>
> —Trevor Potter[1]

In 2005, the Supreme Court's approach to corporate political activity
changed profoundly. The big change in jurisprudence was the result of a big
change in the Court's personnel. Chief Justice William Rehnquist died and Justice Sandra Day O'Connor retired to take care of her ailing husband. President
George W. Bush replaced them with Chief Justice John Roberts and Justice
Samuel Alito. The two departing Justices were moderates in two key area of
the law: campaign finance and corporate power. With the new five-person pro-
corporate and anti-campaign finance reform majority, the Court was free to
change the case law radically. In doing so, the court relied on two pro-corporate
cases from the 1970s, *Bellotti* and *Virginia Pharmacy*—the former involved
expansive corporate political rights, the latter dealt with expansive corporate
commercial speech rights.

Whatever your view about the propriety of corporations gaining new rights,
there is no doubt it is happening, and at a rapid pace. The Supreme Court
started with property and Contract Clause rights and then, with rare exceptions, never stopped expanding corporate rights. But the growth of new rights
has entered a new phase in the last decade within the Court's First Amendment jurisprudence. This is a change, as the First Amendment has often been
thought of as an engine for our democratic process—empowering individual

---

1. Interview with Trevor Potter, President Campaign Legal Ctr. (July 27, 2015).

citizens to make wise democratic choices. As the Supreme Court once explained, "the fundamental premises underlying the First Amendment [is it is] the guardian of our democracy. That Amendment embodies our trust in the free exchange of ideas as the means by which the people are to choose between good ideas and bad, and between candidates for political office."[2]

In contrast to most modern democracies, the United States is noteworthy for its reliance on private funding for nearly all of its elections.[3] Consequently, it is not surprising that one of the rights corporations have been eager to claim has been the right to spend corporate money in elections. It is the privately financed nature of our elections that necessitates some type of campaign finance regulation so that the process is as democratic—and not oligarchic—as possible. The purpose, in short, of money in politics rules, is to protect the influence of average voters on the outcome of the electoral process.

Just as the U.S. Constitution never mentions the word "corporation," it also doesn't mention the words "campaign finance," or anything remotely close. As a result, the Supreme Court has had wide latitude to decide whether campaign finance restrictions are allowed by the Constitution or not. The way that the Court has traditionally dealt with restrictions on money in politics is by framing it in terms of the First Amendment, treating campaign finance as either a subset of the freedom of speech and/or the freedom of association.

For most of the twentieth century, the Court agreed that giving political rights to an individual is different from giving them to a corporation. The reason relates to the particular legal structure of corporations. The corporate structure dictates that shareholders elect the board of directors. Directors hire the officers. The officers hire line employees. The board makes key decisions for the corporation, but typically meets infrequently. The officers run the corporation day to day. Shareholders provide capital, but unless a shareholder is also a board member or a corporate officer, the shareholder does not control what happens day to day at the firm. Shareholders cannot be sued for the corporation's actions.

So how does the corporate structure fit with a constitutional right to spend in politics? Consider a Chief Executive Officer (CEO) or a member of the board. Historically, these individuals spend corporate treasury funds in poli-

2. Brown v. Hartlage, 456 U.S. 45, 60 (1982).
3. International Institute for Democracy & Electoral Assistance, *Political Finance Database*, http://www.idea.int/political-finance/index.cfm (last visited Nov. 11, 2015).

tics at a very high rate.[4] Supreme Court decisions empowering corporations to spend in American elections really empower corporate managers (board members and corporate officers) to spend other people's money in politics. Here the "other people" are shareholders.

One way to think about the corporate structure and political spending is when corporations are banned from a certain type of political spending, that does not mean that business men and women cannot spend in politics; it merely means that they need to spend their own personal money supporting the candidates of their choice. Consequently, when corporate bans are in place, a CEO who is eager to be politically active can be. But that CEO has to reach for his own private credit card if he wants to spend in politics.

In contrast, when the corporation is allowed to spend corporate funds in politics, then the CEO who wants to play in politics can pay for political expenditures using the corporate credit card. When the bill comes due on the corporate credit card, the CEO doesn't pay; rather the corporation, and by extension its investors, foot the bill. So, for example, when News Corp gave $1 million to the Republican Governors Association or Chevron gave $2.5 million to the Congressional Leadership Fund Super PAC, it wasn't the CEOs of either firm who paid for that; rather, it was the corporations that paid for it, and by extension their investors. The millions that just two firms spent on politics could have gone to research and development, improvements to the companies' physical plants, improved wages, more hiring, or higher dividends for investors.

For some, looking at the political spending in past few years since 2010, the spending by individual billionaires of their personal fortunes has so far dwarfed the political spending by corporations at the federal level. Admittedly, billionaire spending does present profound issues, like the impact of the concentrated personal wealth in American elections. An analysis of the 2016 race by the *New York Times* found, "[j]ust 158 families, along with companies they own or control, contributed $176 million in the first phase of the campaign.... Not since before Watergate have so few people and businesses provided so

---

4. Adam Bonica, *Avenues of Influence: On the Political Expenditures of Corporations and Their Directors and Executives* (SSRN Working Paper, Aug. 20, 2013), at 15, http://www.princeton.edu/csdp/events/Bonica11072013/SSRN-id2313232.pdf (last visited Mar. 24, 2014) ("The phenomenally high rates of giving among corporate elites provides a rich data source to examine why and how they give. In fact, the high rate of giving among CEOs and board members that makes this type of analysis feasible is itself notable. Of the sample of directors and CEOs of Fortune 500 companies, at least 83 percent have made political contributions.").

much early money in a campaign, most of it through channels legalized by the Supreme Court's *Citizens United* decision five years ago."[5] But for others, the issue of corporations spending is a far more troubling problem than expenditures from billionaires. The billionaires funding American federal elections, after all, are American citizens and voters.

As worrying as spending by billionaires is, corporations are still in a different category altogether. While corporations can be anything from a mom and pop shop on your corner, to the multinational corporation on every corner, corporate wealth is incredibly concentrated among fewer than two dozen firms. As reported in *The Hill*,

> The majority of corporate cash is amassed in the coffers of 18 U.S. firms—they held 36 percent of all wealth last year, a jump from 27 percent in 2009 with the gap expected to widen further, according to a report from Standard & Poor's, a New York-based credit rater. That means that out of a record $1.53 trillion in cash and short-term investments held by U.S. corporations, the wealthiest 18 held about $535 billion.[6]

Thus, the key question may not be how corporations in general will use their power, but rather how the wealthiest corporations will wield their expanded powers that the Supreme Court is granting them. To answer that question, we first need to explore what rights their corporations have been granted. It may seem odd, but corporate political rights were granted in just two Supreme Court decisions: *Bellotti* and *Citizens United*.

A. *Bellotti*

Before there was *Citizens United*, there was *First National Bank of Boston v. Bellotti*.[7] As attorney Nell Minow states, "[i]n retrospect, *Bellotti* was the beginning of the collapse of notion of any kind of real government oversight of

5. Nicholas Confessore, Sarah Cohen & Karen Yourish, *The Families Funding the 2016 Presidential Election*, N.Y. Times (Oct. 10, 2015), http://www.nytimes.com/interactive/2015/10/11/us/politics/2016-presidential-election-super-pac-donors.html?_r=0.

6. Vicki Needham, *Report: 18 Firms Hold a Third of US Wealth*, The Hill (Aug. 9, 2014), http://thehill.com/policy/finance/economy/214757-report-18-companies-hold-over-a-third-of-us-wealth.

7. First Nat'l Bank of Boston v. Bellotti, 435 U.S. 765, 776 (1978) (Powell, J.).

companies."[8] Mr. Bellotti was the Attorney General of Massachusetts. Massachusetts passed a law that corporations could not make expenditures in ballot measure campaigns. The First National Bank of Boston challenged the law and so it fell to Mr. Bellotti to defend the law. This law had criminal sanctions including fines and up to a year in jail.[9] Citing the First Amendment, the Supreme Court invalidated Massachusetts' law in 1978, which effectively empowered corporations to speak in ballot measure contests.

Justice Powell wrote the majority opinion in *Bellotti* and seized the moment to expand corporate political rights. The approach Justice Powell took in *Bellotti* was subtle and effective. He proclaimed that the First Amendment is concerned with protecting "speech," not the "speaker."[10] It did not matter that the would-be speaker in *Bellotti* was a corporation:

> The speech proposed by appellants is at the heart of the First Amendment's protection.... "there is practically universal agreement that a major purpose of [the First] Amendment was to protect the free discussion of governmental affairs." If the speakers here were not corporations, no one would suggest that the State could silence their proposed speech. It is the type of speech indispensable to decision-making in a democracy, and this is no less true because the speech comes from a corporation rather than an individual. The inherent worth of the speech in terms of its capacity for informing the public does not depend upon the identity of its source, whether corporation, association, union, or individual.[11]

According to Justice Powell and the majority of the Supreme Court, Massachusetts was unconstitutionally singling out corporations as despised speakers. As they ruled, the law "amounts to an impermissible legislative prohibition of speech based on the identity of the interests that spokesmen may represent in public debate over controversial issues[.]"[12] Then Justice Powell wrote, "[i]f a legislature may direct business corporations to 'stick to business,' it also may limit other corporations—religious, charitable, or civic—to their respective 'business' when addressing the public. Such power in government to channel

---

8. Interview with Nell Minow, Vice Chair, ValueEdge Advisors (Aug. 19, 2015).
9. First Nat'l Bank of Boston, 435 U.S. at 768 (Powell, J.).
10. Interview with Robert A.G. Monks (Aug. 17, 2015) ("The thing about *Bellotti* is it was a courageous thing for a young Justice to create the concept that the First Amendment concerns speech and not the speaker.").
11. First Nat'l Bank of Boston, 435 U.S. at 777 (Powell, J.) (footnotes omitted).
12. *Id.* at 784 (Powell, J.).

the expression of views is unacceptable under the First Amendment."[13] But this is an odd list to roll out because the law already forbids charitable groups like 501(c)(3)s from political spending in elections.[14] And churches that get involved in politics risk their tax-exempt status.[15] But the boogey man of the government as censor is a powerful one, and that is what Justice Powell deployed to great effect in *Bellotti*.

In retrospect, that Justice Powell arrived at this conclusion was not surprising. Before Justice Powell became a member of the Supreme Court, as a corporate lawyer he wrote an influential memorandum for the U.S. Chamber of Commerce arguing "the American business executive is truly the 'forgotten man.'"[16] Therefore, "[political] power must be assiduously cultivated; and when necessary, it must be used aggressively and with determination—without embarrassment and without the reluctance which has been so characteristic of American business."[17] Moreover, Powell stressed, the critical ingredient for corporate political success would be coordination: "[s]trength lies in organization, in careful long-range planning and implementation, in consistency of action over an indefinite period of years, in the scale of financing available only through joint effort, and in the political power available only through united action and national organizations."[18]

This is now known as the "Powell Memo." While some, like *American Prospect*'s Mark Schmitt, have maintained that this document's historical sig-

---

13. *Id.* at 785 (Powell, J.).

14. Reagan v. Taxation with Representation of Washington, 461 U.S. 540, 548 (1983) (holding "Congress has not violated [an organization's] First Amendment rights by declining to subsidize its First Amendment activities."); *see also* Donald B. Tobin, *Political Campaigning by Churches and Charities: Hazardous for 501(C)(3)s, Dangerous for Democracy*, 95 Geo. L.J. 1313, 1315 (Apr. 2007) ("In order to deal with the increase in alleged violations of the political campaign ban during the 2004 elections, the IRS instituted a compliance initiative. As part of the compliance initiative, the IRS examined 110 501(c)(3) organizations that were alleged have violated the campaign ban.").

15. *See* Branch Ministries v. Rossotti, 211 F.3d 137 (D.C. Cir. 2000) (upholding revocation of church's tax-exempt status for its purchase of two full-page political ads in a newspaper).

16. Lewis Powell, *Confidential Memorandum: Attack on the Free Enterprise System*, Aug. 23, 1971.

17. Robert Kaiser, So Damn Much Money: The Triumph of Lobbying and the Corrosion of American Government 119–120 (2009) (Noting that before Justice Powell was a member of the Supreme Court, he wrote an influential memorandum for the U.S. Chamber of Commerce in 1971).

18. Powell, Confidential Memorandum: Attack on the Free Enterprise System *supra* note 16.

nificance has been overblown,[19] Robert Monks countered that, "the Powell memo really must be viewed as one of the most successful strategic plans in American history."[20] Norman Ornstein concurred, saying about the memo, "Powell laid the groundwork for the current version of corporate personhood."[21] And Trevor Potter explained, "[w]hat Lewis Powell outlined has become the battle plan for American corporations and American industry in terms of creating a bigger voice in Washington."[22]

A few months after authoring the Powell Memo, President Richard Nixon ran out of southerners to nominate for an open seat on the Supreme Court leaving Mr. Powell in line for the nod. When he was appointed to the Supreme Court, Mr. Powell was a multimillionaire who had served on the board of 11 corporations, including Philip Morris (now Altria). The now infamous Powell Memo did not come up during Powell's Senate confirmation hearing. Instead, the primary topic of conversation was how Powell would sell off his vast stock and bond portfolio before putting on judicial robes.[23] In hindsight, Justice Powell appears to have used *Bellotti* as an opportunity to enshrine his view of the corporation's proper role in the democratic process into constitutional law.

Bellotti was far from a unanimous decision with the Supreme Court split 5–4. Justice Byron White pointed out in his dissent, "[t]he state need not permit its own creation [e.g., corporations] to consume it."[24] Among the dissenters was a young Justice Rehnquist (who would later become Chief Justice of the Supreme Court) who wrote: "[t]his Court decided at an early date, with neither argument nor discussion, that a business corporation is a 'person' entitled to the protection of the Equal Protection Clause of the Fourteenth Amendment [in] *Santa Clara County*[.]"[25] Justice Rehnquist also noted that Congress and 31 states at the time tried to keep corporate money out of politics.[26] Justice Rehnquist's *Bellotti* dissent showed that he did not think business corporations had political speech rights at all: "[a] State grants to a business corporation the

19. Mark Schmitt, *The Legend of the Powell Memo*, AM. PROSPECT (Apr. 27, 2005), http://prospect.org/article/legend-powell-memo.

20. Monks interview *supra* note 10.

21. Interview with Norman Ornstein, Fellow Am. Enterprise Instit. (July 24, 2015).

22. Potter interview *supra* note 1.

23. JOHN NICHOLS & ROBERT W. MCCHESNEY, DOLLAROCRACY HOW THE MONEY AND MEDIA ELECTION COMPLEX IS DESTROYING AMERICA 72–73.

24. First Nat'l Bank of Boston v. Bellotti, 435 U.S. 765, 809 (1978) (White, J., dissenting).

25. *Id.* at 822 (1978) (Rehnquist, J., dissenting) (internal citations omitted).

26. *Id.* at 826 (Rehnquist, J., dissenting).

blessings of potentially perpetual life and limited liability to enhance its efficiency as an economic entity. It might reasonably be concluded that those properties, so beneficial in the economic sphere, pose special dangers in the political sphere."[27] Then Justice Rehnquist concluded that he would have found the Massachusetts law at issue in *Bellotti* constitutional and that the First Amendment is meant to protect natural persons only: "[t]he free flow of information is in no way diminished by the Commonwealth's decision to permit the operation of business corporations with limited rights of political expression. All natural persons, who owe their existence to a higher sovereign than the Commonwealth, remain as free as before to engage in political activity."[28]

The logical result of *Bellotti* is, as Robert Monks joked, "under the Powell doctrine, dogs can have freedom of speech, fire hydrants can have freedom of speech." Becoming more serious, he said, "I do think *Bellotti* was wrongly decided. The notion of corporation as flesh and blood person is simply wrong. A corporation, no matter how you stretch it, or twist it, or put it on its head, a corporation is not a flesh and blood human being."[29]

Between 1978, when *Bellotti* was decided, and 2010, when *Citizens United* was decided, the Supreme Court vacillated on the matter of restricting corporate speech in politics. The statutory backdrop was that corporations were banned from making political contributions to federal candidates under the Tillman Act and banned from making independent expenditures under 1947's Taft-Hartley Act.[30] After 2002, corporations were also banned from making electioneering communications (otherwise known as sham issue ads) as well.[31] The 50 states had a patchwork of different approaches to corporate political spending, some states had corporate expenditure bans, others did not. Plaintiff corporations (and unions who are also covered by these restrictions) challenged them in court over the years.

Pre-*Citizens United*, the Supreme Court had sensibly made a distinction between for-profit corporations and ideological nonprofits. In 1986, in *Massachusetts Citizens for Life,* better known as *MCFL,* the Supreme Court crafted an exception to the federal ban on corporate political spending for ideological non-

---

27. *Id.* at 826–27 (1978) (Rehnquist, J., dissenting).

28. *Id.* at 828 (Rehnquist, J., dissenting).

29. Monks interview *supra* note 10.

30. Pub. L. No. 80–101, 61 Stat. 159 (1947).

31. 2 U.S.C. §441b; *see also* Interview with Frederick A.O. Schwarz, Chief Counsel Brennan Center for Justice at NYU School of Law (July 21, 2015) ("During the *McConnell* litigation, the NRA admitted that there's not a dime's worth of difference between issue ads and electioneering ads.").

profits, so long as the nonprofits were not supported by (and were not effectively acting as straw men for) business corporations. The justification for this distinction between for-profit business corporations and ideological nonprofits was based on differential funding streams.[32] With an ideological nonprofit, say *MCFL* itself, a court could reasonably conclude that all persons who gave money to the anti-abortion group supported its political stances writ large—from supporting pro-life ballot measures to pro-life candidates for elective office. When a donor gave to such an ideological nonprofit, the donor was implicitly consenting to her donation being used in politics.[33] However, this constructive consent does not hold true for either of the primary sources of funds for business corporations: customers and shareholders.[34]

In 1990 in *Austin*, the Supreme Court upheld a Michigan law that banned corporate independent expenditures. In 2003 in *Beaumont,* the Court upheld the Tillman Act's ban on corporate contributions directly to candidates. In 2003, in *McConnell* the Court allowed the Bipartisan Campaign Reform Act's (BCRA's) ban on corporate-funded electioneering communications to stand. But it wouldn't stand for long.

Until *Citizens United*, a century's worth of American election laws prohibited corporate managers from spending a corporation's general treasury funds in federal elections.[35] Pre-existing laws required corporate managers to make political expenditures via separate segregated funds (SSFs), which are also com-

---

32. *MCFL*, 479 U.S. at 258 ("The resources in the treasury of a business corporation, however, are not an indication of popular support for the corporation's political ideas.").

33. *Id.* at 257–58 (1986) ("The resources in the treasury of a business corporation … reflect instead the economically motivated decisions of investors and customers. The availability of these resources may make a corporation a formidable political presence, even though the power of the corporation may be no reflection of the power of its ideas.").

34. Pipefitters Local Union No. 562 v. United States, 407 U.S. 385, 415 n.28 (1972) ("We are of the opinion that Congress intended to insure against officers proceeding in such matters without obtaining the consent of shareholders by forbidding all such [political] expenditures."); United States v. Cong. of Indus. Orgs., 335 U.S. 106, 113 (1948) (explaining Taft-Hartley was motivated by "the feeling that corporate officials had no moral right to use corporate funds for contribution to political parties without the consent of the stockholders …").

35. Until *Citizens United*, the Federal Elections Campaign Act (FECA) prohibited corporations (profit or nonprofit), labor organizations and incorporated membership organizations from making direct contributions or expenditures in connection with federal elections. 2 U.S.C. §441b. The limits have a long vintage. For 69 years, since Taft-Hartley, corporations have been banned from spending corporate treasury money to expressively support or oppose a federal candidate and for 109 years, since the Tillman Act, corporations have been banned from giving contributions directly from corporate treasury funds

monly known as corporate political action committees (PACs), so that share-holders, officers and managers who wanted the corporation to advance a political agenda could designate funds for that particular purpose.[36]

B. *Citizens United*

The historical context that created *Citizens United* originated in the same place as most modern campaign finance laws: with Watergate and its fallout. In response to the underhanded fund raising revealed during Watergate (some of which was legal, but outrageous nonetheless, and some which was patently illegal), Congress adopted the Federal Election Campaign Act of 1974 (FECA). This law did many things, but most importantly, it established hard money limits for contributions to federal candidates, PACs, and political parties; hard money expenditure limits; created the FEC; required disclosure of money in politics; and created the presidential public financial system.

The ink was barely dry on FECA when it was challenged by several plaintiffs in *Buckley v. Valeo*. This case turned out to be a hot mess. *Buckley* is a voluminous *per curiam* decision, which upheld most of FECA, but created a number of loopholes that are still having an impact today. *Buckley* upheld the constitutionality of contribution limits, the creation of the FEC (with a few minor adjustments to the appointment process), disclosure, and the presidential public financing system. The Supreme Court held expenditure limits for individuals were unconstitutional. The Supreme Court's fractured ruling in *Buckley v. Valeo,* when combined with *Bellotti,* set the nation on the path careening toward *Citizens United.*

The *Buckley* court said that in order to regulate a political ad or what is known as an "independent expenditure," it must contain "magic words of express advocacy," which come from *Buckley v. Valeo*'s footnote 52, which listed examples of words that would render an ad subject to regulation under the Federal Election Campaign Act (FECA). The *Buckley* list includes: "vote for," "elect," "support," "cast your ballot for," "Smith for Congress," "vote against," "defeat," and "reject."[37] A basic rule of thumb is if an ad says the word "vote" and shows or names a federal candidate—like "Vote Quimby!" or alternatively

---

to federal candidates. After *Citizens United*, corporations are still banned from direct contributions in federal elections.

36. 11 C.F.R. 100.6; Fed. Election Comm'n, SSFs and Nonconnected PACs (May 2008), http://www.fec.gov/pages/brochures/ssfvnonconnected.shtml.

37. *Buckley*, 424 U.S. at 44, n.52.

"Don't Vote Quimby!"—but was produced independently of a candidate, it is an independent expenditure and can be regulated regardless of the medium used or the day in the election cycle. This means its sponsors can be required to file reports with the Federal Election Commission (FEC), revealing the name of the sponsor and the source of the ad's funding.[38]

Because *Buckley* required disclosure for political ads that contained the "magic words" of express advocacy,[39] this created a loophole that would be exploited for the next 25 years. From 1976 to 2002, hundreds of millions of dollars of corporate and union treasury funds—money that could not legally be used to influence elections at the time—poured into federal campaign ads through the "sham issue ad" loophole.[40] As Trevor Potter noted, "[w]hat we saw in the decade of soft money—the 1990s—was corporate and union money going to the political parties, which a fair reading of the law prohibited.... We also saw spending by corporations and unions in elections through sham issue ads. Corporations and unions at the time were supposed to be banned from funding any public advertising in federal elections."[41] "Sham issue ads" feature a candidate close to an election but avoid *Buckley*'s magic words. To plug this loophole, and other federal loopholes, Congress enacted the Bipartisan Campaign Reform Act of 2002 (BCRA), which created a new category of ads— called electioneering communications—and subjected them regulation and disclosure.

Under BCRA, "electioneering communications" are defined as "any broadcast, cable, or satellite communication that ... refers to a clearly identified candidate ... within 60 days before a general election ... or within 30 days before

---

38. There are many loopholes in the FEC's reporting regime. For example, most nonprofit spenders can evade federal disclosure of underlying donors, if the nonprofit lacks earmarked contributions. *See* Ciara Torres-Spelliscy, *Hiding Behind the Tax Code*, 16 Nexus Chapman's J. Law & Pub. Pol'y 59 (2011).

39. Brennan Ctr. for Justice at NYU School of Law, *The Impact of* FEC v. Wisconsin Right to Life, Inc. *on State Regulation of 'Electioneering Communications' in Candidate Elections, Including Campaigns for the Bench* (Feb. 2008), http://www.brennancenter.org/page/-/Democracy/Impact%20of%20WRTL%20II%20on%20State%20Regulation.pdf?nocdn=1.

40. Craig B. Holman & Luke P. McLoughlin, *Buying Time 2000: Television Advertising in the 2000 Federal Elections* 10–11 (Brennan Ctr. 2001), http://brennan.3cdn.net/efd37f417f16ee6341 _4dm6iid9c.pdf; *see also* McConnell v. FEC, 540 U.S. 93, 197 (2003) (finding political advertising sponsors often hid behind misleading names, such as "Citizens for Better Medicare" [the pharmaceutical industry] or "Americans Working for Real Change" [business groups opposed to organized labor]); Ornstein interview *supra* note 21 ("Aggressive campaign lawyers made the argument that any ad that didn't have magic words could not be regulated.").

41. Potter interview *supra* note 1.

a primary … [and that] can be received by 50,000 or more persons [in the candidate's constituency]."[42] If Bob is a candidate for federal office, these ads need not contain express advocacy words like "Vote for Bob." In laymen's terms, an electioneering communication is typically an ad that trashes the candidate on election eve. In other words, these are the "Bob is the Devil and every policy Bob stands for is wrong" TV and radio ads that run in the 60 days before a general election or 30 days before a primary. Once an ad is deemed a federal electioneering communication, it is subject to federal disclosure requirements. The Supreme Court upheld disclosure of electioneering communications in *McConnell v. FEC* by a vote of eight to one. BCRA also barred corporations and unions from paying for electioneering communications. This ban was also upheld by *McConnell*. But the Court would change its mind seven years later.

Citizens United started as an as-applied constitutional challenge to the corporate electioneering communication regulations in BCRA that *McConnell* in 2003 upheld against a facial challenge. *Citizens United*, the case, started when Citizens United, a nonprofit organization, wanted to broadcast a documentary critical of then-Senator Hillary Clinton called "Hillary the Movie" 30 days before certain Democratic primaries when she was a front-runner for the Democratic nomination for president in 2008. The legal problem was that Citizens United (the nonprofit group) was partially funded by for-profit businesses. Thus, it did not fall squarely under the *MCFL*'s exemption on the ban on corporate money in federal elections for purely nonprofit ideological groups. Consequently, it appeared to regulators at the Federal Election Commission (FEC) that "Hillary the Movie" could not be broadcast without violating the federal ban on corporate electioneering communications. Furthermore, if the film was a covered federal electioneering communication, then the donors to Citizens United would have to be reported to the FEC as funders of a political ad in a federal election. Citizens United took the position that the government could not compel it to name its donors.

When *Citizens United v. FEC* was first heard at the Supreme Court on March 24, 2009, the question was whether Citizens United had to disclose its donors. But oral argument in the case went off the rails for the Acting Solicitor General Malcolm Stewart, arguing the case on behalf of the government, when he had a testy exchange with Justices Alito, Kennedy, and Roberts about whether the government would be able to censor a book under the then-operative corporate ban on electioneering communications. Here's a little taste of how badly the oral argument went:

---

42. 2 U.S.C. §434(f)(3)(A)–(C).

Chief Justice Roberts: If it's a 500-page book, and at the end it says, and so vote for X, the government could ban that? ...

Mr. Stewart:—Yes, our position would be that the corporation could be required to use PAC funds rather than general treasury funds.

Chief Justice Roberts: And if they didn't, you could ban it?

Mr. Stewart: If they didn't, we could prohibit the publication of the book using the corporate treasury funds.[43]

Never mind that the statute in question did not apply to books at all. Based in part of this exchange, which raised the specter of the government banning political books, at least in the hypothetical, the Supreme Court ordered re-argument in *Citizens United* on the issue of whether the Court should overrule *Austin v. Michigan Chamber of Commerce* and *McConnell v. FEC*—two cases that had previously upheld various bans on corporate expenditures in candidate elections. At the re-argument, Solicitor General Elena Kagan had to clarify that the U.S. government was no longer taking the position that it could ban books.[44] But the damage was already done.

In January 2010, after two oral arguments and dozens of briefs, the Supreme Court decided the case. The Supreme Court took *Buckley*'s holding (that independent spending could not corrupt) and combined it with *Bellotti*'s holding (that discriminating against corporate speakers is not allowed) to create the bastard child of *Citizens United*, which bars the government from limiting corporate independent expenditures. But this case gets villainized and exaggerated, so it is important to understand exactly what *Citizens United* did and, just as important, what it did not do.

Citizens United did—

- Hold that corporations have the same First Amendment rights to make independent expenditures as natural people.
- Hold that restrictions that prohibited corporations and unions from spending their general treasury funds on independent expenditures violated the First Amendment.
- Overrule *Austin* and parts of *McConnell*.

---

43. Citizens United v. Federal Election Commission, The Oyez Project at IIT Chicago-Kent College of Law, http://www.oyez.org/cases/2000-2009/2008/2008_08_205 (Oral Argument).

44. Citizens United v. Federal Election Commission, Re-argument Transcript (Sept. 9, 2009), http://www.supremecourt.gov/oral_arguments/argument_transcripts/08-205%5BReargued%5D.pdf.

- Uphold disclosure requirements for political advertisements that mentioned a candidate and were made within 60 days of an election even if they did not expressly advocate for the defeat or election of a candidate.

Citizens United did not—

- Rule on the constitutionality of contribution limits.
- Rule on the constitutionality of pay-to-play laws.
- Rule on the constitutionality of soft-money regulations.
- Rule on the constitutionality of the public financing of elections.

The key change was that *Citizens United* allowed corporations to fund independent expenditures and electioneering communications, or what most people would simply call "political ads."

The issue of expanding corporate citizenship is squarely posed by the text of *Citizens United*. As Professor Tamara Piety noted with dismay, "[t]he opinion in *Citizens United* is replete with rhetoric identifying corporations as 'citizens,' as if they were real persons."[45] For instance in *Citizens United v. FEC*, the Court seems to equate the plaintiff, a nonprofit corporation called "Citizens United" with a group of united citizens, instead of a legal form with tax advantages. The Supreme Court wrote,

> If the First Amendment has any force, it prohibits Congress from fining or jailing citizens, or associations of citizens, for simply engaging in political speech. If the antidistortion rationale were to be accepted, however, it would permit Government to ban political speech simply because the speaker is an association that has taken on the corporate form.[46]

The *Citizens United* opinion reiterates this idea—a false equivalence of human citizens and corporations—in its discussion of the necessity of overruling *Austin*: "*Austin* interferes with the 'open marketplace' of ideas protected by the First Amendment. It permits the Government to ban the political speech of millions of associations of citizens."[47] And the court repeated this approach a third time when comparing the ability of wealthy individuals to spend in election with corporations. As the Court held, "wealthy individuals and unincorporated associations can spend unlimited amounts on independent ex-

45. Tamara R. Piety, Citizens United *and the Threat to the Regulatory State*, 109 MICH. L. REV. FIRST IMPRESSIONS 16 (2010).
46. Citizens United v. Federal Election Comm'n, 558 U.S. 310, 349 (2010).
47. *Id.* at 354 (internal citations omitted).

penditures. Yet certain disfavored associations of citizens—those that have taken on the corporate form—are penalized for engaging in the same political speech."[48]

Justice John Paul Stevens wrote a passionate dissent in *Citizens United*, which included such zingers as "[w]hile American democracy is imperfect, few outside the majority of this Court would have thought its flaws included a dearth of corporate money in politics."[49] And in contrast to the majority opinion, which seems to equate corporations and human citizens, the Stevens dissent addresses human citizens as being distinctly threatened by corporations' incursions into politics:

> In addition to this immediate drowning out of noncorporate voices, there may be deleterious effects that follow soon thereafter. Corporate "domination" of electioneering, [ ] can generate the impression that corporations dominate our democracy. When citizens turn on their televisions and radios before an election and hear only corporate electioneering, they may lose faith in their capacity, as citizens, to influence public policy. A Government captured by corporate interests, they may come to believe, will be neither responsive to their needs nor willing to give their views a fair hearing. The predictable result is cynicism and disenchantment ... On a variety of levels, unregulated corporate electioneering might diminish the ability of citizens to "hold officials accountable to the people," and disserve the goal of a public debate that is "uninhibited, robust, and wide-open[.]"[50]

Justice Stevens hasn't changed his mind since retiring from the bench. In his book, SIX AMENDMENTS, Justice Stevens stated flatly, "[t]he decision in *Citizens United* took a giant step in the wrong direction."[51] Since the Supreme Court decided *Citizens United*, a small cottage industry has sprung up to explain what is wrong with the decision from its departing from precedent,[52] to its being

---

48. *Id.* at 356.

49. Citizens United, 558 U.S. at 479 (Stevens, J., concurring in part and dissenting in part).

50. *Id.* at 470–71 (Stevens, J., concurring in part and dissenting in part).

51. JOHN PAUL STEVENS, SIX AMENDMENTS HOW AND WHY WE SHOULD CHANGE THE CONSTITUTION 78 (2014).

52. Trevor Potter & Bryson B. Morgan, *Campaign Finance: Remedies Beyond the Court*, 27 DEMOCRACY (2013), http://www.democracyjournal.org/27/campaign-finance-remedies-beyond-the-court.php?page=all. ("It is difficult to overstate the impact of the Supreme Court's *Citizens United* decision ... [which] overturned or ignored the Court's own precedents and federal, state, and local statutes that had been in place for more than 60 years."); *see also* Potter interview *supra* note 1 ("Justice Kennedy's statement—that the public will

too broadly written,[53] to its deciding a question not asked by the parties in the case,[54] to its misunderstanding corporations,[55] to its misunderstanding of economics.[56] And as author Elliot Zaret wrote, "[t]o its opponents, [*Citizens United*] was an act of judicial activism, increasing the already enormous amount of influence in the political system of wealthy corporations and extending rights meant for real people to entities that only exist for purposes like liability and contracts. To them, it represents what they see as a corporate takeover of America."[57]

Harvard Professor Laurence Tribe argues that *Citizens United* is blamed by too many for too much.[58] *Citizens United* isn't all bad news for everyone. As

---

not lose confidence in democracy just because they see influence is being bought and sold — is without citation or source, and I believe is incorrect as a matter of fact.").

53. Jeffrey Rosen, *Originalism, Precedent, and Judicial Restraint*, 34 HARV. J. L. & PUB-LIC POL'Y 129, 133 (2013) ("What one cannot be is a restrained originalist or someone who is devoted to precedent or tradition, and still defend the sweeping reasoning of *Citizens United*."); *see also* Interview with Retired Montana Supreme Court Justice James Nelson (Aug. 4, 2015) ("The Supreme Court almost interpreted the First Amendment as being absolute.... No constitutional right is absolute. They could have balanced it against the right to vote, which is a fundamental right. They could have balanced it against the obligation that states have to guarantee free and fair and open elections. They didn't do that.").

54. Ronald Dworkin, *The Decision That Threatens Democracy*, NEW YORK REVIEW OF BOOKS (May 13, 2010), http://www.nybooks.com/articles/archives/2010/may/13/decision-threatens-democracy/ ("The five conservative justices, on their own initiative, at the request of no party to the suit, declared that corporations and unions have a constitutional right to spend as much as they wish on television election commercials specifically supporting or targeting particular candidates.").

55. Lucian A. Bebchuk & Robert J. Jackson, Jr., *Corporate Political Speech: Who Decides?*, 124 HARV. L. REV. 83, 89–90 (2010); Potter interview *supra* note 1 ("The current five-person majority sees corporations differently than the Court has traditionally. They seem to think of corporations as the alter-egos of individuals who are acting collectively."); Joseph F. Morrissey, *A Contractarian Critique of* Citizens United, 15 U. PA. J. CONST. L. 765 (2013).

56. TIMOTHY K. KUHNER, CAPITALISM V. DEMOCRACY MONEY IN POLITICS AND THE FREE MARKET CONSTITUTION 31 ("It would be ironic if the ideology that [Alan] Greenspan recently repudiated — a conceptual framework that assumes a perfect market and resists government efforts to ensure fair play — were discredited within economics but thriving within constitutional law.").

57. Elliot Zaret, *Commercial Speech and the Evolution of the First Amendment*, WASH. LAWYER 25 (Sept. 2015), https://www.dcbar.org/bar-resources/publications/washington-lawyer/articles/september-2015-commercial-speech.cfm. *See also* Interview with Fordham Law Professor Zephyr Teachout (Aug. 10, 2015) ("*Citizens United* was a withering blow.").

58. LAURENCE TRIBE & JOSHUA MATZ, UNCERTAIN JUSTICE THE ROBERTS COURT AND THE CONSTITUTION 91 (2014) ("*Citizens United* became a focal point for debate about the

one election law lawyer explained, "[t]he ability of nonprofits to speak their minds expanded."[59] Another beneficiary of *Citizens United* has been those who have ad space to sell. Craig Aaron reported that "*Citizens United* is propping up the broadcasters." And moreover, "[t]he election season is becoming more valuable than the Olympics for local television stations in swing states. In the last election cycle, broadcasters were actually cutting back on their news to make room for more political ads."[60]

The full impact of *Citizens United* is yet unknown. Harvard Professor Lawrence Lessig noted that independent spending spiked in 2010, up 460%.[61] And studies have shown an increase of negative ads since *Citizens United*.[62] For example, THE NEW SOFT MONEY found: "[i]n 2012 there was $714 million in outside spending in congressional races and 74.22 percent was spent on TV ads. Of that spending, 77 percent was for negative ads spent against a candidate—e.g. trying to tear a candidate down instead of trying to tout the good qualities of a candidate."[63] This is a problem because negative ads can "reduce[] public trust and satisfaction with government"[64] and could have a deleterious impact on the electorate.[65] Media expert Craig Aaron explained, "[t]hey don't run attack ads so that you'll like the other guy a little less. They run attack ads to discourage you from voting at all. Attack ads work and they depress turnout and keep people from participating in the political process."[66]

---

evaporation of faith in responsive government.... *Citizens United* simply cannot bear all that weight.").

59. Interview with Ezra Reese, Partner, Perkins Coie (July 27, 2015).

60. Interview with Craig Aaron, President Free Press (July 27, 2015).

61. LAWRENCE LESSIG, REPUBLIC LOST HOW MONEY CORRUPTS CONGRESS—AND PLAN TO STOP IT 239 (2011).

62. NICHOLS & MCCHESNEY, *supra* note 23, at 119 (referencing studies by Kantar Media's Campaign Media Analysis Group and the Wesleyan Media Project of the 2012 election).

63. Daniel P. Tokaji & Renata E. B. Strause, *The New Soft Money: Outside Spending in Congressional Elections*, ELECTION LAW @ MORITZ AT THE OHIO ST. U. MORITZ COL. OF L., http://moritzlaw.osu.edu/thenewsoftmoney/wp-content/uploads/sites/57/2014/06/the-new-soft-money-WEB.pdf.

64. NICHOLS & MCCHESNEY, *supra* note 23, at 128 (quoting studies from Rutgers and George Washington University).

65. *2012 Shatters 2004 and 2008 Records for Total Ads Aired*, WESLEYAN MEDIA PROJECT (Oct. 24, 2012), http://mediaproject.wesleyan.edu/releases/2012-shatters-2004-and-2008-records-for-total-ads-aired/ ("One of the dominant features of the 2012 election has been the increase in negativity.") (showing data indicating that 88.7% of ads from Democratic groups were negative and 95.2% of ads from Republican groups were negative).

66. Aaron interview *supra* note 60.

Unfortunately for corporate managers, political spending by corporations may be coerced by those in elected office, or their surrogates.[67] Companies frequently "complain they are aggressively solicited by politicians and their intermediaries who take part in the relentless race for campaign cash."[68] Norman Ornstein reported, "[t]he CEOs I know are not thrilled by this decision. It's not like they are sitting around with all this spare cash and thinking 'boy would we like to put it into politics.'"[69] The "shake down" of corporate spenders by politicians in power can be quite costly.[70] As Nicole Gordon explained, the pressure to provide campaign funding is a strong force:

> The corporations have pressure from lawmakers whom they need things from. They need to keep them happy. That is why corporations often give to both sides of the aisle. It is not necessarily about political conviction, but about making sure they have "access" to lawmakers. Indeed, there are corporate executives who would much prefer not to make any campaign spending at all, but they are pressured to do it as long as the law permits it.[71]

And it should be clear that not all companies engage in politics. As investor Timothy Smith reminded us: "[w]e find a lot of companies who tell us that *Citizens United* didn't do us any favors."[72] And he continued, "[a] number of companies that we talk to tell us they don't want to do political spending and never did it. Lots of big companies don't. IBM doesn't do political spending

---

67. Norman J. Ornstein, *J. Byron McCormick Society for Law and Public Affairs Lecture*, 54 Ariz. L. Rev. 481, 491 (2012) ("Now money dominates in a way that we have not seen before.").

68. Heidi Welsh & Robin Young, *Corporate Governance of Political Expenditures: 2011 Benchmark Report on S&P 500 Companies*, Sustainable Invest. Instit. 47, 51 (Nov. 2011).

69. Ornstein interview *supra* note 21.

70. Entrepreneurs should be wary of political corruption. Worldwide, political corruption typically costs businesses dearly. Org. For Econ. Co-Operation & Development, *The Rationale For Fighting Corruption* 2 (2014), http://www.oecd.org/cleangovbiz/49693613.pdf ("corruption distorts market mechanisms, like fair competition, and deters domestic and foreign investments, thus stifling growth and future business opportunities for all stakeholders. IMF research has shown that investment in corrupt countries is almost five percent less than in countries that are relatively corruption-free. The World Economic Forum estimates that corruption increases the cost of doing business by up to 10% on average. Siemens, the German engineering giant, had to pay penalties of US $1.6 billion in 2008 to settle charges that it routinely engaged in bribery around the world.").

71. Interview with Nicole Gordon, Former Executive Director, New York City Campaign Finance Board (Aug. 10, 2015).

72. Interview with Timothy Smith, Walden Asset Management (Aug. 7, 2015).

from their corporate treasury and neither does Procter and Gamble, JP Morgan Chase, or Goldman Sachs."[73]

Just a few days after *Citizens United*, President Obama in his first State of the Union address chastised the Justices sitting in the gallery about the opinion.[74] He stated:

> With all due deference to separation of powers, last week the Supreme Court reversed a century of law that I believe will open the floodgates for special interests—including foreign corporations—to spend without limit in our elections. (Applause.) I don't think American elections should be bankrolled by America's most powerful interests, or worse, by foreign entities. (Applause.) They should be decided by the American people.[75]

Sitting in the audience, Justice Alito was caught on camera mouthing "not true." And ever since then, there has been a lingering question about whether foreign corporate money will get into U.S. elections or not post *Citizens United*.

In *Citizens United* itself, the Supreme Court largely ducks the question of corporations that have foreign investors or corporations that are owned and controlled by foreign sovereigns. The Court merely cryptically said, "[w]e need not reach the question whether the Government has a compelling interest in preventing foreign individuals or associations from influencing our Nation's political process. Cf. 2 U.S.C. §441e (contribution and expenditure ban applied to 'foreign national[s]'). Section 441b is not limited to corporations or associations that were created in foreign countries or funded predominantly by foreign shareholders. Section 441b therefore would be overbroad even if we assumed, *arguendo*, that the government has a compelling interest in limiting foreign influence over our political process."[76] The issue of foreign corporate money had been raised in oral argument and in briefs, but the majority of the Court clearly did not care. But as election lawyer Ezra Reese indicated, "[t]he rule against foreign money being spent in our elections is an important one. You can imagine a parade of horribles were foreign governments allowed to influence U.S. elections."[77]

---

73. *Id.*

74. Adam Liptak, *Supreme Court Gets a Rare Rebuke, in Front of a Nation*, N.Y. TIMES, Jan. 28, 2010, http://www.nytimes.com/2010/01/29/us/politics/29scotus.html?_r=0.

75. Remarks by the President in State of the Union Address, Jan. 27, 2010 https://www.whitehouse.gov/the-press-office/remarks-president-state-union-address.

76. Citizens United v. Federal Election Comm'n, 558 U.S. 310, 362 (2010).

77. Reese interview *supra* note 59.

A year after *Citizens United* two foreign nationals (one named Benjamin Bluman) challenged the long-standing ban on foreigners spending in U.S. elections in a case called *Bluman v. FEC*. Their argument was that the logic of *Citizens United*, that the First Amendment does not discriminate based on the identity of the speaker, should apply to them as well. The lower court in *Bluman* ruled against the foreign plaintiffs stating,

> Plaintiffs … acknowledge that they do not have the right to vote in U.S. elections, but they contend that the right to speak about elections is different from the right to participate in elections. But in this case, that is not a clear dichotomy. When an expressive act is directly targeted at influencing the outcome of an election, it is both speech and participation in democratic self-government. Spending money to contribute to a candidate or party or to expressly advocate for or against the election of a political candidate is participating in the process of democratic self-government.[78]

And the *Bluman* court went on to note, "distinguishing citizens from non-citizens in this context is hardly unusual or deserving of scorn; rather, it is part of a common international understanding of the meaning of sovereignty and shared concern about foreign influence over elections."[79] The Supreme Court summarily affirmed this case without an oral argument.[80] *Bluman* held "there was not a constitutional right for foreign individuals to spend in American elections."[81] As Justice Stevens reasons in his book, Six AMENDMENTS, if we do not want the money of a Canadian person (Mr. Bluman) in our elections because he is not a citizen, it may also follow that we do not want corporate money in elections for the same reason.[82]

But despite the *Bluman* ruling, is foreign corporate money actually getting into our elections? As a matter of statutory law, foreigners are not allowed to spend in an American election. That includes federal, state and local elections. A foreigner can't even pay for a race for dog catcher. Here's the law:

> It shall be unlawful for—(1) a foreign national, directly or indirectly, to make—(A) a contribution or donation of money or other thing of

---

78. Bluman v. FEC, 800 F. Supp. 2d 281, 289–90 (D.D.C. 2011).
79. *Id.* at 292.
80. Bluman v. FEC, 132 S. Ct. 1087 (2012).
81. Potter interview *supra* note 1.
82. STEVENS, *supra* note 51, at 59 ("I shall explain why it is unwise to allow persons who are not qualified to vote—whether they be corporations or nonresident individuals—to have a potentially greater power to affect the outcome of elections than eligible voters have.").

value, or to make an express or implied promise to make a contribution or donation, in connection with a Federal, State, or local election; (B) a contribution or donation to a committee of a political party; or (C) an expenditure, independent expenditure, or disbursement for an electioneering communication (within the meaning of section 434(f)(3) of this title); (2) a person to solicit, accept, or receive a contribution or donation described in subparagraph (A) or (B) of paragraph (1) from a foreign national.[83]

Note that nothing in the statute refers to candidates. It merely bars foreign nationals spending in an American "election." But just as the Tillman Act didn't prevent all corporate money from getting into the Nixon campaign, this part of the law has not stopped all foreign money from getting into U.S. elections. A concrete example occurred in an election in Los Angeles. In 2012, there was a Ballot Measure called the "Safer Sex in the Adult Film Industry Act," which would require actors in pornography to wear condoms. The measure passed with 1,617,866 votes in favor (56.96%) vs. 1,222,681 votes against (43.04%). Spending against Ballot Measure B included $327,000 from two companies tied to Manwin Licensing International. Manwin Licensing International is a foreign corporation located in Luxembourg that runs adult webpages around the world. Its CEO is Fabian Thylmann, who is a German national who works in Belgium.[84]

The FEC received a complaint about the foreign spending in the Los Angeles ballot measure back in 2012,[85] but failed to take action as it deadlocked 3–3. The Democratic commissioners voted to open an investigation while the three Republican commissioners voted to not open the investigation. In 2015, current FEC Chair Ann Ravel revived the matter by filing a memorandum urging the FEC to clarify that ballot measures are covered by 52 USC § 30121, the federal law that bans foreign money in the U.S. elections.[86] On October 1, 2015, the commission deadlocked again, which means there is no clarification from the FEC on whether foreign money is barred from funding American ballot

---

83. 52 U.S.C. § 30121 (formerly 2 U.S.C. § 441e(a)).

84. First General Counsel Report, FEC, re: Complaint by Michael Weinstein against MindGeek & Manwin Licensing International (Aug. 15, 2014), http://eqs.fec.gov/eqsdocsMUR/15044372921.pdf.

85. FEC Complaint from Michael Weinstein against Manwin (Oct. 26, 2012), http://www.aidshealth.org/wp-content/uploads/2012/10/Manwin_FEC-Complaint.pdf.

86. Memorandum from FEC Chair Ann Ravel to the FEC re: State and Local Ballot Measures and the Ban on Foreign National Contributions (Sept. 22, 2015), http://www.aidshealth.org/wp-content/uploads/2015/09/FEC-Ravel-agenda-Measure-B-2015-09-22.pdf.

measures or not.[87] This could affect California's expensive ballot initiatives, state constitutional amendments, and every attempt to legalize marijuana through a ballot measure.

Regarding the Los Angeles affair, FEC Chair Ann Ravel explained "[b]ecause it was a ballot measure, the FEC split 3–3 and said our law didn't cover ballot measures because that is not considered an 'election.' This is absolutely wrong legally because the definition of 'election' that Congress adopted with BCRA changed from 'candidate elections' to just plain 'elections.'"[88] She added with frustration, "[w]e know there was foreign money, and then nothing was done about it."[89] This whole episode with the foreign pornographer spending corporate funds in a Los Angeles election brings us back to President Obama's assertion in his State of the Union that foreign corporate money would be spent in U.S. elections. Trevor Potter stated that foreign money in American elections "may be happening now."[90] He explained how:

> the problem is, many international corporations have significant foreign ownership. Many U.S. corporations have significant foreign ownership. It is easy for a foreign corporation to establish a U.S. registered corporate subsidiary. Many boards of directors have non-U.S. members on their boards. Money is transferred freely around the world. Foreign nations have investments in the U.S. Many Chinese state companies have investments here including in U.S. companies. All of that occurs behind a veil because it is not possible for somebody to know from the public record what the sources of funding are for a U.S. corporation. So saying that companies can spend so long as they have a U.S. charter, opens up the possibility that they will give [foreign money] through the dark money groups.[91]

If Los Angeles is a harbinger, foreign corporate money may well be a factor in the 2016 elections, especially in California, where statewide initiatives generate interest from around the globe.

---

87. Kate Buckley, *Commission Divides Sharply on Scope of Foreign National Ban*, Perkins Coie (Oct. 1, 2015), http://www.lawandpoliticsupdate.com/2015/10/commission-divides-sharply-on-scope-of-foreign-national-ban/.

88. Interview with Ann Ravel, Chair, Federal Election Commission (Nov. 3, 2015).

89. *Id.*

90. Potter interview *supra* note 1.

91. Potter interview *supra* note 1; *see also* Ravel interview *supra* note 88 ("I think there is no question that there is foreign corporate money in elections, but we can't see it.").

The Supreme Court has welcomed corporations to spend in ballot measure campaigns and in candidate elections through *Bellotti* and *Citizens United*. In so doing, the Court overturned federal and state laws that were put in place to keep separation of corporations from the state electoral process. This turn of events has opened the risk of corporate foreign money being injected into American elections. This may already be happening through dark money channels. And disturbingly, foreign money was used in a local election in Los Angeles without any subterfuge, and still, the FEC did not act to discipline the spender. This could broadcast precisely the wrong message to other potential foreign corporate political spenders to jump right into the pool of U.S. elections, because the water's fine.

Chapter 6

Thirty Pieces of Silver

Did you ever expect a corporation to have a conscience, when it has no soul to be damned and no body to be kicked?

—Edward Thurlow[1]

Granting business corporations reasonable commercial speech rights is likely not objectionable, so long as they are subject to democratic controls. But like political rights, religious rights for corporations seem like a profound misfit, like giving a fish a bicycle. And yet the Roberts Court has not only expanded corporate commercial speech rights in *Sorrell v. IMS Health* and political speech rights in *Citizens United*, they have also stepped on juridical thin ice by granting corporations statutory religious rights. The Supreme Court has not granted these rights under the First Amendment, yet. But that could be the next move in the ever-expanding universe of corporate rights.

In 2014, the Supreme Court ruled in *Hobby Lobby* that closely held for-profit corporations could raise religious objections to generally applicable rules—in this case the provision under the Patient Protection and Affordable Care Act (ACA) that employers provide health care coverage that included standard FDA approved birth control options for women.[2] The Supreme Court gave corporations a new power—a power previously reserved to natural persons: the power of religious belief and the attendant protections of the Reli-

---

1. ROBERT A.G. MONKS & NELL MINOW, CORPORATE GOVERNANCE 20 (Fifth ed. 2011) (quoting Edward Thurlow, Lord Chancellor of England).

2. Stuart Kirsch, *Imagining Corporate Personhood*, 37 PoLAR: POL. & L. ANTHR. REV. 207, 207–08 (2014) ("[T]he Supreme Court ruled in *Burwell v. Hobby Lobby Stores, Inc.* (573 U.S. [2014]) that corporations have the right to religious freedom. Consequently, they cannot be compelled to pay for federally mandated health insurance that includes coverage for birth control.").

gious Freedom Restoration Act of 1993 (RFRA).[3] *Hobby Lobby* built on *Citizens United*'s foundations. "Taken together, these two decisions [*Citizens United* and *Hobby Lobby*] extend the rights of for-profit corporations to engage in fundamental freedoms traditionally understood to belong only to individuals or groups of people such as churches and political organizations."[4] Or as Montana Supreme Court Justice Nelson argued, *Hobby Lobby* "is another decision by the U.S. Supreme Court that has created new rights for corporations out of whole cloth that corporations don't enjoy."[5] Whether or not you think this is normatively a good idea, the Supreme Court is still handing out rights to corporations piecemeal, including the new religious statutory right recognized in *Hobby Lobby*.[6] In so doing, as Professor Elizabeth Sepper explained, "a new and potentially expansive doctrine of corporate conscience was born."[7]

A. Background to *Hobby Lobby*

Since *Hobby Lobby* dealt with contraceptives, abortion, and healthcare, here's a little necessary legal background to place *Hobby Lobby* in context. In *Griswold v. Connecticut*, the Supreme Court recognized that married couples have a right to use contraception and that Connecticut's law barring use of contraception violated the constitutional right of marital privacy.[8] In *Eisenstadt v. Baird*, the Supreme Court extended the right to access contraception

---

3. Margaret M. Blair & Elizabeth Pollman, *The Derivative Nature of Corporate Constitutional Rights*, 56 Wm. & Mary L. Rev. 1673, 1729 (2015), http://scholarship.law.wm.edu/wmlr/vol56/iss5/2 (internal citations omitted) ("In a controversial ruling, the Court accorded RFRA free exercise rights to for-profit corporations for the first time.").

4. David Rosenberg, *Goodwill and the Excesses of Corporate Political Spending*, 11 Hastings Bus. L.J. 29, 29 (Winter 2015).

5. Interview with Retired Montana Supreme Court Justice James Nelson (Aug. 4, 2015).

6. Kirsch, *supra* note 2, at 207–08 ("The inconsistency in these rulings—that corporations have the right to free speech and religion, like natural persons, but lack a corresponding right to privacy—suggests that these decisions are being made on a case-by-case basis rather than uniformly applying an established definition of corporate personhood. The metaphor of corporate personhood allows the courts to treat corporations as legal 'persons in some respects and as nonpersons for other purposes' (Berger 2004:181).").

7. Elizabeth Sepper, *Gendering Corporate Conscience*, 38 Harv. J. L. & Gender 193, 193–94 (2015) (footnotes omitted) (citing Burwell v. Hobby Lobby Stores, Inc., 134 S. Ct. 2759, 2759 (2014)).

8. Griswold v. Connecticut, 381 U.S. 479 (1965).

to single people.[9] In 1973 in *Roe v. Wade,* the Supreme Court recognized a constitutional right to abortion.[10]

In 2010, the ACA was passed by Congress. This law expanded access to health care for millions of Americans, mandated that nearly everyone buy health insurance and attempted to expand Medicaid to cover those with lower incomes, so that they too could afford health care coverage. The law also required employers of a certain size to provide basic health care coverage to their employees, including a package of FDA-approved contraceptives for women. If employers did not provide this minimum coverage for employees, the employers faced monetary fines. At the time of the case, the fine was $2,000 per uncovered employee per year.

The Supreme Court upheld the ACA in the face of statutory and constitutional challenges before the law was implemented in 2012 in *National Federation of Independent Business (NFIB) v. Sebelius.*[11] The Court found that the ACA's Medicaid expansion was unconstitutional. Thus, after 2012, states had the choice of whether to expand Medicaid or not.[12] But the Supreme Court upheld the remainder of the challenged portions of ACA.

The other legal background that is necessary to understand *Hobby Lobby* is a law called the Religious Freedom Restoration Act of 1993 (RFRA). The goal of this law is to protect religious freedoms from governmental interference. It was passed in reaction to a case called *Smith,* in which the Supreme Court ruled that the religious use of peyote by two Native Americans was not protected by the First Amendment.

B. *Hobby Lobby* the Case

In *Hobby Lobby,* closely held corporations, with religious families at the helm, objected to a variety of birth control methods that must be covered by employers under the ACA. The definition of a closely held corporation varies, but generally a closely held corporation is not publicly traded, but rather it is owned by a small group of investors. In some cases, all the investors in a closely held corporation are members of the same family. In *Hobby Lobby,* three com-

9. Eisenstadt v. Baird, 405 U.S. 438 (1972).
10. Roe v. Wade, 410 U.S. 113 (1973).
11. National Federation of Independent Business v. Sebelius, 132 S. Ct. 2566 (2012).
12. Kaiser Family Foundation, *Current Status of State Medicaid Expansion Decisions* (2015), http://kff.org/health-reform/slide/current-status-of-the-medicaid-expansion-decision/ (last visited Sept. 1, 2015).

panies raised religious objections to certain types of birth control, essentially confusing them with abortion.

While the corporations who were plaintiffs in *Hobby Lobby* were owned by a small number of individuals, the three firms employed thousands of people:

- Mardel had close to 400 employees.
- Conestoga Wood Specialties had 950 employees.
- Hobby Lobby had more than 13,000 employees.

The rights of these employees were largely ignored by the Supreme Court. As Professor Sepper argued, "*Hobby Lobby* breaks with past doctrine and represents a potentially wide-ranging expansion of religious liberty doctrine. Corporate conscience claims have succeeded—rapidly and mightily—where similar claims had previously failed. As the courts sided with for-profit objectors to the contraceptive mandate, ... the courts treated women as irrelevant to their legal analysis. Women's decisions and earning of benefits were erased from consideration. Any burdens on their rights were immaterial."[13] Instead, the Court focused on the rights of the corporations to raise religious objections to the ACA using RFRA.

The federal government argued neither these companies, nor their owners, had legally cognizable claims under RFRA. According to the government, the companies could not sue because they sought to make a profit for their owners, and the owners could not be heard because the regulations, at least as a formal matter, applied only to the companies and not to the owners as individuals. The Supreme Court rejected the government's argument in *Hobby Lobby*, stating "HHS would put these merchants to a difficult choice: either give up the right to seek judicial protection of their religious liberty or forgo the benefits, available to their competitors, of operating as corporations."[14] The Supreme Court held that corporations can make religious claims under RFRA.

> According to [the federal government]..., these corporations are not protected by RFRA because they cannot exercise religion....
>
> The corporate form alone cannot provide the explanation because, as we have pointed out, HHS concedes that nonprofit corporations can be protected by RFRA.... Furthering their religious freedom also "furthers individual religious freedom." In these cases, for example, allowing Hobby Lobby, Conestoga, and Mardel to assert RFRA claims

---

13. Sepper, *supra* note 7, at 194–95.
14. Burwell v. Hobby Lobby Stores, Inc., 134 S. Ct. 2751, 2767 (2014).

protects the religious liberty of [their owners] the Greens and the Hahns.[15]

RFRA, the law that the Supreme Court applied in *Hobby Lobby*, does not explicitly cover corporations. Rather, the language of the statute said that "[g]overnment shall not substantially burden a *person's* exercise of religion even if the burden results from a rule of general applicability[.]"[16] The law referred only to a "person." In order to make RFRA cover corporations, the majority in *Hobby Lobby* used a separate statute called the Dictionary Act, which includes corporations in the definition of "person."[17]

The Supreme Court found incorporating did not diminish the religious rights of the plaintiffs. Justice Alito held, "[i]n holding that the HHS mandate is unlawful, we reject HHS's argument that the owners of the companies forfeited all RFRA protection when they decided to organize their businesses as corporations rather than sole proprietorships or general partnerships."[18] This was a new approach for the Supreme Court to recognize such religious rights of for-profit corporations.

No one in the case disputed that the families involved had deeply held religious views about contraceptives. What struck many commentators as odd was that the Supreme Court gave the right to object not to the families, but rather to their companies. As the majority wrote,

> corporate law does not require for-profit corporations to pursue profit at the expense of everything else.... For-profit corporations, ... support a wide variety of charitable causes, and it is not at all uncommon for such corporations to further humanitarian and other altruistic objectives.... A for-profit corporation that operates facilities in other countries may exceed the requirements of local law regarding working conditions and benefits. If for-profit corporations may pursue such worthy objectives, there is no apparent reason why they may not further religious objectives as well.[19]

---

15. *Id.* at 2769.

16. 42 U.S. Code § 2000bb–1(a) (emphasis added).

17. Ira C. Lupu, Hobby Lobby *and the Dubious Enterprise of Religious Exemptions*, 38 Harv. J. L. & Gender 35, 78 (2015) (citing Federal Dictionary Act, 1 U.S.C. § 1 (2012); Citizens United v. FEC, 558 U.S. 310 (2010); Hobby Lobby Stores, Inc., v. Sebelius, 723 F.3d 1114, 1133 (10th Cir. 2013) (en banc), *rev'd sub nom.* Burwell v. Hobby Lobby Stores, Inc., 134 S. Ct. 2751 (2014)).

18. *Burwell*, 134 S. Ct. at 2759.

19. *Id.* at 2771.

Indeed, the Supreme Court pointed to the existence of benefit corporations (which will be discussed in Chapter 13)[20] as evidence of the appropriateness of their decision, "[r]ecognizing the inherent compatibility between establishing a for-profit corporation and pursuing nonprofit goals, States have increasingly ... recognized the 'benefit corporation,' a dual-purpose entity that seeks to achieve both a benefit for the public and a profit for its owners."[21] The Supreme Court also noted that corporations like the plaintiffs in the case could be run for any lawful purpose. "[T]he objectives that may properly be pursued by the companies in these cases are governed by the laws of the States in which they were incorporated—Pennsylvania and Oklahoma—and the laws of those States permit for-profit corporations to pursue 'any lawful purpose' or 'act,' including the pursuit of profit in conformity with the owners' religious principles."[22] To many this simply begs the question, as at the time Hobby Lobby brought the case, they were not in compliance with federal law, which meant their actions were not consistent with "any lawful purpose."

Once the Court decided that RFRA applied to closely held corporations, the Court had to analyze whether the ACA's contraceptive provisions burdened the corporations' religious liberty.

> We must decide whether the challenged HHS regulations substantially burden the exercise of religion, and we hold that they do. The owners of the businesses have religious objections to abortion, and according to their religious beliefs the four contraceptive methods at issue are abortifacients. If the owners comply with the HHS mandate, they believe they will be facilitating abortions, and if they do not comply, they will pay a very heavy price—as much as $1.3 million per day, or about $475 million per year, in the case of one of the companies. If these consequences do not amount to a substantial burden, it is hard to see what would.[23]

---

20. At least one CEO of a certified B Corp, Ben Cohen of Ben & Jerry's thinks this absurd leap by the Court. Interview with Ben Cohen, CEO Ben & Jerry's (Nov. 4, 2015) ("The Supreme Court has come up with a lot of misguided decisions and [Hobby Lobby] is just another one. It seems like a big jump for me to say because a benefit corporation chooses to incorporate to include the benefit of the community that that [leads to Hobby Lobby's conclusions.] I don't know how you jump from the existence of a benefit corporation to say that a corporation can have a religion.").

21. Burwell, 134 S. Ct. at 2771.

22. Id.

23. Id. at 2775–76.

Another peculiar part of the case is that the FDA did not classify any of the contraceptives at issue as abortifacients.[24] The families and their corporations believed that they are abortifacients, but there was no scientific support for that assertion. Under most circumstances, it would be the view of the scientists that would prevail. But not so at the Supreme Court. As Justice Alito wrote,

> This argument ... addresses a very different question that the federal courts have no business addressing (whether the religious belief asserted in a RFRA case is reasonable). The Hahns and Greens believe that providing the coverage demanded by the HHS regulations is connected to the destruction of an embryo in a way that is sufficient to make it immoral for them to provide the coverage.... HHS and the principal dissent in effect tell the plaintiffs that their beliefs are flawed. For good reason, we have repeatedly refused to take such a step.[25]

The Supreme Court continued, "it is not for us to say that their religious beliefs are mistaken or insubstantial. Instead, our 'narrow function ... in this context is to determine' whether the line drawn reflects 'an honest conviction,' and there is no dispute that it does."[26] So, not only do corporations get to have religious beliefs, according to *Hobby Lobby*, they get to have unreasonable religious beliefs to boot, and they can use those beliefs to be excused from generally applicable laws like the ACA.[27]

The potential negative fallout from *Hobby Lobby* was not lost on the majority. Taken to its logical conclusion, corporations could raise religious objections to paying taxes or other generic laws. The Court attempted to limit the impact of the case with the following language: "[w]e do not hold ... that for-profit corporations and other commercial enterprises can 'opt out of any law (saving only tax laws) they judge incompatible with their sincerely held re-

---

24. Julie Rovner, *Morning-After Pills Don't Cause Abortion, Studies Say*, NPR (Feb. 22, 2013), http://www.npr.org/sections/health-shots/2013/02/22/172595689/morning-after-pills-dont-cause-abortion-studies-say. ("Both are classified by the Food and Drug Administration as contraceptives.")

25. *Id.* at 2778.

26. *Id.* at 2779.

27. Kara Loewentheil, *The Satanic Temple, Scott Walker, and Contraception: A Partial Account of* Hobby Lobby's *Implications for State Law*, 9 HARV. L. & POL'Y REV. 89, 123 (2015) ("And RFRA, as it is currently usually interpreted, does not require that a religious objector be able to demonstrate that his or her religious belief is canonical or mainstream, or even that the line he or she is drawing is rational or objectively reasonable."); W. David Koeninger, *Removing Access to Health Care from Employer and State Control: The ACA as Anti-Subordination Legislation*, 44 U. BALT. L. REV. 201, 220 (2015).

ligious beliefs.'"[28] On the matter of taxes, which the Court had previously addressed in a case called *Lee*, the Court added, "*Lee* was a free-exercise, not a RFRA, case, but if the issue in *Lee* were analyzed under the RFRA framework, the fundamental point would be that there simply is no less restrictive alternative to the categorical requirement to pay taxes."[29]

Another potential consequence of *Hobby Lobby* would be to grant religious exemptions to publicly traded corporations.[30] This possibility is seemingly foreclosed by the language of the case, which limits the holding to closely held businesses: "[t]hese cases [ ] do not involve publicly traded corporations ... [T]he idea that unrelated shareholders—including institutional investors with their own set of stakeholders—would agree to run a corporation under the same religious beliefs seems improbable.... The companies in the cases before us are closely held corporations ..."[31] The majority in *Hobby Lobby* did not seem bothered by the prospect of there being deep religious disagreements among the owners of a closely held corporation. The basic response was that corporate law rules were up to the task of sorting this out. "The owners of closely held corporations ... might well have a dispute relating to religion ... State corporate law provides a ready means for resolving any conflicts by, for example, dictating how a corporation can establish its governing structure.... Courts will turn to that structure and the underlying state law in resolving disputes."[32]

The Supreme Court further attempted to limit the reach of *Hobby Lobby* by including language that seemingly constrained the case to the contraceptive mandate: "our decision in these cases is concerned solely with the contraceptive mandate. Our decision should not be understood to hold that an insurance-coverage mandate must necessarily fall if it conflicts with an employer's

---

28. *Burwell*, 134 S. Ct. at 2760.

29. *Id.* at 2784.

30. Lupu, *supra* note 17, at 101 n.224 ("The fact that Hobby Lobby and Conestoga Wood Products were closely held, family-run businesses made the argument easier, but there is nothing in the logic of the *Hobby Lobby* majority that restricts religious exercise to such companies. Publicly traded, widely held companies might develop a religious identity, but the impracticality of obtaining internal agreement on the Board of Directors, or among shareholders, as to what that identity is, makes such assertions of corporate religious personhood extremely unlikely.").

31. *Burwell*, 134 S. Ct. at 2774; *see also* Corey A. Ciocchetti, *Religious Freedom and Closely Held Corporations: The* Hobby Lobby *Case and Its Ethical Implications*, 93 Or. L. Rev. 259, 353 (2014) ("The majority limited its *Hobby Lobby* ruling to closely held corporations but did not specifically rule that larger corporations could never qualify for protection. The majority only stated that such challenges were unlikely.").

32. *Burwell*, 134 S. Ct. at 2775.

religious beliefs. Other coverage requirements, such as immunizations, may be supported by different interests[.]"[33]

The Court also tried to prevent *Hobby Lobby* from being used to facilitate all manner of discrimination based on religion. "The principal dissent raises the possibility that discrimination in hiring, for example on the basis of race, might be cloaked as religious practice to escape legal sanction. Our decision today provides no such shield. The Government has a compelling interest in providing an equal opportunity to participate in the workforce without regard to race, and prohibitions on racial discrimination are precisely tailored to achieve that critical goal."[34]

Hobby Lobby was a break from precedent for the Court, which had previously only granted such religious rights to either individuals or nonprofit houses of worship. Judicial expansion of corporate personhood continues with *Hobby Lobby* and now they suddenly have religious views too. As Professor Zephyr Teachout explained, "[t]he Court has provided corporations this collection of rights and responsibilities. It's getting weird with *Citizens United* and *Hobby Lobby* where the anthropomorphization is being taken so seriously that they are getting more rights in other areas like religion."[35] This case raises a host of new questions, including how many closely held companies will assert these new religious rights to escape legal responsibilities and whether the Supreme Court will expand these religious rights to publicly traded firms in the future.

Corporate governance guru Nell Minow finds *Hobby Lobby*'s approach to corporate religious liberty objectionable. She stated *Hobby Lobby* "has turned the First Amendment on its head. What freedom of religion means is that you have the right to practice your religion in your home, in your place of worship, and in your heart. You do not have the right to impose that on other people."[36] She continued, "[t]he courts made a mistake in *Hobby Lobby* of taking at face value any assertion of religious beliefs by the company. In the past they

---

33. *Id.* at 2783 (2014).

34. *Id.* at 2783; Neil S. Siegel & Reva B. Siegel, *Compelling Interests and Contraception*, 47 Conn. L. Rev. 1025, 1026 (2015) ("In *Burwell v. Hobby Lobby Stores*, five Justices concluded that the government has compelling interests in ensuring women (and men) access to contraception.... First, they encompass core concerns of the community in promoting public health and facilitating women's integration in the workplace. Second, they encompass crucial concerns of the employees who are the intended beneficiaries of federal law's contraceptive coverage requirement—concerns that sound in bodily integrity, personal autonomy, and equal citizenship." (footnote omitted)).

35. Interview with Fordham Law Professor Zephyr Teachout (Aug. 10, 2015).

36. Interview with Nell Minow, Vice Chair, ValueEdge Advisors (Aug. 19, 2015).

paid for birth control and their pension fund invested in companies that made
and sell birth control, which puts in question the legitimacy of their assertion
of belief." And she added, "[i]n a commercial context, no one should be able
to impose their religious beliefs on someone else."[37]

Giving corporations religious rights suffers from the same conceptual difficulty of giving corporations political rights: they aren't people and cannot
participate in the same way as a natural person. Professor Richard A. Epstein
acknowledged that, "[i]t is also true that no corporation, recognized by law as
an entity separate from its shareholder owners, celebrates religious holidays,
attends church, performs religious rites, or observes various religious laws."[38]
Thus, there is something wildly inappropriate about granting religious objection under RFRA to business corporations.

The *Hobby Lobby* dissent by Justice Ruth Bader Ginsburg was particularly
withering. As she wrote: "[i]n the Court's view, RFRA demands accommodation of a for-profit corporation's religious beliefs no matter the impact that accommodation may have on third parties who do not share the corporation
owners' religious faith — in these cases, thousands of women employed by
Hobby Lobby and Conestoga or dependents of persons those corporations em-
ploy."[39] As Justice Ginsburg noted, Congress had specifically considered giving employers an opt-out, and Congress rejected this option.[40]

She chastised the majority for forgetting that there were rights of employees at stake in the case as well. As Justice Ginsburg put it, "with respect to free
exercise claims no less than free speech claims, "'[y]our right to swing your
arms ends just where the other man's nose begins.'" This omission has also
caught the eye of academics. "Justice Alito [writing for the majority] did not
explain, however, why the shareholders were the appropriate persons from
whom to derive a religious exemption from an employee health benefit requirement for the corporation, despite one of the corporations involved having more than 13,000 employees, whose religious beliefs were not considered."[41]

Justice Ginsburg drew a strong distinction between religious nonprofits and
for-profit corporations like Hobby Lobby. "Religious organizations exist to foster the interests of persons subscribing to the same religious faith. Not so of

37. *Id.*
38. Richard A. Epstein, *The Defeat of the Contraceptive Mandate in* Hobby Lobby: *Right Results, Wrong Reasons*, 2014 CATO SUP. CT. REV. 35, 43 (2014).
39. Burwell v. Hobby Lobby Stores, Inc., 134 S. Ct. 2751, 2787 (2014) (Ginsburg, J., dissenting).
40. *Id.* at 2788 (Ginsburg, J., dissenting).
41. Blair & Pollman, *supra* note 3, at 1730.

for-profit corporations. Workers who sustain the operations of those corporations commonly are not drawn from one religious community. Indeed, by law, no religion-based criterion can restrict the work force of for-profit corporations."[42] She concluded in dissent: "[w]orking for Hobby Lobby or Conestoga, in other words, should not deprive employees of the preventive care available to workers at the shop next door[.]"[43]

Hobby Lobby holds a sinister potential for a host of other workplace regulations as well. As Professor Frederick Gedicks posited,

> Virtually every law and regulation in the for-profit workplace directs one private party (usually the employer) to provide a benefit to another (usually the employee). The Fair Labor Standards Act directs employers to provide employees the benefits of limited hours and minimum pay; the Occupational Safety and Health Act directs employers to provide employees the benefit of a safe working environment; Title VII of the Civil Rights Act directs employers to provide existing and prospective employees the benefits of an employment market and a work environment free of race, gender, religion, national origin, and disability discrimination; the Employee Retirement Income Security Act directs employees to supply employees the benefits of safe and stable retirement and insurance compensation; the list is almost endless.[44]

Lower courts post-*Hobby Lobby* have been reluctant to extend its reach. For example, the Third Circuit came to the following conclusion: "[a]lthough that person may have a religious objection to what the government, or another third party, does with something that the law requires to be provided (whether it be a Social Security number, DNA, or a form that states that the person religiously objects to providing contraceptive coverage), RFRA does not necessarily permit that person to impose a restraint on another's action based on the claim that the action is religiously abhorrent."[45] And the D.C. Circuit declined to expand *Hobby Lobby*, concluding, "[r]eligious objectors ... have no

---

42. Burwell v. Hobby Lobby Stores, Inc., 134 S. Ct. at 2795 (Ginsburg, J., dissenting).

43. *Id.* at 2804 (Ginsburg, J., dissenting).

44. Frederick Mark Gedicks, *One Cheer for* Hobby Lobby: *Improbable Alternatives, Truly Strict Scrutiny, and Third-Party Employee Burdens*, 38 HARV. J. L. & GENDER 153, 171–72 (2015) (footnotes omitted) (citing Cutter v. Wilkinson, 544 U.S. 709 (2005); Estate of Thornton v. Caldor, 472 U.S. 703 (1985)).

45. Geneva Col. v. U.S. Dep't of Health & Human Servs., 778 F.3d 422, 441 (3d Cir. 2015).

RFRA right to be free from the unease, or even anguish, of knowing that third parties are legally privileged or obligated to act in ways their religion abhors."[46] The Tenth Circuit has also rejected invitations to extend *Hobby Lobby*,[47] as has the Second Circuit.[48]

But once again the Supreme Court is building on its own precedents. *Hobby Lobby* was almost immediately expanded in a terse ruling in *Wheaton College v. Burwell*. *Hobby Lobby* had been limited to objections to a few methods of birth control that the owners of Hobby Lobby had mistaken for abortifacients. Wheaton College objected to all types of birth control coverage. The Supreme Court yielded to this broader religious objection as well.[49] And in late 2015, the Supreme Court granted cert. in another seven cases on religious objections to the ACA's birth control mandate.[50]

The end result of *Hobby Lobby* is a cost shifting from employers to taxpayers. As Chief Justice Leo Strine of the Delaware Supreme Court explained, "[t]he *Hobby Lobby* Court determined that the federal government could not require employers to pay funds into insurance pools to cover medical devices

---

46. Priests for Life v. U.S. Dep't of Health & Human Servs., 772 F.3d 229, 246 (D.C. Cir. 2014) (citation omitted).

47. Little Sisters of the Poor Home for the Aged v. Burwell, No. 13-1540, 2015 WL 4232096, at *4 (10th Cir. July 14, 2015) ("The difference between *Hobby Lobby* and this case is significant and frames the issue here. In *Hobby Lobby,* the plaintiff for-profit corporations objected on religious grounds to providing contraceptive coverage and could choose only between (1) complying with the ACA by providing the coverage or (2) not complying and paying significant penalties. In the cases before us, the plaintiff religious non-profit organizations can avail themselves of an accommodation that allows them to opt out of providing contraceptive coverage without penalty.").

48. Catholic Health Care Sys. v. Burwell, No. 14-427-CV, 2015 WL 4665049, at *8 (2d Cir. Aug. 7, 2015) ("If RFRA plaintiffs needed only to assert that their religious beliefs were substantially burdened, federal courts would be reduced to rubber stamps, and the government would have to defend innumerable actions under demanding strict scrutiny analysis.... Rejecting this possibility, we conclude that the fact that a RFRA plaintiff *considers* a regulatory burden substantial does not make it a substantial burden. Were it otherwise, no burden would be insubstantial." (citations omitted)).

49. Wheaton Coll. v. Burwell, 134 S. Ct. 2806, 2807 (2014) ("the Court orders: If [Wheaton College] informs the Secretary of Health and Human Services in writing that it is a nonprofit organization that holds itself out as religious and has religious objections to providing coverage for contraceptive services, the respondents are enjoined from enforcing against the applicant the challenged provisions of the ... Affordable Care Act and related regulations pending final disposition of appellate review.").

50. Ltr. from U.S. Supreme Ct. to Paul Michael Pohl re: Zubik, et al. v. Burwell, Sec. of H&HS (Nov. 6, 2015), http://www.scotusblog.com/wp-content/uploads/2015/11/14-1418-et-al.-RFRA-Briefing-Proposal-Request-Letter.pdf.

or products for their employees if the corporate employer has a religious objection. Instead, secular taxpayers, and religious taxpayers whose religions do not conflict with the health care at issue, must pay to make up the difference."[51] Consequently, the temptation may be great in the future for business corporations to raise religious objection to shift costs onto those outside the firm. There may even be the incentive to raise bogus religious claims if it will save the corporation money.

---

51. Leo E. Strine, Jr., *Corporate Power Ratchet: The Courts' Role in Eroding "We the People's" Ability to Constrain Our Corporate Creations*, 51 Harv. Civil Rights-Civil Liberties L. Rev. (Forthcoming 2016) (manuscript at 52) (citing Avik Roy, *According to the Supreme Court, Corporations Have More Religious Freedom Than Taxpayers*, Forbes, July 1, 2014).

Part III

Fewer Corporate
Responsibilities

The proper governance of companies will become as crucial to the
world economy as the proper governing of countries.
—James D. Wolfensohn, President of the World Bank[1]

Expanded corporate rights could mean expanded corporate responsibilities. Although corporate rights are expanding, concomitant responsibilities
are not attaching. Instead, corporate responsibilities are being shed, shirked,
and shredded at every turn by certain ambitious firms. As courts have granted
corporations numerous rights, it is important to remember that there are already numerous advantages to being a corporation that are not available to individuals. One key difference, of course, is a person has a body, which means
that corporeal consequences like incarceration can be used as effective sanctions to entice most of us to abide by most laws—from speed limits, to building codes, to taxes. But because a corporation is really just a pile of papers
sitting on file with a secretary of state, these corporeal inducements are not
universally effective. And furthermore, while you or I can only be in one place
at a time, being noncorporeal makes corporations into teleporting shape-
shifters: here for one purpose and across the world for another simultaneously.
This is particularly true of corporations that have intellectual property as their
primary asset. The value of the firm, at least on paper, can slip from jurisdiction to jurisdiction, evading regulators as much as possible, including the tax-

---

1. Commonwealth Association for Corporate Governance, *CACG Guidelines Principles
for Corporate Governance in the Commonwealth Towards Global Competitiveness and Economic Accountability* (Nov. 1999) (quoting James D. Wolfensohn, President of the World
Bank c. 1999).

man. One of the strongest reasons for not giving corporations and humans identical rights is that the corporate form allows for advantages like perpetual life, lower taxes, and limited liability for investors. And their single-minded focus on profit maximization allows them to be used in ways that ignore or devalue moral considerations.

Indeed, their structural advantages allow larger corporations to rival the power of the state, let alone mere individuals. Even back in the 1930s, when Professors Berle and Means were writing, they predicted that

> [t]he rise of the modern corporation has brought a concentration of economic power which can compete on equal terms with the modern state ... The state seeks in some aspects to regulate the corporation, while the corporation, steadily becoming more powerful, makes every effort to avoid such regulation ... The future may see the economic organism, now typified by the corporation, not only on an equal plane with the state, but possibly superseding it as the dominant form of social organization.[2]

Arguably, Professors Berle's and Means' prediction came true. In 2011, *Business Insider* compared corporate revenues with national GDPs and found that many companies had more money than nations.[3]

The problem of big multinational corporations gaining more "citizenship" rights is what Justice Brandeis referred to as the "curse of bigness."[4] Justice Brandeis explored this tension in his famous dissent in the *Liggett* case (which was quoted at length in Chapter 2).[5] As one scholar explained of Brandeis's approach, "[b]elieving strongly that the survival of democracy depended ultimately on a maximum of direct participation by individuals in the decisions that shaped their lives, he was led to stress the virtues of smallness[.]"[6] As UVA Law Professor Richard C. Schragger once put it, "[l]arge-scale shifts in employment, manufacturing base, retail innovation, and demographics have generated anxiety about the nature of corporate capitalism and its relationship to

---

2. ADOLF A. BERLE & GARDINER C. MEANS, THE MODERN CORPORATION & PRIVATE PROPERTY 313 (1932 reprint 2009).

3. Vincent Trivett, *25 US Mega Corporations: Where They Rank If They Were Countries*, BUS. INSIDER (Jun. 27, 2011, 11:27 AM), http://www.businessinsider.com/25-corporations-bigger-tan-countries-2011-6.

4. Louis D. Brandeis, *A Curse of Bigness*, HARPER'S WKLY. 18 (Jan. 10, 1914).

5. *Liggett*, 288 U.S. 517 (Brandeis, J., dissenting in part).

6. SAMUEL J. KONEFSKY, THE LEGACY OF HOLMES AND BRANDEIS: A STUDY IN THE INFLUENCE OF IDEAS 171 (1956).

democracy."[7] And the question of how a corporate behemoth may act in a democratic context is one that is troubling, particularly in a nation with a privately financed electoral system, and especially if that colossus cannot die and refuses to pay into the national treasury for the common good.[8]

---

7. Richard C. Schragger, *The Anti-Chain Store Movement, Localist Ideology, and the Remnants of the Progressive Constitution, 1920–1940*, 90 Iowa L. Rev. 1011, 1016–17 (2005).

8. Marshall Clinard, Corporate Corruption 1 (1990) ("Today, transnational corporations dominate the Western world in much the same manner in which the Roman Catholic Church dominated medieval society.").

Chapter 7

Avoiding the Taxman

> Merchants have no country.
> —Thomas Jefferson[9]

Where exactly are corporations citizens? Norman Ornstein reminded us of a time when the interests of large American corporations and America's national interest were more closely aligned. He urged us to:

> go back to the famous statement of Charles Wilson, the CEO of General Motors, who said in Congressional testimony: 'what's good for General Motors is good for America and vice versa.' The two parts of it are important to put together. What he was saying was if we make a lot of money, that's good for America. But we also understand that if the country doesn't function well and doesn't prosper, then that is bad for General Motors. The later part gets ignored.[10]

But Mr. Ornstein noted that times have evolved since the 1950s. "That was when General Motors was clearly, firmly, an *American* company. Now, General Motors is chartered in the United States. But now, as its board would say, it is a global company. Not only does it have business in countries around the world, its suppliers and parts are from countries around the world. That means that its interests may be at odds with the national interest of the United States."[11] So a real question can be raised about today's General Motors: where does its allegiance lie now?

---

9. Letter from Thomas Jefferson to Horatio G. Spafford, 17 March 1814, http://founders.archives.gov/documents/Jefferson/03-07-02-0167.

10. Interview with Norman Ornstein, Fellow Am. Enterprise Instit. (July 24, 2015).

11. *Id.*

One test of allegiance is does a corporation pay revenues into the national treasury for the common good, and if so, where? If "[t]axes are what we pay for civilized society …" as Justice Oliver Wendell Holmes wrote, then many large corporations are often not paying their fair share.[12] One of the advantages of the corporate form is the ability to be many places at once. Because of their fluidity, "corporations go where diplomats cannot."[13] This facilitates regulatory arbitrage, including the ability to be what tax lawyers euphemistically deem "tax efficient." In plain English, being tax efficient means paying as little tax as possible—preferably zero. In 1935, President Franklin Roosevelt, only half joking, once said, "there is a very great distinction between tax evasion and tax avoidance. Tax avoidance means that you hire a $250,000-fee lawyer, and he changes the word 'evasion' into the word 'avoidance.'"[14] Whether you want to call it evasion or avoidance, many corporations are doing it.

A. American Taxes

1. State and Local Corporate Tax Breaks

Tax breaks are not just a federal phenomenon. Rather, tax breaks are a potent force at the state and local levels. Corporations are offered tax breaks by states and localities that want a corporation to locate there.[15] Certainly states compete, trying to outdo each other in how many tax breaks they can offer to attract firms that will hire their citizens. As Marilyn Friedman articulated in

---

12. Compania General de Tabacos v. Collector, 275 U.S. 87, 100 (1927).

13. ROBERT A.G. MONKS & NELL MINOW, CORPORATE GOVERNANCE 416 (Fifth ed. 2011).

14. Franklin D. Roosevelt, *Excerpts from the Press Conference*, AM. PRESIDENCY PROJECT (July 31, 1935), http://www.presidency.ucsb.edu/ws/?pid=14903.

15. Marilyn Friedman, *To Bail Out or Not to Bail Out: Moral Hazard and Other Ethical Considerations*, 11 GEO. J.L. & PUB. POL'Y 411, 423–24 (2013) ("Another type of government support for corporations … involves substantial incentives given by state and local governments either to keep companies from closing factories and stores and moving elsewhere or to lure them to the localities in the first place. These incentives now add up to about $80 billion per year in the U.S. The incentives take many forms. Story lists 'cash grants and loans; sales tax breaks; income tax credits and exemptions; free services; and property tax abatements.' These incentives come from states and localities that are contending with severe budget deficits. Currently, governments are often cutting worthy expenditures such as those for public schools at the same time that they are paying incentives to corporations." (quoting Louise Story, *As Companies Seek Tax Deals, Governments Pay High Price*, N.Y. TIMES (Dec. 2, 2012), http://www.nytimes.com/2012/12/02/us/how-local-taxpayers-bankroll-corporations.html?pagewanted=all&_r=0)).

this race to the bottom among localities "[c]ompanies may put local governments into bidding wars with each other and may hold out the promise of job creation. However, ... companies appear not to be held accountable for failing to live up to those understandings."[16] Too frequently, the same firm that will locate in your town for a tax break, will also pull up stakes and move to the next town over if the tax package is even sweeter. For example, take the case of Seaboard Corporation in Albert Lea, Minnesota.

> In 1990 the mayor of Albert Lea, Minnesota heralded the re-opening of a hog-processing plant as "quite a Christmas present ... [f]airy tales do come true!" After being enticed with a $2.9 million low-interest loan, property improvements, and a deal on its sewage charges, Seaboard Corporation re-opened what had once been the town's largest employer. In what eventually ended up costing the Federal government, the State of Minnesota, and the town of Albert Lea a combined total of over $41 million, Seaboard created several hundred jobs which paid so little that few residents of Albert Lea even cared to work for the plant. The company eventually resorted to recruiting workers from Mexico and Central America. Then, only four years later, Seaboard closed the plant and moved its operations to a town that offered an even larger economic package. Albert Lea was left with an abandoned slaughter-house, debt, higher utility bills and unemployed migrant workers.[17]

New York State has also experienced a failed escapade in giving tax breaks for little job growth. After spending $47 million to advertise the program known as Start-Up NY, the program only generated 76 jobs.[18] As Emeritus Professor Lawrence Wittner explains, despite giving businesses tax breaks and subsidies to create jobs, "New York State's experience indicates that, when it comes to producing jobs, corporate welfare programs are a bad investment."[19]

---

16. *Id.* at 424.

17. Steven R. Little, Comment, *Corporate Welfare Wars: The Insufficiency of Current Constraints on State Action and the Desirability of a Federal Legislative Response*, 22 HAMLINE L. REV. 849, 849 (1999); Donald L. Barlett & James B. Steele, *The Empire of the Pigs: A Little-Known Company Is a Master at Milking Governments for Welfare*, TIME (Nov. 23, 1998), http://www.cnn.com/ALLPOLITICS/time/1998/11/23/pigs.html.

18. Lawrence Wittner, *Corporate Welfare Fails to Deliver the Jobs: The Sad Case of Start-Up NY*, HUFF. POST (May 28, 2015), http://www.huffingtonpost.com/lawrence-wittner/corporate-welfare-fails-t_b_7454980.html.

19. *Id.*

Louisiana may take the prize for the most short-sighted corporate tax abatement policies. In 1974, Louisiana voters amended the state's constitution, thereby creating an industrial property tax exemption. The Louisiana agency in charge acts as a rubber stamp, granting nearly all tax abatement requests.[20] Kary Moss shared this jaw-dropping anecdote: "[b]idding wars have been premised on a faulty assumption—that the introduction of a business to a local economy will generate a substantial amount of new jobs and growth.... [I]n Baton Rouge ... Exxon Corporation received 27 tax abatements totaling $14,372,600, while the company expected to create just one new permanent job."[21]

The public may have little knowledge about the effectiveness of various tax incentives in creating new jobs in a particular locality or state. This isn't just a matter of the public's lack of curiosity. There is a significant lack of transparency as *Newsweek* reported:

> Transparency and job creation receive great gusts of political lip service. Just not at the same time. Programs for job creation—each state's unique mix of tax breaks and other inducements to new business— are among the least transparent parts of state government ... That prevents people from evaluating corporate-welfare programs, even as politicians tout their benefits.[22]

There are also less noticeable and more subtle ways that corporations get taxpayer subsidies, such as by paying workers less than a living wage and expecting government to pick up the slack. As Nell Minow explained, "companies should not pay full employees so little that they qualify for federal assistance. If the government is paying for employees' food, then the government is really subsidizing the corporation that isn't paying employees enough."[23] This type of indirect subsidy is all but invisible from the outside, as workers are unlikely to tell customers that they need food stamps to make ends meet.[24]

---

20. Kary L. Moss, *The Privatization of Public Wealth*, 23 FORDHAM URB. L.J. 101, 106–107 (1995).

21. *Id.* at 108.

22. McKay Coppins, *The Hidden World of Corporate Subsidies*, NEWSWEEK (Jan 2, 2011), http://www.newsweek.com/hidden-world-corporate-subsidies-66751.

23. Interview with Nell Minow, Vice Chair, ValueEdge Advisors (Aug. 19, 2015).

24. Clare O'Connor, *Report: Walmart Workers Cost Taxpayers $6.2 Billion In Public Assistance*, FORBES (Apr. 15, 2014), http://www.forbes.com/sites/clareoconnor/2014/04/15/report-walmart-workers-cost-taxpayers-6-2-billion-in-public-assistance/.

2. American Federal Tax Loopholes

There are, certainly, some corporate taxes being paid domestically in the U.S. "The Commerce Department ... estimated that corporations earned $2.1 trillion during 2013, and paid $419 billion in corporate taxes. The after-tax profit of $1.7 trillion amounted to 10 percent of gross domestic product during the year[.]"[25] Much more could be paid if tax loopholes were tightened or closed.

The Internal Revenue Code reveals the extent of corporate power in the democratic process, if you know where to look.[26] For example, NASCAR has its own tax break.[27] There is a tax write-off for movie producers for filming in American Samoa.[28] And there's a tax credit for alcohol-based fuel.[29] Andrew Ross Sorkin wrote up some of the more egregious corporate tax loopholes for *The New York Times*. They include the ability of corporations to deduct legal expenses, even if they were defending wrongdoing by the company:

> If individual taxpayers are arrested, admit guilt and reach a civil settlement with the government, they cannot deduct the costs from their returns. But amazingly, a company is allowed to claim those costs as a business expense. JPMorgan Chase, for example, which has agreed to pay billions of dollars in fines for various transgressions, can deduct a large portion—and all the legal expenses—from its taxes.[30]

---

25. Floyd Norris, *Corporate Profits Grow and Wages Slide*, N.Y. Times (Apr. 4, 2014), http://www.nytimes.com/2014/04/05/business/economy/corporate-profits-grow-ever-larger-as-slice-of-economy-as-wages-slide.html?_r=0.

26. Susannah Camic Tahk, *Making Impossible Tax Reform Possible*, 81 Fordham L. Rev. 2683, 2685 (2013) ("These [tax] preferences usually take the form of exclusions, deductions, credits, and special rates, many of which are the hated tax 'loopholes' so bemoaned in popular and academic commentary alike.").

27. Jonathan R. Macey, *Crony Capitalism: Right Here, Right Now*, 37 Harv. J.L. & Pub. Pol'y 5 (2014) ("one could talk for hours about the examples of crony capitalism—for example, the $78 million tax write-off in the new tax bill for NASCAR drivers. That write-off may be very popular—I don't know—but it is crony capitalism.").

28. *Id.* ("Yet another was the tax victory given to companies operating in American Samoa by Chris Dodd—a former Connecticut Senator—who now represents Hollywood's movie studios. He got those companies a two-year extension on a provision allowing film and television producers to expense the first $15 million of production costs incurred in the United States—a kind of wholesale crony capitalism.")

29. Sarah Stodola, *10 Giant Loopholes That Businesses Use To Dodge Taxes*, Fiscal Times (Feb. 10, 2011), http://www.businessinsider.com/corporate-tax-breaks-2011-2?op=1.

30. Andrew Ross Sorkin, *Looking at Some Corporate Tax Loopholes Ordinary Citizens May Envy*, N.Y. Times (Apr. 14, 2014), http://dealbook.nytimes.com/2014/04/14/looking-at-some-corporate-tax-loopholes-ordinary-citizens-may-envy/?_r=0.

Another corporate deduction is for private corporate aircraft.[31] And yet another allows for a deduction for executive stock options.[32] Corporations lobby aggressively for tax loopholes to be included in the U.S. tax laws and they lobby to maintain them. As a result, "U.S. companies, along with their lobbyists and trade groups, are treating Washington, D.C., like a big, swampy strip club, showering it with cash in an effort to fight tax reform laws that might put hundreds of billions of dollars back into government coffers."[33]

3. International Tax Breaks

a. Inversions

Where is Burger King a citizen? A few years ago the answer to this question wasn't that difficult. It was incorporated in Delaware with a principal place of business in Miami, making it an unambiguously American company.[34] Burger King used to be an iconic American brand. Not anymore. It merged with the Canadian company Tim Hortons in 2014[35] and changed its "citizenship" to Canadian for tax purposes.[36] So where is it a citizen now? America? Canada? Both? Neither? Canada for tax purposes, and America for others?

One way for a corporation to do business in the U.S. without paying taxes in the U.S. is to merge with a foreign entity and park its assets abroad. As the

---

31. *Id.* ("Companies that own aircraft can depreciate their planes more quickly than airlines—over five years instead of seven—and claim the deduction. In total, closing the loophole is worth $3 billion to $4 billion over a decade.").

32. *Id.* ("A much larger loophole involves the deduction of executive stock options by the company issuing them. Inexplicably, many of Silicon Valley's newest star companies will be able to shelter a large portion of their profits as a result. Citizens for Tax Justice estimated late last year that a dozen technology companies, including Twitter, LinkedIn and Priceline, 'stand to eliminate all income taxes on the next $11.4 billion they earn—giving these companies $4 billion in tax cuts.'").

33. Mark Gongloff, *U.S. Companies Lobbying Furiously To Save Corporate Tax Loopholes: Study*, Huff. Post (Jun. 18, 2013), http://www.huffingtonpost.com/2013/06/18/companies-lobbying-corporate-tax-loopholes-study_n_3461044.html.

34. Burger King Holdings, Inc., Form 10-k (For the fiscal year ended December 31, 2011), http://www.sec.gov/Archives/edgar/data/1352801/000119312512114564/d26434 5d10k.htm.

35. Burger King Worldwide, Inc. Schedule 14C (Nov. 5, 2014), http://www.sec.gov/Archives/edgar/data/1547282/000119312514398471/d786007ddefm14c.htm.

36. Jamie Sturgeon, *It's official, Tim Hortons, Burger King become One*, Global News (Dec. 12, 2014), http://globalnews.ca/news/1724238/its-official-tim-hortons-burger-king-become-one/.

Washington Post reported on the Burger King deal at the time, "the new Burger King and Tim Hortons parent company would likely station itself in the Ontario province of Canada.... [T]he reason for a headquarter shift across the country's northern border is simple: lower corporate taxes."[37]

What Burger King did is known as an inversion. Professor Sarah A. Wahl explained that a corporate inversion "occurs when an American company legally moves its domicile to a foreign country with lower tax rates in order to reduce its tax burden. After the headquarters is moved, the company utilizes various U.S. tax code provisions to access overseas earnings without paying U.S. taxes."[38] New York-based Pfizer could have become Irish if it completed a merger with Allergan.[39] Brookings' David Wessel mapped the scope of inversions: "it started in the early '80s when some smart tax lawyers figured out that they could do this. Since then, about 50 U.S. companies have reincorporated abroad in an inversion—20 since 2012."[40] As a result, there is growing ambiguity over what constitutes an American company.[41]

One peculiarity of inversions is that on paper it will appear that a tiny foreign company owns a larger U.S. corporation.[42] But really this is mostly a change in the paper address for tax purposes. With a statutory corporate tax rate of 35%, the U.S. has one of the highest rates among OECD nations and this may motivate inversions.[43] Another facilitator of tax inversions is that the

---

37. Roberto A. Ferdman, *Have Taxes Your Way: Why Burger King Wants to Become a Canadian Citizen*, WASH. POST (Aug. 26, 2014), http://www.washingtonpost.com/news/wonkblog/wp/2014/08/25/burger-king-is-mulling-a-move-to-canada-for-breakfast-and-lower-taxes/.

38. Sarah A. Wahl, *The Three Legislative Components Necessary to Curb Corporate Tax Inversions*, 19 N.C. BANKING INST. 297, 299–300 (2015).

39. *Pfizer Would Cut Its Corporate Tax Bill if It Merges with Allergan*, NPR (Nov. 2, 2015), http://www.npr.org/2015/11/02/453885663/pfizer-would-cut-its-corporate-tax-bill-if-it-merges-with-allergan; Dominic Rushe, *Pfizer's $155bn Takeover of Allergan Set to Prompt Tax Row*, THE GUARDIAN (Nov. 23, 2015), http://www.theguardian.com/business/2015/nov/23/pfizer-allergan-agree-160-billion-dollars-deal-tax; Krishnader Calamur, *It's Off: The End of Pfizer's $160 Billion Allergan Merger*, THE ATLANTIC (Apr. 6, 2016).

40. *Pfizer Would Cut Its Corporate Tax Bill if It Merges with Allergan*, *supra* note 39 (quoting Wessel).

41. Minow interview *supra* note 23 ("[i]t is harder and harder to say what's an *American* company and what's not an American company.").

42. Wahl, *supra* note 38, at 299–300 ("Often, tax inversions result in a much smaller foreign holding company owning a significantly larger U.S. operating company. Companies that are inverting are not likely to make any material change in business strategy, operational structure or function. Instead, the inversion is purely a paper transaction motivated by reducing U.S. tax liability.")

43. *Id.* at 299–300.

American the tax code is "so porous that [corporations] can choose from several means of escape."[44]

This raises the issue of where the newly inverted company's loyalties lie. As Norman Ornstein explained, formerly American companies "are relocating their charters from the United States to other countries. So clearly by definition at that point, their interests are no longer grounded or rooted in the United States."[45] He continued, "[t]he idea that the American subsidiaries and its corporate coffers will only reflect the interests of the American subsidiaries and not the [foreign] corporate parents—the owners, the bosses—defies belief."[46] Consider again the *Bluman* case, where the Supreme Court upheld a ban on a Canadian citizen spending money in an American election because he was not a U.S. citizen.[47] Should this logic also apply to Burger King, if it is Canadian for tax avoidance purposes?

The Obama administration adopted rules designed to curb inversions by making it harder for merged entities to bring money back into the United States. And in 2016, the Treasury Department announced additional rules to address the practice of earning stripping.[48] These rules may encourage some companies to reconsider their inversion strategy.[49]

b. The Double Irish

Some companies have gone to even greater lengths to become tax efficient. "Double Irish with a Dutch sandwich'" sounds like something one might order at a gastro pub, but instead this was a complex tax avoidance scheme.[50] The

44. "Tracking Tax Runaways" Bloomberg (updated Apr.13, 2015), http://www.bloomberg.com/infographics/2014-09-18/tax-runaways-tracking-inversions.html.

45. Ornstein interview *supra* note 10.

46. *Id.*

47. *Bluman*, 800 F. Supp. 2d at 289–90.

48. Dep't of Treasury, *Treasury Announces Additional Action to Curb Inversions, Addresses Earning Stripping* (2016).

49. John McKinnon & Damian Paletta, *Obama Administration Issues New Rules to Combat Tax Inversions*, Wall St. J. (Sept. 22, 2014).

50. Jamie Smyth, *Adobe Shows its Creativity with Ireland Tax Base*, Financial Times (Sept. 12, 2013), http://www.ft.com/intl/cms/s/0/6273646e-fb77-11e2-8650-00144fe-abdc0.html#axzz3erfB2ysT ("The 'Double Irish' relies on multinationals setting up two Irish companies, one of which owns the valuable intellectual property central to its products. The first company is tax resident in Ireland and pays royalties to the second company for use of the IP, which generates expenses that reduce the amount of Irish tax it pays. The second company, which is incorporated in Ireland but not tax resident in the country, collects the royalties in a tax haven, thereby avoiding Irish taxes.").

"double Irish with a Dutch sandwich" involves sending profits first through one Irish company, then to a Dutch company and finally to a second Irish company headquartered in a tax haven. The tax avoidance is achieved typically by corporate subsidiaries of the parent company buying and selling goods and services from each other, including intellectual property.[51]

This technique has allowed certain corporations to dramatically reduce their overall corporate tax rates.[52] Use of these tax avoidance methods can make a big difference for a firm's profitability.[53] The United States is one of the big losers from the Double Irish as tax revenues that would have been paid in the United States are diverted elsewhere.[54] This particular tax avoidance method "allowed Apple and other similarly situated companies in Ireland like

---

51. Jesse Ducker, *Google 2.4% Rate Shows How $60 Billion is Lost to Tax Loopholes*, BLOOMBERG BUSINESS NEWS (Oct. 21, 2010), http://www.bloomberg.com/news/articles/ 2010-10-21/google-2-4-rate-shows-how-60-billion-u-s-revenue-lost-to-tax-loopholes ("Income shifting commonly begins when companies like Google sell or license the foreign rights to intellectual property developed in the U.S. to a subsidiary in a low-tax country. That means foreign profits based on the technology get attributed to the offshore unit, not the parent. Under U.S. tax rules, subsidiaries must pay 'arm's length' prices for the rights — or the amount an unrelated company would. Because the payments contribute to taxable income, the parent company has an incentive to set them as low as possible. Cutting the foreign subsidiary's expenses effectively shifts profits overseas."); John T. VanDenburgh, *Closing International Loopholes: Changing the Corporate Tax Base to Effectively Combat Tax Avoidance*, 47 VAL. U. L. REV. 313, 330–32 (2012) ("Earnings Stripping is a tax avoidance technique in which a U.S. corporation sets up a subsidiary in a low-tax country, and then the U.S. corporation uses its U.S. earnings and makes deductible payments to the subsidiary in the form of interest, royalties, or fees. This 'strips' the earnings from the U.S. corporation and transfers the majority of the income to the country with the low tax rate.... In 2006, Google, Inc. (U.S.) implemented a form of earnings stripping when it licensed the rights of its intellectual property to its subsidiary in Bermuda for 'undisclosed' fees.").

52. *Double Irish With A Dutch Sandwich Definition*, INVESTOPEDIA, http://www.investopedia.com/terms/d/double-irish-with-a-dutch-sandwich.asp#ixzz3oC6jUyd4 (last visited Oct. 10, 2015).

53. Alexa Barinka & Jesse Drucker, *IBM Uses Dutch Tax Haven to Boost Profits as Sales Slide*, BLOOMBERG BUSINESS NEWS (Feb. 3, 2014), http://www.bloomberg.com/news/articles/2014-02-03/ibm-uses-dutch-tax-haven-to-boost-profits-as-sales-slide ("IBM ended 2013 with a tax provision $1.84 billion lower than it initially projected, thanks to a tax rate of 15.6 percent — compared with its forecast of 25 percent. Without the lower rate, the company's earnings per share would have fallen from the previous year instead of rising, and net income would have missed analysts' estimates by about 14 percent instead of 2.9 percent, according to data compiled by *Bloomberg*.").

54. Ducker, *supra* note 51 ("Allocating the revenue to Ireland helps Google avoid income taxes in the U.S., where most of its technology was developed.... The profits don't stay with the Dublin subsidiary ... That's largely because it paid $5.4 billion in royalties to

Google, Microsoft, and Twitter to aggressively avoid higher taxes in their home countries."[55]

Apple has been viewed as the largest offender of taking advantage of the Double Irish.[56] *The Economist* reported, "investigators from America's Senate shone a harsh light on a highly profitable unit of Apple that was registered in Ireland, controlled from America—and not paying tax in either country. That this 'stateless-income' structure was perfectly legal highlighted a big loophole in the global system for taxing multinationals."[57] This "holy grail of tax avoidance" allowed Apple to avoid paying $9 billion in taxes in 2012.[58] The Organisation for Economic Co-operation and Development (OECD) estimates that such corporate tax avoidance results in revenue losses between $100 billion and $240 billion every year.[59] However, under pressure from other countries, Ireland has now decided to phase out the Double Irish.[60] Those who were taking advantage of it have five years to stop.[61]

Google Ireland Holdings, which has its "effective centre of management" in Bermuda, according to company filings.").

55. Kelly Phillips Erb, *Ireland Declares 'Double Irish' Tax Scheme Dead*, FORBES, (Oct. 15, 2014 @ 08:50 AM), http://www.forbes.com/sites/kellyphillipserb/2014/10/15/ireland-declares-double-irish-tax-scheme-dead/.

56. Charles Duhigg & David Kocieniewski, *How Apple Sidesteps Billions in Taxes*, N.Y. TIMES (Apr. 28, 2012), http://www.nytimes.com/2012/04/29/business/apples-tax-strategy-aims-at-low-tax-states-and-nations.html?_r=0 ("In 2006, [Apple] reorganized its Irish divisions as unlimited corporations, which have few requirements to disclose financial information.... tax experts say that strategies like the Double Irish help explain how Apple has managed to keep its international taxes to 3.2 percent of foreign profits last year, to 2.2 percent in 2010, and in the single digits for the last half-decade, according to the company's corporate filings.").

57. *New Rules, Same Old Paradigm A Plan to Curb Multinationals' Tax Avoidance Is an Opportunity Missed*, THE ECONOMIST, Oct. 10, 2015, http://www.oecd.org/newsroom/g20-finance-ministers-endorse-reforms-to-the-international-tax-system-for-curbing-avoidance-by-multinational-enterprises.htm.

58. *Death of the Double Irish: The Irish Government Has Announced Plans to Alter One of Its Controversial Tax Policies*, THE ECONOMIST (Oct. 15, 2014), http://www.economist.com/news/business-and-finance/21625444-irish-government-has-announced-plans-alter-one-its-more-controversial-tax-policies.

59. *OECD/G20 Base Erosion and Profit Shifting Project Forwarded to G20 Heads of State in November*, OECD (Oct. 10, 2015), http://www.oecd.org/newsroom/g20-finance-ministers-endorse-reforms-to-the-international-tax-system-for-curbing-avoidance-by-multinational-enterprises.htm. ("Revenue losses ... conservatively estimated at USD 100–240 billion annually, or anywhere from 4–10% of global corporate income tax (CIT) revenues.").

60. *Death of the Double Irish, supra* note 56 ("Last year it made it illegal for firms incorporated in Ireland to have no tax domicile anywhere.").

61. Stephan Castle, Mark Scott, *Ireland to Phase Out 'Double Irish' Tax Break Used by*

The quest to be tax efficient can lead to some very aggressive approaches, including having an office abroad that is little more than a post office box and then asserting that the management of the company is magically happening in that P.O. box. "For example, Google, Inc., a U.S. based corporation, created a subsidiary in the Netherlands, Google Netherlands Holdings, which has no employees or assets but filters through 99.8% of Google's income for tax reasons."[62] Other European tax avoidance gambits are garnering a reaction from regulators. For example, Starbucks and Fiat were handed bills for millions in back taxes by the European Union in late 2015.[63] According to the *Wall St. Journal*, "[t]he European Commission, the EU's executive arm, said ... that tax deals granted to Starbucks in the Netherlands and Fiat in Luxembourg amounted to illegal state subsidies that must be repaid."[64] These companies are likely to appeal these adverse tax rulings.

c. *Other Offshore Tax Havens*

In tax avoidance schemes like the Double Irish, the taxes that are collected are not paid to Ireland. Rather the taxes are paid to a tax haven like the Cayman Islands, the Isle of Man, or Bermuda. A report by U.S. PIRG showed "[a]t least 358 companies, nearly 72 percent of the Fortune 500, operate subsidiaries in tax haven jurisdictions as of the end of 2014."[65] And this report also found, "Fortune 500 companies are holding more than $2.1 trillion in accumulated profits offshore for tax purposes. Just 30 Fortune 500 companies account for 65 percent of these offshore profits. These 30 companies with the most money offshore have booked $1.4 trillion overseas for tax purposes."[66]

And yet, the same firms that bend over backwards to avoid paying taxes to the United States, also take full advantage of selling to U.S. customers, including the U.S. government. Nell Minow finds this unbalanced. She argued, "[y]ou can't have it both ways. If you are going to get the benefits of being an

---

Tech Giants, N.Y. Times (Oct. 14, 2014), http://www.nytimes.com/2014/10/15/business/international/ireland-to-phase-out-tax-advantage-used-by-technology-firms.html?_r=0.

62. VanDenburgh, *supra* note 51, at 328–30.

63. Tom Fairless, *EU Regulators to Require Starbucks, Fiat Pay Millions of Euros in Back Taxes*, Wall St. J. (Oct. 21, 2015), http://www.wsj.com/articles/eu-rules-that-starbucks-fiat-benefited-from-illegal-tax-deals-1445419279.

64. *Id.*

65. Robert S. McIntyre, Richard Phillips & Phineas Baxandall, *Offshore Shell Games 2015 The Use of Offshore Tax Havens by Fortune 500 Companies*, U.S. PIRG & Citizens for Tax Justice 1 (2015), http://www.uspirg.org/sites/pirg/files/reports/USP%20Shell-Games%20Oct15%201.3.pdf.

66. *Id.*

American company and being listed on the American Exchanges, and the privilege of selling to the U.S. government, then you have to be an American company.... [W]e should impose more consequences for companies that are escaping American tax liability while getting these benefits."[67]

B. Corporate Welfare

Some corporations are not just seeking to pay as little tax to the government, they often seek and receive benefits or subsidies at taxpayer expense. Chris Rufer, the founder of The Morning Star Company, wrote an op-ed in the *New York Times* stating, "[a]s someone who started a company that employs approximately 2,500 people ... I used to wonder why so many Americans distrusted big business. I now have a good answer. I have observed too many of my fellow business leaders blatantly work with the government to increase their profits at taxpayer expense."[68] Such special deals between the government and business are often pejoratively called corporate welfare or crony capitalism. The Cato Institute reported in 2012 that "[c]orporate welfare in the federal budget costs taxpayers almost $100 billion a year."[69] Cato argued,

> [w]hile corporate welfare may be popular with policymakers who want to aid home-state businesses, it undermines the broader economy and transfers wealth from average taxpaying households to favored firms. Corporate welfare also creates strong ties between politicians and business leaders, and these ties are often the source of corruption scandals in Washington. Americans are sick and tired of "crony capitalism[.]"[70]

For certain businesses, billions in taxpayer dollars can prop up a single firm as they access multiple federal streams of revenue, a process known as double-dipping. "The double-dipper that stands out from the rest is Boeing. Its more than $18 billion in FY2014 contract awards, combined with the $457 million in federal grants and $64 billion in federal loans and loan guarantees since

---

67. Minow interview *supra* note 23.

68. Chris Rufer, *End this Corporate Welfare*, N.Y. Times (Mar. 23, 2015), http://www.nytimes.com/2015/03/23/opinion/end-this-corporate-welfare.html.

69. Tad DeHaven, *Corporate Welfare in the Federal Budget*, Cato Pol'y Analysis 1 (July 25, 2012), http://object.cato.org/sites/cato.org/files/pubs/pdf/PA703.pdf.

70. *Id.*

2000, make it exceptionally favored by Uncle Sam."[71] Harvard Professor Lawrence Lessig has argued that "[w]e have corporate welfare largely because we have privately funded elections. The 'welfare' is the payback, indirect and legal, but payback nonetheless."[72]

Corporate welfare can take all sorts of forms and often hides in plain sight in congressional legislation like the 2014 farm bill, which included food assistance sent abroad. Vince Smith reported that the 2014 farm bill,

> requires at least 50 percent of all food aid to be carried on U.S. ships that are about twice as expensive to use as other methods of transport. U.S. sourcing requires that almost all food aid provided by the United States is grown by U.S. farmers and then shipped from U.S. ports, which is not the quickest way to get food to, say, sub-Saharan Africa.... [W]hat ... [this] does is generate profits for a few shipping companies and jobs for a few merchant sailors while increasing the cost of delivering emergency food aid to desperately poor households by more than 40 percent.[73]

Other American agricultural and energy policies privilege one type of business over others. Professor Jason Brennan asked readers to "[c]onsider: Why does American Coca-Cola have corn syrup when Mexican Coca-Cola has sugar?"[74] He responded, "[t]he reason: The corn lobby is powerful in the U.S. The U.S. government subsidizes corn and other cereals, feeding nearly $3 billion to large agribusinesses such as, Archer Daniels Midland."[75] Corn is also propped up through federal ethanol polices and sugar tariffs.[76]

The think tank Good Jobs First, which tracks government subsidies, reported in 2015, that "[o]ver the past 15 years, the federal government has provided $68 billion in grants and special tax credits to business, with two-thirds

---

71. Philip Mattera & Kasia Tarczynska, *Uncle Sam's Favorite Corporations: Identifying the Large Companies that Dominate Federal Subsidies*, GOOD JOBS FIRST 4 (Mar. 2015), http://www.goodjobsfirst.org/sites/default/files/docs/pdf/UncleSamsFavoriteCorporations.pdf.

72. LAWRENCE LESSIG, REPUBLIC LOST HOW MONEY CORRUPTS CONGRESS — AND PLAN TO STOP IT 269 (2011).

73. Vince Smith, *One Way the U.S. Is Like Greece: In Both Places, Crony Capitalism is Alive and Well*, U.S. NEWS & WORLD REP. (July 9, 2015), http://www.usnews.com/opinion/economic-intelligence/2015/07/09/in-us-and-greece-crony-capitalism-is-alive-and-well.

74. Jason Brennan, *The Right to Good Faith: How Crony Capitalism Delegitimizes the Administrative State*, 11 GEO. J.L. & PUB. POL'Y 317, 330 (2013).

75. *Id.*

76. *Id.*

of the total going to large corporations."[77] More specifically, they found that federal subsidies were concentrated among fewer than 600 firms, as "582 large companies account for 67 percent of the $68 billion total."[78]

Consider the matter of a beer brewery getting a federal subsidy as highlighted by Cato, "a craft brewery in Michigan recently received $220,000 to help it expand its brewing capacity. That subsidy might be good for the brewery, but it was paid for by raiding the wallets of federal taxpayers, who will have less money to buy their own favored beverages and other products. This handout is also unfair to the hundreds of craft breweries that do not receive federal handouts[.]"[79] In a real way, dolling out corporate subsidies is a way for the government to pick favorites.

Bailouts are another way that the taxpayer has come to the rescue of corporations, especially in the financial sector.[80] This has led to trillions of taxpayer dollars propping up big banks. As Good Jobs First explains, these bailouts have cost taxpayers trillions:

> The biggest aggregate bailout recipient is Bank of America, whose gross borrowing (excluding repayments) is just under $3.5 trillion (including the amounts for its Merrill Lynch and Countrywide Financial acquisitions). Three other banks are in the trillion-dollar club: Citigroup ($2.6 trillion), Morgan Stanley ($2.1 trillion) and JPMorgan Chase ($1.3 trillion, including Bear Stearns and Washington Mutual).[81]

All of this tax avoidance and quest for taxpayer subsidies could be termed socially damaging "rent seeking."[82] When it comes to taxes, corporations (especially the largest ones) are having their cake and eating it too. They shirk the responsibility to pay taxes, and they have their hands out to receive benefits at taxpayer expense. And given that corporations can continue in perpetuity, not only can they shirk taxes in your lifetime, they can shirk them in your grandchildren's lifetimes as well.

---

77. Mattera & Tarczynska, *supra* note 71, at 2.

78. *Id.* ("Six parent companies have received $1 billion or more in federal grants and allocated tax credits (those awarded to specific companies) since 2000; 21 have received $500 million or more; and 98 have received $100 million or more.")

79. DeHaven, *supra* note 69, at 5.

80. Monks & Minow, *supra* note 13, at xviii ("What happened [in the financial crash of 2007–08] was a massive shift of costs as Wall Street externalized the risk on to just about everyone else.").

81. Mattera & Tarczynska, *supra* note 71, at 2.

82. Jason Brennan, *The Right to Good Faith: How Crony Capitalism Delegitimizes the Administrative State*, 11 Geo. J.L. & Pub. Pol'y 317, 328 (2013) ("[a] firm engages in rent seeking when it tries to manipulate the political environment for its own benefit, and this is socially destructive.").

Chapter 8

Get Out of Jail Free

The greatest evil is not now done in those sordid 'dens of crime' that Dickens loved to paint. It is not done even in concentration camps and labour camps. In those we see its final result. But it is conceived and ordered (moved, seconded, carried, and minuted) in clean, carpeted, warmed and well-lighted offices, by quiet men with white collars and cut fingernails and smooth-shaven cheeks who do not need to raise their voices. Hence, naturally enough, my symbol for Hell is something like the bureaucracy of a police state or the office of a thoroughly nasty business concern.

—C.S. Lewis[1]

The non-corporeal nature of corporations, which allows them to sneak around the globe avoiding taxes, can also make corporations hard targets for criminal prosecutors. Criminal prosecutions of corporations still occur, but at the same time, prosecutorial discretion is being used to defer prosecutions or to refuse to prosecute certain (alleged) corporate criminals at all. Here, the fault appears to rest not only with corporations who appear from the outside to have broken the law, but also with prosecutors who refuse to charge them criminally for fear of what the collateral consequences might be.

One objection to the corporate form is that it facilitates grand crimes that individuals would be reticent to commit on their own. Economic theorist William M. Gouge wrote about the moral insulation that corporations facilitate: "[a]s directors of a company, men will sanction action of which they would scorn to be guilty in their private capacity. A crime which would press heavily on the conscience of one man, becomes quite endurable when divided

---

1. C.S. Lewis, *Preface*, The Screwtape Letters (1942).

among many."[2] Culpability for participating in a crime that is done collectively through a corporate structure, especially a large one, may be far more diffuse.[3] A corporate crime is like the Roman Senate killing Julius Caesar on the Ides of March. Unless all 60 Roman Senators are charged with a crime, they all get away with murder, which may be why, on a psychological level, it is easier for an individual to engage in criminality among peers doing the same thing.

But is white-collar crime really worse than petty in-person theft? According to corporate governance experts Robert Monks and Nell Minow, "white collar crime, in absolute terms, is more expensive."[4] They give as an example, "[a] single price-fixing case involving General Electric and Westinghouse in the early 1960s cost the affected consumers more than all of the robberies in the entire country that year."[5] More recently in 2001, the accounting fraud at Enron cost investors $11 billion.[6] And according to the Federal Bureau of Investigation, "white-collar crime is estimated to cost the United States more than $300 billion annually."[7]

A. The History of Corporate Criminal Liability

Just as corporations can sue and be sued, corporations can be held criminally liable. Back in 1909, the Supreme Court first clarified that corporations could properly be defendants in criminal cases requiring a *mens rea*.[8] As the Supreme Court held in *New York Central & Hudson River Railroad v. United States*,

> It is true that there are some crimes which, in their nature, cannot be committed by corporations. But there is a large class of offenses ... wherein the crime consists in purposely doing the things prohibited by

---

2. Arthur M. Schlesinger Jr., The Age of Jackson 335 (1953) (quoting William Gouge, *Paper Money*, Part I at 43 (1835)).

3. Interview with Retired Montana Supreme Court Justice James Nelson (Aug. 4, 2015). (corporations "can act as a concealed vehicle for covering up abuse and wrongdoing.").

4. Robert A.G. Monks & Nell Minow, Corporate Governance 20 (Fifth ed. 2011).

5. *Id.*

6. George J. Benston, *The Quality of Corporate Financial Statements and Their Auditors Before and After Enron*, Cato Institute Pol'y Analysis 12 (Nov. 6, 2003).

7. *White-Collar Crime*, Legal Information Institute at Cornell Law School, https://www.law.cornell.edu/wex/white-collar_crime# (last visited Nov. 28, 2015).

8. New York Cent. & H.R.R. Co. v. U.S., 212 U.S. 481 (1909); Ellen S. Podgor et al., White Collar Crime 23 (2013).

statute. In that class of crimes we see no good reason why corporations may not be held responsible for and charged with the knowledge and purposes of their agents, acting within the authority conferred upon them. If it were not so, many offenses might go unpunished and acts be committed in violation of law where, as in the present case, the statute requires all persons, corporate or private, to refrain from certain practices, forbidden in the interest of public policy.[9]

The Supreme Court continued that corporations were criminally liable under the theory of *respondeat superior*. The Supreme Court also noted that corporations played an outsized role in the economy that demanded legal accountability. "[T]he law ... cannot shut its eyes to the fact that the great majority of business transactions in modern times are conducted through [corporations] ... and to give them immunity from all punishment because of the old and exploded doctrine that a corporation cannot commit a crime would virtually take away the only means of effectually ... correcting [ ] abuses ..."[10] The railroad in the case had challenged the constitutionality of a criminal law applying to a corporation at all. The Supreme Court found it constitutional, stating simply, "the act is valid as to corporations."[11] And the Supreme Court concluded that Congress was acting within its Commerce Clause power in criminalizing corporate actions in interstate commerce.[12]

State courts came to similar conclusions about the culpability of corporations even earlier. In New York, the highest court wrote in 1860: "[l]ike natural persons, they can overleap the legal and moral restraints imposed upon them: in other words, they are capable of doing wrong.... [T]his doctrine of theoretical perfection in corporations would convert them practically into *most mischievous monsters*."[13] Therefore, under state and federal law, corporations can be convicted as criminals.[14]

Shareholders often pay for corporate crime multiple times. "Shareholders in particular pay the costs on all sides: as members of the community, they pay the costs of crime itself; as taxpayers, they pay the costs of prosecutions;

---

9. *Id.* at 494–95 (internal citations omitted).
10. *Id.* at 495–96.
11. *Id.* at 497.
12. *Id.* at 496.
13. Bissell v. Michigan South. R. Co., 22 N.Y. 258, 264, 1860 WL 7904, at *1 (N.Y. 1860) (emphasis added).
14. U.S. v. Philip Morris USA, Inc., 566 F.3d 1095, 1118–119 (D.C. Cir. 2009); U.S. v. Investment Enterprises, Inc., 10 F.3d 263, 266 (5th Cir. 1994); U.S. v. Twentieth Century Fox Film Corp., 882 F.2d 656, 660 (2d Cir. 1989).

as shareholders, they pay the costs of the defense and any penalties."[15] And the problem of how exactly to deter corporate crime is a knotty one given the corporate structure. Columbia Professor John Coffee once observed, "the problem of corporate punishment seems perversely insoluble: moderate fines do not deter, while severe penalties flow through the corporate shell and fall on the relatively blameless."[16]

In the past few decades, corporate crimes have become the new normal. "In 1980, *Fortune* magazine surveyed 1,043 large companies and concluded that a 'surprising' and 'startling' number (about 11 percent) of them had been involved in 'blatant illegalities.' Two years later, *US News and World Report* conducted a similar survey of America's largest 500 companies and found that, in the preceding decade, 115 had been convicted of at least one major crime. In 1990, the *New York Times* found that 25 out of the 100 largest Pentagon contractors had been found guilty of procurement fraud in the preceding seven years."[17] In 1999, *Mother Jones* reported about the 100 top corporate criminals of the 1990s who had criminal fines levied against term ranging from $150,000 to $500,000,000.[18] And in 2002, *Congressional Quarterly* listed corporate criminals who had become household names.[19] From 2002 to 2007, there was a federal Corporate Fraud Task Force that racked up 1,236 convictions.[20]

B. Prosecutorial Discretion

If one looks at Title 18 of the U.S. Code, corporations are criminally liable for all sorts of crimes[21] including conspiracy, RICO, mail and wire fraud, ob-

---

15. ROBERT A.G. MONKS & NELL MINOW, WATCHING THE WATCHERS: CORPORATE GOVERNANCE FOR THE 21ST CENTURY 22 (1996).

16. *Id.* at 23 (quoting John Coffee).

17. MONKS & MINOW, *supra* note 4, at 31.

18. Russell Mokhiber & Robert Weissman, *Top 100 Corporate Criminals of the 1990s*, MOTHER JONES (Sept. 7, 1999), http://www.motherjones.com/politics/1999/09/top-100-corporate-criminals-1990s.

19. Kenneth Jost, *Corporate Crime Are Tougher Regulations and Sentences Needed?*, CQ (Oct. 11, 2002), http://library.cqpress.com/cqresearcher/document.php?id=cqresrre2002101100 (listing Adelphia, Enron, ImClone, Tyco, and WorldCom).

20. ELLEN S. PODGOR ET AL., WHITE COLLAR CRIME 27 (2013).

21. BRANDON L. GARRETT, TOO BIG TO JAIL HOW PROSECUTORS COMPROMISE WITH CORPORATIONS 23 (2014).

struction of justice, and Foreign Corrupt Practices Act (FCPA) violations.[22] Yet corporations are frequently not being prosecuted criminally. Why? This choice appears to be the result of prosecutorial discretion, especially at the U.S. Department of Justice (DOJ). As Judge Emmet Sullivan indicated in 2015, "deferred-prosecution agreements appear to be offered relatively sparingly to individuals, and instead are used proportionally more frequently to avoid the prosecution of corporations …"[23] He noted that Congress allowed for deferred prosecution agreements based in part on juvenile justice programs to rehabilitate young nonviolent offenders. But over time, "the government increasingly now offers … to defer prosecution of a corporation for criminal misconduct in exchange for the payment of a fine and the institution of compliance measures."[24] Why more settlements than prosecutions are happening is a matter of dispute. One explanation for this is the impact of the botched Arthur Andersen prosecution. While Arthur Andersen LLP was organized as a partnership, and not a corporation, it appears to have cast a pall over business prosecutions generally.

After the fraud at Enron became public, its auditor Arthur Andersen was prosecuted.[25] DOJ threw the book at Arthur Andersen because it had multiple previous accounting fraud issues.[26] Arthur Andersen was convicted of a single felony count of obstructing an official government proceeding, and that

---

22. Podgor et al., *supra* note 20, at 24.

23. U.S. v. Saena Tech Corporation, Criminal No. 14-66(EGS) & U.S. v. Intelligent Decisions, Inc., Criminal No. 14-211 (EGS), Memorandum Opinion 26 (Oct. 21, 2015) (Sullivan, J.), https://ecf.dcd.uscourts.gov/cgi-bin/show_public_doc?2014cr0066-45.

24. *Id.* at 68.

25. Kurt Eichenwald, *Enron's Many Strands: The Investigation; Andersen Charged with Obstruction in Enron Inquiry*, N.Y. Times (Mar. 15, 2002), http://www.nytimes.com/2002/03/15/business/enron-s-many-strands-investigation-andersen-charged-with-obstruction-enron.html ("In the first criminal charge ever brought against a major accounting firm, Arthur Andersen has been indicted on a single count of obstruction of justice for destroying thousands of documents related to the Enron investigation …").

26. Francine McKenna, *Why the Ghost of Arthur Andersen No Longer Haunts Corporate Criminals*, MarketWatch (May 21, 2015), http://www.marketwatch.com/story/why-the-ghost-of-arthur-andersen-no-longer-haunts-corporate-criminals-2015-05-21 ("The SEC may have played hardball because Arthur Andersen … was a recidivist. Andersen had previously admitted to its involvement in numerous other fraudulent accounting schemes. The firm had settled criminal charges in 1996 by agreeing to a DPA. Shortly before the Enron fraud…, the SEC fined and censured Andersen and three partners more than $7 million in connection with audits of Waste Management Inc.'s annual financial results. The firm was again permanently enjoined from violating the federal securities laws."); *see also* Garrett, *supra* note 21, at 22 ("Andersen was already on thin ice as a recidivist.").

conviction barred Andersen from auditing the financial statements of publicly traded companies.[27] The Fifth Circuit Court of Appeals affirmed the conviction.[28] During the litigation, Arthur Andersen imploded, and thousands of employees, most of whom had nothing to do with the Enron fraud, lost or left their jobs.[29] By one count, 28,000 people lost their jobs at Arthur Andersen.[30] On appeal at the Supreme Court, Arthur Andersen won its case because of a flawed jury instruction, but the business was already ruined.[31] As Professor Brandon Garrett put it, this was a lose-lose situation for all involved. "The case ended in twin disasters for the company and the prosecutors: a conviction that destroyed the firm yet was thrown out on appeal by the U.S. Supreme Court."[32]

In 2005, the DOJ decided not to pursue Arthur Andersen's prosecution further after the loss at the Supreme Court.[33] The *Washington Post* reported, "a Justice Department spokesman[] said Andersen's nearly defunct status amounted to a 'heavy factor' in the government's decision not to retry the firm."[34] This ex-

---

27. Jonathan Weil & Alexei Barrionuevo, *Arthur Andersen Is Convicted on Obstruction-of-Justice Count*, WALL ST. J. (June 16, 2002), http://www.wsj.com/articles/SB1023469 305374958120.

28. Arthur Andersen LLP v. United States, 544 U.S. 696, 698 (2005) ("As Enron Corporation's financial difficulties became public in 2001, petitioner Arthur Andersen LLP, Enron's auditor, instructed its employees to destroy documents pursuant to its document retention policy. A jury found that this action made petitioner guilty of violating 18 U.S.C. §§ 1512(b)(2)(A) and (B).... The Court of Appeals for the Fifth Circuit affirmed.").

29. Lawrence D. Finder & Ryan D. McConnell, *Devolution of Authority: The Department of Justice's Corporate Charging Policies*, 51 ST. LOUIS U. L.J. 1, 14–15 (2006) (footnotes omitted).

30. Charles Lane, *Justices Overturn Andersen Conviction*, WASH. POST (June 1, 2005), http://www.washingtonpost.com/wp-dyn/content/article/2005/05/31/AR2005053100491.html ("The Chicago-based firm has a staff of only 200 left out of the 28,000 people who once worked there.").

31. Arthur Andersen LLP v. United States, 544 U.S. 696, 698 (2005) ("We hold that the jury instructions failed to convey properly the elements of a 'corrup[t] persua[sion]' conviction under § 1512(b), and therefore reverse."); *see also* GARRETT, *supra* note 21, at 86 ("In 2001, Andersen had more than 85,000 employees, but by the end of 2002, only 3,000 remained."); Lane, *supra* note 30.

32. GARRETT, *supra* note 21, at 13.

33. Carrie Johnson, *U.S. Ends Prosecution of Arthur Andersen*, WASH. POST (Nov. 23, 2005), http://www.washingtonpost.com/wp-dyn/content/article/2005/11/22/AR2005112 201852.html ("The Justice Department yesterday abandoned its prosecution of Arthur Andersen LLP, walking away from one of the signature cases in its drive to eradicate corporate fraud.").

34. *Id.*; Michael Cohn, *Andersen to Pay Additional $38M for WorldCom Audits*, ACCTG. TODAY (Oct. 18, 2012), http://www.accountingtoday.com/news/arthur-andersen-settlement-worldcom-audits-64365-1.html ("Andersen voluntarily surrendered its CPA license in 2002

perience has appeared to chasten prosecutors, who are now incredibly reluctant to bring criminal charges against a corporation for fear of the collateral consequences associated with charging a company criminally.[35] The impact on the corporate defendant bar is also a factor. The destruction of Arthur Andersen has also acted a catalyst for defense lawyers to cut plea deals with the government more readily, instead of duking it out in court.[36] The lesson from Arthur Andersen from the corporate side could well have been that even winning a case in court did not save the firm, and thus the prudent course of action is to settle early with federal prosecutors.[37] Whatever the cause, following Arthur Andersen, "the use of pre-trial agreements exploded."[38] For instance, the DOJ decided to settle with accounting firm KPMG instead of prosecuting that firm criminally in 2005.[39]

Former U.S. Attorneys Lawrence D. Finder and Ryan D. McConnell note that another driving force in deferred and nonprosecution is the U.S. Attor-

---

in the wake of auditing and accounting scandals at its clients WorldCom and Enron. Most of its partners joined other auditing firms as clients also fled to competing firms.").

35. Geoff Colvin & Ryan Derousseau, *Power Sheet*, FORTUNE (Sept. 11, 2015), http://fortune.com/2015/09/11/power-sheet-september-11-2015/ ("when a corporation ... is convicted of a crime, who actually suffers? ... By charging the company, not just the individuals involved, Justice immediately ended the firm's 89-year history; no company will hire an indicted auditor.").

36. Candace Zierdt & Ellen S. Podgor, *Corporate Deferred Prosecutions Through the Looking Glass of Contract Policing*, 96 Ky. L.J. 1, 3–4 (2007–2008) ("corporations are deprived of basic contract rights as a result of the over-powering prosecutorial power used in reaching these agreements.").

37. Charles Doyle, *Corporate Criminal Liability: An Overview of Federal Law*, CONGRESSIONAL RESEARCH SERVICE 12 (Oct. 30, 2013) https://www.fas.org/sgp/crs/misc/R43293.pdf ("The common perception is that the announcement of its indictment sounds a large corporation's death knell. Consequently, a large corporation, threatened with the prospect of indictment, may be inclined to accept a deferred prosecution agreement or a non-prosecution agreement at terms particularly favorable to the government.").

38. Finder & McConnell, *supra* note 29, at 14–15 (footnotes omitted).

39. Johnson, *U.S. Ends Prosecution of Arthur Andersen*, *supra* note 33 ("Justice Department officials took a markedly different approach with accounting giant KPMG LLP earlier this year. That firm was allowed to pay $456 million and institute stark changes to its business practices as part of a deal in which it avoided criminal prosecution over its sale and marketing of abusive tax shelters. KPMG could still face legal jeopardy if it violates the terms of the August agreement."); McKenna, *supra* note 26 ("Andersen's fellow global public accounting firm, KPMG, was also threatened with a criminal indictment for tax fraud in 2005 but ultimately spared by then Attorney General Alberto Gonzales ... [who] said, '[this] reflects the reality that the conviction of an organization can affect innocent workers and others associated with the organization, and can even have an impact on the national economy.'").

ney's Manual, which guides the behavior of attorneys working at DOJ. "The U.S. Attorneys' Manual ... notes that '[t]he offender must acknowledge responsibility for his or her behavior, but is not asked to admit guilt.' Finally, after completion of the pre-trial diversion agreement, the Manual confirms a declination of prosecution—every corporate defendant's dream."[40] However, as financial reporter Francine McKenna explains, more than the Arthur Andersen episode explains the reluctance of DOJ to go after corporations criminally. A memo written by then-Deputy Attorney General Eric Holder also had a significant impact on corporate prosecutions. As Ms. McKenna wrote: "DOJ was concerned about potential collateral consequences of criminal prosecutions of corporations long before Andersen. Eric Holder ... wrote in 1999 that government officials could take into account collateral consequences when prosecuting corporate crimes."[41] The Holder memo has eight factors for prosecutors to consider when deciding whether to charge a corporation criminally, including "[c]ollateral consequences, including disproportionate harm to shareholders and employees not proven personally culpable[.]"[42] The Holder Memo explained collateral consequence in the following manner:

> In the corporate context, prosecutors may take into account the possibly substantial consequences to a corporation's officers, directors, employees, and shareholders, many of whom may, depending on the size and nature (e.g., publicly vs. closely held) of the corporation and their role in its operations, have played no role in the criminal conduct, have been completely unaware of it, or have been wholly unable to prevent it.... Virtually every conviction of a corporation ... will have an impact on innocent third parties, and the mere existence of such an effect is not sufficient to preclude prosecution of the corporation. Therefore, in evaluating the severity of collateral consequences, various factors already discussed, such as the pervasiveness of the criminal conduct and the adequacy of the corporation's compliance programs should also be considered in determining the weight to be given to this factor.[43]

---

40. Finder & McConnell, *supra* note 29, at 12–13 (citing U.S. DEP'T OF JUSTICE, UNITED STATES ATTORNEYS' MANUAL 9–22 (1997)).

41. McKenna, *supra* note 26.

42. Finder & McConnell, *supra* note 29 at 8–9 (2006) (citing Holder memo).

43. Memorandum from Eric Holder, Deputy Att'y Gen., U.S. Dep't of Justice to Component Heads and U.S. Attorneys on Bringing Criminal Charges Against Corps. (June 16, 1999), http://www.justice.gov/sites/default/files/criminal-fraud/legacy/2010/04/11/charging-corps.PDF.

Matt Taibbi argued in his book THE DIVIDE that Holder's 1999 Memo was the basis for how Attorney General Holder ran the Department of Justice under President Obama. "Holder couldn't have known it at the time, but through his 1999 Collateral Consequences memo, he had designed a get-out-of-jail-free policy for a kind of company that hadn't existed yet: the too-big-to-fail mega firm that simply couldn't be reined in with conventional criminal laws."[44] Even Attorney General Holder himself told Congress in March 2013. "'I am concerned that ... if we do bring a criminal charge it will have a negative impact on the national economy, perhaps even the world economy.'"[45] At least during the Enron days, the DOJ was willing to step toe to toe with Arthur Andersen. As Deputy Attorney General Larry Thompson said at the time, "'[i]t would be unfortunate for a criminal justice system if any individual or any entity could say that he or she or it was too big or too important to be indicted.'"[46] The reticence to prosecute corporations for wrongdoing is remarkable, especially after the 2008 financial crisis which caused the Great Recession. [47]

UVA Law Professor Brandon Garrett has written about the ways prosecutors compromise with defendant companies in criminal cases. As Professor Garrett explained, "[s]ome companies are not just 'too big to fail' but also 'too big to jail': they are considered to be so valuable to the economy that prosecutors may not hold them accountable for their crimes."[48] Professor Garrett noted that "by 2003, the overriding goal of corporate prosecution was to try to rehabilitate a firm's culture, not to punish."[49] To be clear, it's not the case that there are zero criminal prosecutions of corporations. In fact, there were 2,000 criminal convictions in the 11 years that Professor Garrett studied. Yet Professor Garrett concluded that, after conducting his study of prosecutorial discretion, "the more troubled I have become. Prosecutors allow many large companies to avoid an indictment or a conviction, largely freeing them from judicial oversight. From 2001 through 2012, 58 percent of the companies re-

---

44. MATT TAIBBI, THE DIVIDE: AMERICAN INJUSTICE IN THE AGE OF THE WEALTH GAP 18–19 (2014).

45. McKenna, *supra* note 26 (quoting Holder).

46. *Andersen Indictment and Consequences*, FORBES (Mar. 15, 2002), http://www.forbes.com/2002/03/15/0315topnews.html (quoting Thompson).

47. Taibbi, *supra* note 44, at 18 (corporations "raced around the earth in search of tax, labor, and other advantages. The whole world with its myriad sets of laws and rules presented endless opportunities for regulatory arbitrage. It would be harder for the cop on the beat to chase an offender that simultaneously existed everywhere and nowhere.").

48. GARRETT, *supra* note 21, at 47.

49. *Id.*

ceiving deferred prosecution or non-prosecution agreements were publicly listed on a U.S. stock exchange[.]"[50]

Financial institutions, in particular, seem to benefit from deferred and non-prosecution agreements.[51] And this has struck many Americans as unjust. At the time of the 2008 financial crisis, there was a growing disconnect between pay and performance[52] as CEOs (and other top managers) of major financial firms continued to be paid generously while leading their companies into bankruptcy or other financial ruin.[53] As one reporter expounded during the 2008 financial crisis, "[t]he guys who ran the recently collapsed Lehman Bros., Merrill Lynch, Bear Stearns, Fannie Mae, and Freddie Mac all prove one thing. You don't always get what you pay for."[54] Adding insult to injury, many of the banks that precipitated the financial crisis were both bailed out at taxpayer expense and not prosecuted.

Undoubtedly, the bailout of the banks left a sour impression in the minds of many Americans.[55] A *Washington Post* column written in 2013, five years after the financial crisis, promised a list of the CEOs that had been prosecuted

---

50. *Id.*

51. *Id.* at 65.

52. Gretchen Morgenson, *Say-on-Pay Gets Support at Verizon*, N.Y. TIMES (May 19, 2007), http://www.nytimes.com/2007/05/19/technology/19verizon.html (quoting Brian Foley, "People were frustrated with the way management had been paid relative to performance....").

53. Alyce Lomax, *Is Shareholder "Say on Pay" Working?*, MOTLEY FOOL (Apr. 3, 2014), http://www.fool.com/investing/general/2014/04/03/is-shareholder-say-on-pay-work ing.aspx ("For years, CEO pay rose largely unchecked in America. Although leaders who build great companies deserve pay commensurate to their accomplishments, too many underperforming or lackluster CEOs make astronomical amounts of money at shareholders' expense. It's odd that one class of workers tends to make millions—often without a performance review."); *see also* Interview with Nell Minow, Vice Chair, ValueEdge Advisors (Aug. 19, 2015) ("CEO pay is excessive. It is not related to performance.").

54. Eve Tahmincioglu, *Can wild CEO Pay be Tamed? Probably Not*, MSNBC.COM (Sept. 1, 2008), http://www.nbcnews.com/id/26963309/ns/business-stocks_and_economy/t/can-wild-ceo-pay-be-tamed-probably-not/#.VKYP5orF_pA ("Big paychecks for jobs not well done: Lehman Bros.' Richard Fuld, $40 million. Merrill Lynch's Stanley O'Neal, $46 million. Bear Stearns' James Cayne, $40 million. Freddie Mac's Richard Syron, just shy of $20 million. Fannie Mae's Daniel Mudd, $12.2 million."); Interview with Robert A.G. Monks (Aug. 17, 2015) ("Say on pay has raised consciousness, but it hasn't curbed high executive compensation.").

55. Jacob S. Hacker & Nathaniel Loewentheil, *How Big Money Corrupts the Economy*, 27 DEMOCRACY (2013), http://www.democracyjournal.org/27/how-big-money-corrupts-the-economy.php?page=all ("Middle-class Americans are losing their ... economic security, and they believe government isn't looking out for them. Asked in mid-2010 whom

because of mortgage or bank fraud contributing to the financial crisis. It stated simply: "No one."[56] The financial services industry seems particularly immune from criminal and other sanctions.[57] When a federal judge had the temerity to reject a SEC settlement with Citigroup arising out of alleged financial fraud, he was overturned on appeal by a higher court.[58]

According to Professor Jennifer Taub, the problem of "too big to fail" has gotten worse, not better, in the years since the financial crisis, as banks are even bigger and more concentrated than they were in 2007. As she writes:

> Seven years after the financial crisis began, many of the conditions that helped cause the near collapse of our banking system—and that were used to rationalize the multi-trillion dollar U.S. government rescue—endure. The top six bank holding companies are considerably larger than before ... Compensation incentives fail to discourage mismanagement and illegality, given that when legal fees, settlements, and fines mount, it is usually the shareholders, not the corporate executives, who pay.[59]

Meanwhile, these financial services industries are politically powerful, as the President of Demos Heather McGhee reminded us: "[t]he financial services, real estate and insurance sector contains the most profligate contributors and spenders in politics today. Over the past 20 years they have been the biggest

---

government had helped 'a great deal' during the downturn, 53 percent of Americans said banks and financial institutions. Forty-four percent pointed to large corporations.").

56. Neil Irwin, *This Is a Complete List of Wall Street CEOs Prosecuted for their Role in the Financial Crisis*, Wash. Post (Sept. 12, 2013), https://www.washingtonpost.com/news/wonk/wp/2013/09/12/this-is-a-complete-list-of-wall-street-ceos-prosecuted-for-their-role-in-the-financial-crisis/.

57. Monks interview *supra* note 53 ("The financial service industry has created a new level of 'capture' of government by private industry. They have more effectively freed themselves from governmental supervision and effective regulation than has the industrial sector."); *see also* Interview with Warren Langley, Former President of the Pacific Stock Exchange (July 14, 2015) ("The financial services industry has more conflicts of interest than any other industry.").

58. SEC v. Citigroup Global Markets Inc., No. 11-5227 (L) (2d Cir. 2014), https://www.documentcloud.org/documents/1182923-court-overrules-judge-who-blocked-bank-settlement.html; *see also* Ben Protess & Matthew Goldstein, *Overruled, Judge Still Left a Mark on S.E.C. Agenda*, N.Y. Times (June 4, 2014), http://dealbook.nytimes.com/2014/06/04/appeals-court-overturns-decision-to-reject-s-e-c-citigroup-settlement/.

59. Jennifer Taub, *Still Too Big To Fail: Opportunities for Regulatory Action Seven Years after the Bear Stearns Rescue*, Corporate Reform Coalition 4 (May 7, 2015), http://www.citizen.org/documents/still-too-big-to-fail-crc-report.pdf.

financial beneficiaries of deregulation. The bankruptcy bill of 2005 was written by the credit card industry and was accompanied with bipartisan campaign contributions. This law made it harder for unsecured debtors to modify or discharge debt in bankruptcy, which makes credit cards a less risky business model."[60] And once again, we may have financial firms that are too big to fail because of the structure of privately financed elections.[61] It's also possible that one is not causally connected to the other and both are just happening simultaneously. Ultimately, this is an empirical question. But it is an empirical question that is hard to unravel because of the dark money problem. It's impossible to test whether Bank X is spending in support of Congressman Y and getting special treatment, when the political money is untraceable.

The trends of leniency shown to the financial services industry in terms of deferred and non-prosecutions may just be a piece of a larger trend. As a study from the Transactional Records Access Clearinghouse (TRAC) at Syracuse University showed, white-collar criminal prosecutions are hitting a 20-year low.[62] This study found,

> [f]ederal prosecution of individuals identified by the government as white collar criminals is at its lowest level in the last twenty years, according to the latest data from the Justice Department ... During the first nine months of FY 2015, the government brought 5,173 white-collar crime prosecutions. If the monthly number of these kinds of cases continues at the same pace until the end of the current fiscal year on September 30, the total will be only 6,897 such matters — down by more than one-third (36.8%) from levels seen two decades ago — despite the rise in population and economic activity in the nation during this period.[63]

This study turns on what the definition of "white-collar crime" is.[64]

---

60. Interview with Heather McGhee, President, Demos (Aug. 11, 2015).

61. Taub, *supra* note 59, at 22 ("seven years after the [financial] crisis began, it may be time for Congress to step in where regulators have either left gaps ... Such action in the public interest, however, would require a sufficient number of legislators who truly serve the public and are not influenced by both overt and hidden political spending by financial firms.").

62. *Federal White Collar Crime Prosecution at 20-Year Low*, TRANSACTIONAL RECORDS ACCESS CLEARINGHOUSE (July 29, 2015), http://trac.syr.edu/tracreports/crim/398/.

63. *Id.*

64. The TRAC study used the Department of Justice's definition, but this definition could be underinclusive, and thus the measurement may undercount white collar crime prosecutions. *See also* Ellen S. Podgor & Lucian E. Dervan, *'White Collar Crime': Still Hazy*

And a more troubling study from George Mason University found a trend of deferred prosecutions or nonprosecutions of publicly traded corporations that were accused of breaking criminal laws.[65] The George Mason study found, "[a]greements with public companies to resolve criminal allegations grew substantially over the 1997–2011 period. In 1997, only 11 criminal cases involving public companies were settled, but rapid growth began around 2005, leading to a four-fold increase in the number of settlements by 2011."[66]

The impression that is hard to escape is that corporations are being excused from legal responsibilities that average citizens endure for far smaller criminal infractions. After all, the United States imprisons more people per capita than any other nation. The latest data available shows that U.S. state and federal prisons held an estimated 1,561,500 inmates on December 31, 2014.[67] Meanwhile, deferred prosecutions for individuals are strikingly low.[68] Yet, for large corporations, the same criminal rules don't seem to apply.

After All These Years, 50 (3) Ga. L. Rev. (Forthcoming 2016), available at http://ssrn.com/abstract=2628751.

65. Cindy R. Alexander & Mark A. Cohen, *Trends in the Use of Non-Prosecution, Deferred Prosecution, and Plea Agreements in the Settlement of Alleged Corporate Criminal Wrongdoing*, George Mason U. Sch. of Law Ctr for Law & Economics 1 (Apr. 2015), http://masonlec.org/site/rte_uploads/files/Full%20Report%20-%20SCJI%20NPA-DPA%2C%20April%202015%281%29.pdf.

66. *Id.* at 28.

67. Press Release, Bureau of Justice Statistics, *U.S. Prison Population Declined One Percent in 2014* (Sept. 17, 2015), http://www.bjs.gov/content/pub/press/p14pr.cfm.

68. U.S. v. Saena Tech Corporation, *supra* note 23, at 72 ("Department of Justice statistics indicate that in fiscal year 2012, there were a total of 253 pretrial diversions for individual defendants, accounting for 0.9% of the reasons why Assistant United States Attorneys declined to prosecute.").

Chapter 9

Death and Chocolate

Even where businesses act in violation of domestic laws or international conventions protecting human rights, limited domestic law enforcement capabilities undermine the force of accountability standards.
—Council on Foreign Relations[1]

International human rights law has evolved in reaction to new challenges. The experience of the Holocaust in Europe and World War II led to the creation of new institutions like the United Nations and a new consensus about human rights as embodied in the Universal Declaration of Human Rights. Since World War II, international law has imposed obligations on nation states to protect human rights.[2] Now that there are corporations with more resources than nation states, should they also be liable for human rights violations, especially if they colluded with state actors to cause the human rights abuses?[3] Certain firms have been sued in American courts for aiding and abetting human rights abuses from murder, rape and torture to child slavery—some of the original sins of the German Holocaust.[4] However, under recent Supreme

1. *The Global Human Rights Regime Issue Brief*, Council on Foreign Relations (June 19, 2013), http://www.cfr.org/human-rights/global-human-rights-regime/p27450.

2. Universal Declaration of Human Rights, G.A. Res. 217 (III) A, U.N. Doc. A/RES/217(III) (Dec. 10, 1948); International Covenant on Civil and Political Rights, Dec. 16, 1966, S. Exec. Rep. 102-23, 999 U.N.T.S. 171; UN General Assembly, International Covenant on Economic, Social and Cultural Rights, Dec. 16, 1966, United Nations, Treaty Series, vol. 993, p. 3.

3. Vincent Trivett, *25 US Mega Corporations: Where They Rank If They Were Countries*, Bus. Insider (Jun. 27, 2011, 11:27 AM), http://www.businessinsider.com/25-corporations-bigger-tan-countries-2011-6.

4. Dr. Jennifer Zerk, *Corporate Liability for Gross Human Rights Abuses Towards a Fairer and More Effective System of Domestic Law Remedies*, Office of the UN High Commis-

Court decisions, it is becoming increasingly difficult for plaintiffs to find relief in U.S. courts.

If certain corporations are picking and choosing the responsibilities that they must abide by, one responsibility they are trying to avoid assiduously is being held liable for human rights laws. Logically, one way to avoid such liability is to never take any action that could be misconstrued as a human rights violation. This is not how specific corporations are avoiding this legal peril. Instead, some corporations are facilitating human rights abuses and then making legal arguments in courts about why they should not be held responsible. These corporations clearly do not want the responsibility of answering for aiding and abetting violations of these international law norms. The question is: will courts excuse them from this set of responsibilities? Indeed, certain corporations have given themselves black eyes in the area of human rights abuses, especially in the Third World.[5] These actions have also led to a complex set of legal questions including: can corporations be held legally accountable? And if so, where? Consider, for example, the chocolatiers Nestle or Hershey's. If they are knowingly buying from farms that use child slaves as laborers—a universally condemned human rights abuse—should they be held legally accountable for facilitating this slavery? The story of chocolate and child slavery will be discussed in more detail below. But first, here's how the human rights law of holding corporations accountable (or not) in the United States is developing.

A. *Doe v. Unocal*

Human rights litigator Marco Simons at Earth Rights International explained, "[m]ost of our litigation in U.S. courts is directly against corporations who are alleged to have to committed various egregious violations of human rights and contributed to environmental degradation of vulnerable commu-

---

SIONER FOR HUMAN RIGHTS 13 (2013), http://www.ohchr.org/Documents/Issues/Business/ DomesticLawRemedies/StudyDomesticeLawRemedies.pdf ("After the Second World War, senior managers and representatives of several companies were convicted in military courts of grave human rights abuses as a result of their contributions, through their respective business activities, to aggression and atrocities carried out by the Nazi regime. In the decades since, there have been numerous allegations, from almost every part of the world, of corporate involvement in gross human rights abuses either directly, or by reason of their associations with State authorities, militia or rebel groups, police and security providers.").

5. Interview with Retired Montana Supreme Court Justice James Nelson (Aug. 4, 2015) ("Human beings are being beaten to a pulp around the world ... by two institutions that should be working for them: one is government and the other is big business.").

nities."[6] He continued, "[i]ncreasingly, corporations, especially large multinational corporations, are both heavily implicated in enabling abuses and partnering with the state in abusive projects, as well as rivaling the power of the state in many circumstances."[7] Take for example the abuses meted out by certain extractive industries building oil pipelines abroad, including in Burma where the building of an oil pipeline resulted in multiple abusive and violent practices including "summary executions of villagers who lived there."[8] As Marco Simons narrated:

> Essentially what Unocal and its French partner Total did was partner with the Burmese government in order to use the Burmese military as their security force. They were using the Burmese military both to recruit labor for projects in support of the pipeline and provide security for the pipeline corridor. In the course of doing so, they engaged in widespread forced labor practices as well as in a series of widespread human rights abuses including torture, rape, and murder.[9]

These events in Burma led to an unprecedented legal case attempting to hold the corporate actors responsible.[10] Victims along the pipeline in Burma sued Unocal and its executives using the Alien Tort Statute in a ground breaking case, *Doe v. Unocal*, which established the principle that corporations could be sued in U.S. courts for complicity in human rights abuses.[11] The federal

---

6. Interview with Marco Simons, General Counsel EarthRights International (July 9, 2015).

7. *Id.*

8. Katie Redford, Introduction to Lisa Girion's *Pipeline to Justice* (2003) in the *L.A. Times* in Global Muckraking 100 Years of Investigative Journalism from around the World (Anya Schiffin ed.) at 140 (2014).

9. Simons interview *supra* note 6.

10. Doe v. Unocal Corp., 963 F. Supp. 880, 891 (C.D. Cal. 1997) (allowing suit to go forward); *see also* the parallel state court case Doe I v. Unocal Corp., 2002 WL 33944505 ("Unocal Defendants' Motion for Summary Judgment Based on Absence of Vicarious Liability is DENIED.").

11. *Doe v. Unocal* Case History, Earth Rights International, http://www.earthrights.org/legal/doe-v-unocal-case-history (last visited Sept. 3, 2015); *see also* Doe v. Unocal Corp., 248 F.3d 915, 920 (9th Cir. 2001) ("According to plaintiffs' complaint, defendants, through the SLORC military, intelligence and/or police forces, have used and continue to use violence and intimidation to relocate whole villages and force farmers living in the area of the proposed pipeline to work on the pipeline.... Plaintiffs allege defendants' conduct has caused plaintiffs to suffer death of family members, assault, rape and other torture, forced labor, and the loss of their homes, in violation of California law, federal law and customary international law.") (denying jurisdiction over the French corporation Total).

district judge who first heard the case, ruled, "[the Burmese] Plaintiffs have alleged that [Unocal and Total] were and are jointly engaged with the state officials in the challenged activity, namely forced labor and other human rights violations in furtherance of the pipeline project. These allegations are sufficient to support subject-matter jurisdiction under the [Alien Tort Statute]."[12]

The Alien Tort Statute (ATS) is one of America's oldest, enacted by the very first Congress.[13] The ATS is incredibly terse. It reads,

> Alien's action for tort:
> The district courts shall have original jurisdiction of any civil action by an alien for a tort only, committed in violation of the law of nations or a treaty of the United States.[14]

That is the whole statute. But it has been given new life in the hands of human rights attorneys who are using it to bring suits against multinational companies that they allege have aided and abetted human rights violations. Although the *Unocal* case was eventually settled,[15] its trip through both federal and state courts, "put global corporations on notice that they could be held accountable for their involvement in human rights abuses where they operate, sending a strong message of deterrence and forcing them to factor human rights risks into their bottom line."[16]

---

12. Doe v. Unocal Corp., 963 F. Supp. 880, 891 (C.D. Cal. 1997); Doe I v. Unocal Corp., 395 F.3d 932, 962 (9th Cir. 2002) ("we REVERSE the District Court's grant of summary judgment in favor of Unocal on Plaintiffs' [Alien Tort Statute] claims for forced labor, murder, and rape.") This Ninth Circuit opinion was vacated when the Ninth Circuit agreed to hear the case en banc. Doe I v. Unocal Corp., 395 F.3d 978, 979 (9th Cir. 2003) ("The three-judge panel opinion shall not be cited as precedent by or to this court or any district court of the Ninth Circuit, except to the extent adopted by the en banc court."). Then the case was settled before the Ninth Circuit could rule again. Doe I v. Unocal Corp., 403 F.3d 708 (9th Cir. 2005).

13. Lyle Denniston, Kiobel: *Made Simple*, SCOTUS BLOG (July 6, 2012), http://www.scotusblog.com/2012/07/kiobel-made-simple/.

14. 8 U.S.C. § 1350 (1789).

15. *Doe v. Unocal* Case History, *supra* note 11.

16. Katie Redford, Introduction to Lisa Girion's *Pipeline to Justice?* (2003) in *L.A. Times* in GLOBAL MUCKRAKING 100 YEARS OF INVESTIGATIVE JOURNALISM FROM AROUND THE WORLD (Anya Schiffin ed.) at 140-141 (2014).

B. *Kiobel v. Royal Dutch Petroleum*

In a partial rebuke to the *Doe v. Unocal* approach of allowing ATS claims against corporations, in 2010, the Second Circuit issued a split opinion in *Kiobel v. Royal Dutch Petroleum Co.*, ruling that the U.S. courts did not have jurisdiction over Shell for alleged human rights abuses in Nigeria. In particular, the appellate court ruled that corporations could not be held liable under the Alien Tort Statute (ATS).[17] This was an outlier approach to the ATS.[18]

In contrast to the Second Circuit's methodology, contemporaneously Judge Judith W. Rogers of D.C. Circuit held in *Doe v. Exxon* that,

> [g]iven that the law of every jurisdiction in the United States and of every civilized nation, and the law of numerous international treaties, provide that corporations are responsible for their torts, it would create a bizarre anomaly to immunize corporations from liability for the conduct of their agents in lawsuits brought for shockingly egregious violations of universally recognized principles of international law.[19]

Similarly, the Seventh Circuit's Judge Posner concluded "[i]t is neither surprising nor significant that corporate liability hasn't figured in prosecutions of war criminals and other violators of customary international law. That doesn't mean that corporations are exempt from that law."[20] No other court besides the Second Circuit in *Kiobel* had ever come to the conclusion of law that the ATS could not be used to litigate against a corporate actor.[21]

When *Kiobel* was appealed to the Supreme Court, one of the key questions was: can a corporation be sued (or not) under the Alien Tort Statute? A 2012 case called *Mohamad v. Palestinian Authority,* which had excused corporations from being defendants under Torture Victim Protection Act, found that the

---

17. Kiobel v. Royal Dutch Petroleum Co., 621 F.3d 111, 148 (2d Cir. 2010).

18. Romero v. Drummond Co., Inc., 552 F.3d 1303, 1315 (11th Cir. 2008) (stating that "the law of th[at] Circuit is that [the ATS] grants jurisdiction from complaints of torture against corporate defendants"); *see also* Herero People's Reparations Corp. v. Deutsche Bank, A.G., 370 F.3d 1192, 1193, 1195 (D.C. Cir. 2004); Wiwa v. Royal Dutch Petroleum Co., 226 F.3d 88, 91–92 (2d Cir. 2000); Beanal v. Freeport-McMoran, Inc., 197 F.3d 161, 163 (5th Cir. 1999); Abdullahi v. Pfizer, Inc., 562 F.3d 163, 174 (2d Cir. 2009); Sarei v. Rio Tinto, PLC, 550 F.3d 822, 831 (9th Cir. 2008) (en banc).

19. Doe v. Exxon Mobil Corp., 654 F.3d 11, 57 (D.C. Cir. 2011), *vacated on other grounds*, 527 Fed. Appx. 7 (D.C. Cir. 2013) (quotations omitted).

20. Flomo v. Firestone Natural Rubber Co., 643 F.3d 1013, 1019 (7th Cir. 2011).

21. *Id.* at 1017 ("The outlier [on corporate liability] is the split decision in *Kiobel v. Royal Dutch Petroleum Co.*, 621 F.3d 111 (2d Cir. 2010).").

term "individual," at least in that Act, only included natural persons.[22] Would the Court apply similar reasoning in *Kiobel*? Much to the chagrin of many involved in the case on both sides, the Supreme Court was not clear in answering this question in its final *Kiobel* opinion, which while 9–0, was spread over four different opinions, and displayed a range of disagreements among the Justices.

But before there was a Supreme Court case, there were atrocities in Nigeria. In the 1950s, Shell Petroleum Development Company of Nigeria (SPDC) found oil in Ogoniland, Nigeria.[23] The indigenous people of the region, the Ogoni, alleged that Shell's oil wells, pipeline, and consequent oil spills had spoiled arable land in the area negatively impacting their ability to farm the land for both food and income. The legitimate complaints by the Ogoni included toxic pollution from "daily gas flaring, and resultant emissions of carbon monoxide, carbon dioxide, soot, methane, and other substances that reduce soil fertility and pollute the water used for drinking and fisheries."[24] According to the United Nations, much of Ogoniland is still contaminated from the oil production.[25]

In 1990, members of the local Ogoni population formed the Movement for the Survival of the Ogoni People (MOSOP). MOSOP started a "campaign against Royal Dutch/Shell, the region's largest oil producer, demanding that it stop its environmental devastation of the Ogonis' indigenous lands."[26] Journal-

---

22. Kiobel v. Royal Dutch Petroleum, The Oyez Project at IIT Chicago-Kent College of Law, http://www.oyez.org/cases/2010-2019/2011/2011_10_1491 (oral argument at 0:00–4:07); *Mohamad v. Palestinian Authority*, 566 U.S. _ (2012).

23. Bruno Pierri, *A New Entry into the World Oil Market: Nigeria and Its Relations with the Atlantic Powers, 1967–1973*, 1(2) EUNOMIA 105–150 (2012).

24. Chinedu Reginald Ezetah, *International Law of Self-Determination and the Ogoni Question: Mirroring Africa's Post-Colonial Dilemma*, 19 LOY. L.A. INT'L & COMP. L.J. 811, 814–15 (1997).

25. United Nations Environmental Programme, *UNEP Ogoniland Oil Assessment Reveals Extent of Environmental Contamination and Threats to Human Health; Drinking Water Pollution in Some Places So Serious Immediate Emergency Action Needed; Full Environmental Restoration May Take Up to 30 Years with Calls for an Initial US$1 Billion Fund to Kick-Start Clean-Up* (Aug. 4, 2011), http://www.unep.org/disastersandconflicts/Portals/155/countries/nigeria/press_release_ogoniland_en.pdf ("The environmental restoration of Ogoniland could prove to be the world's most wide-ranging and long term oil clean-up exercise ever undertaken if contaminated drinking water, land, creeks and important ecosystems such as mangroves are to be brought back to full, productive health.").

26. Clifford Bob, Introduction to Ken Saro-Wiwa's *The Coming War in the Delta* (1990) in *Sunday Times* in GLOBAL MUCKRAKING 100 YEARS OF INVESTIGATIVE JOURNALISM FROM AROUND THE WORLD (Anya Schiffin ed.) at 118 (2014).

ist Ken Saro-Wiwa[27] wrote at the time, the Ogoni people "are faced by a Company—Shell—whose management policies are racist and cruelly stupid, and which is out to exploit and encourage Nigerian ethnocentricism."[28] MOSOP was particularly effective at organizing and in 1993, in commemoration of the United Nations Year of Indigenous People, "MOSOP mobilized 300,000 Ogoni (out of 500,000 total population) to come out in support of the Ogoni Bill of Rights and of its demand to Shell, in a day of non-violent demonstrations."[29]

The corporate response to MOSOP's nonviolent organizing in Nigeria was swift, relentless and violent:[30]

> Shell asked its business partner, the dictatorial Nigerian government, for help. In response to Shell's request, the Nigerian government launched a hostile campaign toward the Ogoni people which included 'extrajudicial executions, rapes, looting, beatings, shooting, and arrests and detentions completely lacking in due process protections.'... Nigerian security forces have attacked, burned and destroyed several Ogoni villages and homes under the pretext of dislodging officials and supporters of the Movement of the Survival of Ogoni People (MOSOP). These attacks have come in response to MOSOP's nonviolent campaign in opposition to the destruction of their environment by oil companies.[31]

---

27. Marion Campbell, *Witnessing Death: Ken Saro-Wiwa and the Ogoni Crisis*, 5 POST-COLONIAL STUDIES 39, 39–40 (2002) ("Ken Saro-Wiwa ... was part of an intellectual elite that had easy access to influential and lucrative government positions [in Nigeria]; the stumbling block for him was his Ogoni ethnicity in a region dominated by the Igbo.").

28. *Ken Saro-Wiwa, The Coming War in the Delta* (1990) in *Sunday Times* in GLOBAL MUCKRAKING 100 YEARS OF INVESTIGATIVE JOURNALISM FROM AROUND THE WORLD (Anya Schiffin ed.) at 119 (2014).

29. Elizabeth A. Wilson, *Kiobel, the ATS, and Human Rights Litigation in U.S. Courts*, 107 AM. SOC'Y INT'L L. PROC. 155, 157 (2013).

30. Robert Dufresne, *The Opacity of Oil: Oil Corporations, Internal Violence, and International Law*, 36 N.Y.U. J. INT'L L. & POL. 331, 336–37 (2004) ("The case of Shell operating in Ogoniland in Nigeria is notorious: The Ogoni people campaigned against the alliance between the federal government and multinational oil corporations, articulating their claims in terms of minority rights and claims against exploitation and pollution. Contestation by the Ogonis intensified and was repeatedly met by repression.").

31. Kathleen Morris, *The Emergence of Customary International Law Recognizing Corporate Liability for Violations of International Human Rights and Environmental Law*, 11 GONZ. J. INT'L L. 4 (2008).

Ken Saro-Wiwa was specifically targeted for his leadership role in MOSOP.[32] The trial and death of the author brought negative notoriety to Nigeria as the trial was internationally condemned as a fraud.[33] Before his death even "the Pope pleaded for clemency,"[34] but to no avail. His family ended up suing Shell in a case called *Wiwa*.[35] The *Wiwa* case was settled with Shell on the eve of trial for $15.5 million.[36]

The 12 plaintiffs in the *Kiobel* case, filed in 2002, alleged many of the same claims as the *Wiwa* plaintiffs, accusing Royal Dutch Petroleum and Shell Transport and Trading (Shell) of "torture, prolonged arbitrary detention, and crimes against humanity during the mid-1990s, charging Shell with complicity with the military dictatorship in Nigeria."[37] Ms. Kiobel, the named lead plaintiff, was Mr. Kiobel's widow. According to Amnesty International: "[i]n January 1995, when Ms. Kiobel visited her husband Barinem in a Nigerian prison to bring him some food, she was stripped, beaten and thrown into a cell herself."[38] Barinem Kiobel and Ken Saro-Wiwa were executed alongside seven other activists from the Ogoni region of Nigeria in 1995.[39]

The original question in *Kiobel* heard by the Supreme Court was whether the Alien Tort Statute could be applied to corporations. Shell's position was,

---

32. Dufresne, *supra* note 30, at 336–37.

33. Morris, *supra* note 31, at 4.

34. *Id.*

35. Wiwa v. Royal Dutch Petroleum Co., No. 96 CIV. 8386 (KMW), 2002 WL 319887, at *2 (S.D.N.Y. Feb. 28, 2002).

36. Ed Pilkington, *Shell Pays Out $15.5m over Saro-Wiwa Killing*, THE GUARDIAN (June 8, 2009), http://www.theguardian.com/world/2009/jun/08/nigeria-usa.

37. Jennifer Green, *The Rule of Law at a Crossroad: Enforcing Corporate Responsibility in International Investment through the Alien Tort Statute*, 35 U. PA. J. INT'L L. 1085, 1097–1101 (2014); *see also* Ingrid Wuerth, *Kiobel v. Royal Dutch Petroleum Co.: The Supreme Court and the Alien Tort Statute*, 107 AM. J. INT'L L. 601, 604 (2013) ("Events in Ogoniland provided the basis for several lawsuits filed in the United States against an individual and entities related to the corporation now known as Royal Dutch Shell. These cases include *Kiobel*. The complaint alleged that Royal Dutch Petroleum Company (incorporated in the Netherlands), Shell Transport and Trading Company (incorporated in England), and Shell Petroleum Development Company of Nigeria (incorporated in Nigeria) aided and abetted the Nigerian military in committing extrajudicial killing, torture, crimes against humanity, and other human rights violations. The plaintiffs, including Esther Kiobel, whose husband was one of the men sentenced to death and executed in 1995, now live in the United States, where they have been granted political asylum.").

38. Erica Razook, *Corporate Accountability Comes Before the U.S. Supreme Court*, AMNESTY INTERNATIONAL (Mar. 2, 2012), http://blog.amnestyusa.org/africa/corporate-accountability-comes-before-the-u-s-supreme-court/.

39. *Id.*

"corporations are not responsible for human rights abuses under such circumstances; that individual employees who are complicit in torture, summary executions and other crimes against humanity can be held liable, but not corporations."[40] But after the first oral argument, the Supreme Court set the case for re-argument. In re-argument, the question changed radically to whether the Alien Tort Statute could apply extraterritorially (beyond the U.S. shores),[41] despite the fact that "[t]here was nothing about extraterritoriality in the Second Circuit [in *Kiobel*]."[42] In *Kiobel*, the Supreme Court indicated that they presume that all U.S. laws end at the shore of the U.S., unless Congress has made it clear that they intend for a particular law to apply abroad. As the Supreme Court noted, "[f]or us to run interference in ... a delicate field of international relations there must be present the affirmative intention of the Congress clearly expressed.... The presumption against extraterritorial application helps ensure that the Judiciary does not erroneously adopt an interpretation of U.S. law that carries foreign policy consequences not clearly intended by the political branches."[43]

One of the ways the Supreme Court conceptualized *Kiobel* is that the case presented a "foreign cubed" fact pattern. "Foreign cubed" means that the lawsuit was filed by foreign plaintiffs against foreign defendants, alleging violations that happened in a foreign location. So one way to think about the *Kiobel* case is: should foreign cubed cases be heard in U.S. courts? The Supreme Court said no. The reasoning from the Court was because this was a "foreign cubed" problem, it would be inappropriate for the U.S. Supreme Court to weigh in on the matter. But on closer inspection, legitimate questions about the Supreme Court's formulation can be raised. For one, is Shell truly a "foreign defendant"? Shell has multiple contacts with the United States. It has an entire web of gas stations in America. Shell Energy North America has an office in Houston, Texas. Its shares trade on the New York Stock Exchange (ticker NYSE: RDS.A). So going back to the characterization of *Kiobel* as a foreign cubed problem, Shell may be Dutch, but it certainly is availing itself of many benefits of locating on American soil, taking American investments and earning profits from American motorists, who pump gas from their American pumps. There's also a reasonable question about how "foreign" the plaintiffs were since "at the time

---

40. Ka Hsaw Wa, *When Big Business and Human Rights Collide*, L.A. Times (Feb. 26, 2012), http://articles.latimes.com/2012/feb/26/opinion/la-oe-ka-nigerians-20120226/2.

41. Kiobel v. Royal Dutch Petroleum, The Oyez Project at IIT Chicago-Kent College of Law, http://www.oyez.org/cases/2010-2019/2011/2011_10_1491 (re-argument at 0:00–3:45).

42. Simons interview *supra* note 6.

43. Kiobel v. Royal Dutch Petroleum Co., 133 S. Ct. 1659, 1664 (2013).

that they brought the suit the plaintiffs were U.S. asylees in the United States."[44] Yet, these facts did not matter to the Supreme Court.

The Supreme Court only obliquely addressed the matter of whether corporations could be defendants in an Alien Torts Statute claim. As the Court concluded:

> On these facts, all the relevant conduct took place outside the United States. And even where the claims touch and concern the territory of the United States, they must do so with sufficient force to displace the presumption against extraterritorial application. Corporations are often present in many countries, and it would reach too far to say that mere corporate presence suffices. If Congress were to determine otherwise, a statute more specific than the ATS [Alien Tort Statute] would be required.[45]

And even though Justice Breyer would argue about other aspects of the case, he didn't dispute this point about "mere corporate presence." In his concurring opinion, he wrote,

> [I]t would be farfetched to believe, based solely upon the defendants' minimal and indirect American presence, that this legal action helps to vindicate a distinct American interest, such as in not providing a safe harbor for an "enemy of all mankind." Thus I agree with the Court that here it would "reach too far to say" that such "mere corporate presence suffices."[46]

The textual analysis conducted by the Supreme Court in *Kiobel* will strike some as disingenuous. For example, the Supreme Court stated, "nothing in the text of the statute suggests that Congress intended causes of action recognized under it to have extraterritorial reach.... Nor does the fact that the text reaches 'any civil action' suggest application to torts committed abroad; it is well established that generic terms like 'any' or 'every' do not rebut the presumption against extraterritoriality."[47] This may strike many readers as odd and counterintuitive. Another reading of "any civil action" would be *any* civil action no matter where in the world it arises.[48] But alas, the conclusion of the

44. Simons interview *supra* note 6.
45. Kiobel v. Royal Dutch Petroleum Co., 133 S. Ct. 1659, 1669 (2013) (internal citation omitted).
46. *Id.* at 1678.
47. *Id.* at 1665.
48. By contrast to the Supreme Court's approach, the Second Circuit in *Filartiga* did

Supreme Court was that the Alien Tort Statute does not apply foreign companies acting abroad, causing harm to foreign individuals.

A plausible justification for the result in *Kiobel* is a concern that opening U.S. federal courts to claims similar to Kiobel's widow's would result in Americans being sued abroad, perhaps at times inappropriately. As the Supreme Court explained, "[m]oreover, accepting [Ms. Kiobel's] view would imply that other nations, also applying the law of nations, could hale our citizens into their courts for alleged violations of the law of nations occurring in the United States, or anywhere else in the world."[49]

In concluding that "mere corporate presence" is not enough to confer jurisdiction over Shell under the Alien Tort Statute, *Kiobel* raises the troubling question of where multi-national corporations can be held accountable for their actions. After *Kiobel*, federal courts are much less hospitable to claims arising from abroad about human rights abuses under the Alien Tort Statute when the corporation is a foreign corporation. This means U.S. asylees who have been granted political asylum in the United States because of the human rights abuses inflicted on them in their homelands, must turn to state courts, instead of federal courts, to seek redress using state law remedies.[50] This is why the next case is potentially so damaging to such human rights plaintiffs. But interestingly, a strict reading of *Kiobel* still leaves the door open to plaintiffs to sue domestic corporations, a topic to which we will return momentarily.

C. *Daimler AG v. Bauman*

Kiobel was troubling for many who thought of the U.S. courts as one of the places that human rights victims could seek legal redress. If *Kiobel* was bad, *Daimler* decided one year later, also unanimously, is potentially worse.

---

not find extraterritoriality to be a bar to suit. Filartiga v. Pena-Irala, 630 F.2d 876, 878 (2d Cir. 1980) ("we hold that deliberate torture perpetrated under color of official authority violates universally accepted norms of the international law of human rights, regardless of the nationality of the parties. Thus, whenever an alleged torturer is found and served with process by an alien within our borders, [ATS] provides federal jurisdiction.").

49. *Kiobel*, 133 S. Ct. at 1669.

50. Additionally, plaintiffs could sue corporations in the corporation's home country. This has happened to Shell, which has been sued in the Netherlands for alleged environmental damage in Nigeria. Shell has not been sued over the Saro-Wiwa/Kiobel events in the Netherlands. See Milieu Defensie Friends of the Earth Netherlands, *Dossier Shell in Nigeria* https://milieudefensie.nl/english/shell/courtcase/documents (last visited Nov. 23, 2015).

Before *Daimler*, the Supreme Court's approach to general jurisdiction over foreign corporations was "when the cause of action does not arise out of or relate to the foreign corporation's activities in the forum State ... [a] court may assert general jurisdiction over foreign (sister-state or foreign-country) corporations to hear any and all claims against them when their affiliations with the State are so 'continuous and systematic' as to render them essentially at home in the forum State."[51] This was distinct from a state asserting specific jurisdiction over a foreign corporation for events arising out of the defendant corporations' actions within the state.[52]

The nub of the issue in *Daimler* was whether California's long arm statute could be used to get general jurisdiction over Mercedes-Benz USA, LLC (MBUSA), a subsidiary of DaimlerChrysler Aktiengesellschaft in a case in which Daimler's Argentinian subsidiary, Mercedes-Benz Argentina (MB Argentina) was accused of human rights abuses in Argentina. As the Supreme Court summarized the case: "[t]he complaint alleged that during Argentina's 1976–1983 'Dirty War,' Daimler's Argentinian subsidiary, Mercedes-Benz Argentina (MB Argentina) collaborated with state security forces to kidnap, detain, torture, and kill certain MB Argentina workers, among them, plaintiffs or persons closely related to plaintiffs. Damages for the alleged human-rights violations were sought from Daimler under the laws of the United States, California, and Argentina."[53]

This was a long shot because the Supreme Court has only allowed general jurisdiction over a foreign corporation once in 1952.[54] In two other cases raising the issue of general jurisdiction, the Supreme Court had refused to allow it under the due process clause.[55] The Supreme Court decided that in *Daimler* that it would not be constitutional for California to assert jurisdiction over

---

51. Helicopteros Nacionales de Colombia, S.A. v. Hall, 466 U.S. 408, 414 (1984) (citing Int'l Shoe Co. v. Washington, 326 U.S. 310, 317 (1945)).

52. *Helicopteros*, 466 U.S. at 414 n.8 ("[w]hen a State exercises personal jurisdiction over a defendant in a suit arising out of or related to the defendant's contacts with the forum, the State is exercising 'specific jurisdiction' over the defendant.") (citation omitted).

53. Daimler AG v. Bauman, 134 S. Ct. 746, 750–51 (2014).

54. Perkins v. Benguet Consolidated Mining Co., 342 U.S. 437, 447–48 (1952)(subjecting a Filipino corporation to general jurisdiction after it had moved its operations to Ohio).

55. Helicopteros Nacionales de Colombia, S.A. v. Hall, 466 U.S. 408 (1984) (due process would be violated in subjecting a Colombian corporation to general jurisdiction in Texas); Goodyear Dunlop Tires Operations, S.A. v. Brown, 131 S. Ct. 2846 (2011) (two foreign subsidiaries of a North Carolina parent corporation were not subject to general jurisdiction in North Carolina).

Daimler for its actions in Argentina under the due process clause of the Fourteenth Amendment. As the Supreme Court concluded, "Daimler is not 'at home' in California, and cannot be sued there for injuries plaintiffs attribute to MB Argentina's conduct in Argentina."[56] In reaching this conclusion, the Court compared Daimler's worldwide sales to its sales in California and found, "California sales account for 2.4% of Daimler's worldwide sales."[57] And this small percentage was not enough for the Supreme Court to grant general jurisdiction over Daimler.

The Supreme Court indicated a strong preference for considering the locus of incorporation and its principal place of business as locations where general jurisdiction could be applied. As Justice Ginsburg wrote in *Daimler*, those locations "have the virtue of being unique — that is, each ordinarily indicates only one place — as well as easily ascertainable."[58] The Supreme Court declined the plaintiffs' request to find general jurisdiction based on the defendant companies' continuous contacts with the state of California. The Court's response was:

> neither Daimler nor MBUSA is incorporated in California, nor does either entity have its principal place of business there. If Daimler's California activities sufficed to allow adjudication of this Argentina-rooted case in California, the same global reach would presumably be available in every other State in which MBUSA's sales are sizable. Such exorbitant exercises of all-purpose jurisdiction would scarcely permit out-of-state defendants "to structure their primary conduct with some minimum assurance as to where that conduct will and will not render them liable to suit."[59]

The Supreme Court also stated that the lower court had erred in failing to consider the international consequences of allowing a suit against Daimler to go forward in California.[60] And accordingly, the Supreme Court reversed the lower court's decision, thereby dismissing Daimler from the suit.

Like *Kiobel* before it, *Daimler* was a 9–0 decision. Only Justice Sonia Sotomayor in her concurrence hinted at the possible negative consequences of the Supreme Court's approach in *Daimler*. Justice Sotomayor noted that in contrast to thinking of California as merely the source of 2.4% in sales, "[e]ach

---

56. Daimler AG v. Bauman, 134 S. Ct. at 751.
57. *Id.* at 752.
58. *Id.* at 760 (internal citations omitted).
59. *Id.* at 761–62 (internal citations omitted).
60. *Id.* at 763 (Sotomayor, J., concurring in the judgment).

year, [Daimler] distributes in California tens of thousands of cars, the sale of which generated billions of dollars in the year this suit was brought."[61]

Justice Sotomayor criticized her fellow Justices for getting their jurisdictional analysis backwards. She argued, "the Court's focus on Daimler's operations outside of California ignores the lodestar of our personal jurisdiction jurisprudence: A State may subject a defendant to the burden of suit if the defendant has sufficiently taken advantage of the State's laws and protections through its contacts in the State; whether the defendant has contacts elsewhere is immaterial."[62] The analysis of jurisdiction before *Daimler* had been, "[that] the touchstone principle of due process in this field, [was] the concept of reciprocal fairness. When a corporation chooses to invoke the benefits and protections of a State in which it operates, the State acquires the authority to subject the company to suit in its courts."[63] And as Justice Sotomayor wrote critically:

> Are these contacts sufficient to permit the exercise of general jurisdiction over Daimler? The Court holds that they are not, for a reason wholly foreign to our due process jurisprudence. The problem, the Court says, is not that Daimler's contacts with California are too few, but that its contacts with other forums are too many.... In recent years, Americans have grown accustomed to the concept of multinational corporations that are supposedly "too big to fail"; today the Court deems Daimler "too big for general jurisdiction."[64]

The beneficiaries of the *Daimler* rule, as Justice Sotomayor notes in her concurrence, will be the largest enterprises as they will have the lowest percentage of sales in any given state. Meanwhile, the jurisdictional "losers" will be smaller enterprises whose sales may be concentrated in just a few states. As she said, "the proportionality approach will treat small businesses unfairly in comparison to national and multinational conglomerates. Whereas a larger company will often be immunized from general jurisdiction in a State on account of its extensive contacts outside the forum, a small business will not be."[65] Justice Sotomayor would have disposed of the case on *Kiobel*-like grounds, in that it presented a foreign-cubed fact scenario, such that California's "exercise of ju-

61. *Id.* (Sotomayor, J., concurring in the judgment).
62. *Id.* at 764 (Sotomayor, J., concurring in the judgment).
63. *Id.* at 768 (Sotomayor, J., concurring in the judgment).
64. *Id.* at 763–64 (Sotomayor, J., concurring in the judgment).
65. *Id.* at 772 (Sotomayor, J., concurring in the judgment).

risdiction would be unreasonable given that the case involves foreign plaintiffs suing a foreign defendant based on foreign conduct, and given that a more appropriate forum is available."[66]

Reading *Kiobel* and *Daimler* together is bad news for U.S. asylees who want to sue foreign corporations for human rights abuses in U.S. Courts. But like *Kiobel*, *Daimler* may still leave the door open to suing domestic corporations for foreign torts.

D. The Aftermath of *Kiobel* and *Daimler*

Despite *Kiobel* and *Daimler*, lower courts have not been deterred in seeking to hold corporate tortfeasors accountable under the Alien Tort Statute and other theories of liability for corporate complicity in human rights abuses. Under *Kiobel*'s reasoning, if a corporation had more than "mere corporate presence" in the United States, that corporation might still be liable under the Alien Tort Statute. As one attorney laid out the argument, "[w]hile 'mere corporate presence' is not enough, where more is alleged, corporate ATS liability can be established. This important sentence—indeed, the whole [*Kiobel*] decision—would be superfluous if corporations can never be ATS defendants."[67]

Lower courts have largely adopted this reasoning. A Southern District of New York court allowed a suit against American corporations IBM and Ford to go forward under the Alien Tort Statute for alleged misdeeds under the apartheid regime in South Africa.[68] This case, *In Re: Apartheid Litigation*, may indicate the future path of similar human rights cases. Originally, this case included Daimler AG as a defendant, but in light of *Kiobel* and *Daimler* discussed above, the foreign corporate defendants were dismissed from the case.[69] However, the domestic corporate defendants Ford and IBM remained in the case. In the opinion of the district court judge, "[n]othing in the text, history or

---

66. *Id.* at 764 (Sotomayor, J., concurring in the judgment).

67. Douglas J. Pepe, *Corporate Liability Under Alien Tort Statute in the Second Circuit*, N.Y. L. J. (Feb. 17, 2015).

68. Jennifer Green, *The Rule of Law at a Crossroad: Enforcing Corporate Responsibility in International Investment through the Alien Tort Statute*, 35 U. Pa. J. Int'l L. 1085, 1111 (2014) (citing In Re: Apartheid Litigation, No. 1:02-md-01499-SAS (S.D.N.Y. Apr. 17, 2014).

69. In re South African Apartheid Litig., No. 02 MDL 1499, 2013 WL 6813877, at *1–2 (Dec. 26, 2013).

purposes of the ATS indicates that corporations are immune from liability on the basis of federal common law."[70] Therefore, the judge granted "plaintiffs' motion for an order finding that corporations may be held liable under the ATS[.]"[71] This case had a pending petition for cert. before the Supreme Court as this book was finalized. The Second Circuit accepted the concept of corporate liability but reversed the decision on the grounds that the evidence did not establish the proper mens rea of "purposeful" action.[72]

One of the best examples of this approach to the Alien Tort Statute litigation involves the harvesting of chocolate by some of America's favorite candy bar makers. In *Doe I v. Nestle USA, Inc.*, a case that was filed in 2005 against Nestle USA, Archer Daniels Midland, and Cargill for aiding and abetting child slavery in Cote d'Ivoire (the Ivory Coast), the Ninth Circuit refused to dismiss the suit just because the defendants were corporations.[73] How cacao (an element of chocolate which is also known as cocoa) is harvested is why this case arose:

> The seeds of the cacao tree, from which chocolate is produced, are bitter. So too is the story of how this sweet confection gets to our mouths. Much of the world's cocoa is picked by tiny hands, those of children as young as seven or eight, in places like Ivory Coast, which supplies more than 30 percent of the global harvest. An estimated six hundred thousand children work in cocoa fields there, wielding machetes, handling dangerous pesticides, often toiling far from home and rarely going to school. Some are sold or bonded into slavery.[74]

---

70. In re South African Apartheid Litigation, 15 F.Supp.3d 454, 464 (S.D.N.Y. 2014).

71. *Id.* at 465; *see also* Licci ex rel. Licci v. Lebanese Canadian Bank, SAL, 732 F.3d 161, 174 (2d Cir. 2013).

72. In re South African Apartheid Litigation, 796 F.3d 160 (2d Cir. 2015).

73. Specifically the defendants in this case are Defendants Nestle, S.A. (based in Switzerland), Nestle, U.S.A., and Nestle Cote d'Ivoire, S.A. (collectively "Nestle"); Cargill, Incorporated ("Cargill, Inc."), Cargill Cocoa (based in the United States), and Cargill West Africa, S.A. (collectively "Cargill"); and Archer Daniels Midland Company ("Archer Daniels Midland").

74. Robert Friedman, Introduction to Christian Parenti's *Chocolate's Bittersweet Economy* (2008) in *Fortune* in GLOBAL MUCKRAKING 100 YEARS OF INVESTIGATIVE JOURNALISM FROM AROUND THE WORLD (Anya Schiffin ed.) at 40 (2014); *see also* Luz Estella Nagle, *Selling Souls: The Effect of Globalization on Human Trafficking and Forced Servitude*, 26 WIS. INT'L L.J. 131, 140–41 (2008) ("One of the world's most popular agricultural products, dependent on trafficked labor to 'subsidize' global market prices, is cocoa. In 2005, in the United States alone, the chocolate industry imported over $870 million of cocoa beans for processing in the United States ... Trafficked children working in West African cocoa farms

In 1998 UNICEF (United Nations Children's Fund) documented evidence that Ivory Coast chocolate farmers were using enslaved children from Burkina Faso and Mali.[75] The U.S. Congress reacted, albeit three years later, by introducing legislation that would have mandated labels on chocolate to disclose the use of child slave labor.[76] But, "[i]ndustry fought back, and a compromise was reached establishing a voluntary protocol by which chocolate companies would wean themselves from child labor, then certify that they had done so ... [T]he U.S. Department of Labor contracted with Tulane University to monitor progress."[77] The Engel-Harkin Protocol (or Cocoa Protocol) was signed in September 2001.[78] But even years after the industry had promised to self-regulate, "[t]he problem ... was that no one—not the manufacturers, not the government, not the middlemen who buy beans from farmers and sell them to exporters such as Cargill, Archer Daniels Midland, and Barry Callebaut, not even the organizations set up to help implement the reforms—was enforcing the voluntary code."[79] As reported in *Fortune*, "[t]his type of child labor isn't sup-

---

face some of the most hazardous and exhausting working conditions. Child slaves work excessive hours, are forced to do highly repetitive tasks, spray pesticides with no protection, are subjected to physical abuse from overseers, and receive little or no health care. In 2003, a report by Global Exchange noted that the M&M/Mars Corporation and other major chocolate manufacturers conspired to hold down cocoa prices in the world market, 'thereby reducing cocoa farmers' incomes and fomenting abusive child labor practices, including child slavery.'").

75. Friedman, *supra* note 74, at 41.

76. H. Amdt. 142 to P.L. 107–76, FY2002 Agriculture, Rural Development and Food and Drug Administration (FDA) Appropriations (would have authorized $250,000 for the FDA to develop a label for chocolate indicating that no child slave labor had been used in the growing and harvesting of the chocolate).

77. Christian Parenti, *Chocolate's Bittersweet Economy* (2008) in *Fortune* in Global Muckraking 100 Years of Investigative Journalism from around the World (Anya Schiffin ed.) at 42 (2014).

78. Abby Haglage, *Lawsuit: Your Candy Bar Was Made by Child Slaves*, The Daily Beast (Sep. 30, 2015), http://www.thedailybeast.com/articles/2015/09/30/lawsuit-your-candy-bar-was-made-by-child-slaves.html.

79. Friedman, *supra* note 74, at 41; *see also* Tobias Barrington Wolff, *The Thirteenth Amendment and Slavery in the Global Economy*, 102 Colum. L. Rev. 973, 992 (2002) ("One recent example that has received worldwide attention is the farming of cocoa beans in West Africa, particularly in Ivory Coast. West African nations produce more than 40 percent of the world's cocoa. Child laborers, many of them imported from neighboring Mali and Burkina Faso, are sometimes forced to work as slaves on cocoa farms and plantations. The cocoa beans that they produce are imported to the United States, processed at plants in Wisconsin, Minnesota, and California, and turned into chocolate products sold throughout the domestic market.").

posed to exist in the Ivory Coast.... Yet today child workers, many under the age of 10, are everywhere."[80]

The lawsuit against Nestle is an attempt to hold the companies who trade in chocolate accountable. The plaintiffs, a group of John Does who were forced to work as child slaves on West African cocoa plantations, filed a class action in the United States District Court for the Central District of California, alleging that the defendants were liable under the Alien Tort Statute (ATS) for aiding and abetting child slavery in the Ivory Coast. When asked by a reporter why they were suing these particular companies, they replied, "[w]e have evidence against Nestlé," adding, "[i]f we find evidence that Mars or Hershey were complicit, we will add them to the suit."[81] The Plaintiffs "said they filed in the Northern District of California because Mali lacks basic laws and the Ivory Coast's courts are 'notoriously corrupt.'"[82] Incidentally, Hershey's may have its own problems as indicated in a lawsuit brought by one of its institutional shareholders seeking more information about its alleged use of child slaves.[83] And in late 2015, Hershey's, Mars and Nestle were sued again in a class action for allegedly not labeling their products as being produced with slave labor.[84]

---

80. Parenti, *supra* note 77, at 42.

81. Deborah Orr, *Slave Chocolate?* FORBES (Apr. 7, 2006), http://www.forbes.com/forbes/2006/0424/096.html.

82. Jack Bouboushian, *9th Circuit Digs into Nestle Child Slavery Suit*, BUSINESS & HUMAN RIGHTS RESOURCE CENTRE (Sept. 5, 2014), http://business-humanrights.org/en/9th-circuit-digs-into-nestle-child-slavery-suit.

83. Louisiana Municipal Employees' Retirement System v. Hershey, No. 7996-ML (Del. Ch.) (special master's report) ("Despite these commitments from industry members and governments, child labor and human trafficking continue to be a pervasive problem in cocoa farming. Approximately 70 percent of the world's supply of cocoa beans, and the largest percentage of Hershey's supply, comes from West African nations, including Ghana and the Ivory Coast."); *see also* Rulings of the Court From Oral Argument on Exceptions to the Master's Final Report, La. Mun. Police Emps. Ret. Sys. v. Hershey Co., No. 7996-ML (Del. Ch. Mar. 18, 2014), http://www.law.du.edu/documents/corporate-governance/disclosure/lampers/hershey-ruling.pdf ("the allegations in the complaint, read in the doubly plaintiff-friendly manner that is required in this procedural posture, support a reasonable inference of possible violations of law in which Hershey may be involved. And those possibilities are sufficient, in the words of our Supreme Court, 'to warrant further investigation.'").

84. Abby Haglage, *Lawsuit: Your Candy Bar Was Made by Child Slaves*, THE DAILY BEAST (Sep. 30, 2015), http://www.thedailybeast.com/articles/2015/09/30/lawsuit-your-candy-bar-was-made-by-child-slaves.html ("[A] class action lawsuit [was] filed Monday against Hershey and two of its competitors, Mars and Nestle. The complaints, filed by three California residents, allege that the companies are guilty of false advertising for failing to disclose the

The Ninth Circuit, citing to previous Circuit precedent in *Nestle*, said that corporations did not have blanket immunity from Alien Tort Statute claims.[85] The Ninth Circuit held, "[w]e conclude that the prohibition against slavery is universal and may be asserted against the corporate defendants in this case."[86] Nestle and its co-defendants had tried to have the case dismissed.[87] The Ninth Circuit disagreed reading the facts alleged in the plaintiff's complaint in the light most favorable to the plaintiffs, and concluded that if true, the plaintiffs would be able to prove their case against Nestle. The Ninth Circuit's ruling was quite blistering considering a mere motion to dismiss was in front of them. For example:

> We conclude that the plaintiffs' allegations ... state a claim for aiding and abetting slavery. All international authorities agree that "at least purposive action ... constitutes aiding and abetting[.]" ... Reading the allegations in the light most favorable to the plaintiffs, one is led to the inference that the defendants placed increased revenues before basic human welfare, and intended to pursue all options available to reduce their cost for purchasing cocoa. Driven by the goal to reduce costs in any way possible, the defendants allegedly supported the use of child slavery, the cheapest form of labor available. These allegations explain how the use of child slavery benefitted the defendants and furthered their operational goals in the Ivory Coast, and therefore, the allegations support the inference that the defendants acted with the purpose to facilitate child slavery.[88]

The Ninth Circuit was careful to say merely doing business was not enough to trigger liability. But here the Court considered the allegations that the corporations "allegedly intended to support the use of child slavery as a means of reducing their production costs. In doing so, the defendants sought a legitimate goal, profit, through illegitimate means, purposefully supporting child slavery."[89] In 2015, a petition to rehear the *Nestle* case by the full Ninth Circuit sit-

---

use of child slavery on their packaging. Without it, the plaintiffs claim, the companies are deceiving consumers into 'unwittingly' supporting the child slave labor trade.").

85. Doe I v. Nestle USA, Inc., 766 F.3d 1013, 1021 (9th Cir. 2014).

86. *Id.* at 1022.

87. In a motion to dismiss under Federal Rule of Civil Procedure 12(b)(6), the court assumes that the facts alleged in the complaint are true. *Bell Atlantic Corp. v. Twombly*, 550 U.S. 544, 555–556 (2007).

88. *Id.* at 1024–1025.

89. *Id.* at 1025–1026.

ting *en banc* was denied.[90] In 2016, the Supreme Court denied a petition for cert. from Nestle in the case.[91]

There is a real sense in which it is tragic that litigation is needed to address this issue. Some chocolatiers like Royal Verkade have decided to use 100 percent Fair Trade chocolate and sugar.[92] "Fair Trade" is a third party certification that indicates, among other attributes, that the producer of a good has been paid a reasonable price and that the good has not been produced using forced labor.[93] And other businesses have made similar choices to use more Fair Trade ingredients. As Ben Cohen, the Ben of Ben & Jerry's Ice Cream, explained, "we started to use a high percentage of Fair Trade ingredients in our ice cream. That helps the income of the peasant farmers that are growing the coffee or the chocolate or the vanilla." And Mr. Cohen added finding ethically sourced chocolate "is not that hard. You just have to pay attention. If you place no criteria on finding raw materials, then it's easier to find. Just like it's easier to find middle of the road chocolate in terms of taste and quality, than it is to find high quality chocolate. But it's not hard to find responsibly grown chocolate if you're looking for it."[94] If more food manufacturers who use chocolate in their products made this choice, perhaps the market driving slavery in the cacao harvest would abate.[95]

---

90. Doe I v. Nestle USA, Inc., 788 F.3d 946, 946 (9th Cir. 2015).

91. Nestle USA Inc. v. Doe I, No. 15-349 (U.S. Jan. 11, 2016) (cert. denied).

92. Dr. Ranee Khooshie Lal Panjabi, *Sacrificial Lambs of Globalization: Child Labor in the Twenty-First Century*, 37 Denv. J. Int'l L. & Pol'y 421, 442–43 (2009); Dave Gram, *Ben & Jerry Back Social Mission Bill*, Rutland Herald (Apr. 12, 2010), http://www.rutland-herald.com/apps/pbcs.dll/article?AID=/20100412/NEWS03/4120354/1004/NEWS03?template=printart ("Greenfield and Cohen said Unilever, which still employs both of them, generally has been good about pursuing a social mission, but could have been better. They cited the company's recent announcement that it would source chocolate, nuts and other ingredients from suppliers that observe 'fair trade' practices designed to avoid exploiting agricultural workers in developing countries.").

93. World Fair Trade Organization, *10 Principles of Fair Trade* (Oct. 2013), http://wfto.com/fair-trade/10-principles-fair-trade.

94. Interview with Ben Cohen, CEO Ben & Jerry's (Nov. 4, 2015).

95. Dr. Ranee Khooshie Lal Panjabi, *Sacrificial Lambs of Globalization: Child Labor in the Twenty-First Century*, 37 Denv. J. Int'l L. & Pol'y 421, 442–43 (2009); Dave Gram, *Ben & Jerry Back Social Mission Bill*, Rutland Herald (Apr. 12, 2010), http://www.rutland-herald.com/apps/pbcs.dll/article?AID=/20100412/NEWS03/4120354/1004/NEWS03?template=printart ("Greenfield and Cohen said Unilever, which still employs both of them, generally has been good about pursuing a social mission, but could have been better. They cited the company's recent announcement that it would source chocolate, nuts and other ingredients from suppliers that observe 'fair trade' practices designed to avoid exploiting agricultural workers in developing countries.").

But with several major chocolate companies refusing to self-regulate to re-solve the labor issues in the cacao harvest, litigators are pushing forward with the legal tools they have at their disposal. Human Rights attorney Marco Si-mons reasoned,

> Despite *Kiobel* and *Daimler,* there are still a lot of tools available to pursue corporations, especially Western corporations, who are engaged in harmful practices around the world. So the overall picture of accountability is one of progress. Corporations today are far less likely to conclude that they are immune or untouchable when it comes to legal liability no matter where in the world they operate.[96]

Many corporate defendants are continuing to argue in court that they cannot be held accountable for human rights abuses abroad using the Alien Tort Statute. Thus, it may take another trip to the Supreme Court, perhaps in one of the lower court cases mentioned in this chapter, before the law is perfectly clear about if, and when, corporations are excused from liability under laws that allow human rights victims some legal recourse.

---

96. Simons interview *supra* note 6.

Chapter 10

Fracturing Politics

Fracking. Who would have allowed this without money in politics?
— Phil Radford, Former Executive Director of Greenpeace[1]

One of the most fraught topics for corporations and the democracies they inhabit is environmental policy. Avoiding the taxman is just the one of the responsibilities that certain corporations will try to avoid. Environmental stewardship is another responsibility certain firms try to avoid like Typhoid Mary in turn-of-the-century New York. Because of the scale of multinational corporate actors (producing and shipping products worldwide), these corporations have an enormous role in not only shaping the physical environment that they inhabit, but they can also affect the health of the land, water, and air that all humans occupy. How good or bad a firm is to the environment depends on their business model. For many firms, their environmental impacts are modest, and they voluntarily take prudent steps to remediate harms and act sustainably. At the other extreme are fossil fuel companies, whose practice of pushing environmental costs on to others has been done on an industrial scale.

The topic of environmental impacts of corporations could be its own book, so this chapter will highlight one of the more extreme examples: the role of extractive industries and what that shows about the relationship among corporations, democracy, power, the environment, and science. The exemplar that demonstrates the environmental dangers posed by extractive industries is hydraulic fracturing to release natural gas (better known as *fracking*) and the chemicals that are used—frequently secretly—in the process.

There are some basic expectations around chemicals in America in the twenty-first century—that they are highly regulated for public safety by the federal gov-

---

1. Interview with Phil Radford, Former Executive Director of Greenpeace (Aug. 5, 2015).

ernment, that they are kept away from drinking water supplies, and that they can't be used recklessly without triggering crippling liability. These assumptions hold true for a host of chemicals, but not the ones used in fracking.[2] The story of why the United States is failing to regulate fracking chemicals comprehensively at the federal level is part of a broader narrative about our Congress not coping with climate change or our energy dependency on fossil fuels; the power of lobbying by the oil and gas industry; the reverence in the legal system for corporate trade secrets; and a pass-the-buck mentality that assumes some regulator somewhere is protecting key natural resources like drinking water.

If successful lobbying is one of the key measures of power, then as the former Executive Director of Greenpeace Phil Radford argues,

> [t]he fact that Congress has not passed a new major environmental law since 1980 (the Superfund law on toxic waste) is evidence of corporate power. If you look at issues like global warming that are incredibly pressing right now or the loss of 42% of our bees in U.S. this year that pollinate one in three bites of food that we eat ... these are real issues that have major consequences on the American people and the world and Congress is still siding with corporations.[3]

Often what industry wants from Congress is for Congress to do nothing at all. Congress is frequently only too willing to oblige.

Twenty-five years ago, Marshall Clinard drew a bleak picture of corporate environmental impacts: "in spite of government controls, the corporate world still pollutes air, water, and soil on a wide scale."[4] Things have not necessarily improved in the past quarter century. A concrete example is offered by Former President of the Pacific Stock Exchange, Warren Langley, "[l]ook at the fracking in Bakken oil fields. Look at how unsafe that is. And how much pollution there is. The oil companies claim, it's all fine.... But they are trying to shift the cost to state or federal government and ultimately to the taxpayer."[5]

One problem that extractive industries have is one faced by all for-profit corporations—the tyranny of the bottom line and how to maximize profits.

---

2. David B. Spence, *Federalism, Regulatory Lags, and the Political Economy of Energy Production*, 161 U. PA. L. REV. 431, 449–50 (2013) ("this federal regulatory superstructure does not always regulate environmental, health, and safety risks associated with fracking in the same way it regulates other industries. Fracking operations enjoy some exemptions from federal environmental regulation.").

3. Radford interview *supra* note 1.

4. MARSHALL CLINARD, CORPORATE CORRUPTION 13 (1990).

5. Interview with Warren Langley, Former President of the Pacific Stock Exchange (July 14, 2015).

A classic excuse for cutting environmental corners is the need for profit max-imization for shareholders. But this excuse rings hollow because as Dr. Marcy Murninghan argues, "[s]hareholders care about more than just the money that is in their pocket. They would also like to be able to walk to the corner and buy a gallon of milk that is not tainted, and they'd like to walk there and back without getting shot."[6]

The pressure to maximize the bottom line pushes all for-profit corpora-tions, and extractive industries in particular, to externalize as many costs as possible. Robert Monks has even called corporations "externalizing ma-chine[s]."[7] An externalized cost is one that is incurred by the firm, but paid for by someone else. "A typical externality is pollution. If I am downwind of some factory that belches smoke into the atmosphere, the productive activity of that factory imposes a cost on me to which I have not consented and for which the free market provides no compensation."[8] Mr. Monks, who once ran a coal company, noted that "[c]oal is the cheapest BTU because they have external-ized all of the liabilities like the health care costs of workers and neighbors being paid for at public cost."[9] He offered this stark assessment of corpora-tions' relationship to environmental degradation, noting: "I started to wonder whether we had created a death machine in corporations."[10]

Most corporations have a financial incentive, at least in the short term, to foist the environmental costs of producing goods and services onto others. The others who bear these costs are frequently taxpayers, who foot the bill for en-vironmental remediation or the costs of health care for individuals who are too poor to pay for their own healthcare through programs like Medicaid. The costs can also be borne by neighbors, if the environmental impact is so great that nearby land is no longer arable or nearby water is no longer potable.

Corporations, particularly those with the largest negative environmental impacts, have incentives to resist all attempts to make them internalize the costs and pay for their impacts. As a result, they engage in extensive lobbying efforts to resist new laws and regulations, to deregulate laws that are already on the books, to try to litigate away existing regulations,[11] and to capture reg-

---

6. Interview with Dr. Marcy Murninghan, corporate governance expert (July 24, 2015).

7. ROBERT A.G. MONKS & NELL MINOW, CORPORATE GOVERNANCE 12 (Fifth ed. 2011).

8. ANDREW B. SCHMOOKLER, THE ILLUSION OF CHOICE: HOW THE MARKET ECONOMY SHAPES OUR DESTINY 55 (1993).

9. Interview with Robert A.G. Monks (Aug. 17, 2015).

10. *Id.*

11. There are many ongoing litigations challenging various environmental regulations by two of the biggest business trade associations. *See* West Virginia v. EPA, No. 15-1363

ulators, who have decision-making power on how laws on the books are enforced.[12] There are many tactics that can be deployed to escape environmental responsibilities, from exploiting information asymmetries, to hiding the facts, to lying about the facts, to trying to curry favor with the decision maker through legal and illegal means. But it should also be clear that many firms can be a force for good in environmental stewardship. Before we get to those good actors, let's look at what some of the worst actors are doing.

A. Exploiting Informational Asymmetries

Environmental protection is partially a classic collective action problem, or what Plato called the tragedy of the commons. Everyone wants clean air and water, but the individual impetus to protect the water or air may be quite low. First, the average person is busy dealing with work, school, and family obligations. There is little time for altruism, especially to solve complex, long-term problems. And second, there is the problem of expertise. Average people are unlikely to believe that they have the requisite proficiency to debate the intri-

---

(D.C. Cir. Oct. 23, 2015) (arguing against Section 111(d) of the Clean Air Act because it constitutes a "massive executive power grab" by the EPA with respect to the electricity sector and is costly for businesses, consumers, and families); Chamber of Commerce v. EPA, No. 4:15-cv-00386-JED-PJC (N.D. Okla. July 10, 2015) (arguing against the "Waters of the U.S." rule that expands the areas regulated by the Clean Water Act because it takes away states' ability to determine how they will use land and water resources and because the EPA failed to assess the economic harm of the regulation before implementation); Chamber of Commerce v. EPA, No. 15-9552 (10th Cir. July 23, 2015) (arguing against the "Waters of the U.S." rule that expands the areas regulated by the Clean Water Act because it takes away states' ability to determine how they will use land and water resources and because the EPA failed to assess the economic harm of the regulation before implementation); Am. Forest & Paper Assoc. v. EPA, No. 13-1123 (D.C. Cir. Apr. 29, 2011) (seeking review of EPA's regulation, "Commercial and Industrial Solid Waste Incineration Units: Reconsideration and Final Amendments; Non-Hazardous Secondary Materials That Are Solid Waste"); Petition for Administrative Stay Pending Judicial Review of Carbon Pollution Emission Guidelines for Existing Stationary Sources: Electric Utility Generating Units, Chamber of Commerce v. EPA (2015) (No. EPA-HQ-OAR-2013-0602) (challenging the EPA's promulgation of the Clean Air Act that purports to phase out states use of fossil fuels to create electricity).

12. Michael Smallberg, *POGO Speaks at National Government Ethics Summit*, POGO.ORG (Oct. 15, 2014), http://www.pogo.org/blog/2014/10/20141015-pogo-speaks-at-national-government-ethics-summit.html ("'regulatory capture' [is] when a regulated industry is able to sway policies in its favor and away from the public interest.... When an agency becomes captured, it's easier for powerhouse firms to sway contracting decisions, regulations, and other government policies.").

cacies of environmental protection. While citizens can state the general proposition that they want clean air to breathe and fresh water to drink, they may have nothing sensible to say about which of a dozen chemicals would be dangerous to human health and in which concentrations. Financially interested corporations can frequently afford the experts to frame their side of the story. The public may not have this luxury. Corporations can exploit this information deficit while lobbying regulators. As Deborah Goldberg of Earth Justice explained,

> [w]e work on shutting down coal-fired power plants. What we have discovered is that for the most part, the regulatory proceedings that are conducted by the PUCs [Public Utility Commissions] are attended only by the industry. So when we come into these proceedings and bring a different perspective, it is sometimes the first time that the PUC has heard the voice of the public in this context. Some states have consumer advocates, but they don't have environmental advocates. We actually had a situation in Kentucky where we had appeared in one proceeding, and we were invited back to a second proceeding, because the PUC recognized that without us there, they didn't get an accurate and full picture. But you can only imagine that, if they are hearing only from one side, we face the ultimate in industry capture.[13]

She added, PUC proceedings "are extremely technical. In order to participate in a meaningful way, you need to bring in scientific experts that cost a lot of money. So it is prohibitive both from a procedural perspective and from a financial perspective for an ordinary citizen to intervene."[14] Corporations rely on these informational asymmetries to control the terms of the debate. It is easy to win an argument when the other side lacks the capacity to gather the evidence in its favor. In some instances, corporations have taken the next step, actively seeking to impede the collection of evidence through the use of the trade secrets doctrine.

B. Hiding the Facts

One way that corporations game the regulatory system is by asserting trade secret protection. Professor David Levin argued, "[s]ecrecy, and its attendant

---

13. Interview with Deborah Goldberg, Managing Attorney Northeast Office of Earth Justice (July 22, 2015).
14. *Id.*

goals of pecuniary gain and commercial competition, conflict with the methods and purpose of transparent and accountable democratic governance."[15] And yet as Professor Levine noted, "the breadth of application of the trade secrecy doctrine continues to expand."[16] Asserting trade secrets over chemicals has been a favored tactic of the extractive natural gas industry. Phil Radford stressed, "[f]racking is the most egregious example [of the use of trade secrets]. You can be sued for exposing the chemicals that are poisoning your community because of trade secrets, which is just unbelievable."[17] The potential negative impacts on human health from fracking include exposure to chemicals known to cause cancer.[18]

Environmental attorney Deborah Goldberg explains how the use of trade secrets works in the real world to shield the public from the truth,

> Wyoming ... [has] trade secret protections of various different kinds. This meant that all of the information would go to the agency, but not all information would necessarily go to the public, because anything that was proprietary would be held by the agency.... Halliburton, would routinely submit blanket trade secret claims. Even if there

---

15. David S. Levine, *Secrecy and Unaccountability: Trade Secrets in our Public Infrastructure*, 59 Fla. L. Rev. 135, 138 (2007).

16. *Id.* at 139–40 (footnote omitted).

17. Radford interview *supra* note 1.

18. Brie DeBusk Sherwin, *Chocolate, Coca-Cola, and Fracturing Fluid: A Story of Unfettered Secrecy, Toxicology & the Resulting Public Health Implications of Natural Gas Development*, 77 Ohio St. L.J. (forthcoming 2016), *available at* http://ssrn.com/abstract=2616550 ("Between 2005 and 2009, hydraulic fracturing companies used approximately ninety-five products that contained thirteen known carcinogens, including benzene, naphthalene, and acrylamide.") (citing Bernard D. Goldstein, et al., *The Role of Toxicological Science in Meeting The Challenges and Opportunities of Hydraulic Fracturing*, 139(2) Toxicological Sci. 271, 271–83 (2014); A.L. Israel, et al., *Concerns About Shale Gas Risks Among interested and Affected Parties*, Workshop on Risks of Unconventional Shale Gas Development. National Academy of Sciences, Washington, D.C. (2013), http://sites.nationalacademies.org/ DBASSE/BECS/CurrentProjects/DBASSE069201; United States House of Representatives Committee on Energy and Commerce Minority Staff, Chemicals Used in Hydraulic Fracturing, (Apr. 2011), http://democrats.energycommerce.house.gov/sites/ default/files/documents/Hydraulic-Fracturing-Chemicals-2011-4-18.pdf; FracFocus, https://fracfocus.org/ (last visited Mar. 10, 2015); Envtl. Integrity Project, Fracking's Toxic Loophole (Oct. 22, 2014), http://environmentalintegrity.org/wp-content/uploads/ FRACKINGS-TOXIC-LOOPHOLE.pdf; *Find a Well*, FracFocus, file:///Users/bsherwin/ Downloads/42-127-35771-00-00-1132014%2015111%20PM-924-BlackBrush%20O%20 20G%20LLC%20(1).pdf (accessed on Feb. 28, 2015) (Well API # 42-127-35771); *Material Safety Data Sheet (MSDS) for 8002-05-09s18*, Marathon Oil (Dec. 7, 2010), http://www.marathonpetroleum.com/brand/content/documents/mpc/msds/0110MAR001.pdf.

was just one proprietary chemical they used in fracking, they would claim trade secret protection for everything they were using. The Wyoming agency basically would routinely grant all of the trade secret claims without reviewing them.[19]

There is some disclosure of fracking fluid chemicals if the drilling is done on federal (as opposed to state) lands.[20] But among federal regulators, the assertion of corporate trade secrets has a powerful impact because it is illegal for federal employees to reveal corporate trade secrets.[21] This part of the federal law is little used if reported cases are the metric.[22] Regardless of how little this law is prosecuted, it may still have a chilling effect on federal employees who have proprietary information from disclosing it, even if disclosing the information is key to protecting human health. Additionally, through reverse-FOIA suits, companies can ask for courts to enjoin the government from releasing proprietary information and the government must respect such court orders.[23]

Abstractions about trade secrets are a bloodless and boring business, until they're not. Consider the experience of a nurse helping a patient and then falling ill because the chemicals that patient walked in to the ER with were not regulated federally and were hidden under a miasma of corporate trade secrets. This isn't a hypothetical. Dr. Gretchen Goldman reported, "[t]here was a nurse in Colorado. She was taking care of a worker who had spilled fracking chemicals on himself. She had several organ failures. She was very close to death.

---

19. Goldberg interview *supra* note 13.

20. Daniel J. Corbett, *Secret Recipes: Fracking Fluid Fracas*, MONDAQ (Aug. 6, 2015), http://www.mondaq.com/article.asp?articleid=418568&signup=true&newsub=1 ("the Department of the Interior's Bureau of Land Management (BLM) has recently imposed rules that require companies to publicly disclose chemical additives used in fracking if the wells are located on lands managed by the BLM or on Indian reservations. However, this only affects roughly one-fifth of fracking operations nationwide.").

21. Trade Secrets Act, 18 U.S.C.A. § 1905 (West, P.L. 114-49) ("Whoever, being an officer or employee of the United States or of any department or agency thereof, ... discloses, or makes known ... the trade secrets, ... of any person, firm, partnership, corporation, or association; ... shall be fined under this title, or imprisoned not more than one year, or both; and shall be removed from office or employment.").

22. U.S. v. Wallington, 889 F.2d 573, 574 (5th Cir. 1989).

23. In *GTE Sylvania, Inc. v. Consumers Union of the United States, Inc.*, 445 U.S. 375 (1980), a unanimous Supreme Court held that information may not be obtained under the FOIA when the agency holding the material has been enjoined from disclosing it by a federal district court.

Her doctors asked the company and the company would not tell them what chemicals she was exposed to because of trade secrets. This woman nearly died."[24] Her name is Cathy Behr. *Newsweek* related Behr's story this way:

> Cathy Behr says she won't forget the smell that nearly killed her. An emergency-room nurse in Durango, Colo.'s Mercy Regional Medical Center, Behr was working the April 17 day shift when Clinton Marshall arrived complaining of nausea and headaches. An employee at an energy-services company, Weatherford International, Marshall, according to Behr, said that he was caught in a 'fracturing-fluid' spill.... The chemical stench coming off Marshall's boots was buckling, says Behr. Mercy officials took no chances. They evacuated and locked down the ER, and its staff was instructed to don protective masks and gowns.[25]

As reported by the *Denver Post*, here is what happened to Behr. She helped her patient remove his boots and shower off, all the while exposing herself unprotected to the chemicals that had been on him. She lost her sense of smell and her vision blurred. Then her organs started to fail.[26] "Trying to figure out how to treat her, [Behr's doctor] called Weatherford ... to learn which chemicals it uses to make ZetaFlow, the fluid both were exposed to. The company denied him the information, saying it was a trade secret."[27] The spokesman for the company involved (Weatherford) compared the chemicals in the fracking fluid ZetaFlow to chocolate:

> Weatherford this week had an even more contemptuous way of describing the health effects of its ZetaFlow. 'It's got parameters that you need to work in, that you need to be mindful of when you're using it. That's sort of a given. I mean, if I ate too much chocolate, that could be hazardous to my health, too,' said spokeswoman Christine McGee. Behr—a wife and mother who is back at work and mostly recovered after nearly losing her life in April—had this response to McGee:

24. Interview with Dr. Gretchen Goldman, Union of Concerned Scientists (July 28, 2015).

25. Jim Moscou, *Oil & Gas Exploration: Is 'Fracking' Safe?*, Newsweek (Aug. 19, 2008), http://www.newsweek.com/oil-gas-exploration-fracking-safe-87557.

26. Susan Greene, *Oil Secret Has Nasty Side Effect*, Denver Post (July 24, 2008), http://www.denverpost.com/news/ci_9976257.

27. *Id.*

'Chocolate, huh? Let's give those boots to her and have her take a couple of deep breaths.'[28]

Newsweek noted that the Material Safety Data Sheet for ZetaFlow contains trade secret assertions for proprietary chemicals: "[i]n a copy of its Material Safety Data Sheet—which details ingredients, health warnings, fire hazards, and more—ZetaFlow contains methanol and two undisclosed 'proprietary' compounds."[29]

Under OSHA's rules employers are allowed to hide proprietary chemicals by asserting that they are protected trade secrets. "The chemical manufacturer, importer, or employer may withhold the specific chemical identity ... from the safety data sheet, provided that: The claim that the information withheld is a trade secret ..."[30] However, even under the OSHA regulations, "[t]he specific chemical identity and percentage is made available to health professionals, employees, and designated representatives" in emergencies.[31] But the reflexive assertions of trade secrets make chemical disclosures essentially worthless. In a study of 944 Material Safety Data Sheets for the oil and gas industry, researchers found "that a mere 14% specified the complete chemical contents of the product, and for almost half of the products, less than 1% of the chemical makeup of the product could be determined."[32]

Despite the indifference that was shown to her and her health, Behr said she "harbors no ill-feelings toward the industry, noting the jobs and economic benefit it has brought to her area. 'I always thought that the industry probably took chances,' she [said]. 'But I always thought someone was watching them. I really did think that.'"[33] As Behr's story inspired calls for more disclosure of chemicals used in fracking, the industry ginned up more legal claims to defend itself. "The oil and gas industry officials argued that forcing companies to reveal the information would force it take its business outside of Colorado. One oil and gas executive likened it to asking the Coca-Cola company to disclose the formula for Coke."[34] Then Halliburton took the argument one step

---

28. *Id.*

29. Moscou, *supra* note 25.

30. OSHA Hazard Communication Standards Regarding Trade Secrets, 20 C.F.R. 1910.1200(i)(1), (i)(1)(i–iv) (2012).

31. *Id.*

32. Matthew McFeeley, *Falling Through the Cracks: Public Information and the Patchwork of Hydraulic Fracturing Disclosure Laws*, 38 Vt. L. Rev. 849, 857–58 (2014).

33. Moscou, *supra* note 25.

34. Brie DeBusk Sherwin, *Chocolate, Coca-Cola, and Fracturing Fluid: A Story of Unfettered Secrecy, Toxicology & the Resulting Public Health Implications of Natural Gas Develop-*

further, arguing that revealing the chemicals in fracking fluid would be an unconstitutional taking of their property:

> "A disclosure to members of the public of detailed information ...
> would result in an unconstitutional taking of [Halliburton's] prop-
> erty," the company told Colorado's Oil and Gas Conservation Com-
> mission.... Then Halliburton fired a major salvo: If lawmakers forced
> the company to disclose its recipes, the letter stated, it "will have lit-
> tle choice but to pull its proprietary products out of Colorado." The
> company's attorneys warned that if the three big fracking companies
> left, they would take some $29 billion in future gas-related tax and
> royalty revenue with them over the next decade.[35]

Halliburton's takings argument is a strained one that flies in the face of Supreme
Court precedent.[36] In 2015, in *Horne v. Department of Agriculture*, the Supreme
Court, reaffirming an earlier case from 1984, stated: "in *Ruckelshaus v. Monsanto Co.*, we ... recognized that 'a voluntary submission of data by an applicant' in exchange for the ability to participate in a regulated market 'can hardly
be called a taking.'"[37]

The corporate assertion of trade secrets has also slowed litigation by those
injured by fracking. As environmental attorney Deborah Goldberg noted, "[i]f
you have medical problems, you might be able to sue for personal injury, but
those cases are taking a long time to develop, in large part, because the industry did such a good job of concealing the chemicals it was using.... It's only
since we've been getting more disclosure that plaintiffs have been able to trace
the connection in a way that has been generating winning verdicts."[38]

---

ment, 77 Ohio St. L.J. (forthcoming 2016), *available at* http://ssrn.com/abstract=2616550
(citing Eric Frankowski, *Gas Industry Secrets and a Nurse's Story*, High Country News
(July 28, 2008), https://www.hcn.org/wotr/gas-industry-secrets-and-a-nurses-story).

    35. Abrahm Lustgarten, *Buried Secrets: Is Natural Gas Drilling Endangering U.S. Water
Supplies?*, Pro Publica (Nov. 13, 2008), http://www.propublica.org/article/buried-secrets-
is-natural-gas-drilling-endangering-us-water-supplies-1113.

    36. Horne v. Dep't of Agric., 135 S. Ct. 2419, 2430 (2015) ("[In] *Ruckelshaus v. Mon-
santo Co....* we held that the Environmental Protection Agency could require companies
manufacturing pesticides, fungicides, and rodenticides to disclose health, safety, and environmental information about their products as a condition to receiving a permit to sell
those products. While such information included trade secrets in which pesticide manufacturers had a property interest, those manufacturers were not subjected to a taking because they received a 'valuable Government benefit' in exchange—a license to sell dangerous
chemicals.") (citing Ruckelshaus v. Monsanto Co., 467 U.S. 986 (1984)).

    37. *Id.* at 2440–41 (citing Ruckelshaus v. Monsanto Co., 467 U.S. 986 (1984)).

    38. Goldberg interview *supra* note 13.

C. Lying about the Facts

In these fights over regulations at state and federal agencies, the approach of extractive industries is often to use their informational advantage to outmaneuver the public. But what happens when the facts and the science are on the side of the public instead of the industry? Then, corporate tactics can shift into an all-out disinformation campaign. And this is what has happened in the battle over climate change denial at the congressional level. Despite reports from NASA predicting food shortages caused by climate change,[39] reports from the White House that climate change threatens infrastructure,[40] reports from the U.S. military that climate change poses an existential national security threat,[41] and reports from the United Nations that climate change will have significant negative impacts on individuals and ecosystems,[42] Congress has been slow to act or failed to act at all.[43] As a 2014 U.S. military report on climate change

39. Peter Schwartz & Doug Randall, *An Abrupt Climate Change Scenario and Its Implications for United States National Security*, NASA JET PROPULSION LABORATORY 2 (Oct. 2003), http://training.fema.gov/hiedu/docs/crr/catastrophe%20readiness%20and%20response%20-%20appendix%202%20-%20abrupt%20climate%20change.pdf (The report explores how such an abrupt climate change scenario could potentially de-stabilize the geo-political environment, leading to skirmishes, battles, and even war due to resource constraints such as: 1) Food shortages due to decreases in net global agricultural production[,] 2) Decreased availability and quality of fresh water in key regions due to shifted precipitation patters, causing more frequent floods and droughts [and] 3) Disrupted access to energy supplies due to extensive sea ice and storminess").

40. *Findings from Select Federal Reports: The National Security Implications of a Changing Climate*, WHITE HOUSE (May 2015), https://www.whitehouse.gov/sites/default/files/docs/National_Security_Implications_of_Changing_Climate_Final_051915.pdf ("The present day effects of climate change are being felt from the Arctic to the Midwest. Increased sea levels and storm surges threaten coastal regions, infrastructure, and property. In turn, the global economy suffers, compounding the growing costs of preparing and restoring infrastructure.").

41. *National Security and the Accelerating Risks of Climate Change*, CNA MILITARY ADVISORY BOARD iii (May 2014), https://www.cna.org/cna_files/pdf/MAB_5-8-14.pdf ("The nature and pace of observed climate changes—and an emerging scientific consensus on their projected consequences—pose severe risks for our national security.").

42. Intergovernmental Panel on Climate Change, *Climate Change 2014 Synthesis Report Fifth Assessment Report*, UNITED NATIONS (2014), http://ar5-syr.ipcc.ch/.

43. Juliet Eilperin & Steven Mufson, *EPA Proposes Cutting Carbon Dioxide Emissions from Coal Plants 30% by 2020*, WASH. POST (June 2, 2014), https://www.washingtonpost.com/national/health-science/epa-to-propose-cutting-carbon-dioxide-emissions-from-coal-plants-30percent-by-2030/2014/06/01/f5055d94-e9a8-11e3-9f5c-9075d5508f0a_story.html ("Ever since a climate bill stalled in the Senate four years ago, environmental and public health ac-

warned, "[t]ime and tide wait for no one ... We are dismayed that discussions of climate change have become so polarizing and have receded from the arena of informed public discourse and debate. Political posturing and budgetary woes cannot be allowed to inhibit discussion and debate over what so many believe to be a salient national security concern for our nation."[44]

Because science is a search for objective truths about the known universe, believing in its outcomes really should not be a matter of partisan politics. Two plus two should equal four, whether you are a Republican or a Democrat. And yet again and again, political ideology appears to block understanding and acceptance of facts. As Yale Professor Dan Kahan wrote, "public debate about science is strikingly polarized. The same groups who disagree on 'cultural issues'—abortion, same-sex marriage and school prayer—also disagree on whether climate change is real.... [Yet] [t]he ability of democratic societies to protect the welfare of their citizens depends on finding a way to counteract this culture war over empirical data."[45]

Battles over environmental policy that involve extractive industries (such as coal, oil, and gas) have turned into large-scale fights over science. So far, the Supreme Court has sided with mainstream scientific consensus that climate change is real.[46] But on Capitol Hill, Dr. Gretchen Goldman of the Union of Concerned Scientists noted, "[w]e see science get used as a political football."[47] And when asked how she sees corporations attacking science in policy making, she said,

> Any time we see something that might threaten business as usual, like a new public health protection, or a new environmental protection ... Then we see this pattern: we see companies and their agents—trade associations, lobbying firms and PR firms—we see them come on board and interfere with the science. They will downplay the risks that the science shows. Sometimes they will try to discredit the researcher. And sometimes they will hire their own

---

tivists have been pressing Obama to use his executive authority to impose carbon limits on the power sector, which accounts for 38 percent of the nation's carbon dioxide emissions.").

44. *National Security and the Accelerating Risks of Climate Change, supra* note 41, at iii.

45. Dan Kahan, *Fixing the Communications Failure,* 463 NATURE 296 (Jan. 21, 2010).

46. Massachusetts v. EPA , 549 U.S. 497, 504 (2007) ("A well-documented rise in global temperatures has coincided with a significant increase in the concentration of carbon dioxide in the atmosphere. Respected scientists believe the two trends are related.... carbon dioxide ... is therefore a species—the most important species—of a 'greenhouse gas.' ").

47. Goldman interview *supra* note 24.

scientists to spout the industry talking points through a science lens. Often that is bogus science."[48]

Deborah Goldberg agreed with her assessment, reporting from her perspective, "[t]here is a really negative impact of corporate money on policy-making. We see huge PR campaigns with less than fully accurate information, where there are conscious efforts to undermine good science and demonize the scientists who do it. And the stranglehold on our Congress in opposition to environmental protection is very extreme. If ever there were an argument for regulating money in politics, the environment would be it."[49] Meanwhile, Phil Radford stated that oil companies "took a play out the book of big tobacco. The strategy was to create a scientific debate to slow action.... You have 95% of scientists saying climate change is real. You have Shell and Chevron and coal industry funding scientists on the other side to make it look like there is a scientific debate."[50]

As environmental law professor Katrina Kuh described Congress' lack of action in the face of climate science, "it feels like you are in one of those dreams and you are screaming and no one hears you and no sound comes out."[51] Corporations in the extractive industries have tried to create the false impression for the public that there is serious debate about climate change. Dr. Goldman reports that this is a real problem. She indicated,

> [w]e still see the funding of researchers to spout the industry talking points to shed doubt on the climate debate. This year there was the revelation that Exxon Mobil and Southern Company had been funding Willie Soon, a researcher at the Harvard-Smithsonian Center for Astrophysics. He's been doing work to try to undermine [climate] science and had been paid by the industry to do that without disclosing those affiliations and conflicts of interest. And it continued years past the point when Exxon had said that it had stopped funding [climate] skeptics.[52]

48. *Id.*

49. Goldberg interview *supra* note 13.

50. Radford interview *supra* note 1; Tamara R. Piety, *The Corporate First Amendment, Why Protection for Commercial and Corporate Speech Does Not Advance First Amendment Values*, Corporate Reform Coalition, 37–40 (July 20, 2015), http://www.citizen.org/documents/crc-corporate-free-speech-report.pdf ("Recall that the tobacco companies are the ones who popularized the tactic of creating doubt and controversy around health warnings. And they industriously attempted to suggest to smokers who were worried about the health effects of smoking, through the colors on the package and terms such as "light," that light cigarettes were less damaging to their health. And they were successful....").

51. Interview with Hofstra Law Professor Katrina Fischer Kuh (Sept. 11, 2015).

52. Goldman interview *supra* note 24.

Presently, the New York Attorney General is investigating Exxon to see whether its stances on climate change violated New York's Martin Act by basically telling the investing public one thing, while telling internal audiences something different and contradictory.[53]

Professor Kuh noted, "[t]he difficulty with climate change is it is a slow moving disaster."[54] As a result, evidence of its effects are not always readily apparent. Still, there are some victims of the warming climate in the United States already. "The most readily identifiable climate victims in the United States are the native villagers of Kivalina who are presently being relocated from where they live on the Chukchi Sea in the Arctic because rising temperatures have so reduced the ice that used to surround their island that it is now disappearing to erosion. The Army Corps of Engineers has a relocation process underway."[55] The villagers tried to sue corporations for contributing to global warming.[56] This legal effort was unsuccessful.[57]

D. Capturing Decision Makers

Beyond taking advantage of information asymmetries, hiding the facts, or obfuscating, another approach is to try to control the actual decision makers. This is known as regulatory capture and it is another problem that seems to follow extractive industries like slime after a slug. Craig Aaron explained regulatory capture as "[t]he industries that are supposed to be regulated are calling the shots among the regulators.... You have a government agency that is really an extension of the corporations."[58] The problem of regulatory capture

---

53. Marilyn Geewax, *N.Y. Attorney General Investigates Whether Exxon Mobil Lied On Climate Change*, NPR (Nov. 5, 2015), http://www.npr.org/sections/thetwo-way/2015/11/05/454917914/new-york-attorney-general-investigating-exxonmobil-on-climate-change.

54. Kuh interview *supra* note 51.

55. *Id.*

56. Native Village of Kivalina v. ExxonMobil Corp., 696 F.3d 849, 853 (9th Cir. 2012) ("The Native Village of Kivalina ... alleges that massive greenhouse gas emissions emitted by the Energy Producers have resulted in global warming, which, in turn, has severely eroded the land where the City of Kivalina sits and threatens it with imminent destruction. Kivalina seeks damages under a federal common law claim of public nuisance.").

57. *Id.* at 858 ("Our conclusion obviously does not aid Kivalina, which itself is being displaced by the rising sea. But the solution to Kivalina's dire circumstance must rest in the hands of the legislative and executive branches of our government, not the federal common law.").

58. Interview with Craig Aaron, President Free Press (July 27, 2015) ("The communications industry loves to push the discussion to be as technical and obscure as possible. Let's

may be the most acute in the area of environmental law, where a few motivated polluters may outmaneuver the uncoordinated general public. Phil Radford illuminated, "[i]n California, there are 2,500 waste water disposal areas from fracking, many of which are polluting water bodies near L.A. and throughout California that are the source of water for drinking and irrigating crops. Investigations into the regulators shows that they are completely inept, corrupt and captured by industry."[59]

Federal administrative agencies, like the Environmental Protection Agency (EPA), may only hear from industry, and not the public, during the rulemaking process—thereby skewing the results. Often the public relies on the EPA itself to be the expert to counter the corporate narrative. And indeed, the EPA and other regulatory bodies can play this role as the "people's expert." But if a regulatory agency like the EPA is captured by the firms it is meant to regulate, then the public interest may be left on the cutting room floor as the captured agency problematically parrots back what corporate experts suggested they put in the final agency rules. As a result, who is in charge of the agency matters, and it is important to note that who is in charge of an agency changes as the presidency changes. Sometimes there are dedicated administrators and other times there are not.[60] During the George W. Bush Administration, Massachusetts sued the EPA for failing to enforce part of the Clean Air Act.[61] The EPA had taken the position that it did not have the authority to regulate greenhouse gases.[62] The Supreme Court agreed with Massachusetts that the EPA did have this authority and was not doing its job, holding, "EPA has offered no reasoned explanation for its refusal to decide whether greenhouse gases cause or contribute to climate change."[63] A document released from the EPA in 2009 revealed, "the George W. Bush administration had concluded in December 2007 that greenhouse gas emissions from motor vehicles were endangering public welfare and needed to be reg-

have days and days of expert testimony. Your average member of the public can barely sit through it. It doesn't help that the FCC has hearings during the day. You basically have to be an insider to even know it's going on.").

59. Radford interview *supra* note 1.

60. Eilperin & Mufson, *supra* note 43 ("The Environmental Protection Agency proposed a regulation Monday that would cut carbon dioxide emissions from existing coal plants by up to 30 percent by 2030 compared with 2005 levels, taking aim at one of the nation's leading sources of greenhouse gases.").

61. Massachusetts v. EPA, 549 U.S. 497 (2007).

62. *Id.* at 511.

63. *Id.* at 534; *but see* Michigan v. EPA, 576 U.S. __, 135 S. Ct. 2699 (2015) (invalidating EPA rule for an insufficient cost benefit analysis).

ulated under the Clean Air Act. The 29-page EPA analysis—labeled 'Deliberative, Do Not Distribute'—ticked through the climate-changing effects that heat-trapping gases have on air pollution, precipitation patterns, sea-level rise, glacial melting and wildlife patterns."[64]

Regulatory capture can take many forms, from the dull to the lurid. For instance, "following the BP Oil Spill, numerous accounts of industry influence in the well approval process showed that the Minerals Management Service cut corners in environmental review—in large part due to industry pressure to allow drilling to move forward quickly."[65] Arguably this agency was simply acting wildly inappropriately. Former Executive Director of Greenpeace Phil Radford described,

> [a]fter the BP Deep Water Horizon spill in the Gulf, we found out that the agency which was charged with regulating the oil industry was just out of control. Big parties with cocaine. Lots of trips on the dime of the oil industry. The oil industry had undue influence over that agency. Industries are working harder and harder to try to control the agency that regulates them in addition to Congress.[66]

This characterization of the Minerals Management Service is no exaggeration.[67] The MMS is now defunct. It was replaced with the Bureau of Ocean Energy Management (BOEM) and the Bureau of Safety and Environmental Enforcement (BSEE).

And why stop at trying to capture regulators if you can capture Congress itself? The reason there wasn't a federal law on the books to protect Cathy Behr was a failure at the congressional level. But here it wasn't a case of congressional omission. Rather, it was an affirmative act by Congress that caused this

---

64. Darren Samuelson & Robin Bravender, *EPA Releases Bush-Era Endangerment Document*, N.Y. Times (Oct. 13, 2009), http://www.nytimes.com/gwire/2009/10/13/13greenwire-epa-releases-bush-era-endangerment-document-47439.html.

65. Hari M. Osofsky & Hannah J. Wiseman, *Hybrid Energy Governance*, 2014 U. Ill. L. Rev. 1, 20 (2014).

66. Radford interview *supra* note 1.

67. *POGO: DOI's Minerals Management Service Wins "Worst Misconduct Abuse" Award*, POGO.org (Sep. 10, 2008), http://www.pogo.org/about/press-room/releases/2008/nr-ogr-20080910.html#sthash.BqlWUDjZ.dpuf ("the Department of Interior OIG have documented evidence that employees at the Department of Interior's Minerals Management Service (MMS) have accepted gifts, ski vacations, and sex from industry personnel. The charges illustrate the improper relationship between the regulatory agency and the oil and gas industry that it is tasked with over-seeing.").

problem: the enactment of the Halliburton loophole, a clear example of the power of corporate lobbying.[68] This loophole exempts fracking from the Clean Water Act and other environmental laws.[69] As Professor Elisabeth Radow clarifies, "passage of certain provisions of the Energy Policy Act of 2005, advanced by former Halliburton CEO-turned-Vice-President, Richard Cheney, exempted the oil and gas industry from the Safe Drinking Water Act and the Clean Water Act, and substantially stripped the EPA of its authority to regulate hydraulic fracturing."[70]

And the carve-out from the Safe Drinking Water Act and the Clean Water Act is only the start. As Deborah Goldberg explains:

> There are loopholes or exclusions from all of the major [federal] environmental laws for the oil and gas industry. They very successfully lobbied not to be covered by our major hazardous waste laws … There are major carve-outs from the Clean Water Act, from the Clean Air Act, from the Safe Water Drinking Act, from the National Environmental Policy Act. You name it. Any federal environmental law that affects the oil and gas industry allows that industry to operate in ways that other industries would never be permitted to operate.[71]

With fracking chemicals exempted from many federal laws, this leaves states on the front lines to regulate them. While there is an argument that states will be more careful than the federal government because they may be more politically responsive to local constituencies, the opposite can also happen as the

---

68. Joseph P. Tomain, *Shale Gas and Clean Energy Policy*, 63 CASE W. RES. L. REV. 1187, 1210 (2013) ("Unfortunately, the EPA, pursuant to the Energy Policy Act of 2005, is prohibited from regulating hydraulic fracturing operations under the Safe Drinking Water Act. This gaping loophole is known as the 'Halliburton exception' named for the oil and gas industry firm that lobbied for it and patented hydraulic fracturing in the 1940s.").

69. Kevin Grandia, *How Cheney's Loophole Is Fracking Up America*, HUFF. POST (May 25, 2011), http://www.huffingtonpost.com/kevin-grandia/how-cheneys-loophole-is-f_b_502924.html ("In 2005, at the urging of Vice President Cheney, fracking fluids were exempted from the Clean Water Act after the companies that own the patents on the process raised concerns about disclosing proprietary formulas—if they had to meet the Act's standards they would have to reveal the chemical composition which competitors could then steal. Fair enough, but this also exempts these companies from having to meet the strict regulations that protect the nation's freshwater supply.").

70. Elisabeth N. Radow, *Citizen David Tames Gas Goliaths on the Marcellus Shale Stage: Citizen Action as a Form of Dispute Prevention in the Internet Age*, 12 CARDOZO J. CONFLICT RESOL. 373, 382 (2011).

71. Goldberg interview *supra* note 13.

states compete in the classic race to the bottom to attract industry to locate in a particular state.[72] And the conservative lobbying group ALEC has pushed states to adopt policies that ignore climate science. As Lisa Graves related,

> ALEC's corporate board has presided over decades of climate change denial. ALEC has argued to their lawmakers that climate change is not happening or that if it is going on that it is good for you.... They have deployed a range of [state] bills to stop addressing climate change. They have tried to stop renewable energy contracts of states, they have tried to stop regional climate agreements, and they are trying to stop the EPA from having any authority over carbon.[73]

An alarming example of how states are trying to lure fracking to their backyards is the an inconspicuous law called Act 13, passed by Pennsylvania in 2012. Two of the subsections, when read together, restricted doctors from informing anyone, including other physicians, about the contents of fracking chemical mixtures. "The purpose of the 'Medical Gag Rule' was to provide a necessary layer of protection for trade secret exemptions claimed by the companies for proprietary information.... In July 2014, the Pennsylvania Commonwealth court addressed this very provision and upheld the 'gag order' provision of Act 13. In fact, the opinion of a majority of the judges was that doctors 'have nothing to worry about' with the law."[74] In a federal case, a doctor challenged Act 13, but the case was dismissed because the courts concluded that the doctor had not been injured, *yet*.[75]

---

72. McFeeley, *supra* note 32, at 859 ("In general, states perform poorly on almost all metrics [of fracking chemical disclosure].").

73. Interview with Lisa Graves, Executive Director Center for Media & Democracy (July 17, 2015).

74. Sherwin, *supra* note 34; Janet L. Dolgin, *Physician Speech and State Control: Furthering Partisan Interests at the Expense of Good Health*, 48 NEW ENG. L. REV. 293, 308 (2014); Susan Phillips, *Science and the Fracturing Boom: Missing Answers*, NPR (May 17, 2012), http://www.npr.org/2012/05/17/152268501/pennsylvania-doctors-worry-over-fracturing-gag-rule; *Rodriguez v. Krancer*, No. 3:12-CV-1458, 2013 WL 574866, 1 (M.D. Pa. July 27, 2013); Katie Colaneri & Susan Phillips, *Commonwealth Court Throws Out Several Challenges to Act 13, Including 'Doctor Gag Rule' [UPDATED]*, NPR (July 17, 2014), https://stateimpact.npr.org/pennsylvania/2014/07/17/commonwealth-court-throws-out-several-challenges-to-act-13-including-doctor-gag-rule-updated)).

75. Rodriguez v. Secretary of Pennsylvania Dept. of Environmental Protection of Pennsylvania, 604 Fed. Appx. 113, 115 (3d Cir. 2015) ("District Court [found] that Rodriguez has failed to allege an injury-in-fact.").

E. Taking Responsibility

Again, not every industry is acting like the oil and gas industry. There are plenty of firms who are doing the right thing. Caring about the environment and caring about the bottom line do not have to be at loggerheads. As Daniel C. Esty and Andrew S. Winston argued in their book GREEN TO GOLD, "[o]ur economy and society depend on natural resources. To oversimplify, every product known to man came from something mined or grown ... [A]n environmental lens is not just a nice strategy tool or a feel-good digression from the real work of a company. It's an essential element of business strategy in the modern world."[76] Ironically, while huge multinationals can cause epic damage, they are also in the position to be a helpful force on environmental stewardship across national boundaries. As Nell Minow explains, Walmart has used its market share and supply chain to influence environmental policy for the better:

> The good and bad news is corporations are in a better position to address environment issues than any government. Walmart has done more than the Oslo Accords to improve environmental conditions in China by saying to their manufacturers to up their game or else we won't buy from you anymore.[77]

And Former Executive Director of Greenpeace Phil Radford notes that progress can be made with environmental stewardship by the largest technology companies. He reports,

> Apple, Google, Facebook and a whole set of companies have committed to Greenpeace to make the cloud 100% clean energy. Servers for the cloud are 2% of worldwide electricity use. Cloud computing is one of the fastest growing drivers of energy consumption. But these major players committed that the server farms that they use will be 100% renewable.[78]

---

76. DANIEL C. ESTY & ANDREW S. WINSTON, GREEN TO GOLD 3 (2006).

77. Interview with Nell Minow, Vice Chair, ValueEdge Advisors (Aug. 19, 2015); *see also* Interview with Timothy Smith, Walden Asset Management (Aug. 7, 2015) ("Walmart is requiring companies that provide goods and services for them to increase environmental standards and increase disclosure. They are using the power of their supply chain to do better by the environment.").

78. Radford interview *supra* note 1.

And in another success story, "[i]n Brazil, Greenpeace worked with McDonald's and Burger King who pushed suppliers to stop deforestation of the rain forest for beef."[79]

The urge to externalize environmental costs continues at many firms. This leads to pitched legislative battles over what types of environmental regulations can be passed to protect the integrity of water, air, and land. So far, extractives industries win a victory every day that the Halliburton loophole continues at the federal level. States are put to the hard choice of how to regulate their natural resources responsibly in the face of federal failures to regulate. These choices are even more difficult to make in the face of a noise machine of misinformation about the underlying science, especially as industries hide the facts through trade secrets. The story of a nurse harmed by fracking chemicals hidden behind a veil of trade secrets should give lawmakers pause. We can and must do better. We need energy. But we also need reasonable environmental protections.

---

79. *Id.*

Part IV

The Push Back

Thus far, this book has painted a rather dire and unflattering picture of corporations. And to be fair, thus far it has focused on case law that involves some of the most egregious types of corporate behavior, and the most aggressive legal arguments that have been deployed to absolve them. Historically, there have always been various strains of resistance in America to the inevitability of corporate domination, like Justice Brandeis's dissent in the *Liggett* case, where he laid out the history of the race to the bottom for corporate governance laws.[1] Today, corporations are facing resistance to their expansion of rights without concomitant responsibilities. They face opposition from investors, customers, and lawmakers. They also face an interesting new resistance from more morally grounded fellow entrepreneurs, who do not want profit-seeking behavior to be their lodestar.

---

1. Stephen W. Baskerville, Of Laws and Limitations: An Intellectual Portrait of Louis Dembitz Brandeis 309–10 (1994) (citing Letter from Louis D. Brandeis to Frank A. Fetter (Nov. 26, 1940) in 5 Letters of Louis D. Brandeis 648 (Melvin I. Urofsky & David W. Levy, eds., 1971–78); Letter from Louis D. Brandeis to Felix Frankfurter (Oct. 18, 1935) in Felix Frankfurter Papers, Library of Congress, Washington, D.C., Box 28; *Liggett*, 288 U.S. at 548–64 (Brandeis, J., dissenting)).

Chapter 11

Shareholders Remember They Own the Joint

If we cannot keep corporations out of our democracy, then we must have more democracy in our corporations.

—David G. Yosifon[2]

Shareholders are the forgotten stepchild of the corporate world. They are often treated as if they should be seen and not heard. Or to put it more bluntly, that they should turn over their money and then never make a peep. This passive role is not accepted by active investors, who have clamored for—and received—more rights to participate in corporate democracy. The discussion below is limited largely to shareholder proposals on corporate proxies trying to encourage firms to be better corporate citizens of one stripe or another. But this is just a subset of shareholders' democratic rights to vote within the corporate structure. And some shareholders have tried other tactics to get corporations to change their behavior, including lawsuits.

To review, corporations have a particular legal structure. The board of directors makes the key decisions for the corporation. The board is elected by the shareholders, who own equity in the corporation. The board has a fiduciary duty to act in the shareholders' best interests. The board hires officers to run the corporation day-to-day. Shareholders typically have no say (with some narrow exceptions) on the day-to-day management of ordinary business. But

---

2. David G. Yosifon, *It's Law, But It Shouldn't Be*, Room for Debate, N.Y. Times (Apr. 16, 2015), http://www.nytimes.com/roomfordebate/2015/04/16/what-are-corporations-obligations-to-shareholders/its-law-but-it-shouldnt-be.

shareholders do get to vote on retaining the board yearly, as well as on managerial and shareholder proposals on the corporate proxy.[3]

The word "equity" is a miniature Rorschach test. For those working on social justice, "equity" means justice and fairness—it is a synonym for equality. For those who work on Wall St., "equity" is an ownership stake in a company. The etymology of the word reveals the roots of both meanings:

> "Equity" derives from the Latin word for horse, equus. When soldiers came back from various wars they would get a horse, a form of property. This was at a time when Roman society was pretty much stratified between two tiers, composed of aristocrats and slaves. There was no such thing as a middle class. The government rewarded returning warriors with a horse and allowed them to farm and create a family. The horse was a piece of property that distinguished the ex-soldier from the emperor and the slave. That gave them a stake in society.[4]

The idea is thus premised on the idea of fairness as well as creating stakeholders in society. So whether you are talking about a corporation's "equity," as in its social justice, or its "equity," as in ownership of the company, shareholders are center stage in the debate.

Investors can be a very heterogeneous group, geographically, ideologically, and even temporally. Some will only hold a stock for less than a day. Others will be invested for decades. While high-frequency traders may only own a stock for a fraction of a second, there are still investors who hold investments for years, and who worry about the long-term profitability of firms. Here, the emphasis is primarily on these longer-term investors, who have an interest in the long-term sustainability of a firm. The paradigmatic examples of long-term investors are institutional investors like public pension funds.[5]

A. Corporate Democracy

Often, phrases have multiple meanings, like the double meanings of "equity." Problematically, these double meanings allow people to talk past each

---

3. Lisa M. Fairfax, Shareholder Democracy: A Primer on Shareholder Activism and Participation 7 (2011) ("State law is the primary source of shareholders' voting rights.").

4. Interview with Dr. Marcy Murninghan, corporate governance expert (July 24, 2015).

5. Interview with Heidi Welsh, Executive Director Sustainable Investment Institute (July 8, 2015) ("Public funds are looking at the very long term. They will tell you that they think of investing perpetually for the 20-year-old that just started working.").

other. One phrase that has multiple meanings is "corporate democracy." After all, "corporate democracy" could describe the incursion of corporations into the political process. But here, "corporate democracy" is meant to have the connotations it has in the world of corporate governance, referring to those voting rights that investors have within the corporate structure.[6]

American courts have held repeatedly that a core component of American corporations are the "procedures of corporate democracy"—a phrase Justice Kennedy used in his *Citizens United* majority opinion. What Justice Kennedy meant by "procedures of corporate democracy" is not entirely self-evident, as he neglected to provide a definition. Typically, in corporate law, the way that shareholders hold managers accountable is through voting their proxy card at an annual or special meeting of shareholders. On a typical corporate proxy card, there are four items that are subject to a shareholder vote on an annual basis: (1) the election of directors, (2) the appointment of auditors/accountants, (3) management proposals and (4) shareholder proposals.[7] After the enactment of Dodd-Frank, shareholders in publicly traded firms have the right to vote on a fifth category: executive compensation.[8] And each of these five categories could be properly thought of as a subject of "corporate democracy."[9]

Although Justice Kennedy failed to provide a definition, previous Supreme Court opinions have articulated what the Court means by the phrase "corporate democracy." In 1964 in *Borak*, the Supreme Court noted that federal securities laws are meant to empower "fair corporate suffrage."[10] Then in 1991, in *Virginia Bankshares*, the Supreme Court quoted the legislative history of the Securities Exchange Act of 1934 highlighting the centrality of shareholders' voting rights: "[a]ccording to the House Report, Congress meant to promote the 'free exercise' of stockholders' voting rights, and protect ... [them] from

---

6. Frank Pasquale, *Two Meanings of Corporate Governance*, Concurring Opinions (Sept. 14, 2010), http://concurringopinions.com/archives/2010/09/two-meanings-of-corporate-governance.html.

7. *Sample Proxy Card*, SEC, https://www.sec.gov/spotlight/proxymatters/proxy_sample.htm (last visited March 29, 2015).

8. Dodd-Frank Section 951(a)(2); Exchange Act Section 14A(a)(2); 15 U.S.C. §78n-1(a)(2).

9. Ciara Torres-Spelliscy, *Corporate Democracy from Say on Pay to Say on Politics*, 30(2) Constitutional Commentary 431 (Summer 2015).

10. J. I. Case Co. v. Borak, 377 U.S. 426, 431 (1964) ("The section stemmed from the congressional belief that '[f]air corporate suffrage is an important right that should attach to every equity security bought on a public exchange.'") (quoting H.R. Rep. No. 73-1383, at 13 (1934)).

abuses exemplified by proxy solicitations that concealed what the Senate Report called the 'real nature' of the issues to be settled by the subsequent [shareholder] votes."[11] Thereby, the Supreme Court affirmed the importance of shareholders' right to meaningfully participate in the management of the corporations that they own.

Given Delaware's prominent role in American corporate law, another useful source for defining the meaning of "corporate democracy" is Delaware case law.[12] Delaware is the center of gravity for American corporate law because so many firms choose Delaware as their locus of incorporation. As the *New York Times* reported in 2012, "[n]early half of all public corporations in the United States are incorporated in Delaware. Last year, 133,297 businesses set up here. And, at last count, Delaware had more corporate entities, public and private, than people—945,326 to 897,934."[13]

The Delaware courts have been quite protective of corporate democracy.[14] As one of the lower courts in Delaware concluded, "shareholder franchise is the ideological underpinning upon which the legitimacy of [corporate] directorial power rests."[15] Or as the Supreme Court of Delaware once explained, "[b]ecause of the overriding importance of voting rights, this Court and the Court of Chancery have consistently acted to protect stockholders from unwarranted interference with such [voting] rights."[16] In a 2012 case, the Delaware Supreme Court reaffirmed these earlier precedents, stating in no uncertain terms: "[s]hareholder voting rights are *sacrosanct*. The fundamental governance right possessed by shareholders is the ability to vote for the directors the

---

11. Virginia Bankshares, Inc. v. Sandberg, 501 U.S. 1083, 1103 (1991).

12. MM Cos. v. Liquid Audio, Inc., 813 A.2d 1118, 1127 (Del. 2003) (explaining Delaware's courts "have remained assiduous in carefully reviewing any board actions designed to interfere with or impede the effective exercise of corporate democracy by shareholders, especially in an election of directors").

13. Leslie Wayne, *How Delaware Thrives as a Corporate Tax Haven*, N.Y. Times (June 30, 2012), http://www.nytimes.com/2012/07/01/business/how-delaware-thrives-as-a-corporate-tax-haven.html.

14. Unocal Corp. v. Mesa Petroleum Co., 493 A.2d 946, 959 (Del. 1985) ("If the stockholders are displeased with the action of their elected representatives, the powers of corporate democracy are at their disposal to turn the board out.").

15. Blasius Indus., Inc. v. Atlas Corp., 564 A.2d 651, 659 (Del. Ch. 1988); *id.* at 663 ("The theory of our corporation law confers power upon directors as the agents of the shareholders; it does not create Platonic masters.").

16. Paramount Communications, Inc. v. QVC Network Inc., 637 A.2d 34, 42 (Del. 1994); Williams v. Geier, 671 A.2d 1368, 1381 (Del. 1996) (where "stockholders control their own destiny through informed voting ... [t]his is the highest and best form of corporate democracy").

shareholder wants to oversee the firm. Without that right, a shareholder would more closely resemble a creditor than an owner."[17]

B. History of Shareholder Voting Rights on Political Issues

The idea that shareholders could change the social and political behavior of the companies they own using the mechanisms of corporate democracy has been around for decades.[18] Heidi Welsh provided some historical perspective that there have been shareholder resolutions on topics as varied as nuclear weapons to South African Apartheid: "[s]hareholder resolutions reflect what is going on in society and the issues of the day."[19]

Back in the early 1950s, James Peck, working with civil rights lawyer Bayard Rustin,[20] tried to get Greyhound to allow a shareholder vote on ending racial segregation on Greyhound buses.[21] Peck and Rustin were both grass-roots activists who participated in direct protests to try to end segregation, in addition to the more staid approach of going through the SEC and courts.[22] In a no-action let-

17. EMAK Worldwide, Inc. v. Kurz, 50 A.3d 429, 433 (Del. 2012) (emphasis added).

18. Leila N. Sadat-Keeling, *The 1983 Amendments to Shareholder Proposal Rule 14a-8: A Retreat from Corporate Democracy?*, 59 Tul. L. Rev. 161, 168–69 (1984) (citing *Peck v. Greyhound Corp.*, 97 F. Supp. 679 (S.D.N.Y. 1951)) ("[B]etween 1944 and 1971, not one shareholder proposal was able to muster judicial support for its inclusion. Thus, when the late 1960's and 1970's brought an increase in shareholder proposals, the law clearly disfavored their proponents.").

19. Welsh interview *supra* note 5.

20. Richard Marens, *Inventing Corporate Governance: The Mid-Century Emergence of Shareholder Activism*, 8 J. Bus. & Mgmt. 365, 372 (2002) ("He [James Peck] and Bayard Rustin, both then working for the Congress of Racial Equality, each bought a share of stock in Greyhound as the price of admission to the annual shareholder's meeting in 1948 with the intention of raising the issue of integrating bus seating in the South."); Raymond O. Arsenault, *You Don't Have to Ride Jim Crow*, 34 Stetson L. Rev. 343, 364 (2005).

21. Eric Engle, *What You Don't Know Can Hurt You: Human Rights, Shareholder Activism and Sec Reporting Requirements*, 57 Syracuse L. Rev. 63, 78 (2006) ("Apparently 'leave the driving to us' once meant 'get in the back of the bus.'").

22. Daniel Levine, Bayard Rustin and the Civil Rights Movement 53 (2000) ("The sixteen [men], including Bayard Rustin ... were experienced in nonviolent demonstrations."); *State v. Johnson*, 51 S.E.2d 186, 186 (N.C. 1949) ("[T]he defendants ... Bayard Rustin, Igal Roodenko and Joseph A. Felmont, the first two being colored men and the latter two white men, boarded one of the busses ... [t]he defendants Rustin and Roodenko ... were sitting together in ... [t]hey were requested by the bus driver to take the proper seats which were designated, but they refused to move."); *People ex rel. Hearn v. Parilli*, 1 Misc. 2d 201, 204

ter, the SEC sided with Greyhound, holding that Peck's shareholder proposal was excludable from the company's proxy under then-applicable SEC Rule 14a-8. (Rule 14a-8 sets the parameters for what is allowed on the proxy of a publicly traded company.) As Mr. Peck wrote about his efforts at the time: "in my case the SEC ruled that no social issue is a proper subject for action by stockholders.... The issue, therefore, is much broader than segregation on Greyhound's southern buses."[23] In litigation following the SEC's no action letter, the court also sided with Greyhound.[24] But it was on exhaustion of remedies grounds.[25] In 1952, the SEC clarified which subjects were proper for inclusion on the proxy, fencing out most social and political issues.[26] And during the 1960s and 1970s, the SEC sided with companies that wanted to keep "political matters" off the proxy.[27] The few political matters that were left on the proxy saw little support.[28]

(N.Y.S. 1955) ("[D]efendants [including Bayard Rustin and James Peck] as pacifists, intended to and did willfully disobey the official orders incident to the air raid drill that was being conducted under the New York Defense Emergency Act.").

23. James Peck, *Minority Stockholders vs. Jim Crow—Continued, in* THE CRISIS 367, 368 (June/July 1952).

24. D. A. Jeremy Telman, *Is the Quest for Corporate Responsibility A Wild Goose Chase? The Story of* Lovenheim v. Iroquois Brands, Ltd., 44 AKRON L. REV. 479, 489–90 (2011) ("the court denied Peck's motion to enjoin Greyhound from soliciting proxies and holding its shareholder meeting unless Peck's proposal was included in Greyhound's proxy materials, finding that Peck had failed to exhaust available administrative remedies. The court believed that Peck must first pursue SEC review of its staff's no-action letter before seeking the injunction.").

25. *Liberalizing Sec Rule 14a-8 Through the Use of Advisory Proposals*, 80 YALE L.J. 845, 864 n.45 (1971) ("In one of the few court cases involving the shareholder proposal rule, this release [the SEC Securities Exchange Act of 1934 Release No. 3638] was used to justify the omission from Greyhound's proxy of a proposal recommending that management consider the advisability of abolishing the segregated seating system in the South.").

26. Thomas W. Joo, *Corporate Governance and the "D-Word"*, 63 WASH. & LEE L. REV. 1579, 1588 (2006) ("As a shareholder of Greyhound Corporation, Peck attempted to use the federal shareholder proposal rule to advance a resolution against segregated bus seating. The SEC advised Greyhound in 1951 that it need not allow shareholders to use the proposal rule for 'political' issues and codified this position in a 1952 amendment to the rule."); Marilyn B. Cane, *The Revised SEC Shareholder Proxy Proposal System: Attitudes, Results and Perspectives*, 11 J. CORP. L. 57, 76 (1985) ("By 1952 the Commission promulgated specific rules which delineated 'proper subject.' Among those proposals which could be excluded (i.e., those not proper subjects) were those relating to general political, social or economic matters.).

27. Henry G. Manne, *Shareholder Social Proposals Viewed by an Opponent*, 24 STAN. L. REV. 481, 486 (1972) ("*Peck v. Greyhound Inc.* is the only proposal dealing with what we now term a 'social issue'... Now, only twenty years later, it is almost eerie to contemplate the lack of public concern that the case aroused.").

28. Dale A. Oesterle & Alan R. Palmiter, *Judicial Schizophrenia in Shareholder Voting*

But things changed radically with a D.C. Circuit Court case brought by shareholders of the Dow Chemical Company called the *Medical Committee for Human Rights v. SEC*. In 1970, the D.C. Circuit embraced strong corporate democracy rights for shareholders:

> It is obvious to the point of banality to restate the proposition that Congress intended ... to give true vitality to the concept of corporate democracy. The depth of this commitment is reflected in the strong language employed in the legislative history: Even those who in former days managed great corporations were by reason of their personal contacts with their shareholders constantly aware of their responsibilities. But as management became divorced from ownership and came under the control of banking groups, men forgot that they were dealing with the savings of men and the making of profits became an impersonal thing. When men do not know the victims of their aggression they are not always conscious of their wrongs.... Fair corporate suffrage is an important right that should attach to every equity security bought on a public exchange.[29]

The shareholders at Dow were trying to use a shareholder resolution to implore the firm to stop producing the chemical weapon napalm for the Vietnam War.[30] In the *Medical Committee for Human Rights* case, the D.C. Circuit dramatically expanded the rights of shareholders in publicly traded firms under SEC Rule 14a to vote on political and social issues through shareholder resolutions on corporate proxy cards. As the Court explicated: "there is a clear and compelling distinction between management's legitimate need for freedom to apply its expertise in matters of day-to-day business judgment, and management's patently illegitimate claim of power to treat modern corporations with their vast resources as personal satrapies implementing personal political or moral predilections."[31] This case proved to be a watershed moment for in-

---

Cases, 79 Iowa L. Rev. 485, 487 (1994) ("During the 1950s and 1960s, proxy contests were still infrequent, and insurgents were still unsuccessful; management-sponsored initiatives won and shareholder-sponsored initiatives lost, each by wide margins.").

29. Med. Comm. for Human Rights v. SEC, 432 F.2d 659, 676 (D.C. Cir. 1970) (citing H.R. Rep. No. 73-1383, at 5, 13 (1934)).

30. The shareholders in question were the Medical Committee for Human Rights (MCHR), which provided emergency medical care for civil rights workers in Mississippi in the 1960s. Medical Committee for Human Rights, Med. Comm. For Human Rights 1, 2, http://www.crmvet.org/docs/64_mchr.pdf (solicitation pamphlet).

31. Med. Comm. for Human Rights v. SEC, 432 F.2d 659, 681 (D.C. Cir. 1970); *see also* Roosevelt v. E.I. Du Pont de Nemours & Co., 958 F.2d 416, 421 (D.C. Cir. 1992) ("Access

creasing the scope of permissible shareholder proposals.[32] Shortly thereafter, the SEC changed Rule 14a-8 to allow for shareholder proposals on social and political matters.[33] Rule 14a-8 now empowers shareholder resolutions on issues like transparency of corporate political spending, environmental matters, and other corporate social responsibility issues.

C. Socially Responsible Investing

The inheritors of Peck, Rustin, and the Medical Committee for Human Rights' legacy are today's socially responsible investors. Shareholder actions asking for more socially responsible behavior by companies have taken off in the past two decades with socially responsible investing (or SRI). SRI is a growing sector of shareholding in the United States[34] as well as globally.[35] While once thought to be a distraction that would go away,[36] SRI has matured to the point

---

to management proxy solicitations to sound out management views and to communicate with other shareholders on matters of major import is a right informational in character, one properly derived from section 14(a) and appropriately enforced by private right of action." (internal citation omitted)).

32. *See e.g.,* Lovenheim v. Iroquois Brands, Ltd., 618 F. Supp. 554, 556, 561 (D.D.C. 1985) (in light of "ethical and social significance" of a shareholder proposal on animal cruelty, court granted preliminary injunction barring a corporation from excluding from its proxy materials shareholder proposal regarding pate de foie gras production).

33. Adoption of Amendments Relating to Proposals by Security Holders, Exchange Act Release No. 12,999, 41 Fed. Reg. at 52,994, 52,998 (Nov. 22, 1976).

34. Virginia Harper Ho, *"Enlightened Shareholder Value": Corporate Governance Beyond the Shareholder-Stakeholder Divide*, 36 J. CORP. L. 59, 88 (2010) ("Support for emerging conceptions of enlightened shareholder value is further amplified by its natural overlap with much of the SRI movement, which now accounts for more than 12% of all professionally managed investments in the United States, or $3.07 trillion assets under management.").

35. Jacob Park & Sonia Kowal, *Socially Responsible Investing 3.0: Understanding Finance and Environmental, Social, and Governance Issues in Emerging Markets*, 18 GEO. PUB. POL'Y REV. 17, 26–27 (2013) ("The global effects of increasing SRI in China.... SRI has the potential to advance a deeper set of social, environmental, and ethical business norms on the global level and is finally becoming a market reality, if not a force, in a number of emerging economies.").

36. Michael S. Knoll, *Ethical Screening in Modern Financial Markets: The Conflicting Claims Underlying Socially Responsible Investment*, 57 BUS. LAW. 681, 681 (2002) ("The proponents of socially responsible investment (SRI) claim that as of the end of 1999, $1.5 trillion was invested in the United States using social criteria. That is up from $40 billion in 1984, which implies an annualized compound rate of increase of twenty-seven percent. Moreover, rather than slowing down, SRI has been accelerating.").

where returns on socially responsible investments are equal to or greater than other investments[37] as major institutional investors have adopted the approach.[38]

Even the venerable Wharton Business School reports, "[t]imes have changed. There remain company chieftains who take a Friedman-esque view, of course, but many more have made CSR [Corporate Social Responsibility] a priority. Ten years ago, for instance, only about a dozen Fortune 500 companies issued a CSR or sustainability report. Now the majority does."[39] Wharton continued, "[m]ore than 8,000 businesses around the world have signed the UN Global Compact pledging to show good global citizenship in the areas of human rights, labor standards and environmental protection."[40]

This is really a remarkable evolution. Think back to when Mr. Peck and Mr. Rustin were trying to get Greyhound to allow a shareholder vote on racial segregation in the 1950s. They could not convince the company, the SEC, or the courts that social issues were an appropriate topic for a corporate proxy. How times have changed. But now, socially responsible investors can influence corporate behavior, and the SEC and courts typically allow social topics onto corporate proxies. Timothy Smith of Walden Asset Management reported on the development of these trends that, "[o]ne trend in SRI is the tremendous growth of mainstream investment managers and pension funds being involved in ESG [Environmental, Social, and Governance] issues. Now we have the Principals for Responsible Investing with investors with $58 trillion in assets under management saying that ESG must be taken into account in the investment process because they effect the bottom line. And you have the Carbon Disclosure Proj-

---

37. Sarah Pickering, *Our House: Crowdfunding Affordable Homes with Tax Credit Investment Partnerships*, 33 Rev. Banking & Fin. L. 937, 975 (2014) ("[T]here is evidence that certain forms of SRI may outperform traditional investments in periods of financial crisis. Much in the same way that the conservative lending practices of smaller financial institutions insulated their losses in the most recent financial crisis, SRI also experiences stability in economic downturns.").

38. Li-Wen Lin, *Corporate Social and Environmental Disclosure in Emerging Securities Markets*, 35 N.C. J. Int'l L. & Com. Reg. 1, 6–7 (2009) ("SRI has evolved from eccentric practices by a small club of faith-based investors to innovative strategies by a large community of financially-sophisticated investors. Major asset management companies offer a variety of SRI products. Large institutional investors ... (e.g. CalPERS, the largest public pension fund in the United States), have adopted responsible investment principles.").

39. *From Fringe to Mainstream: Companies Integrate CSR Initiatives into Everyday Business*, Wharton Univ. Pa. (May 23, 2012), http://knowledge.wharton.upenn.edu/article/from-fringe-to-mainstream-companies-integrate-csr-initiatives-into-everyday-business/.

40. *Id.*

ect with investors with $95 trillion under management asking companies about their carbon footprint. Mainstreaming is real."[41]

Heidi Welsh keeps track of shareholder support for issues on corporate proxies and she recounted, "[i]n the last decade shareholder support for environmental and social issues has more than doubled. It went from an average of 10% to 20%."[42] Many firms are apparently responding to pressure from SRI investors[43] by including reporting about Corporate Social Responsibility (CSR).[44] As Robert Monks quipped, "SRI proposals are having an impact on corporate behavior. If you work very hard, the way you know you are successful is if the corporation hires a vice president who is in charge of coping with you."[45]

The battle over corporate political spending between firms and their shareholders could be seen as just a subset of topics that socially responsible investors are worried about. These investors want more transparency on a host of issues besides money in politics. Timothy Smith of Walden Asset Management reasoned: "[a]s investors we support companies being transparent on key issues including climate change, diversity, and governance. And we think transparency regarding where shareholder money is spent for lobbying and political spending is in the investors' best interest."[46]

D. A Sleeping Giant Awakes After *Citizens United*

Even though shareholders have a broad ability to raise issues on the proxy, investors often neglect this power or fail to vote their proxies at all. The founder of Vanguard, Jack Bogle, in his 2005 book urged shareholders to engage more:

---

41. Interview with Timothy Smith, Walden Asset Management (Aug. 7, 2015); *see also* Interview with Warren Langley, Former President of the Pacific Stock Exchange (July 14, 2015) ("[s]ocially responsible investing is on the rise. I was looking at Schwab and there is a box you can tick for socially responsible investments. That is a sign of how mainstream it is now.").

42. Welsh interview *supra* note 5.

43. Michael R. Siebecker, *A New Discourse Theory of the Firm After* Citizens United, 79 Geo. Wash. L. Rev. 161, 173 (2010) ("A 2008 survey of international business leaders conducted by IBM indicates that 68% of those surveyed focus on CSR [corporate social responsibility] activities to generate new revenue and that 54% believe current CSR activities give their company an advantage over competitors.").

44. *Id.* at 127 ("In 2008, 86% of companies in the S&P 100 Index included information about social and environmental business practices on their websites.").

45. Interview with Robert A.G. Monks (Aug. 17, 2015).

46. Timothy Smith interview *supra* note 41.

[b]y and large, all we have heard from these owners is the sound of silence. If the owners don't give a damn about the triumph of managers' capitalism, it is fair to ask, who on earth should? Stock owners must demand that directors and managers alike honor the primacy of their interests. The corporation, after all, is their property.[47]

Mr. Bogle was essentially complaining that investors were asleep at the wheel. But there was a change in tone among many investors after 2010 because *Citizens United* awoke a slumbering giant, the American shareholder.[48] Ever since 2010, shareholders have been trying to make their desires heard around the ability of corporations to spend more money in elections. By all objective measures, "[s]hareholder resolutions on corporate political activity really blossomed after 2010."[49]

Corporate political activity, as unleashed by *Citizens United* and *Bellotti*, presents a new set of quandaries for investors, in part because investors bear the risk if the corporate political activity goes badly. Former FEC Chair, Trevor Potter, contended, "[t]here are problems that corporations face if they get involved in controversial political activity which could injure the shareholders' equity. A political controversy could result in boycotts and loss of good will. Shareholders are punished if the company gets it wrong."[50]

Here recalling the corporate structure is important. When the Supreme Court granted corporations the power to spend in politics, as a practical matter, this empowered officers and directors of corporations to direct corporate resources into politics.[51] And as the Chief Justice of the Delaware Supreme Court reminds us,

> Most Americans have become 'forced capitalists' who must give over a large portion of their wealth to the stock market to fund their re-

---

47. JOHN C. BOGLE, THE BATTLE FOR THE SOUL OF CAPITALISM 60 (2005).

48. Adolf A. Berle, *Corporate Powers as Powers in Trust*, 44 HARV. L. REV. 1049, 1049 (1931) (Berle explained that, "all powers granted to a corporation or the management of a corporation … are necessarily and at all times exercisable only for the ratable benefit of all the shareholders as their interest appears").

49. Welsh interview *supra* note 5.

50. Interview with Trevor Potter, President Campaign Legal Ctr. (July 27, 2015).

51. Kent Greenfield, *The Stakeholder Strategy*, 26 DEMOCRACY (2012) http://www.democracyjournal.org/26/the-stakeholder-strategy.php?page=all ("The reason why corporate political speech is so corrosive to democracy is that the benefits and prerogatives of the corporate form are marshaled to bolster the speech of a tiny sliver of the financial and managerial elite. The fact that corporations speak is not itself a problem; whom they speak for is.").

tirements and their children's educations. As a result, the actual human beings whose capital is invested by these intermediaries do not directly vote on who sits on corporate boards, do not have the option to buy and sell the securities of particular companies on any basis, and only retain very limited rights of exit from the market without facing expropriatory levels of taxation.[52]

The corporate structure makes it difficult for shareholders to influence how corporate managers spend money in politics, even if managers are spending in ways that are detrimental to shareholders.[53]

When the Supreme Court upheld the disclosure of money in politics as perfectly constitutional in *Citizens United*, the Justices presumed that corporate political spending would be transparent. But one of the troubling things about the political spending post-*Citizens United* is how much of it has been "dark money" or, in other words, from an untraceable source. Between 2010 and today, at least $600 million in spending in federal elections has been dark money. Much of this dark money is flowing through trade associations, thus it is reasonable to surmise that some of that dark money is corporate. More than $67 million of this money was routed through the Chamber of Commerce, an opaque business trade association.[54] A presumably high percentage of that money was from corporate sources.

As the law stands now, corporations can legally refuse to tell investors where they are spending in politics. Trevor Potter stated, "[t]here is an odd aspect to the Kennedy opinion [in *Citizens United*] because he says shareholders will know how their corporations are spending their money and they can take appropriate action. But as we see, they don't know. He must have assumed that the name of the company would be on the ads."[55] In 2015, Justice Kennedy

---

52. Leo E. Strine, Jr. & Nicholas Walter, *Conservative Collision Course?: The Tension Between Conservative Corporate Law Theory and* Citizens United, 100 CORNELL L. REV. 335, 370 (2015) (internal citations omitted).

53. ROBERT A.G. MONKS & NELL MINOW, CORPORATE GOVERNANCE 41 (Fifth ed. 2011) (because corporate political contributions "are allocated according to the priorities of the managers, not the shareholders, that power distorts the ability of the marketplace to discipline corporations.").

54. U.S. Chamber of Commerce Outside Spending Summary 2012, CTR FOR RESPONSIVE POLITICS, https://www.opensecrets.org/outsidespending/detail.php?cycle=2012&cmte=C90013145 (showing 2012 spending at $32,255,439); US Chamber of Commerce Outside Spending Summary 2014, CTR FOR RESPONSIVE POLITICS, https://www.opensecrets.org/outsidespending/detail.php?cycle=2014&cmte=C90013145 (showing 2012 spending at $35,472,011).

55. *Id.*

spoke at Harvard and said, "certainly, in my own view, what happens with money in politics is not good." He was still focused on disclosure as a panacea. Furthermore, Justice Kennedy said that we "live in this cyber age. We don't have to wait three months for a report. A report can be done in 24 hours."[56] But these "reports" he alluded to simply do not exist.

Just because the money is not transparent for voters or investors does not mean that the politicians who benefit from dark money are similarly unaware of its sources. Lisa Graves verified, "[o]ften politicians know exactly who is giving money to outside dark money groups in many instances.... The only people who are left in the dark are the American people."[57] This might be why Transparency International ranked the United States so low on its corruption perceptions index.[58]

Spending through social welfare groups is one way corporate political spending goes dark; another way dark money is created is through trade groups.[59] In 2010, Investor Responsibility Research Center found that a supermajority (86%) of the S&P 500 lacks stated policies on corporate political spending through dark money conduits.[60] Warren Langley, the former President of the Pacific Stock Exchange, finds the lack of transparency of corporate political activity disconcerting. As he put it: "[i]t is troubling that corporations can

---

56. Dean of Harvard Law School Martha Minow interview with Justice Anthony Kennedy (Oct. 22, 2015), https://www.youtube.com/watch?v=ZHbMPnA5n0Q (see mins 57:30–1:00:00).

57. Interview with Lisa Graves, Executive Director Center for Media & Democracy (July 17, 2015).

58. Press Release, Transparency International, *Corruption Perceptions Index 2014: The United States Scores Well But Lags Many Other Developed Nations* (Dec. 3, 2014), http://www.transparency-usa.org/documents/CorruptionPerceptionsIndex2014TI-USA-pressrelease.pdf.

59. Interview with Dr. Gretchen Goldman, Union of Concerned Scientists (July 28, 2015) ("Between the trade groups and the c4s, there is less and less transparency."); CTR. FOR POL. ACCOUNTABILITY, THE 2015 CPA-ZICKLIN INDEX OF CORPORATE POLITICAL DISCLOSURE AND ACCOUNTABILITY 14 (2015), *available at* http://files.politicalaccountability.net/index/CPA-Zicklin_Index_Final_with_links.pdf ("While more companies at the top of the S&P 500 are bringing sunlight by disclosing their political spending, there continues to be resistance to disclosing payments to (c)(4) nonprofit organizations that are permitted to conceal their donors.").

60. Press Release, IRRC Institute, *Study Finds 86% of S&P 500 Companies Have Not Disclosed Indirect Political Expenditure Policies, Only 20% Disclose Spending; First Comprehensive Political Spending Governance Analysis Finds Few Boards Engaged in Oversight Despite Potential Corporate Risks* (Oct. 14, 2010), http://www.businesswire.com/news/home/20101014005545/en/Study-Finds-86-SP-500-Companies-Disclosed#.VdIwdlNVhHw.

spend money on politics and they don't have to tell investors about it. Shareholders need to make thoughtful decisions, but there is this big hole called 'political contributions' that are not disclosed."[61] He continued, "[t]he SEC hasn't required disclosure of corporate political spending. And the Federal Accounting Standards Board [FASB] haven't required it either."[62] Because corporations are not required to disclose their political spending, many shareholders suspect, but cannot confirm, that some of the dark money in American elections is corporate money.

Not all corporate political spending is completely obscured. The public can see from voluntary disclosures at select firms, and Super PACs, that managers are using corporate resources (and not just their own personal funds) in politics.[63] According to the Center for Responsive Politics, in the 2012 federal election, Chevron (ticker CVX) gave $2.5 million to the Congressional Leadership Fund Super PAC. Clayton Williams Energy (ticker CWEI) gave $1 million to American Crossroads Super PAC. Chesapeake Energy (ticker CHK) gave $250,000 to the Make Us Great Again Super PAC. Scotts Miracle Gro (ticker SMG) gave $200,000 to Restore our Future Super PAC. CONSOL Energy (ticker CNX) and Hallador Energy (ticker HNRG) each gave $150,000 to Restore our Future Super PAC. And Pilot Corp (Ticker 7846 on the Tokyo Nikkei) gave $100,000 to the American Crossroads Super PAC.[64]

The story was much the same in the 2014 midterm. In 2014, Alliance Resource Partners, L.P. (Ticker ARLP on NASDAQ) gave $1,500,000 to American Crossroads and Hallador Energy (ticker HNRG) gave the group $200,000;[65] meanwhile KapStone Paper and Packaging Corp. (Ticker KS) gave $1,250,000 and BB&T (Ticker BBT) gave $156,925 to Freedom Partners Action Fund;[66]

---

61. Langley interview *supra* note 41.

62. *Id.*

63. Moving Forward a Coalition of Labor Unions, Small Bus., Public Safety, & Firefighters Associations Major Funding by Chevron, Recipient Committee Campaign Statement Cover Page (Nov. 4, 2014), https://s3.amazonaws.com/s3.documentcloud.org/documents/1312372/chevron-contribs.pdf; Potter interview *supra* note 50 ("An unintended, un-thought of, consequence of *Citizens United* are Super PACs. The Supreme Court didn't say anything about Super PACs.").

64. *2012 Top Donors to Outside Spending Groups*, CTR FOR RESPONSIVE POLITICS, https://www.opensecrets.org/outsidespending/summ.php?cycle=2012&disp=D&type=O&superonly=N (last visited Mar. 17, 2015).

65. *American Crossroads, 2014 All Donors*, CTR FOR RESPONSIVE POLITICS, https://www.opensecrets.org/outsidespending/contrib.php?cmte=C00487363&cycle=2014 (last visited Mar. 17, 2015).

66. *Freedom Partners Action Fund 2014 All Donors*, CTR FOR RESPONSIVE POLITICS, https://www.opensecrets.org/outsidespending/contrib.php?cmte=C00564765&cycle=2014.

Chevron (ticker CVX) and Alliance Resource Partners, L.P. (Ticker ARLPT on NASDAQ) gave $1,000,000 each to the Congressional Leadership Fund, while Apollo Education Group Inc. (Ticker APOL on NASDAQ) and Swisher (Ticker SWSH on NASDAQ) gave a more modest $50,000 each.[67] Meanwhile, corporate spending also took place at the state and local levels.[68] Chevron made headlines in 2014 when it spent approximately $3 million in a municipal election in California.[69]

A big fight over dark money between corporate shareholders and corporate managers is happening presently on corporate proxies[70] because many investors believe that "[t]here should be complete and total transparency of every penny spent on lobbying or campaign contributions and on the process of allocating them."[71] They are introducing shareholder proposals to achieve that end. A

---

67. *Congressional Leadership Fund 2014 All Donors*, CTR FOR RESPONSIVE POLITICS, https://www.opensecrets.org/outsidespending/contrib.php?cmte=C00504530&cycle=2014.

68. Jane Mayer, *State for Sale*, NEW YORKER (Oct. 10, 2011), http://www.newyorker.com/magazine/2011/10/10/state-for-sale ("Bob Phillips ... argues that the Court's decision, in *Citizens United v. Federal Election Commission*, has been a 'game changer,' especially in the realm of state politics. In swing states like North Carolina—which the Democrats consider so important that they have scheduled their 2012 National Convention there—an individual donor, particularly one with access to corporate funds, can play a significant, and sometimes decisive, role.").

69. Michael Hiltzik, *How Chevron Swamps a Small City with Campaign Money and Bogus News*, L.A. TIMES (Oct. 13, 2014), http://www.latimes.com/business/hiltzik/la-fi-mh-chevron-deluge-of-campaign-money-20141013-column.html#page=1 ("Chevron has poured an astounding $2.9 million into three campaign committees in Richmond.... The figures suggest that Chevron is preparing to spend at least $33 for the vote of every resident of the city 18 or older.").

70. Nell Minow, Editor & Co-Founder, The Corporate Library, *The Diane Sanger Memorial Lecture to the SEC Historical Society* (Mar. 17, 2010), http://c0403731.cdn.cloudfiles.rackspacecloud.com/collection/programs/sechistorical-podcast-031710-transcript.pdf ("Companies that want to avoid more new rules should begin to reach out to their shareholders to explain their procedures and criteria for political campaign and lobbying contributions and be able to show how they support both the brand and long-term shareholder returns."); Liz Bartolomeo, *The Political Spending of 501(c)(4) Nonprofits in the 2012 Election*, SUNLIGHT FOUNDATION (May 21, 2013), http://sunlightfoundation.com/blog/2013/05/21/the-political-spending-of-501c4-nonprofits-in-the-2012-election/ ("We often use the term 'dark money' to describe these groups since they can spend an unlimited amount on independent expenditures and electioneering communications yet they do not have to disclose their donors."); Report to the House of Delegates, ABA Section of Administrative Law and Regulatory Practice, 4 (2013) (citing Ciara Torres-Spelliscy, *Hiding Behind the Tax Code, The Dark Election of 2010 and Why Tax-Exempt Entities Should be Subject to Robust Federal Campaign Finance Disclosure Laws*, 16 NEXUS: CHAP. J.L. & POL'Y 59, 79 (2010–2011)).

71. Interview with Nell Minow, Vice Chair, ValueEdge Advisors (Aug. 19, 2015).

typical shareholder resolution on the topic requests periodic disclosure of political expenditures, including payments to trade associations and other tax exempt organizations.[72]

Even before *Citizens United,* many shareholders expressed displeasure with the ability of corporations to spend in politics. A poll in 2006 found "a striking 85 percent [of shareholders] agreed that the 'lack of transparency and oversight in corporate political activity encourages behavior' that threatens shareholder value. 94 percent supported disclosure and 84 percent backed board oversight and approval of 'all direct and indirect [company] political spending.'"[73] In 2006, shareholder resolutions calling for more transparency of corporate political spending gained the support of 20% or more of the vote at 11 major companies.[74]

After *Citizens United* in 2010, pressure from investors increased markedly as evidenced by an uptick in filings of shareholder resolutions on corporate political spending.[75] Between 2010 and 2012 investors filed 282 shareholder resolutions about corporate political spending at publicly traded companies. Nearly 80% simply asked for more transparency.[76] Shareholder proposals on political spending continued to be filed in the intervening years.[77] In 2014, there were more than 130 shareholder resolutions about corporate political activity. Again, most of them were asking for more disclosure and less dark money.[78] In 2014,

---

72. Shareholder Resolution filed by Trillium Asset Management Corporation Requesting Political Contributions by Ford Motor Company (2010), http://www.onlineethicalinvestor.org/eidb/wc.dll?eidbproc~reso~9143 (asking for semiannual reporting on Ford's political expenditures).

73. Press Release, Ctr. for Political Accountability, *Shareholders See Risky Corporate Political Behavior As Threat to Shareholder Value, Demand Reform, CPA Poll Finds* (Apr. 5, 2006), http://www.politicalaccountability.net/index.php?ht=a/GetDocumentAction/i/1267.

74. Timothy Smith & Bruce Freed, *Social Investment—Highlights from 2006 Proxy Season,* Greenmoneyjournal.Com (Oct. 10, 2006), http://www.politicalaccountability.net/index.php?ht=d/ArticleDetails/i/373.

75. Murninghan interview *supra* note 4 ("Shareholders are demanding more transparency of political spending.").

76. Letter to Elizabeth M. Murphy, Sec'y, U.S. Sec. & Exch. Comm'n, from Heidi Welsh, Exec. Dir., Sustainable Inv. Inst. (Oct. 30, 2012), http://www.sec.gov/comments/4-637/4637- 1149.pdf.

77. *The 2012 CPA-Zicklin Index of Corporate Political Accountability and Disclosure,* Ctr. for Political Accountability 15–16 (Sep. 25, 2012).

78. *Shareholder Resolutions,* US SIF The Forum for Sustainable and Responsible Investment (2015), http://www.ussif.org/resolutions; *see also* Heidi Welsh, Mid-Year Review: Corporate Political Activity Proposals in the 2014 Proxy Season, Sustainable Inv. Instit. 1, 10 (2014), https://si2news.files.wordpress.com/2014/08/si2-2014-proxy-season-mid-year-review-corporate-political-activity-excerpt.pdf ("A broad coalition of investors

shareholder proposals asking for more transparency received shareholder votes averaging 23.7%.[79] According to As You Sow, which tracks social responsible investing, "[h]alf of the 19 proposals earning more than 40 percent dealt with these concerns [e.g. political spending], while proponents racked up 28 withdrawals after reaching accords with management in nearly every instance."[80] Investors are interested not just in corporate spending in elections, they are also interested in corporate spending on lobbying.[81]

Shareholders have won some of these votes asking for transparency. In 2014, five public firms had a majority of their shareholders vote in favor of such political transparency. Those firms were Sallie Mae, Lorillard, and Valero Energy, where a majority voted for disclosure of lobbying[82]—and Dean Foods and Smith & Wesson, where a majority voted for disclosure of campaign spending.[83] These victories can be added to the win at Sprint Nextel in 2011, which also received a majority vote in favor of transparency.[84] One driver of high

---

continued to file resolutions asking companies to tell stockholders and the public more about what they spend on political campaigns and lobbying, both directly and most particularly through intermediary groups.").

79. Welsh, *supra* note 5, at 9; *id.* at 10 ("In all, shareholders have filed 530 resolutions on these subjects in the last five years, with 136 in 2014.").

80. Heidi Welsh & Michael Passoff, *Proxy Preview 2014*, As You Sow 15 (2014).

81. Welsh interview *supra* note 5 ("Lately lobbying has increased substantially as an issue on the proxy statement.").

82. Sara Murphy, *What Companies Don't Want You to Know About the Millions They Spend*, Motley Fool (July 13, 2014), http://www.fool.com/investing/general/2014/07/13/what-companies-dont-want-to-know-about-the-mil.aspx (referencing majority vote at Sallie Mae); Form 8-K for Lorillard, Inc., May 16, 2014, http://biz.yahoo.com/e/140516/lo8-k.html (showing majority vote at Lorillard); Form 8-K for Valero Energy Corporation, May 1, 2014, http://app.quotemedia.com/data/downloadFiling?webmasterId=101533&ref=9571747&type=HTML&symbol=VLO&companyName=Valero+Energy+Corp.&formType=8-K&dateFiled=2014-05-05 (showing majority vote at Valero).

83. Form 8-K for Dean Foods Company, May 20, 2014, http://services.corporate-ir.net/SEC/Document.Service?id=P3VybD1hSFIwY0RvdkwyRndhUzUwWlc1cmQybDZZWEprTG1OdmJTOWtiM2R1Ykc5aFpDNXdhSEEvWVdOMGFGXOXVQVkJFUmlacGNHHRm5aVDA1TmpFd05ERTJKbk4xWW5OcFpEFOdz09JnR5cGU9MiZmbj05NjEwNDE2LnBkZg== (showing majority vote at Dean Foods); Form 8-K for Smith & Wesson Holding Corp, Sept. 26, 2014 http://biz.yahoo.com/e/140926/swhc8-k.html (showing majority vote at Smith & Wesson).

84. *Proxy Season Update: CPA Resolution Wins 53.3% at Sprint; Tops 40% at State Street, Windstream, RR Donnelley, Lorillard*, Ctr for Political Accountability News Letter (May 2011), http://www.politicalaccountability.net/index.php?ht=a/GetDocumentAction/i/5379; Welsh interview *supra* note 5 ("On occasion shareholder votes on political spending get majority votes.... [And t]here have been a lot that have received 30–40% of the vote or more.").

votes in favor of disclosure of corporate political spending may be the largest proxy advisor, the Institutional Shareholder Services' (ISS's) pro-disclosure stance.[85] Surely part of what is motivating shareholders to seek more transparency is the sneaking suspicion that corporate political spending may not be for the benefit of shareholders at all. Stanford Professor Pamela Karlan explained, a year after *Citizens United*, "[t]hat corporate managers might spend corporate funds not to maximize the shareholders' welfare but to maximize their own is a very real danger."[86]

Shareholder concerns may be justified, as some empirical studies show shareholders are not typically the beneficiaries of corporate political activity. Professors Michael Hadani and Douglas A. Schuler reported, "[w]e find that firms' political investments are significantly and negatively related to market valuation and firms' cumulative political investments are likewise significantly and negatively related to market valuation and return on sales (ROS)."[87] Professors Aggarwal, Meschke, and Wang found

> that [corporate political] donations are negatively correlated with future excess returns. An increase in soft money and 527 Committee donations of $10,000 is associated with a reduction in excess returns of 7.4 basis points in the following year.... this reduction in shareholder value far outstrips the dollar value of the donations. This suggests that political donations may be a useful window into the presence of wider agency problems within firms.[88]

And when they know about corporate political spending, some shareholders are objecting. For example, Target's institutional investors wanted to know

85. Institutional Shareholder Services, Inc., 2012 U.S. Proxy Voting Summary Guidelines 64 (2012), http://www.issgovernance.com/files/2012USSummaryGuidelines1312012.pdf.

86. Pamela Karlan, *Me Inc.*, Boston Rev. (July 1, 2011), http://www.bostonreview.net/pamela-karlan-corporate-personhood.

87. Michael Hadani & Douglas A. Schuler, *In Search of El Dorado: The Elusive Financial Return On Corporate Political Investments*, 34 J. Strat. Mgmt. 165, 166 (2013).

88. Rajesh Aggarwal, Felix Meschke, & Tracy Wang, *Corporate Political Donations: Investment or Agency?*, 14 Bus. & Pol., vol. 1, art. 3 (Apr. 2012); *see also* Andre Douglas Pond Cummings, *Procuring "Justice"?: Citizens United, Caperton, and Partisan Judicial Elections*, 95 Iowa L. Rev. Bull. 89, 109 (2010) ("There is little evidence to suggest that these executives will be careful, thoughtful, or responsible with the new ability to spend shareholder funds at their disposal.").

how $150,000 got into the governor's race in Minnesota in 2010.[89] Simultane-
ously, the Nathan Cummings Foundation objected to spending by News Corp.[90]

Many firms have increased the transparency of their political spending under
pressure from investors and the Center for Political Accountability (CPA).[91]
Heidi Welsh found, "[f]irms have become more transparent about corporate
political spending over the past decade."[92] The CPA, which tracks corporate
political activity, reported in 2015 that although there was substantial progress
on improved corporate political spending transparency, there was still significant work to do given the magnitude of dark money.[93] This report also noted
that 145 firms had adopted the CPA's model for disclosure.[94]

Some corporations have taken a leadership role in advocating transparent
politics for corporations.[95] Unfortunately, even the disclosure that is available
from some firms, or from some governmental agencies, is not easily compa-
rable across firms, apples to apples.[96] Or as one shareholder related: "[it is] increasingly a game of whack-a-mole: as soon as a company agrees to disclose

---

89. Jennifer Martinez & Tom Hamburger, *Target Feels Backlash from Shareholders*, L.A.
Times, Aug. 19, 2010, http://articles.latimes.com/2010/aug/19/nation/la-na-target-share-
holders-20100820.

90. Michael D. Shear, *News Corp. Shareholder Objects to G.O.P. Donations*, N.Y. Times
(Oct. 13, 2010), http://thecaucus.blogs.nytimes.com/2010/10/13/news-corp-shareholder-
objects-to-g-o-p-donations/?_r=0.

91. Peter Overby, *More Corporations Shed Light on Political Spen*ding, NPR.org (Oct.
27, 2011), http://www.npr.org/2011/10/27/141767870/more-corporations-shed-light-on-po-
litical-spending (noting Charles Grezlak, head of government affairs for Merck, discussed
how increased political spending disclosure can be a good thing for companies, because "we
need trust among consumers, we need trust among physicians who prescribe our products.").

92. Welsh interview *supra* note 5.

93. Ctr. for Pol. Accountability, *supra* note 59, at 8.

94. *Id.* at 10; Timothy Smith interview *supra* note 41 (estimating that "[t]here are 150
firms who are doing good disclosure of corporate political spending.").

95. Dan Bross & Trevor Potter, *Contribution Clarity*, Corporate Responsibility Magazine, Vol 3. No 2 (March/April 2012), http://www.thecro.com/content/contribution-clar-
ity ("We believe corporations subject themselves to perhaps unwarranted criticism and risk
by not sharing with stakeholders a broad overview of their governance philosophy related
to participation in the political process.").

96. *Confronting Corporate Money in Politics A Guide for Individual & Institutional Investors*, US SIF Foundation 3 (2014), http://www.ussif.org/Files/Publications/Corpo-
rate_Money_in_Politics.pdf ("Information that is publicly available on [corporate] political
spending is scattered among several federal, state and local government agencies and is available in widely varying formats ill-suited to providing investors with a clear picture of corporate efforts to influence the political system.").

one avenue of contributions, the money starts flowing through another avenue."[97] This dark money problem[98] has prompted academics and over one million investors to ask for more disclosure of corporate political spending for all publicly traded firms by clamoring for a new rule from the SEC.[99]

One sign of improvement is there are more internal controls at many firms over political spending than there were in 2010. At the time that *Citizens United* was decided, even the board of directors could be uninformed about corporate political spending.[100] Heidi Welsh reported, "[m]ore companies have internal policies on corporate political spending including at the board level."[101] The Center for Political Accountability found that the glass was half full/half empty on board involvement as some were doing it well,[102] while many firms still needed improvement.[103]

97. Christopher P. Skroupa, *Investors Want Disclosure of Corporate Political Contributions and Lobbying Expenditures*, FORBES (Apr. 20, 2012), http://www.forbes.com/sites/christopherskroupa/2012/04/20/investors-want-disclosure-of-corporate-political-contributions-and-lobbying-expenditures-2/ (quoting Scott Zdrazil Head of Corporate Governance for Amalgamated Bank); *id.* ("Zdrazil emphasizes the importance of being mindful that, 'Companies increasingly "report" but do not include all avenues by which they are funneling money into politics.'").

98. Brief for United States Representatives Robert Brady, et al. as Amici Curiae Supporting Respondents, American Tradition Partnership, Inc. v. Bullock, 132 S. Ct. 2490 (U.S. 2012) ("Citizens and shareholders are too often unable to see, as the Court put it, "whether elected officials are 'in the pocket' of 'so-called moneyed interests,'" and are thus unable "to hold corporations and elected officials accountable for their positions and supporters." (quoting *McConnell v. Fed. Election Comm'n*, 540 U.S. 93, 259 (2003) (opinion of Scalia, J.)").

99. Lucian A. Bebchuk & Robert J. Jackson, Jr., *Shining Light on Corporate Political Spending*, 101 GEO. L.J. 923, 966 (2013) ("To the extent that a company's political spending is consistent with shareholder interests, there is no reason to expect that disclosure would deter directors and executives from such spending. And to the extent that disclosure deters directors and executives from engaging in spending that is disfavored by the company's shareholders, discouraging that spending should be considered a benefit, not a cost, of the proposed disclosures.").

100. Jill Fisch, *The "Bad Man" Goes to Washington: The Effect of Political Influence on Corporate Duty*, 75 FORDHAM L. REV. 1593, 1613 (2006) ("Political contributions are generally not disclosed to the board or shareholders, nor are political expenditures generally subject to oversight as part of a corporation's internal controls. The lack of oversight makes it difficult for corporate decision makers and stakeholders to evaluate the costs and benefits of political activity.").

101. Welsh interview *supra* note 5.

102. Ctr. for Pol. Accountability, *supra* note 59, at 20 ("Data from the 2015 Index indicate that fewer than half of companies in the S&P 500 have some level of board oversight of their political contributions and expenditures.").

103. *Id.* at 17 ("Of the 497 companies included in the Index, 435 (87.5 percent) had at

E. Shareholder Suits

Another path to the truth is litigation, and some investors have taken this route. In 2013, the Comptroller of the State of New York, in his capacity as a shareholder, sued Qualcomm to get it to reveal its political expenditures under Section 220 of Delaware General Corporation Law.[104] Qualcomm settled the suit and agreed to be transparent about its political spending.[105] Some of the spending Qualcomm revealed was money going to the U.S. Chamber of Commerce, which, as discussed above, is a dark money conduit. In one report, Qualcomm gave $500,000 to the Chamber—$262,500 of which was for non-deductible (read political) purposes.[106] In 2015, the New York Comptroller sued Oracle using the same theory, to try to get more transparency from the firm.[107]

Shareholders have also used their inspection rights under Delaware law to seek information about corporate complicity in human rights violations.[108] An institutional investor at Hershey's sued the company to get more information about its potential use of child slavery in its supply chain, as discussed in more

---

least some level of policy posted on their websites. Some of these policies are comprehensive and robust while others are not fully formed.").

104. 8 Del. C. § 220.

105. Nicholas Confessore, *State Comptroller Sues Qualcomm for Data About Its Political Contributions*, N.Y. TIMES (Jan. 3, 2013).

106. Qualcomm Incorporated, *Disclosures Under Political Contributions and Expenditures Policy Fiscal Year 2014* (Sept. 30, 2013—Sept. 28, 2014) (Amounts Paid In Fiscal Year 2014), http://files.shareholder.com/downloads/QCOM/201997084x0x800323/BDA640B4-68FD-41FD-88A0-CB523C3B2AA5/Fiscal_2014_Disclosures.pdf.

107. Freeman Klopott, *Oracle Sued by N.Y. Pension Over Political-Giving Disclosure*, BLOOMBERG (Oct. 28, 2015), http://www.bloomberg.com/news/articles/2015-10-28/oracle-sued-by-new-york-pension-fund-over-political-funding.

108. Jef Feeley, *Hershey Investors Suing Over Child Labor Can Pursue Files*, BLOOMBERG (Mar. 19, 2014), http://www.bloomberg.com/news/articles/2014-03-18/hershey-judge-says-shareholders-can-seek-child-labor-files-1- ("Hershey Co … was ordered to face a lawsuit by investors seeking to force it to turn over records about cocoa from African farms that may use illegal child labor. A Louisiana pension fund raised legitimate questions about Hershey executives' knowledge of how much of the company's cocoa, grown in West Africa, may have been produced by child slaves, Delaware Chancery Court Judge Travis Laster said yesterday."); Tiffany Hsu, *Hershey Sued Over African Cocoa Farm Child Labor Accusations*, L.A. TIMES (Nov. 2, 2012), http://articles.latimes.com/2012/nov/02/business/la-fi-mo-hershey-cocoa-child-labor-20121102 ("The pension fund claims that Hershey's board knew that its ingredients came from West African suppliers sourcing from farms built on illegal child and forced labor.… It also alleges that Hershey 'has flouted domestic and foreign law' related to human trafficking.").

detail in relation to another chocolatier in Chapter 9.[109] The shareholder, Louisiana Municipal Employees' Retirement System, wanted to see Hershey's books and records under Section 220 of Delaware General Corporation Law.[110] Hershey wanted the court to dismiss the case. In 2014, the Delaware trial judge refused to dismiss, thereby siding with the investors and transparency.[111]

F. Divestment

In addition to staying and slugging it out with firms through shareholder proposals on political and social issues, truly disenchanted shareholders can take the Wall St. Walk—that is to say they can sell their shares. Or if they are really motivated, they can urge across-the-board divestment by others.[112] Of all of the tactics discussed in this book, divestment may be one of the most controversial. Human Rights lawyer Marco Simons argues in favor of divestment in certain extreme circumstances. He stated that divestment is appropriate when "a shareholder would be morally complicit in a serious abuse when they profit from that company.... The question is: Has it gotten to the point where to be an investor in that corporation would be to be complicit in illegal, immoral or outrageous behavior?"[113]

Or as Adam Kanzer of Domini Social Investments wrote about divestment after the massacre at Sandy Hook Elementary in Newtown, Connecticut, where 20 first graders were killed by a former student:

> Newtown presents a very concrete example of what a violation of
> the duty of loyalty looks like. If you use my money to make a weapon

---

109. Gabrielle Palmer, *Stockholder Inspection Rights and an "Incredible" Basis: Seeking Disclosure Related to Corporate Social Responsibility*, 92 Denv. U.L. Rev. On. 125, 135-36 (2015) (citing Rulings of the Court From Oral Argument on Exceptions to the Master's Final Report, La. Mun. Police Emps. Ret. Sys. v. Hershey Co., No. 7996-ML (Del. Ch. Mar. 18, 2014).

110. 8 Del. C. §220.

111. Rulings of the Court From Oral Argument on Exceptions to the Master's Final Report, La. Mun. Police Emps. Ret. Sys. v. Hershey Co., No. 7996-ML ("the motion to dismiss is denied.").

112. *Unburnable Carbon 2013: Wasted Capital and Stranded Assets*, Carbon Tracker & The Grantham Research Institute, LSE (2013) ("This is the ultimate sanction for many investors which would require some of the previous options to have been exhausted, and may only apply to the most extreme cases where companies have refused to take other action. This may require investors to believe that the company's strategy puts value at risk.").

113. Interview with Marco Simons, General Counsel EarthRights International (July 9, 2015).

that kills my child, don't tell me that in 20 years I'll retire with more money as a result. If you claim that decision was made in my best interest, you have no right to call yourself a fiduciary....

Semiautomatic weapons are now widely available, not solely as a function of consumer demand, but also due to the ready availability of investor capital and investor demand for expanding markets. Is there any limit to these demands? *The New York Times* reports that industry strategies to increase market share now include an aggressive push to get guns into the hands of children ...

This is your return on investment: Children touting semiautomatic weapons. Whether communicated through private or public equity ownership, the message, no doubt, has been the same—make more, and get these weapons into as many hands as possible.

Whether they like it or not, pension funds are, in fact, agents of social change.... When we allocate billions of capital, we are also sketching out the parameters of future societal possibilities.[114]

In the 1960s, 1970s, and 1980s, shareholders used divestment campaigns to pressure South Africa to end Apartheid.[115] The South Africa divestment campaign included various different tactics ranging from church groups disrupting shareholder meetings, to encouraging corporate boards to adopt a fair labor code known as the Sullivan Principles.[116] States and municipalities who were shareholders because of their public pension funds also took a leadership role in the divestment effort against South Africa.[117]

---

114. Adam Kanzer, *Divesting is an Exercise in Real Fiduciary Care Duty of Loyalty should not Ignore Other Human Beings and Social Issues*, PENSIONS & INVESTMENTS (Feb. 18, 2013), http://www.pionline.com/article/20130218/PRINT/302189995/divesting-is-an-exercise-in-real-fiduciary-care.

115. Heather M. Field, *Throwing the Red Flag: Challenging the NFL's Lessons for American Business*, 38 J. CORP. L. 381, 396 (2013) ("as the public increasingly rallied against South African apartheid, shareholders (in particular, states and localities) increasingly divested themselves of South African companies, choosing to invest elsewhere.").

116. NAOMI KLEIN, NO LOGO MONEY, MARKETING, AND THE GROWING ANTI-CORPORATE MOVEMENT, 337 (1999); Murningham interview *supra* note 4 ("The Sullivan Principles were a set of fair labor principles. The idea was that the market could make change in society. The Sullivan Principles included opportunity and fairness in hiring, promotion and pay.").

117. Grace A. Jubinsky, *State and Municipal Governments React Against South African Apartheid: An Assessment of the Constitutionality of the Divestment Campaign*, 54 U. CIN. L. REV. 543, 544–5 (1985) (Connecticut, Maryland, Massachusetts, Michigan, and Nebraska all passed their own divestment laws, and at least twenty-seven states had considered di-

Chief Counsel at the Brennan Center, Fritz Schwarz actually helped with two different phases of the effort to divest from South Africa. He explained that after he wrote an article urging companies to leave South Africa,[118] "we (the American Committee on Africa) set up a boycott against six banks that announced $50,000 in loans to South Africa."[119] In the 1980s when he was New York City's top lawyer, he raised the issue again. He encouraged New York City to use its buying power to impact South Africa in a positive way. Mr. Schwarz recalled, "[w]hen I was New York Corporation Counsel, Mayor Ed Koch said a South African boycott was ridiculous. I went to see Ed and I suggested he appoint a commission to look at the issue of South Africa. I must have done a good job because when he announced the Commission, which I chaired, he said, 'the question is should the City do something to attack this uniquely evil government.'"[120] This Commission urged divestment.[121] Mr. Schwarz reported, "Nelson Mandela said that New York City's divestment and pressure were key in ending Apartheid in South Africa."[122] In contrast, Dr. Murninghan, who also worked on ending Apartheid, argued, "[d]ivestment alone did not topple South Africa." She continued, "[c]ompanies left South Africa because of selective contracting laws that cities and towns and states passed. For example, the entity would say to IBM, 'We won't buy your typewriters if you stay in South Africa,' or to Ford, 'We won't buy your cars for our police force if you stay in South Africa.' That's what made a difference."[123] Some debate the effectiveness and appropriateness of divestment as a tactic. As Nell Minow explained, "[t]he happiest day for the [company] is the day that activist investors divest because they don't have to deal with you anymore. By definition you have sold your stock to someone who doesn't care. It would be better to stay as an investor and push them to do better."[124]

---

vestment legislation by 1985.); Frederick A. O. Schwarz, Jr., *Lawyers for Local Government Have Unique Responsibilities and Opportunities to Influence Public Policy*, 53 N.Y.L. Sch. L. Rev. 375, 404–405 (2009) (describing Mr. Schwarz's early involvement in New York City's divestment initiatives and his confidence that Mayor Ed Koch was "proud of being an early leader in the pressure against [A]partheid from America, which clearly helped to accelerate change in South Africa").

118. Interview with Frederick A.O. Schwarz, Chief Counsel Brennan Center for Justice at NYU School of Law (July 21, 2015).

119. *Id.*

120. *Id.*

121. *Id.*

122. *Id.*

123. Murninghan interview *supra* note 4.

124. Minow interview *supra* note 71.

Despite such potential drawbacks, divestment is also a strategy that is currently in use. There is a wide-ranging effort to get universities and foundations to divest their endowments from fossil fuels to address climate change and to incentivize investments in cleaner energy technologies.[125] Here fossil fuels include coal, oil, and gas.[126] Only a handful of smaller universities have actually divested, with the notable exception of Stanford, which has chosen to divest from coal only.[127] One foundation that has chosen to divest from fossil fuels is the Rockefeller Family Foundation.[128] This is notable because the Rockefeller fortune was made through Standard Oil.[129] Harvard University, which has the largest endowment in the world, has been subject to a campaign to convince the trustees to divest from fossil fuels.[130] So far, Harvard has not budged on

---

125. Adam Vaughan, *Fossil Fuel Divestment: A Brief History*, THE GUARDIAN (Oct. 8, 2014), http://www.theguardian.com/environment/2014/oct/08/fossil-fuel-divestment-a-brief-history ("the campaign to get institutions to pull their financial investments as a way of tackling climate change has seen a total of $50bn divested so far, according to the US Fossil Free campaign."); Emma Howard, *A Beginner's Guide to Fossil Fuel Divestment*, THE GUARDIAN (June 23, 2015).

126. Damian Carrington, *Fossil Fuel Lobby Goes on the Attack Against Divestment Movement*, THE GUARDIAN (Feb. 11, 2015), http://www.theguardian.com/environment/damian-carrington-blog/2015/feb/11/fossil-fuel-lobby-goes-on-the-attack-against-divestment-movement ("In a similar vein, but closer to fighting than laughing, is the claim that coal is 'the bedrock of modern life' from the American Energy Alliance, a group with links to the fossil fuel industry.").

127. Steven Davidoff Solomon, *Colleges Use Anti-Apartheid Strategies to Battle Fossil Fuels*, N.Y. TIMES (Feb. 10, 2015), http://dealbook.nytimes.com/2015/02/10/using-anti-apartheid-divestment-strategies-to-battle-fossil-fuels/?_r=0 ("Stanford and a handful of other colleges have pledged to divest their endowments of such investments, but ... most of them, including Harvard and Yale, have demurred.").

128. *Rockefellers to Sell Oil Assets as Part of $50B Global Warming Fight*, CBC NEWS (Sept. 22, 2014) ("The Rockefellers, who made their vast fortune on oil, will on Monday join and other philanthropies and high-wealth individuals in a pledge to sell and get out of a total of $50 billion US worth of fossil fuel assets.").

129. Vaughan, *supra* note 125 ("'We are quite convinced that if he were alive today ... he would be moving out of fossil fuels...,' said Stephen Heintz of John D. Rockefeller, as he announced that the heirs to one of America's most famous dynasties, which was built on oil, were pulling their philanthropic funds out of fossil fuels.").

130. Matt Rocheleau, *Prominent Alumni Ramp Up Pressure on Universities to Divest*, BOS. GLOBE (Feb. 20, 2015), http://www.bostonglobe.com/metro/2015/02/19/alumni-with-hold-donations-join-student-protests-pressure-colleges-divest-from-fossil-fuels/WgWZ1SQKEAxigN6Gl1pRrI/story.html ("powerful alumni of Harvard University ... called for other graduates to join the effort ... 'Divestment is effective,' said the letter, whose signatories included Portman, Kennedy, former US senator Tim Wirth, philosopher Cornel West, director Darren Aronofsky, and architect Maya Lin. 'While we can't bankrupt the oil

the issue.[131] But there may be collateral benefits to divestment campaigns, like impacting public opinion.[132] Fritz Schwarz stated of the current fossil fuel divestment movement, "I don't advocate for divestment campaigns as a general matter. But in the case of South Africa there was a moral imperative. And now with the existential threat of climate change, the fossil fuel divestment campaign for university endowments has a similar moral force since the impact of climate change would not be limited to one country, but would be felt globally by all people."[133]

G. Push Back to the Push Back

Shareholders act in the midst of a dynamic system. As they raise issues, corporations and their advocates react. Timothy Smith of Walden Asset Management noted, "[t]here has also been push back by companies and trade associations who are not happy with shareholders flexing their muscles. The U.S. Chamber of Commerce is trying to change the proxy rules to limit shareholder proposals."[134] Not to be outdone by shareholders' petitioning the SEC for improved rules, the U.S. Chamber of Commerce and other trade associations filed a petition with the SEC asking for the Commission to amend Rule 14a-8 to make it more difficult for shareholders to have their proposals on social and political items included on corporate proxies.[135] Currently, shareholders can relist their shareholder proposals if the proposal received a certain percentage of the shareholder vote. Under Rule 14a-8(i)(12), a shareholder proposal that gets three percent of the vote in the first year on the proxy can

---

companies, we can start to politically bankrupt them, complicating their ability to dominate our political life.'").

131. John Schwartz, *Harvard Students Move Fossil Fuel Stock Fight to Court*, N.Y. TIMES (Nov. 19, 2014), http://www.nytimes.com/2014/11/20/us/harvard-students-move-fossil-fuel-divestment-fight-to-court.html?_r=0 ("Harvard students, frustrated by the university's refusal to shed fossil fuel stocks from its investment portfolios, is looking beyond protests and resolutions to a new form of pressure: the courts.... The 11-page complaint, with 167 pages of supporting exhibits, asks the court to compel divestment on behalf of the students and 'future generations.'").

132. Langley interview *supra* note 41 ("[d]ivestment by university endowments of fossil fuels is influencing public opinion on climate change now.").

133. Schwarz interview *supra* note 118.

134. Timothy Smith interview *supra* note 41.

135. U.S. Chamber of Commerce et al., Petition For Rulemaking Regarding Resubmission of Shareholder *Proposals Failing to Elicit Meaningful Shareholder Support*, SEC Petition No. 4-675 (2014), http://www.sec.gov/rules/petitions/2014/petn4-675.pdf.

be relisted; a shareholder proposal that gets six percent of the vote in the second year on the proxy can be relisted; and a shareholder proposal that gets 10 percent of the vote in the third year (or later) on the proxy can be relisted.[136] The U.S. Chamber would prefer that these thresholds be much higher, thereby barring shareholder votes on a range of topics.[137]

Corporate democracy within the corporate structure has been used for decades to raise shareholders' issues of concern to the attention of corporate managers. This power has been used to file shareholders' proposals ranging from racial segregation and nuclear power to transparency of dark money. Those investors who are particularly frustrated with corporate intransigence on these topics can get more aggressive by suing or divesting. However, divesting is a tricky tool to use to impact corporations because it can leave stocks in the hands of passive investors, who do not care about negative corporate practices.

---

136. SEC Rule 14a-8(i)(12).
137. *Id.*

Chapter 12

There's an App for That

Consumers are shopping with their values.[1]
—Katie Kerr Holcomb, Director of Communications at the B Lab

While only half of American households own investments, nearly every American household contains consumers. Consequently, one force that can drive corporate behavior is the preferences of customers. The choice for the consumer is binary: to buy or not to buy, that is the question. But when customers act in concert—like surging to buy one toy at Christmas or see one film over the Fourth of July weekend—fortunes are made and blockbusters are born. But likewise, if customers coordinate to reject a brand, a store, or a product, the impact can be quite pronounced. Such customer boycotts have a self-limiting dynamic because they are difficult to organize and sustain. But technology may be changing the consumer boycott. Like so much in our smart phone lives, if you want to learn more about the corporation and their political and social stances, well, guess what? There's an app for that.

One manifestation of the power of *Citizens United* has been the well-documented practice of CEOs telling their employees how to vote in upcoming national elections.[2] Employees—especially in a down economy—don't have a lot of ability to speak back to this type of bullying.[3] But customers have sig-

---

1. Interview with Katie Kerr Holcomb, Director of Communications B Lab (Aug. 24, 2015).

2. Steven Greenhouse, *Here's a Memo from the Boss: Vote This Way*, N.Y. TIMES (Oct. 26, 2012) http://www.nytimes.com/2012/10/27/us/politics/bosses-offering-timely-advice-how-to-vote.html ("the Supreme Court's *Citizens United* decision has freed companies from those restrictions, and now several major companies, including Georgia-Pacific and Cintas, have sent letters or information packets to their employees suggesting—and sometimes explicitly recommending—how they should vote this fall.").

3. Jason Bent, *Curtailing Voter Intimidation by Employers After* Citizens United, 43 STETSON L. REV. 595 (2014); Alexander Hertel-Fernandez, *Employer Political Coercion: A Grow-*

nificant leeway to react to what they find to be morally repugnant corporate behavior. Customers are not just driven by price. A large percentage of them cares about the morals behind the products that they purchase.[4]

A. Boycotts

Frequently customers who have signed contracts with corporations, and later have objections to corporate behavior, may find it difficult to sue the corporation in court because of aggressive mandatory arbitration clauses, which have been upheld by the Supreme Court.[5] Yet the customer still has the power of the purse. If a company is caught being too obnoxious, it risks a backlash of consumer boycotts.[6]

Boycotts can originate from all quarters for a number of reasons, from the political left, right, or center; because of social stances by the CEO; labor prac-

---

ing Threat, AMERICAN PROSPECT (Nov. 23, 2015), http://prospect.org/article/employer-political-coercion-growing-threat.

4. *Global Consumers are willing to Put Their Money Where Their Heart is when it Comes to Goods and Services from Companies Committed to Social Responsibility*, NIELSEN (June 17, 2014), http://www.nielsen.com/us/en/press-room/2014/global-consumers-are-willing-to-put-their-money-where-their-heart-is.html (showing 55% of online consumers from 60 countries were "willing to pay more for product and services provided by companies that are committed to positive social and environmental impact." And 40% of North American respondents had made a sustainable purchase in the previous six months.); John Peloza & Jingzhi Shang, *Investing in Corporate Social Responsibility to Enhance Customer Value*, HARV. L. SCH. FORUM ON CORPORATE GOVERNANCE & FIN. REG. (Feb. 28, 2011), http://corpgov.law.harvard.edu/2011/02/28/investing-in-corporate-social-responsibility-to-enhance-customer-value/ (CSR could lead "to outcomes such as increased customer loyalty, willingness to pay premium prices, and lower reputational risks in times of crisis.").

5. AT&T Mobility LLC v. Concepcion, 131 S. Ct. 1740 (2011) (upholding arbitration agreement between customers, who files punitive class action suit, and telephone company); CompuCredit Corp. v. Greenwood, 132 S. Ct. 665 (2012) (upholding arbitration agreement between customers, who file action asserting a violation of Credit Repair Organization Act, and credit card marketer); Shearson/American Express, Inc. v. McMahon, 107 S. Ct. 2332 (1987) (upholding arbitration agreement between customers, who allege violations of the Securities Exchange Act and RICO, and broker); Dean Witter Reynolds, Inc. v. Byrd, 105 S. Ct. 1238 (1985) (upholding arbitration agreement between investor, who files suit for violations of federal and state law, and securities broker-dealer).

6. NAOMI KLEIN, NO LOGO MONEY, MARKETING, AND THE GROWING ANTI-CORPORATE MOVEMENT 288 (1999) ("'No one want to be in the limelight because they are the target of community protests or boycotts,' one advertising executive told Advertising Age.").

tices abroad or domestically; environmental impacts; product safety; or political spending, to name just a few motivations. For example, when Nike became the poster child for sweatshop labor in the 1990s, the result was customers refusing to buy the trademarked swoosh.[7]

The Supreme Court has recognized that customer boycotts to make a political point are First Amendment activities in *Claiborne Hardware*.[8] As professor Gary Minda explained, this case was about a civil rights boycott of a hardware store in Mississippi, "the Court found the civil rights boycott in *Claiborne Hardware* to be constitutionally protected. The boycott advanced constitutional objectives because it was aimed at pursuing the goal of equality for African-Americans rather than narrow self-interest."[9]

Customer boycotts are notoriously difficult to organize because consumers are not a natural constituency. They can live all over the globe and can disagree about what is objectionable corporate behavior. But this hasn't stopped attempts at organized boycotts since before the United States was a nation until today. Some of these early boycotts were led by founding fathers, who tried to align American colonists' purchases with their politics. For instance, Alexander Hamilton and John Jay led boycotts in New York against merchants engaged in the slave trade.[10]

The link between democratic participation and ethical consumption is a theme that boycott organizers have invoked explicitly throughout American history. As Professor Glickman related in his book BUYING POWER, "[t]he renewed popularity of boycotts over a range of issues, from the high cost of milk and meat, to racist practices at stores, to unhappiness with foreign governmental policies and even to dissatisfaction with theatrical performances and prices, demonstrated that Americans used their pocketbooks to achieve their social and political goals."[11]

---

7. Jeff Ballinger, *Introduction to Analyzing the Added Value of the Shoe Industry for Workers* (1991) in *Media Indonesia* in GLOBAL MUCKRAKING 100 YEARS OF INVESTIGATIVE JOURNALISM FROM AROUND THE WORLD (Anya Schiffin ed.) at 45 (2014) ("The struggle against Nike and other major U.S. footwear and clothing brands that underpaid their workers in factories throughout the developing world led to the major consumer boycott of the 1990s.").

8. National Association for the Advancement of Colored People v. Claiborne Hardware Company, 458 U.S. 886 (1982).

9. GARY MINDA, BOYCOTT IN AMERICA HOW IMAGINATION AND IDEOLOGY SHAPE THE LEGAL MIND 132–3 (1999) (quoting Justice Stevens).

10. Theresa J. Lee, *Democratizing the Economic Sphere: A Case for the Political Boycott*, 115 W. VA. L. REV. 531, 538–39 (Winter 2012) (internal citation omitted).

11. LAWRENCE B. GLICKMAN, BUYING POWER: A HISTORY OF CONSUMER ACTIVISM IN AMERICA, 203 (2009).

If properly organized, a boycott by customers can persist for years. For instance, "[t]he granddaddy of modern brand-based actions is the boycott against Nestle, which peaked in the late seventies. The campaign targeted the Swiss company for its aggressive marketing of costly baby formula as a 'safer' alternative to breast-feeding in the developing world."[12] The reason Nestle angered so many was they were encouraging poor women to buy formula when breast milk would have been better for their children and free to boot. "[A]ny action that discourages breastfeeding is dangerous, its consequences measured in sick and dead children. For the food industry, however, more sales mean bigger profits, and in the absence of regulations profits determine policy."[13] The impact of pushing baby formula on impoverished women was "causing what pediatrician and professor Derrick Jelliffe calls 'commerciogenic malnutrition.'"[14] In other words, Nestle was being both hazardous and greedy. As a result, boycotting Nestle for its baby formula sales policies lasted for years, eventually leading to the adoption of the International Code of Marketing of Breastmilk Substitutes by the World Health Organization in 1981.[15] There are disputes to this day about whether Nestle is complying with this international code.[16]

B. There's an App for That

One of the ways customers reacted negatively to the news of Target's political spending in 2010 to support a Republican gubernatorial candidate in Minnesota was by boycotting. Viral videos on YouTube showed flash mobs protesting in Target stores or consumers more simply and damningly returning merchandise to Target retailers. After all this upheaval, Target agreed to place more internal controls on its political spending.[17] Target, of course, is

12. KLEIN, *supra* note 6, at 336.

13. Mike Muller, Introduction to Mike Muller's *Milking the Poor* (1975) in *The Guardian* in GLOBAL MUCKRAKING 100 YEARS OF INVESTIGATIVE JOURNALISM FROM AROUND THE WORLD (Anya Schiffin ed.) at 180 (2014).

14. *Id.* at 180–81.

15. World Health Organization, *The WHO/UNICEF International Code* (1981), http://archive.babymilkaction.org/regs/thecode.html.

16. Jill Krasny, *Every Parent Should Know The Scandalous History of Infant Formula*, BUS. INSIDER (Jun. 25, 2012), http://www.businessinsider.com/nestles-infant-formula-scandal-2012-6?op=1.

17. Kim Geiger & Noam N. Levey, *Target changes political donations policy after controversy*, L.A. TIMES (Feb. 19, 2011), http://articles.latimes.com/2011/feb/19/nation/la-na-target-20110219.

just one retailer. Should other retailers be worried? In a word, yes. An election-eve poll conducted by Bannon Communications in October 2012 asked, "would you refuse to buy a company's product or services based on their political spending?" A staggering 79% of Americans polled responded that yes, they would be willing to stop buying a company's products based on corporate politicking, with 36.7% stating that they would be very willing to stop buying.[18]

Against this backdrop of a corporate constitutional right to spend in politics thanks to *Citizens United*[19] (and its predecessor *Bellotti*),[20] and an increasingly polarized customer base, entering from stage left and stage right are new technologies to empower consumers to tap into databases to learn the politics behind mass-marketed brands.[21] New applications for smart phones like Buycott, Buypartisan, and 2nd Vote allow customers to quickly discern whether the products they are buying are associated with corporate spenders that they find politically objectionable. Once consumers know a brand's politics, they may alter their purchasing patterns accordingly. When customers think of the "bad behind the good,"[22] this alienation can spread like a contagion to far-flung corners of the world through democratizing technologies.[23]

One fact that impeded boycotts from being launched or sustained in the past was the high transaction costs of organizing them. Boycotts require communications to vast numbers of people informing consumers about what is being boycotted and why, as well as whether the object of the boycott has changed their behavior in a positive way. In the 1970s, boycotts were coordi-

---

18. Bannon Communications, *PhonetiCall Corporate Reform National Survey Top Lines*, Q10A, (2012), http://www.citizen.org/documents/toplines.pdf; Liz Kennedy, *Citizens Actually United: The Bi-Partisan Opposition to Corporate Political Spending and Support for Common Sense Reform*, DEMOS (Oct. 25, 2012), http://www.demos.org/publication/citizens-actually-united-bi-partisan-opposition-corporate-political-spending-and-support.

19. Citizens United v. Fed. Election Comm'n, 558 U.S. 310 (2010).

20. First National Bank of Boston v. Bellotti, 435 U.S. 765 (1978).

21. Drew DeSilver, *How The Most Ideologically Polarized Americans Live Different Lives*, PEW RESEARCH (June 13, 2014), http://www.pewresearch.org/fact-tank/2014/06/13/big-houses-art-museums-and-in-laws-how-the-most-ideologically-polarized-americans-live-different-lives/.

22. GLICKMAN, *supra* note 11, at 79 (explaining how abolitionists linked everyday products with the suffering of the slaves who produced them. "[Abolitionist] Garnet ... wished, through such imagery, to convey the bad behind the good.").

23. Michael Luciano, *The 'Boycott Burger King' Hashtag Is Perfect For Privileged Yuppies*, THE DAILY BANTER (Aug. 26, 2014), http://thedailybanter.com/2014/08/boycott-burger-king-hashtag-perfect-lazy-privileged-yuppies/.

nated in churches, social meetings, and face-to-face encounters in front of a picketed store. Organizing an old-style boycott required phone trees and newsletters. All of this takes time, money, and resources—both on the part of the boycott organizer and on the part of the consumer who needs to keep a running tally of what is copacetic to buy at the grocery store this week. Busy shoppers may not have time for all of this.[24] But with technological innovation, many of those old barriers began to disappear.

With the advent of social media, modern boycotts can catch fire much quicker. Smartphone technology is potentially solving the time-intensive organizational problem presented by the traditional boycott. And the modern corporation should take notice. For once, the consumer does not have to be part of a pre-existing large membership group to get pulled into a boycott effort. Rather, boycotts can be more atomized, self-driven, and miniature. Call it a "micro-boycott," if you will. A micro-boycott is one where an individual is not prompted by others, but rather individually decides to stop buying a particular good or service. As Professor Gary Minda put it, "[w]ith little capital, lots of imagination, and some luck, anyone can organize a cyberboycott. The boycott can be initiated without speakers and listeners revealing their identities."[25] Boycotts may be particularly effective in the hands of Millennials and other young digital natives,[26] who are both technologically connected, and a sought-after target demographic for retailers.[27]

As distinguished from a boycott, a "buycott" is when a consumer buys the products of companies whose behavior is admired by the consumer.[28] Buy-

---

24. Ashlee Kieler, *If A Boycott Works, It's Not Just Because People Stopped Buying Stuff,* Consumerist (May 17, 2014), http://consumerist.com/2014/05/17/if-a-boycott-works-its-not-just-because-people-stop-buying-stuff/.

25. Minda, *supra* note 9, at 185–6.

26. Larry Atkins, *Hashtag Activism Is a Good Thing, Despite Its Conservative Critics,* Huff. Post (July 29, 2014), http://www.huffingtonpost.com/larry-atkins/hashtag-activism-is-a-goo_b_5368173.html ("Twitter is the equivalent of the town square or the National Mall in Washington, D.C. for Millennials. Most of them do not read physical newspapers or watch Meet the Press…. It's not that they are stupid; it's that they receive news and information in a different way than their parents and grandparents.").

27. Klein, *supra* note 6, at 403 ("a leader in exile of Burma's elected National League for Democracy, observed that 'PepsiCo very much takes care of its image. It wanted to press the drink's image as "the taste of a young generation," so when the young generation participates in boycotts, it hurts that effort.'").

28. Monroe Friedman, *A Positive Approach to Organized Consumer Action: The "Buycott" as an Alternative to the Boycott,* 19 J. Consumer Pol'y 439, 440 (Dec. 1996); Glick-man, *supra* note 11, at 72 ("[Free produce activists] were the first consumer activists to

cotts, like boycotts, have a long lineage in America, dating back to founding father Benjamin Franklin. As Professor Glickman explained, "many free producers were doubtless aware of the maple sugar craze of the 1790s, in which Benjamin Franklin and others encouraged entrepreneurial Americans to market the sweet sap of the maple tree as an alternative to slave-grown cane sugar. The successful marketing of maple sugar, claimed one advocate, would 'diminish so many strokes of the whip, which our luxury draws upon the blacks.'"[29]

App makers have sought to modernize the practices adopted by Ben Franklin and his cohorts. As of May 2013, Buycott is also a popular application available on various smartphone platforms.[30] It allows users to create an account and join "campaigns" that align with the users' beliefs. The point of the program is to make it easier "for consumers to make sure what's in their cart is aligned with what's in their heart."[31] As its creator explained: "I see Buycott as the next stage for how people can organize themselves using technology."[32]

Once campaigns are selected, Buycott users can scan the barcode of a product using their smart phone's camera. The application alerts a user when a particular product is owned by a company that conflicts with one of the campaigns a user has followed (boycott) or is aligned with a user's campaign (buycott).[33] The application provides users with information on the company producing the product like corporate office address, brands owned by the company, contact information, and links to the company's website and social media sites.[34]

In contrast to Buycott, BuyPartisan allows shoppers to scan the bar codes on products and to learn about the politics of the corporation behind it.[35] As

---

propose what scholars today call the 'buycott,' a commercial alternative to abstention, and the first to suggest labeling ethical goods.").

29. GLICKMAN, *supra* note 11, at 63.

30. BUYCOTT APP, http://www.buycott.com/ (last visited Aug. 1, 2013).

31. M. Joy Hayes, *Buycott App Makes It Easier to Put Your Money Where Your Ideals Are*, DAILYFINANCE (June 12, 2013), http://www.dailyfinance.com/2013/06/12/buycott-app-put-your-money-where-your-ideals-are/.

32. Sonya James, *Q&A: Ivan Pardo, Creator of Buycott, on Politically Savvy Consumerism*, ZDNET.COM (Aug. 16, 2013), http://www.zdnet.com/article/qa-ivan-pardo-creator-of-buycott-on-politically-savvy-consumerism/.

33. M.J. Angel, *To Buy or Boycott—Brands Beware*, SYDNEY MORNING HERALD (July 29, 2013), http://www.smh.com.au/action/printArticle?id=4599088.

34. BUYCOTT APP, *supra* note 30.

35. John Brownlee, *How Republican Is Whole Foods? I Used An App To Find Out*, FAST COMPANY, Aug. 29, 2014, http://www.fastcodesign.com/3035033/how-republican-is-whole-foods-i-used-an-app-to-find-out ("a review by a liberal customer who used BuyPartisan

the *L.A. Times* described it, "[b]y compiling campaign finance data from the top Fortune 500 companies and matching it with their products, the app lets consumers scan their groceries and immediately find out which political party stands to profit most from the sale."[36] The process is user friendly. After scanning the bar code, "within seconds data are displayed on the screen. A red and blue bar breaks down the percentage of Republican and Democratic support the manufacturer and its employees provided, while a green bar signifies 'other.' "[37] The data on the partisanship of the firms is based on the political spending of the CEO, board, corporate PACs, and employees.[38]

While Buycott allows users to keep track of buycotts and boycotts, "BuyPartisan doesn't directly urge users to boycott products, but that's likely how many consumers will use it."[39] *The Economist* doesn't like the idea of consumers bringing their partisanship into the grocery store. In a hostile review of the BuyPartisan App, the magazine clucked, "the prissiest Americans are haunted by a different fear: that they may buy cheese made by someone whose opinions they do not share."[40] *The Washington Post* editorial page agreed: "[i]f the app succeeds, it would be a sign that Democrats and Republicans aren't even willing to do business with one another any longer.... [W]e hope BuyPartisan fails."[41]

App developers are undeterred. Some App makers are targeting particular audiences espousing particular political viewpoints. An App called 2nd Vote, which works on the same principles as Buycott and Buypartisan, but is being targeted at conservative consumers. This App will alert users whether a particular product is associated with gun control or pro-choice spending, among other issues. As *Politico* explained "2nd Vote is designed to allow conservative voters to see how companies score on five issues: gun rights, abortion, the en-

bemoaned, "Spoiler: it's almost impossible to buy anything in Whole Foods without, in a roundabout way, supporting the Republican Party.").

36. Rebecca Bratek, *Smartphone App Reveals the Politics in Your Shopping Cart*, L.A. Times (Aug. 25, 2014), http://www.latimes.com/nation/la-na-buy-partisan-20140825-story.html.

37. *Id.*

38. *Id.*

39. *Id.*

40. *BuyPartisan Voting with your Wallet an App that Brings Partisan Rage to the Grocery Store*, The Economist (Sept. 13, 2014), http://www.economist.com/news/united-states/21616976-app-brings-partisan-rage-grocery-store-voting-your-wallet.

41. Editorial Board, *Democrat? Republican? There's an app for that*, Wash. Post, Aug. 17, 2014, http://www.washingtonpost.com/opinions/democrat-republican-theres-an-app-for-that/2014/08/17/1d4b3086-2323-11e4-86ca-6f03cbd15c1a_story.html.

vironment, same-sex marriage and federal subsidies[.]"[42] And 2nd Vote gives "each company a score from 1 to 10[.] The app rates everything from the airline industry to Internet businesses as actively liberal, passively liberal, passively conservative and actively conservative."[43] According to press reports, Buycott has 1.5 million users, and Buypartisan and 2nd Vote have 100,000 users each. But the potential is quite striking, as it could take the human organizer, and many man-hours, out of organizing a boycott and could lead to powerful simultaneous micro-boycotts.

C. Customers Flex Their Muscles

No one can be certain what the future may hold for the politically active corporation, but the recent experience of corporations being pressured to leave American Legislative Exchange Council (better known as ALEC) may presage the future. As Bill Moyers jibed, ALEC is "the most influential corporate-funded political force most of America has *never* heard of."[44] ALEC is a 501(c)(3). Among other things, ALEC's legislative members introduce model legislation in state capitols around the country.[45] Some of these model ALEC bills have become state laws.[46] After a leak at ALEC, many of their internal documents were published by *Pro Publica* and the Center for Media and Democracy, which made clear that the use of model ALEC legislation was propagating nationwide.[47]

---

42. Tal Kopan, *App Grades Companies on Their Political Bent*, Politico (Oct. 22, 2013), http://www.politico.com/story/2013/10/app-grades-companies-on-their-political-bent-98697.html#ixzz3UvxZ1JqQ.

43. *Id.*

44. *United States of ALEC*, Moyers & Co (Sept. 28, 2012).

45. Molly Jackman, *ALEC's Influence over Lawmaking in State Legislatures*, Brookings, (Dec. 6, 2013), http://www.brookings.edu/research/articles/2013/12/06-american-legislative-exchange-council-jackman ("First, ALEC model bills are, word-for-word, introduced in our state legislatures at a non-trivial rate. Second, they have a good chance—better than most legislation—of being enacted into law.").

46. *Full Show: United States of ALEC—A Follow-Up*, Moyers & Co. (June 21, 2013), http://billmoyers.com/episode/full-show-united-states-of-alec-a-follow-up/ ("In state houses around the country, hundreds of pieces of boilerplate ALEC legislation are proposed or enacted that would, among other things, dilute collective bargaining rights, make it harder for some Americans to vote, and limit corporate liability for harm caused to consumers—each accomplished without the public ever knowing who's behind it.").

47. Lois Beckett, *Our Step-By-Step Guide to Understanding ALEC's Influence on Your State Laws*, ProPublica (Aug. 1, 2011), http://www.propublica.org/article/our-step-by-step-guide-to-understanding-alecs-influence-on-your-state-laws.

The President of Demos, Heather McGhee, explicated ALEC's power: "[w]hat we know from political science and from political outcomes is that organization and money are the coin of the realm in terms of influencing elected officials. ALEC is a very good example of both of those things. ALEC is operating in nearly every legislature in the country. They are able to translate conservative economic and environmental ideas into actionable legislation. They are also able to coordinate legislators all over the country with money."[48] ALEC is not some fly-by-night organization.[49] It has been around since 1973. And ALEC's business model has been incredibly successful in terms of recruiting legislators. There are approximately 2,000 legislators who are members of ALEC out of approximately 7,000 legislators in the United States (or nearly 30% of the nation's lawmakers).[50] The other members of ALEC are corporations.

Lisa Graves explained ALEC's basic structure: "[i]t's really a membership group of corporations who want to influence state legislators. Lawmakers pay $50 a year. Sometimes the taxpayer pays for them to be members of ALEC. Corporations pay tens of thousands of dollars to be members of ALEC. What corporations get out of that is one-stop shopping for state legislators across the country."[51] She continued, "at ALEC conferences, corporations literally vote as equals with state legislators on bills before the bills are introduced in state legislatures and become law."[52] Meanwhile, Phil Radford, former Executive Director of Greenpeace, had little positive to say about ALEC's political influence over state lawmaking:

> ALEC is one of the most outrageous examples of pay to play. State leaders all convene. Companies pay to have a membership to get in front of the state leaders. Companies and legislators sit down together and co-author bills. In the ALEC meetings ... companies are writing the laws with veto power. Many state legislators push those bills through their states. This is not what our founding fathers pictured when they pictured democracy.[53]

---

48. Interview with Heather McGhee, President Demos (Aug. 11, 2015).

49. Alan Greenblatt, *ALEC Enjoys a New Wave of Influence and Criticism*, GOVERNING (Dec. 2011), http://www.governing.com/topics/politics/ALEC-enjoys-new-wave-influence-criticism.html.

50. American Legislative Exchange Council, Membership http://www.alec.org/membership/ (last visited Nov. 27, 2015).

51. Interview with Lisa Graves, Executive Director Center for Media & Democracy (July 17, 2015).

52. *Id.*

53. Interview with Phil Radford, Former Executive Director of Greenpeace (Aug. 5, 2015).

While money in politics and voting rights are not always directly linked, ALEC shows one of the examples of where voter suppression can be linked to corporate backed lobbying. To wit, ALEC has been one of the forces pushing for the widespread adoption of voter ID legislation, that many voting rights advocates worry suppress the ability of minorities, students and the elderly to vote.[54] Elizabeth Kennedy of Demos stated, "ALEC was behind the lock step voter ID laws that spread like wildfire moving through a drought stricken countryside after 2010. This raises the specter of a confluence of economic power and attempts to restrict people power by cutting off access to the ballot box."[55]

One of the states that adopted a voter ID law was North Carolina. Professor Zephyr Teachout indicated, "[o]ne thing that is so troubling about ALEC is it is leveraging North Carolina racism to limit access to the polls." She continued, "[w]ith ALEC, politicians who want to limit access to the polls for racist reasons get hooked up with corporations who want to limit the access to polls for tax reasons. It is very dangerous and unhealthy and sick. The most efficient way to serve ALEC's donors is to have less democracy."[56]

Good government groups had complained about ALEC for years.[57] But the public's disenchantment with ALEC came with the death of an unarmed teenager in Florida. After the highly publicized killing of African American teenager Trayvon Martin at the hands of George Zimmerman, national attention by the media focused on the Florida Stand Your Ground law that Zimmerman used as a defense.[58] Demos President Heather McGee noted that ALEC

---

54. Sarah Childress, *Why Voter ID Laws Aren't Really About Fraud*, PBS (Oct. 20, 2014), http://www.pbs.org/wgbh/frontline/article/why-voter-id-laws-arent-really-about-fraud/ ("Richard Posner, in a recent scathing critique of these laws, calling the expressed concern about fraud a 'a mere fig leaf' and that they instead 'appear to be aimed at limiting voting by minorities, particularly blacks.'"); Suevon Lee, *Everything You've Ever Wanted to Know About Voter ID Laws*, ProPublica (Nov. 5, 2012), http://www.propublica.org/article/everything-youve-ever-wanted-to-know-about-voter-id-laws. ("Voting law opponents contend these laws disproportionately affect elderly, minority and low-income groups that tend to vote Democratic.").

55. Interview with Elizabeth Kennedy, Counsel Demos (Aug. 12, 2015).

56. Interview with Fordham Law Professor Zephyr Teachout (Aug. 10, 2015).

57. Nathan Newman & David Sirota, *Forget D.C.— The Battle Is in the States*, In These Times (Feb. 20, 2006), http://inthesetimes.com/article/2509.

58. Courteney Keatinge & David Eaton, *Political Contributions A Glass Lewis Issue Report*, Glass Lewis & Co 11 (2013) http://politicalaccountability.net/index.php?ht=a/GetDocumentAction/i/7544 ("Zimmerman, who told police he shot Martin in self-defense, was released by police the evening of the shooting as a result of Florida's 'Stand Your Ground' law.").

move "into voting rights beyond economic ideas and their move into 'stand your ground' or 'kill at will' laws that gave cover to George Zimmerman's killing of Trayvon Martin, prompted groups like Color of Change to bring a new spotlight to the life-and-death consequences of ALEC."[59] Many felt that Zimmerman got away with murder.[60] Public interest groups rightly pointed out that "Stand Your Ground" laws[61] had been adopted in many states at the urging of ALEC.[62]

In protest of not only the Stand Your Ground Laws, but also certain voter suppression laws, an advocacy group called Color of Change gathered 85,000 signatures and threatened to boycott certain consumer companies if they did not leave ALEC,[63] demonstrating that on occasion, a full boycott is not even necessary to change corporate behavior if the threat of a boycott is credible.[64]

59. McGhee interview *supra* note 48.

60. *33% Believe Zimmerman Guilty of Murder in Trayvon Martin Case*, RASMUSSEN REPORTS (Mar. 28, 2012), http://www.rasmussenreports.com/public_content/lifestyle/general_lifestyle/march_2012/33_believe_zimmerman_guilty_of_murder_in_trayvon_martin_case.

61. William Alan Nelson II, Esq., *Post*-Citizens United: *Using Shareholder Derivative Claims Of Corporate Waste To Challenge Corporate Independent Political Expenditures*, 13 NEV. L.J. 134, 157–58 (2012) (internal citations omitted) (" 'ALEC promotes business-friendly legislation in state capitols and drafts model bills for state legislatures to adopt.' However, the organization has also supported 'controversial measures, including voter-identification laws and stand[-]your[-]ground laws.' ").

62. Anthony Kammer, *Privatizing the Safeguards of Federalism*, 29 J.L. & POL. 69, 121 (2013) ("according to … ALEC's tax filings, … in 2009, …'legislative dues came to $82,891, and all the corporate tax-free donations and other income amounted to $6.1 million.' Notwithstanding ALEC's official nonpartisan status as a 501(c)(3) organization, both its leadership and legislative members are predominantly Republican.") (internal citations omitted).

63. Press Release, *ColorOfChange.org Applauds Coca-Cola's Decision to Pull its Support of ALEC Civil Rights Organization Calls on More Corporations to Follow Suit and End Their Support of ALEC* (April 4, 2012), http://colorofchange.org/press/releases/2012/4/4/colorofchangeorg-applauds-coca-colas-decision-pull/; Tiffany Hsu, *Coca-Cola, Kraft Leave Conservative ALEC after Boycott Launched*, L.A. TIMES (Apr. 6, 2012), http://articles.latimes.com/2012/apr/06/business/la-fi-mo-coca-cola-kraft-alec-20120406 ("Within hours of advocacy group Color of Change launching a boycott against Coca-Cola for its participation on ALEC's Private Enterprise Board, the soft drink giant issued a statement saying that it had 'elected to discontinue its membership.' ").

64. David Ferguson, *Coke and Pepsi Abandon Conservative Group Over Voter ID, Gun Laws*, THE RAW STORY (Apr. 5, 2012), http://www.rawstory.com/rs/2012/04/05/coke-and-pepsi-abandon-conservative-group-over-voter-id-gun-laws/ ("The advocacy group Color of Change began a call-in campaign on Wednesday threatening a boycott of Coca-Cola and its products. The company announced within hours that it will not be renewing their membership in ALEC."); Kieler, *supra* note 24 ("Brayden King's report…, which studies 221

Within hours, Coke was one of the first to exit ALEC.[65] Shortly thereafter, Kraft left ALEC[66] as did many other Fortune 500 companies.[67] At this point, more than 100 firms have left ALEC.[68]

Corporations must consider how customers will react, including the risk that if customers become too disenchanted, they will boycott firms. Technology is offering customers more tools to learn whether they are buying products that are backed by firms that are politically, socially or culturally aligned with the customers' core values. And the threatened boycott associated with ALEC demonstrates the power of customers. Even though ALEC has existed since 1973, and has approximately 2,000 legislators as members, under the threat of a consumer boycott, firms disassociated themselves from ALEC.

---

boycotts between 1990 and 2005, found companies were more likely to give in to boycotter's demands when the issue garnered a great amount of press coverage.").

65. Barbara Liston & Martinne Geller, *Coke Withdraws from Group that Backs Stand Your Ground Law*, REUTERS (Apr. 10, 2012), http://uk.reuters.com/article/2012/04/10/usa-coke-alec-idUKL2E8F54P120120410 ("Coca-Cola Co is dropping its membership in a conservative national advocacy group that supports 'Stand Your Ground' laws such as the one being used as a defense in the Florida killing of an unarmed black teenager, Trayvon Martin. The move by the world's biggest soft drink maker comes as corporate America faces increased scrutiny from consumers and shareholder activists over lobbying and political spending.").

66. Nelson, *supra* note 61, at 157–58 (internal citations omitted).

67. Paul Bedard, *Coke Caves in Face of Democratic Boycott Threat*, WASH. EXAMINER (Apr. 4, 2012), http://washingtonexaminer.com/article/444346 ("The Coca-Cola Company has elected to discontinue its membership with the American Legislative Exchange Council (ALEC). Our involvement with ALEC was focused on efforts to oppose discriminatory food and beverage taxes, not on issues that have no direct bearing on our business. We have a long-standing policy of only taking positions on issues that impact our Company and industry."); Joel Connelly, *Amazon Cited "Public Concerns," Quits Right-Wing Legislative Group*, SEATTLE P.I., (May 24, 2012), http://www.seattlepi.com/local/connelly/article/Amazon-cites-public-concerns-quits-right-wing-3583140.php?cmpid=emailarticle&cmpid=emailarticle; *Wal-Mart Ending Membership in Conservative Group*, REUTERS (May 31, 2012), http://www.reuters.com/article/2012/05/31/us-walmart-alec-idUSBRE84U05N20120531?irpc=932 ("Maggie Sans, Wal-Mart vice president of public affairs and government relations, said in a May 30 letter addressed to ALEC's national chairman and executive director. 'We feel that the divide between these activities and our purpose as a business has become too wide. To that end, we are suspending our membership in ALEC.'"); Rebekah Wilce, *National Board for Professional Teaching Standards Cuts Ties to ALEC*, PR WATCH (May 1, 2012), http://www.prwatch.org/news/2012/05/11491/national-board-professional-teaching-standards-cuts-ties-alec ("Given recent events, the new NBPTS President and CEO decided to discontinue engagement with ALEC.").

68. *Corporations that Have Cut Ties to ALEC*, SOURCE WATCH, Nov. 29, 2012, http://www.sourcewatch.org/index.php/Corporations_Who_Have_Cut_Ties_to_ALEC.

Chapter 13

The End of the Bottom Line

You never change things by fighting the existing reality. To change
something, build a new model that makes the existing model obsolete.
— Architect R. Buckminster Fuller[1]

What is the ethical entrepreneur to do if she wants to start a for-profit business? Given the moral pitfalls that can be laid at the feet of the traditional C
corporation, should the entrepreneur put her heart, mind, and soul into building a C corp and hope she won't be crushed by the tyranny of the bottom line?
Or is there another path? Since 2010, there is another way of constructing a
business—the benefit corporation. At the very same time the Supreme Court
was handing out more and more powers to the traditional corporation, a small
but significant change, pushed by morally grounded business people, has created a new corporate form that insists on building social responsibility into
the corporate structure.

The tyranny of the bottom line can lead to all sorts of antisocial corporate
behaviors. The traditional C corp is incentivized to maximize profits, which
leads to negative externalities that push the costs of environmental impacts
onto others, like taxpayers, and to minimize labor costs by using child and in-
voluntary labor.

One of the most extreme examples of corporate callousness and disregard
for human life in the face of making money was the continued marketing of
Ford's Pinto, which the company knew could catch fire in certain types of col-
lisions—thereby burning, maiming, or killing passengers.[2] Ford had conducted

---

1. Buckminster Fuller Institute, *Greenwave Wins the 2015 Fuller Challenge* (Oct. 21,
2015), https://bfi.org/dymaxion-forum/2015/10/greenwave-wins-2015-fuller-challenge
(quoting R. Buckminster Fuller).
2. Robin Paul Malloy, *Equating Human Rights and Property Rights—The Need for Moral*

a cost-benefit analysis about the cost of recalling the Pinto, and other similarly flawed vehicles.[3] Even though it would have only cost $11 per vehicle to improve the safety of the Pinto, the costs of paying for deaths and burn victims was lower, and Ford delayed a recall.[4] After press reports of the tendency of Ford Pintos to catch fire became public, Ford finally decided to recall the Pinto, but it wasn't soon enough. In 1978 three women died in their Pinto when it exploded in a car crash. They died before Ford's recall letters went out. A prosecutor in Indiana decided to charge Ford criminally,[5] but in the end, the jury found Ford not guilty.[6]

Whether it's environmental degradation, child labor, or exploding Pintos, the root cause appears to be the pressure to maximize profits. Too frequently, the economic incentive is in conflict with the public interest. But this is not an inevitable conclusion. Past generations had a sense that business and social responsibility went hand-in-hand. Even when Berle and Means were writing in the 1930s, they had contemporaries like Professor E. Merrick Dodd arguing for what we'd now call corporate social responsibility. As Dodd wrote, "there is in fact a growing feeling not only that business has responsibilities to the community, but that our corporate managers who control business should voluntarily and without waiting for legal compulsion manage it in such a way as to fulfill those responsibilities."[7]

Dr. Marcy Murninghan reminds us that even the language that is used in business has ethical overtones. "The vocabulary of Wall St. and vocabulary of theology are very much the same. Think about terms such as equity, trust, value, denomination, redemption. That is because the words themselves signal cer-

---

Judgment in an Economic Analysis of Law and Social Policy, 47 Ohio St. L.J. 163, 175–176 (1986) ("A lack of moral judgment was evident in the 'real world' dilemma of the Ford Motor Company and the exploding Pinto automobile.... Consumer use revealed that a design flaw had made the car a virtual time bomb.").

3. Gary T. Schwartz, *The Myth of the Ford Pinto Case*, 43 Rutgers L. Rev. 1013, 1020–1021 (1991).

4. William Shaw & Vincent Barry, Moral Issues in Business 8th ed. 83–86 (2001); W. Kip Viscusi, *Pricing Lives for Corporate Risk Decisions*, 68 Vand. L. Rev. 1117, 1133–1135 (2015).

5. Brandon L. Garrett, Too Big to Jail How Prosecutors Compromise with Corporations 130 (2014). It is rare but not unheard of to charge a corporation with physical harm. *See also* Granite Construction Co. v. Superior Court of Fresno County, 149 Cal.App.3d 465, 197 Cal. Rptr. 3 (Cal. App. 1983) (permitting a corporate prosecution for manslaughter).

6. Garrett, *supra* note 5, at 131.

7. E. Merrick Dodd, *For Whom Are Corporate Managers Trustees?*, 45 Harv. L. Rev. 1145, 1153 (1931–1932).

tain kinds of ethical commitment and community obligations."[8] Dr. Murning-han found consideration of the public interest in the U.S. securities laws: "[i]f you look at the 1933 and 1934 enabling legislation that created the SEC and the Investment Company Act of 1940, the public interest is mentioned hundreds of times, almost always in the same sentence as 'protect shareholders.'"[9]

Can business do well by doing good? Being environmentally prudent can actually make good business sense, particularly in the long term. The Green-est CEO in America, Ray Anderson of Interface, was quoted as saying "'I always make the business case for sustainability ... It's so compelling. Our costs are down, not up. Our products are the best they have ever been.... And the goodwill in the marketplace—it's just been astonishing.'"[10] One thing that may be holding back other CEOs from following in Ray Anderson's footsteps is the traditional corporate structure that places profit maximization above all else.[11]

A. Benefit Corporation Laws

Instead of trying to jerry-rig the traditional model, a few creative thinkers founded a nonprofit called the B Lab, and decided perhaps it was finally time for a new model.[12] That model is the benefit corporation (also known as the "B Corp"). Generally, benefit corporation laws allow for the creation of a for-profit business entity that also has a social mission. This business form has caught fire. Why? One explanation is "[t]here was a cultural shift. Social im-pact is becoming more important to American citizens in general—maybe be-cause of the recession or all the recent corporate scandals."[13]

The speed of adoption of benefit corporation legislation has been nothing short of astounding.[14] In 2010, Maryland became the first state to allow for

---

8. Interview with Dr. Marcy Murninghan, corporate governance expert (July 24, 2015).
9. *Id.*
10. Emily Langer, *Ray Anderson, 'Greenest CEO in America,' Dies at 77*, WASH. POST, Aug. 10, 2011, https://www.washingtonpost.com/local/obituaries/ray-anderson-greenest-ceo-in-america-dies-at-77/2011/08/10/gIQAGoTU7I_story.html.
11. Interview with Ben Cohen, CEO Ben & Jerry's (Nov. 4, 2015) ("Other older forms of corporations require the corporation to solely maximize profits. In some instances, they prevent a corporation from factoring social benefit into their decision making systems.").
12. Jay Coen Gilbert, *On Better Businesses at TEDxPhilly* (Dec. 1, 2010) (asking "how do we evolve capitalism?"), https://www.youtube.com/watch?v=mGnz-w9p5FU.
13. Katie Kerr Holcomb, Director of Communications B Lab (Aug. 24, 2015).
14. Cohen interview *supra* note 11 ("I'm surprised at how fast it has taken off. A lot of credit has to go the people who started B Lab. They are doing a fantastic job. It really said

benefit corporations. In late 2011, two of the biggest states by population—New York and California—also adopted benefit corporation laws, bringing the grand total to seven states. But because so many corporations are incorporated in Delaware, the big question was whether Delaware would follow suit. It took two years, but on July 17, 2013, the governor of Delaware signed benefit corporation legislation into law, signaling a seismic shift in corporate law. By 2015, 30 states plus the District of Columbia had adopted the legislation. Before the existence of benefit corporation laws, socially conscious entrepreneurs were put to a difficult and limiting choice: either take the charitable route and incorporate as a nonprofit or incorporate as a for-profit and face potential lawsuits from shareholders for not maximizing profits whenever a "charitable" action was taken using corporate funds.

In an age when bipartisanship seems to be waning, the B Lab reported, "[b]enefit corporation laws cross party lines."[15] And the B Lab explains why so many states and the District of Columbia adopted the legislation so quickly. "Policy makers like the following three things about the benefit corporation legislation: (1) it provides more freedom for business (2) it doesn't cost the state anything, and (3) it shows that your state is a leader to attract new businesses to the state."[16]

The sales pitch to lawmakers to adopt the new business form has been relatively simple, as CEO Davis Smith reports from his vantage point in Utah. Mr. Smith indicated, "I testified in the Utah legislature in support of the benefit corporation legislation. The bill was unanimously approved in Utah." And he continued, "[t]he only questions that I got from lawmakers were (1) why didn't you just incorporate as a nonprofit? So I responded, I would not have been able to raise venture capital for a nonprofit. And (2) the other question was why not incorporate as a C corp and then do good things? Then I explained the liability protection that directors get under the benefit corporation bill."[17] Benefit corporation legislation requires boards to take into consideration the interests of constituencies other than shareholders. This means that shareholders are foreclosed from suing the board merely because the directors considered the public's benefit when making business choices. Though no one really knows what will happen when a disenchanted shareholder sues the board of a benefit corporation either for taking the public benefit into account, or

---

a lot when\Delaware, the state where most corporations choose to incorporate in, adopted the B Corp law.").

15. Holcomb interview *supra* note 13.

16. *Id.*

17. Interview with Davis Smith, CEO Cotopaxi (Sept. 2, 2015).

alternatively not taking the public benefit into account enough, because "[t]he benefit corporation laws are untried in court."[18]

The model legislation to create benefit corporations was created by the B Lab, but laws differ by state. For example, here is the structure of the Delaware Public Benefit Corporation Law. Under Delaware law, a "public benefit corporation" is

> a for-profit corporation organized ... that is intended to produce a public benefit or public benefits and to operate in a responsible and sustainable manner. To that end, a public benefit corporation shall be managed in a manner that balances the stockholders' pecuniary interests, the best interests of those materially affected by the corporation's conduct, and the public benefit or public benefits identified in its certificate of incorporation.[19]

The Delaware law requires that the benefit corporation's certificate of incorporation (otherwise known as its corporate charter) contain a statement clarifying one or more public benefits that the corporation will pursue. Delaware law defines a "public benefit" as "a positive effect (or reduction of negative effects) on 1 or more categories of persons, entities, communities or interests (other than stockholders in their capacities as stockholders) including, but not limited to, effects of an artistic, charitable, cultural, economic, educational, environmental, literary, medical, religious, scientific or technological nature."[20] Thus, one of the big differences between a traditional Delaware C corporation and a Delaware B corporation is that the benefit corporations must have a stated public benefit and that benefit must take into consideration interests other than just those of shareholders. In a traditional Delaware C corporation, the interests of shareholders are primary. This has been reaffirmed by Delaware case law. In a case arising between eBay and craigslist called *eBay Domestic Holdings, Inc. v. Newmark*, the Delaware court stated,

> Jim and Craig [the founders of craigslist] did prove that they personally believe craigslist should not be about the business of stockholder wealth maximization, now or in the future.... The corporate form in which craigslist operates, however, is not an appropriate vehicle for purely philanthropic ends, at least not when there are other stockholders interested in realizing a return on their investment. Jim and

---

18. Holcomb interview *supra* note 13.
19. 8 Del. Gen. Corp. Law §362, http://delcode.delaware.gov/title8/c001/sc15/.
20. *Id.*

Craig opted to form craigslist, Inc. as a *for-profit Delaware corporation* and voluntarily accepted millions of dollars from eBay as part of a transaction whereby eBay became a stockholder. Having chosen a for-profit corporate form, the craigslist directors are bound by the fiduciary duties and standards that accompany that form. Those standards include acting to promote the value of the corporation for the benefit of its stockholders. The "Inc." after the company name has to mean at least that.[21]

Giving shareholders a fair return on investment must drive the board of a traditional Delaware C corporation. But the duties of a board of directors of Delaware benefit corporations are different. The statutory law specifies: "[t]he board of directors shall manage or direct the business and affairs of the public benefit corporation in a manner that balances the pecuniary interests of the stockholders, the best interests of those materially affected by the corporation's conduct, and the specific public benefit ... identified in its certificate of incorporation."[22] This does not mean that directors have legally binding duties to individuals outside of the corporate structure. All of the duties still run between the board and shareholders. The law also allows for exculpatory clauses for directors.[23]

Delaware's benefit corporations are required to report to shareholders at least every two years, explaining how the corporation has promoted the public benefit identified in the certificate of incorporation.[24] This statement must include (1) the objectives set by the board to promote the public benefit; (2) the metrics the board is using to measure the corporation's progress in achieving those goals; (3) factual information based on those metrics regarding the corporation's success in meeting the objectives; and (4) an assessment of the corporation's success in promoting the public benefit. Delaware benefit corporations can opt to make this statement public, but are not required to do

---

21. eBay Domestic Holdings, Inc. v. Newmark, 16 A.3d 1, 34 (Del.Ch. 2010).

22. 8 Del. Gen. Corp. Law § 365, http://delcode.delaware.gov/title8/c001/sc15/.

23. *Id.*; Delaware law § 102(b)(7) allows exculpatory clauses in a corporation's charter eliminating personal liability of a director to shareholders for monetary damages for breach of fiduciary duty, provided that such clause does not eliminate liability (1) for "any breach of the director's duty of loyalty," (2) "for acts or omissions not in good faith or which involve intentional misconduct or a knowing violation of law," and (3) "for any transaction from which the director derived an improper personal benefit." Delaware law § 145 allows for indemnification and interim advancement of expenses with respect to proceedings to which a person "was or is made a party ... by reason of the fact that the person is or was a director, officer, employee or agent of the corporation ..."

24. 8 Del. Gen. Corp. Law § 366, http://delcode.delaware.gov/title8/c001/sc15/.

so. They can also opt to use a third-party standard (like the ones provided by the B Lab, Fair Trade, or LEED), but, again, are not required to do so.[25]

Under Delaware law, stockholder derivative suits against public benefit corporations are limited to stockholders who own at least two percent of the corporation's outstanding shares or, if the corporation is publicly traded, the lesser of shares worth $2 million or two percent of the shares. These shareholders can sue to enforce § 365(a).[26] Again, § 365(a) requires the board to balance the interest of investors with the public interest.[27] No one else, including members of the public who are supposed to be benefited by a particular Delaware benefit corporation, can sue the directors for failing to materialize an actual benefit. But the two percent shareholders can sue to make the board balance profitability with public benefits.

The Delaware law was amended in 2015 to make it even easier for corporations to switch to becoming benefit corporations.[28] For example, the name of the corporation no longer must contain the words "public benefit corporation."[29] Another change was that previously a vote of 90% of existing shareholders would have to vote in favor of converting a traditional C corporation into a benefit corporation. But under the new 2015 law, only a two-thirds vote is required to make this conversion.[30]

B. Certified B Corps

Admittedly the language can get a little murky, because in addition to Delaware public benefit corporations, there are also benefit corporations in other states that use slightly different nomenclatures, and there are also "Certified B Corps" that are not necessarily organized as benefit corporations in any state.[31] In contrast to benefit corporations (described above), a "Certified B Corp" is a corporation that has been certified by the B Lab to meet rigorous standards. The B-Lab certification is a third-party standard requiring compa-

---

25. *Id.*

26. 8 Del. Gen. Corp. Law § 367, http://delcode.delaware.gov/title8/c001/sc15/.

27. 8 Del. Gen. Corp. Law § 365(a), http://delcode.delaware.gov/title8/c001/sc15/.

28. Del. Sen. Bill No. 75 (2015), http://legis.delaware.gov/LIS/lis148.nsf/vwLegislation/SB+75/$file/legis.html?open.

29. *Id.*

30. *Id.*

31. Ryan Honeyman, *What's the Difference Between Certified B Corps and Benefit Corps?*, TRIPLE PUNDIT (Aug. 26, 2014), http://www.triplepundit.com/2014/08/whats-difference-certified-b-corps-benefit-corps/.

nies to meet social, sustainability, and environmental performance standards, accountability standards, and to be transparent to the public. The B Lab recertifies firms every two years.[32]

The B Lab explains the certification process for becoming a Certified B Corp:

> The first step is to score an 80 out of 200 on the B impact assessment to measure and manage your impact on your workers, your community and the environment. After your answers are verified, the next step is legal. You need to put stakeholders in your foundational documents so that you are legally required to consider them when making decisions. The last step is to sign a term sheet and to sign the declaration of interdependence that lays out our beliefs.[33]

Many benefit corporations are also Certified B Corps, but not every Certified B Corp is a benefit corporation, especially if it was founded before 2010.

Entrepreneur Davis Smith, who incorporated one of the first Delaware benefit corporations, said the creation of benefit corporations was a welcome evolution: "[t]he way capitalism currently operates doesn't address serious existing and emerging social issues. We need capitalism to continue to evolve. At one point in America, we had children working in factories. My hope is that over the next century we'll see a continued evolution of capitalism where businesses look beyond their bottom line for ways they can positively impact their communities and the world."[34]

C. Benefits to Benefit Corporations

For socially minded entrepreneurs, the benefit corporation form allows a third path separate from the rigid for-profit/not-for-profit dichotomy that existed before 2010. And indeed, hiring likeminded, socially responsible employees may be facilitated by the benefit corporation form. As the B Lab's Katie Holcomb asserted, "[f]or entrepreneurs, the benefit corporation law ... helps them protect their mission as they grow, bring in capital, and new leadership. They can protect their legacy. It reduces their liability because they can't get

32. Interview with Warren Langley, Former President of the Pacific Stock Exchange (July 14, 2015) ("B Lab has provided a validation of a company's commitment to high socially responsible standards.").

33. Holcomb interview *supra* note 13.

34. Davis Smith interview *supra* note 17.

sued for not maximizing profit, which could happen under the old form. It attracts the best talent. Millennials want to work for more than a company. They want to work for a cause. And it attracts capital because there are investors that want to invest in B Corps."[35]

CEO of Cotopaxi Davis Smith agreed that being a benefit corporation helped in hiring his employees. "Being a benefit corporation is a great advantage when you are building your team.... [because] Millennials want their work to be meaningful.... Within the first two months of our launch, we had nearly 400 unsolicited job applicants."[36] Ben Cohen of Ben & Jerry's, which is a Certified B Corp, reported that hiring is one of the things that makes benefit corporations and Certified B Corps attractive ways to do business. As Mr. Cohen said, "[t]here's a growing number of potential employees that want to factor in a concern for the community. They want to do more than just earn a living. They want to work for corporations that are doing something more than just maximizing profits, often at the expense of the community."[37] He continued that when employees are treated well, "[w]hat you get back is employees who work a heck of a lot harder for you and that are out there promoting your business and your products to everyone they know. You are getting the cream of the crop of potential employees because they want to work for a company that they can believe in, a company that has a heart and a soul.... And it makes money."[38] His partner, Jerry Greenfield (the Jerry of Ben & Jerry's), stated, "I look forward to the time when [B corporations are] legal in all 50 states in this country. I think the idea that businesses exist simply to make money for the shareholders is just a much too narrow definition of what value is. Money is not value; value is not money."[39]

The B Corp/benefit corporation structure also makes it much easier for a firm to make choices that build in long-term environmental sustainability even when it would cause a short-term financial loss. Adam Lowry, the CEO of Method, which is both a Certified B Corp and a public benefit corporation, told *The New York Times* why the company decided to install a 240-foot windmill and solar arrays on their factory in Chicago: "'If our only mandate was the cheapest costs now, we'd have made a decision to use coal-fired energy,' he said. 'But climate change is the biggest environmental challenge we face, and

---

35. *Id.*

36. Davis Smith interview *supra* note 17.

37. Cohen interview *supra* note 11.

38. *Id.*

39. Sustainable Business Oregon, *Interview, Ben & Jerry's Co-Founder Jerry Greenfield*, YouTube (Nov. 3, 2011), https://www.youtube.com/watch?v=wlFesF-Zjp4.

financially, in seven to eight years, we're going to be in a much better position because we'll be getting cheaper energy.' "[40]

Katie Holcomb harkened back to the sentiments expressed by Dr. Murningham that business and social responsibility are not natural enemies. Speaking of benefit corporations, Ms. Holcomb said, "this isn't a brand new idea. If you look at original purpose of corporations, businesses were about the community and supporting the community. It was only in the recent years that the focus became short termism and the focus on quick profits that things got out of hand. This is an old concept that has come back around. And we are just formalizing it."[41]

As of 2015, in the United States there are more than 3,000 benefit corporations.[42] Companies that are Certified B Corps or benefit corporations are in a wide range of industries, including food, cleaning products, investments, and even a power company. Green Mountain Power, Vermont's largest electricity provider, was the first utility to become a Certified B Corp.[43] Among the thousands of benefit corporations and hundreds of Certified B Corps are Method Products, EO Products, Ben & Jerry's, Patagonia, King Arthur Flour, Change.org, Trillium Asset Management, and Warby Parker. The B Corp/benefit corporation phenomenon is also global, as B Lab Founder Jay Coen Gilbert explains.

[N]early 800 leading businesses from more than 60 industries and nearly 30 countries have earned B Corporation certification.... [W]ith benefit corporations, consumers and investors have another tool to clearly identifying those companies walking the talk and access the social and environmental performance data they need to make more informed choices.[44]

Of course, one key question for any entrepreneur is how to get a new idea for a business off the ground and actualized as a real enterprise. Venture cap-

40. Hiroko Tabuchi, *Etsy I.P.O. Tests Pledge to Balance Social Mission and Profit*, N.Y. Times (Apr. 16, 2015), http://www.nytimes.com/2015/04/17/business/dealbook/etsy-ipo-tests-pledge-to-emphasize-social-mission-over-profit.html?_r=0.

41. Holcomb interview *supra* note 13.

42. *Id.*

43. Wilson Ring, *Green Mountain Power Certified as Socially Conscious*, Burlington Free Press (Dec. 1, 2014), http://www.burlingtonfreepress.com/story/money/2014/12/01/green-mountain-power-become-bcorp/19727103/.

44. Jay Coen Gilbert, et al., *Today Marks a Tipping Point in the Evolution of Capitalism*, Forbes (July 7, 2013), http://www.forbes.com/sites/skollworldforum/2013/07/17/today-marks-a-tipping-point-in-the-evolution-of-capitalism/.

ital is a way to kick-start a business. But if venture capitalists don't believe in benefit corporations, then lack of access to seed capital could prove devastating. Fortunately for B corporations, venture capitalists do not appear to be shying away from this new business form. Examples of successful venture capital rounds for Certified B Corps/benefit corporations include: Cotopaxi, a socially conscious outdoor gear company that raised $6.5 million in Series A funding;[45] Ello.co, the ad-free social media network, which raised $5.5 million in venture capital funding;[46] and Yerdle, an app for exchanging used goods, which raised $5 million from venture capital funds in their Series A funding round from investors.[47] As Ben Cohen rationalized, "[t]here are lots of investors that want to factor in social concerns. If they have a choice between making money by investing in a corporation that's not helping the community versus making money with a corporation that is helping the community, many people choose to invest their money in ways that is more beneficial to the community in general."[48]

Benefit corporations and Certified B Corps are so new that predicting their future path is impossible. But two developments may indicate some longevity: (1) public corporations now have subsidiaries that are Certified B Corps: Plum Organics, which is a subsidiary of Campbell's Soup[49] and Ben & Jerry's, which is a subsidiary of Unilever; and (2) Certified B Corps, such as Rally Software[50] and Etsy,[51] have successfully gone public. As reported by *The New York Times*, "Etsy declares in its public offering prospectus that it wants to change the decades-old conventional retail model of valuing profits over community. It states that its reputation depends on maintaining its B Corp status by contin-

45. Anthony Ha, *Cotopaxi Raises $6.5M to Sell Socially Conscious Outdoor Gear*, TechCrunch (Mar. 24, 2015), http://techcrunch.com/2015/03/24/cotopaxi-series-a/.

46. Jonathan Shieber, *Ello Raises $5.5 Million, Legally Files as Public Benefit Corp. Meaning No Ads Ever*, TechCrunch (Oct. 23, 2014), http://techcrunch.com/2014/10/23/ello-raises-5-5-million-legally-files-as-public-benefit-corp-meaning-no-ads-ever/.

47. *Who Is Investing in Benefit Corps?*, BenefitCorp.net, http://benefitcorp.net/investors/who-investing-benefit-corps (last visited Sept. 4, 2015).

48. Cohen interview *supra* note 11.

49. Plum Organics, B Lab (last visited Nov. 9, 2015), https://www.bcorporation.net/community/plum-organics.

50. Peri Schweiger & Jackie Marcus, *Etsy and the B Corp IPO: Sustainability Meets Wall Street*, Triple Pundit (Apr. 27, 2015), http://www.triplepundit.com/2015/04/etsy-and-the-b-corp-ipo-sustainability-meets-wall-street/.

51. Tabuchi, *supra* note 40 ("Etsy ... became only the second for-profit company to go public out of more than 1,000 companies that have [B Corp] certification. Etsy shares closed on Thursday at $30, almost twice their initial public offering price, in one of the most closely watched market debuts this year.").

uing to offer employees stock options and paid time for volunteering, [and] paying all part-time and temporary workers 40 percent above local living wages[.]"[52]

Benefit corporations and Certified B corporations may be a model for a desirable corporate citizen: one that creates jobs, desired products, and has a socially responsible mission that is not entirely profit driven.[53] Or as Timothy Smith of Walden Asset Management explained, "[t]he philosophy of B Corps that acknowledges that all stakeholders are valued is what corporate social responsibility and sustainability is all about."[54]

Corporations are still evolving. The Certified B Corp/benefit corporation phenomenon shows there is an appetite for more morally and environmentally responsible business among entrepreneurs. This business model has caught fire quickly, with 30 states and the District of Columbia offering firms the option, with businessmen and businesswomen creating 3,000 such firms. Furthermore, publicly traded corporations with subsidiaries that are Certified B Corps and publicly traded Certified B Corps will test the long-term viability of this model. Because it is so new, it is difficult to predict whether benefit corporations will have unforeseen negative consequences.

---

52. *Id.*

53. Robert A. Katz & Antony Page, *The Role of Social Enterprise*, 35 Vt. L. Rev. 59, 86 (2010).

54. Interview with Timothy Smith, Walden Asset Management (Aug. 7, 2015).

Chapter 14

Changing the Rules of the Game

The welfare of the people shall be the supreme law.

—Cicero[1]

After the Supreme Court rules, the political branches typically react. And the Court's expansion of corporate rights while shrinking responsibilities has generated a slew of reactions from Congress, the Executive and the States. However, because many of the rulings about corporate power have been on constitutional grounds, the ability of other parts of the government to react is severely curtailed. Indeed, the Supreme Court has gone so far with some of the opinions which have been discussed in this book, that citizens through the nation have been inspired to call for amending the U.S. Constitution. The Supreme Court has painted itself into a corner with its corporatization of the First Amendment, but it still has the ability to step out of that corner and choose a different path. And the opening left on the bench by the death of Justice Scalia could be an opportunity for the newly reconstituted Supreme Court to reverse some of its recent controversial 5–4 decisions.

As will be discussed below, reforms of the role of corporations in our democracy could happen under a few broad categories: (1) strengthening democracy, (2) reforming corporations, (3) changing the jurisprudence, or (4) using the Constitution's Article V amendment process.

Enacting these reforms will take action at all levels of government. While the market may push traditional C corporations toward being better through

---

1. CICERO, DE LEGIBUS (book III, part III, sub. VIII) (The original Latin is "Salus populi suprema lex esto").

pressure from investors, customers, and competition from new corporate forms like the benefit corporation, government regulations nonetheless are still needed to provide clear rules for modern corporations. Even Adam Smith recognized that regulation was needed to maintain the common good. As Smith wrote, "those exertions of the natural liberty of a few individuals, which might endanger the security of the whole society, are, and ought to be, restrained by the laws of all governments[.]"[2]

A key aspect of why empowering corporations in politics is so problematic is that corporations are not as internally democratic as the democratic political systems they inhabit.[3] One of the most troubling aspects of corporate political activity is that corporations will get to set their own rules of engagement. Our historical experience has demonstrated that laws are necessary to incentivize corporations to act in ways that create fewer and less severe negative externalities.[4] Because "corporations have power now that would be an anathema to the framers sense of self-governance,"[5] there must be regulations to moderate the corporate excesses in the environment, human rights, and tax avoidance, just to name a few.[6]

In other countries, the reaction to vast inequality in economic or political power has inspired violent revolutions. And we are in a time of growing income inequality.[7] Analysts at Citigroup in 2005 declared that "the U.S. is a Plutonomy" or, in other words, that "economic growth is powered by and largely consumed by, the wealthy few."[8] But democracy offers a way of reaching con-

---

2. THE OXFORD HANDBOOK OF ADAM SMITH 388 (Christopher J. Berry & Maria Pia Paganelli & Craig Smith eds.) (2013).

3. Interview with Nell Minow, Vice Chair, ValueEdge Advisors (Aug. 19, 2015) ("[c]orporations should not be establishing public policy because they are terrible at it and they are not accountable the way the government is.").

4. ROBERT A.G. MONKS & NELL MINOW, CORPORATE GOVERNANCE 50 (Fifth ed. 2011) ("The only way to make sure that corporate management cannot merely externalize its costs on to the community is to have government, accountable through the political process, make the ultimate determination when the issue involves a trade-off of corporate profits against social goals."

5. Interview with Fordham Law Professor Zephyr Teachout (Aug. 10, 2015).

6. MONKS & MINOW, supra note 4, at 91 ("Corporations need to have some say in the government process affecting them, but not so much that they undercut the judgment of government, either.").

7. Interview with Elizabeth Kennedy, Counsel, Demos (Aug. 12, 2015). ("Even Pikety in CAPITAL says the answer to inequality is democracy. If that is true, then we really need a more robust democracy.").

8. Ajay Kapur, Niall Macleod & Narendra Singh, Equity Strategy Plutonomy, Buying Lux-

sensus without violence. Justice Sandra Day O'Connor touted the nonviolent attributes of democracy. As she said, "democracy forces society to come together and deliberate. Instead of attempting to change laws and government by means of violence and threats, democracy elevates the importance of debate.... For these reasons, democracy is one of the most powerful tools we have available to us to combat the spread of violence."[9] Democracy is the antidote to impersonal and unaccountable corporate power.[10]

However, one unresolved matter is how corporations and humans will coexist in a modern democracy. The worry is that corporate actors, especially the largest and the wealthiest, will have an insurmountable advantage over real citizens in getting their voices heard in the democratic process. Reporter William Greider argues, "[i]f corporations are citizens, the other citizens—the living, breathing kind—necessarily become less important to the process of self-government."[11]

Thomas Mann and Norman Ornstein lament in their book It's Even Worse Than It Looks, that because of the makeup of the FEC and the Supreme Court, "the path to restrictions on an out-of-control money system after Citizens United is steeply uphill."[12] And indeed these two challenges have made campaign finance reform very challenging. Judge Posner worries that reform is hampered because "[l]imited terms in office (with or without term limits) truncate politicians' time horizons; and interest-group politics, operating with vast sums of money on a complex decentralized system of government strongly biased to the status quo, has little trouble pushing needed reforms off beyond those horizons."[13] But difficult is not impossible. Consider the success of the

---

ury, Explaining Global Imbalances, CITIGROUP (Oct. 16, 2005), available at http://delong.typepad.com/plutonomy-1.pdf.

9. Justice Sandra Day O'Connor, Remarks at the Inaugural Sandra Day O'Connor Distinguished Lecture Series Lubbock, Texas November 16, 2007, 41 TEX. TECH L. REV. 1169, 1170 (2009).

10. ARTHUR M. SCHLESINGER JR., THE AGE OF JACKSON 335-36 (1953) ("the only alternative to tyranny or anarchy was the growth of the public conscience, and the natural expression of the public conscience was the democratic government.").

11. WILLIAM GREIDER, WHO WILL TELL THE PEOPLE? THE BETRAYAL OF AMERICAN DEMOCRACY 349 (1992); Kennedy interview supra note 7 ("[c]orporations are a legal fiction that exist to further profit, but now they are out of the box. And they are challenging the ability of people to create rules for society through the democratic process.").

12. THOMAS E. MANN & NORMAN ORNSTEIN, IT's EVEN WORSE THAN IT LOOKS: HOW THE AMERICAN CONSTITUTIONAL SYSTEM COLLIDED WITH THE NEW POLITICS OF EXTREMISM 152 (2012).

13. RICHARD A. POSNER, THE CRISIS OF CAPITALIST DEMOCRACY 387 (2010).

benefit corporation legislation. In five years, 30 states adopted the new model. Here's where policies may change.

A. Strengthening Democracy

While Congress has been stalled or deadlocked, states have led the way in implementing an array of policy changes in response to *Citizens United*. Leadership among the states in democratic innovation is an American tradition. As the Brennan Center's Fritz Schwarz related, "Justice Brandeis knew that the real wisdom of federalism was that a courageous state could be a laboratory for democracy and an example for other states."[14] Recall that *Citizens United* directly affected the laws of 24 states that had previously banned corporations or unions, or both, from making political expenditures.[15] By 2012, 20 states took the opportunity, as they altered their laws to comply with the Supreme Court decision, to amend their laws to improve disclosure of money in politics.[16] States have continued to change their laws to adapt to the modern political campaign, which includes corporate spending. Here are a few examples of the variety of approaches the states have tried in recent years.

In 2013, Utah amended its campaign finance law to require more robust reporting of money flowing through corporations that is used for political expenditures. A corporation is required to file a financial disclosure report with Utah once it spends $750 in a calendar year for political purposes (supporting or opposing candidates) or political issues (supporting or opposing ballot measures). One aspect of the Utah law that is unique is it respects donor intent. Donors to non-profit corporations can specify that donations are not to be used for political expenditures. But if a donor does not so specify, then the corporation has an obligation to tell the donor (1) their donation could be used for political spending and (2) that the name of the donor may be disclosed in the corporation's filing with Utah.[17] Another aspect of Utah report-

---

14. Interview with Frederick A.O. Schwarz, Chief Counsel Brennan Center for Justice at NYU School of Law (July 21, 2015).

15. National Conference of State Legislatures, *Life After* Citizens United 6-7 (2010), http://www.ncsl.org/research/elections-and-campaigns/citizens-united-and-the-states.aspx.

16. Robert M. Stern, *Sunlight State By State After* Citizens United, CORPORATE REFORM COALITION (June 2012), https://www.citizen.org/documents/sunlight-state-by-state-report.pdf.

17. Utah Code 20A-11-702; Utah H.B. 43 (2013), http://le.utah.gov/~2013/bills/static/hb0043.html.

ing is the corporation must report whether it is a state contractor or bidding for a state contract.[18]

In 2014, Delaware amended its laws to require more disclosure for corporate political donors and to close loopholes. The text of the Delaware law provides:

> Any person other than an individual or a political committee which makes a contribution to a political committee shall notify such political committee in writing of the full names and mailing addresses of:
> (1) All persons who, directly or otherwise, own a legal or equitable interest of 50% or greater ... in such corporation, partnership or other entity, or that no such persons exist; and
> (2) A responsible party, if such contribution would cause the aggregate amount of contributions by such entity during the election period to exceed $100.[19]

Delaware has identical contribution limits for humans and corporations.[20] But under this law, an individual cannot use contributions through multiple shell corporations to evade Delaware's individual contribution limits.[21] This law also lowered the reporting of underlying donors from $1,200 to $100 to provide more transparency. Legislative notes accompanying the legislation indicate that "responsible party" means "someone who shares or exercises direction or control over the entity's activities."[22]

In 2013, Maryland amended its campaign finance laws to strengthen disclosure, close corporate loopholes and improve anti-pay-to-play measures.[23] The law went into effect in 2015. To close what is known as the LLC loophole, Maryland aggregates corporate contributions from related entities. Under the Maryland law "[c]ontributions by two or more business entities shall be considered as being made by one contributor if: (i) one business entity is a wholly

---

18. *Corporate Disclosures*, Utah Elections, http://elections.utah.gov/campaign-finance/corporate-disclosures (last visited Nov. 10, 2015).

19. Del. Code § 8012(e), http://delcode.delaware.gov/title15/c080/sc02/index.shtml.

20. *Contribution Table Maximum Contribution Limit Per Election Period*, Delaware Elections, http://elections.delaware.gov/information/campaignfinance/pdfs/contributiontable.pdf.

21. Del. Code § 8012(e); Delaware Elections, *Campaign Finance Section Corporate Contribution Notice*, http://elections.delaware.gov/pubs/cf_corporate_contribution_notice.pdf.

22. Del. S.B. No. 186 (2014), http://www.legis.delaware.gov/LIS/lis147.nsf/vwLegislation/SB+186/$file/legis.html?open.

23. Md. H.B. 1499 (2013), http://mgaleg.maryland.gov/2013RS/chapters_noln/Ch_419_hb1499E.pdf.

owned subsidiary of another; or (ii) the business entities are owned or controlled by at least 80% of the same individuals or business entities."[24] If an individual owns 100% of a dozen corporations, all 12 businesses will be subject to a single corporate contribution limit. Such a person does not get to give 12 times through each corporation.

Maryland also directly addresses the problem of dark money flowing through 501(c)(4) social welfare organizations and 501(c)(6) trade associations by making them register with the state within 48 hours and disclose the five largest donors from the past year if the nonprofit spends more than $6,000 in Maryland's elections. The same holds true for 527 political organizations.[25] Additionally, independent spenders over a $10,000 threshold must file reports with the state within 48 hours listing any donors who gave $6,000 or more.[26] The new law requires persons doing business with Maryland with contracts of $200,000 or more, and persons employing lobbyists over a $500 threshold, to file a Disclosure of Contributions.[27] Finally, Maryland is the first state to require corporations to report their political spending directly to shareholders.[28]

Montana changed its law in 2015 to require disclosure of who is funding electioneering communications in addition to independent expenditures. In Montana, electioneering communications are

> a paid communication that is publicly distributed by radio, television, cable, satellite, internet website, newspaper, periodical, billboard, mail, or any other distribution of printed materials, that is made within 60 days of the initiation of voting in an election, that does not support or oppose a candidate or ballot issue, that can be received by more than 100 recipients in the district voting on the candidate or ballot issue, and that: (i) refers to one or more clearly identified candidates in that election; (ii) depicts the name, image, likeness, or voice of one or more clearly identified candidates in that election; or (iii) refers to a political party, ballot issue, or other question submitted to the voters in that election.[29]

---

24. *Id.*

25. *Id.*

26. *Id.*

27. Maryland Elections, *Disclosure of Contributions* (Jan. 16, 2015), http://www.elections.state.md.us/campaign_finance/disclosure_of_contributions.html.

28. Md. H.B. 1499.

29. Mt. S.B. 289 (2015), http://leg.mt.gov/bills/2015/sesslaws/ch0259.pdf.

Montana's definition is broader than the definition of electioneering communications at the federal level (as discussed in more detail in Chapter 5), as Montana covers non-broadcast media, ballot issues, and applies an additional 30 days before primaries.[30]

In 2014, Pennsylvania passed a new law that restricts the so-called "reverse revolving door."[31] Under the Pennsylvanian law "[n]o individual who has been employed by an offeror within the preceding two years may participate in the evaluation of proposals."[32] What this means in plain English is that if an individual who was in the private sector moves into a government position, then that individual cannot help his old private sector firm gain a contract with Pennsylvania for two years.

The most comprehensive change happened in Arkansas in 2014. The state amended its constitution by ballot measure to improve campaign finance,[33] banning contributions to candidates from corporations and unions.[34] Under the new Arkansas Constitution, "[l]obbyists are prohibited from giving gifts to lawmakers under a new 'no cup of coffee rule'—so named because there is no allowance for gifts of nominal value, so even a cup of coffee would be a prohibited gift."[35] Unlike Pennsylvania, which addressed the reverse revolving door, Arkansas addressed the revolving door of government workers going to work for the private sector. Under the Arkansas law, members of the General Assembly cannot lobby the government for two years after leaving the government.[36]

Providing candidates an alternative to privately financed elections in the form of public financing is another option to improve democratic outcomes.[37] Nicole

30. Ciara Torres-Spelliscy, *Transparent Elections after* Citizens United (Brennan Ctr. 2011).

31. Pa H.B. 201 (2014), http://www.legis.state.pa.us/cfdocs/billInfo/bill_history.cfm?syear=2013&sind=0&body=H&type=B&bn=201.

32. *Id.*

33. Ar. H.J.R. 1009 (2014), http://www.arkleg.state.ar.us/assembly/2013/2013R/Bills/HJR1009.pdf.

34. *Id.*

35. Andrew Garrahan, *New Arkansas Campaign Finance, Lobbying, and Ethics Laws Take Immediate Effect*, INSIDE POL. L. (Nov. 7, 2014), http://www.insidepoliticallaw.com/2014/11/07/new-arkansas-campaign-finance-lobbying-and-ethics-laws-take-immediate-effect-2/.

36. Ar. H.J.R. 1009 (2014), http://www.arkleg.state.ar.us/assembly/2013/2013R/Bills/HJR1009.pdf.

37. Zephyr Teachout, *The Supreme Court's* McCutcheon v. FEC *ruling leaves a campaign finance void*, WASH. POST ("Our candidates don't have to be beggars at the feet of oligarchs.... Public-funding systems transform candidates from beggars into statesmen.").

Gordon, who oversaw New York City's well-regarded public financing system, stated, "[p]ublic funding in elections, in particular through a matching funds system for small contributions by individuals, is the single most important change that can be implemented."[38] New York City has provided public financing to candidates for city office for more than two decades. Los Angeles, San Francisco, Tallahassee, Florida, and Montgomery County, Maryland, among many other municipalities, also provide public financing. And in 2015, Seattle's voters approved a ballot measure to implement public financing there, too.[39]

At the state level, Arizona, Maine, and Connecticut have robust public finance systems that allow candidates to run for office using public funds after they demonstrate a required threshold of public support from their constituents. In 2015, Maine voters voted to strengthen the public financing system, improve disclosure and enhance campaign finance violation penalties.[40]

States are not always in a race to the bottom. They can be in a race to the top. In addition to fixing the financing of elections, another approach to improve democracy is making registering to vote easier. Staying registered to vote in most states is surprisingly difficult given modern mobility. Moving state to state, or town to town, can often result in inadvertent disenfranchisement because the onus is on the voter to register and re-register. Whether a voter can vote in state elections after moving depends on state law. For most states, voter registration closes approximately 30 days before an election. Some states provide citizens with the ability to register the day of the election. Rules in other states range between extremes. North Dakota doesn't require voters to register at all. Louisianans have to re-register if they move between parishes.[41]

California and Oregon have led the way in improving voter registration by adopting automatic voter registration.[42] Under these laws, voters will be automatically registered and individuals must actively opt out if they wish to be

---

38. Interview with Nicole Gordon, Former Executive Director, New York City Campaign Finance Board (Aug. 10, 2015).

39. Justin Miller, *The New Public Option*, Am. Prospect (Fall 2015), http://prospect.org/article/can-campaign-finance-be-reformed-bottom.

40. Paul Blumenthal, *Maine, Seattle Pave Next Path for Campaign Finance Reform*, Huff. Post (Nov. 4, 2015), http://www.huffingtonpost.com/entry/campaign-finance-reform_563a14fee4b0b24aee482a20.

41. Ciara Torres-Spelliscy, *The Jobless Could Swing the Election—If They're Actually Registered to Vote*, The Atlantic (Sept. 13, 2012), http://www.theatlantic.com/politics/archive/2012/09/the-jobless-could-swing-the-election-if-theyre-actually-registered-to-vote/262239/.

42. For more details on the differences between California and Oregon's approaches *see* Melanie Mason, *Q&A Here's How California's New Voter Registration Law Will Work*, L.A.

unregistered. This is unique because the default in most states is that a citizen is not registered to vote and must opt in. In California, the automatic registration is linked to getting a driver's licenses. At the California DMV, the driver will be asked if they do not want to be registered to vote.[43] California Secretary of State Alex Padilla views the law as a way to boost civic participation. He said, "'[w]e want to serve as a contrast to what we see happening in other states, where they are making it more difficult to register or actually cast a ballot. I think that's flat out un-American, and we can show a different, better way with the automatic registration system.'"[44] The California automatic registration law is particularly expected to help minority voters because Latino and Asian American citizens are currently registered to vote at low rates in California.[45] The Oregon law works in a similar way. Those age 18 and older with an Oregon driver's license are automatically registered to vote.[46] In Oregon, the state conducts elections by mail and all automatically registered voters will be sent ballots.

At the federal level, things can be more complicated. One of the problems that has been highlighted again and again in this book are the myriad dilemmas caused by privately financed elections; but as Trevor Potter, President of the Campaign Legal Center, indicated, "[t]here is a long list of desirable reforms."[47] In Congress, democracy reforms were introduced on the fifth anniversary of *Citizens United*, including The Government by the People Act, which would provide for public financing of elections for congressional races. Here's how it would work:

> First, it would amplify the voices of ordinary citizens by matching small contributions with public funds, up to a 9:1 ratio, for candi-

---

Times (Oct. 16, 2015), http://www.latimes.com/politics/la-me-pol-ca-motor-voter-law-20151016-html-htmlstory.html.

43. *Id.*

44. Ian Lovett, *California Law Will Automatically Register Drivers to Vote*, N.Y. Times (Oct. 10, 2015), http://www.nytimes.com/2015/10/11/us/california-law-will-automatically-register-drivers-to-vote.html?_r=1.

45. Khorri Atkinson, *California Set to Automatically Register Millions of Voters*, MSNBC.com (Oct. 12, 2015), http://www.msnbc.com/msnbc/california-set-automatically-register-millions-voters.

46. Russell Berman, *Should Voter Registration Be Automatic?*, The Atlantic (Mar. 20, 2015), http://www.theatlantic.com/politics/archive/2015/03/should-voter-registration-be-automatic/388258/ ("any eligible Oregonian with a driver's license will be automatically registered to vote and will receive a ballot by mail weeks before Election Day.").

47. Interview with Trevor Potter, President Campaign Legal Ctr. (July 27, 2015).

dates who forgo big contributions. Second, it would empower more Americans to participate in campaigns by providing a refundable tax credit for small contributions.[48]

Other reforms introduced include bills to improve disclosure in elections, and a bill to improve coordination rules for Super PACs and nonprofits.[49] However, present partisan deadlocks make congressional campaign finance reforms unlikely to pass in the near term.

B. Corporate and Securities Law Reforms

Besides lessening the reliance of politicians on private money and empowering voters, another approach to reform is improving corporate governance through corporate and securities laws to increase disclosure, provide shareholder consent, and require better internal controls within the corporate structure.

For public companies, an improvement in disclosure could be achieved through congressional legislation. Disclosure of who is paying for political ads helps the voter to place the ad in context. As Trevor Potter explained, "[i]f an ad is about smoking, it matters whether that ad is from the tobacco companies or the American Lung Association."[50]

In addition to disclosure, shareholders need a way to meaningfully consent to corporate political spending. Such a system already exists in the U.K. Ever since 2000, the U.K. has required companies that spend in politics either in the U.K., and now in the E.U. as well, to get shareholder consent to a corporate political budget before corporate resources are spent in politics.[51]

The appetite for shareholder consent may be growing. In 2014, an industry group called the CFA Institute did a survey of 1,500 financial analysts to ask them about corporate political spending. The survey found that "62% of

---

48. Press Release, *U.S. PIRG Applauds Reintroduction of Reform Legislation on the Fifth Anniversary of* Citizens United, U.S. PIRG (Jan. 21, 2015), http://www.uspirg.org/news/usp/us-pirg-applauds-reintroduction-reform-legislation-fifth-anniversary-citizens-united.

49. Paul Blumenthal, *Democrats Link Middle Class Woes to Need for Campaign Finance Reform*, HUFF. POST (Jan. 21, 2015), http://www.huffingtonpost.com/2015/01/21/democrats-campaign-finance-reform_n_6517648.html?1421872778.

50. Potter interview *supra* note 47.

51. Ciara Torres-Spelliscy & Kathy Fogel, *Shareholder-Authorized Corporate Political Spending in the United Kingdom*, 46 U. SAN FRAN. L. REV. 479 (Spring 2012).

respondents either agree or strongly agree that shareholders should have a say in who gets [political] contributions."[52] Providing shareholders with a consent mechanism for corporate political expenditures would require a change of law either at the state or federal level. Using its Commerce Clause Power, Congress could pass a law that required shareholder approval for publicly traded companies. One tactic is to try to get Congress to adopt the U.K. approach to corporate political spending, which requires prior authorization via shareholder vote.[53] Congressional legislation to provide shareholder approval of corporate political spending has been introduced in Congress several sessions in a row,[54] but so far these bills have not progressed in the legislative process.[55] This is a troubling development. As Lisa Graves said, "[y]ou would think it would be uncontroversial to require, as has been proposed federally, corporations to get shareholder consent before the company engages in political spending that alienates consumers and thus depresses revenues."[56]

Using their Tenth Amendment power, states could do the same for firms that are incorporated in their state. Bills to provide shareholder approval of corporate political budgets have been introduced in several states, including

52. Political Contribution Disclosure Survey Results, CFA INST. 1, 3 (2014), http://www.cfainstitute.org/Survey/political_contribution_survey_final.pdf.

53. Potter interview *supra* note 47 ("The British have a system that requires shareholder approval of corporate political spending. That would make sense because under our tax laws this is not a business expense that can be deducted.").

54. Jennifer S. Taub, *Money Managers in the Middle: Seeing and Sanctioning Political Spending After* Citizens United, 15 N.Y.U. J. LEGIS. & PUB. POL'Y 443, 447 (2012) ("There are efforts to require advance consent of corporate political spending. On the Congressional front, a pending bill called the Shareholder Protection Act (SPA), which was introduced in 2010 and again in 2011, would require corporations to both disclose certain direct and indirect political expenditures and obtain advance consent by a majority of the outstanding shares before dedicating funds toward those political activities.").

55. Bill Summary & Status — 111th Congress (2009–2010) — H.R.4790, THOMAS, http://thomas.loc.gov/cgi-bin/bdquery/z?d111:HR04790:@@@R (showing the Shareholder Protection Act of 2010, H.R. 4790, was reported out of the Committee on Financial Services in House Report 111-620, but no floor vote was taken); Michael Megaris, *The SEC and Mandatory Disclosure of Corporate Spending by Publicly Traded Companies*, 22-SUM KAN. J.L. & PUB. POL'Y 432, 440 (2013) ("The stated purpose of the Shareholder Protection Act (SPA) was to 'amend the Securities Exchange Act of 1934 to require shareholder authorization before a public company may make certain political expenditures.' The bill, as evidenced by the timing of its introduction, was drafted in direct response to the Supreme Court decision in *Citizens United*. The bill, unfortunately, never made it out of committee reviews.").

56. Interview with Lisa Graves, Executive Director Center for Media & Democracy (July 17, 2015).

Maine, New York, California, Wisconsin, Maryland, and Pennsylvania, but so far none has become law.[57] One bill in Connecticut to empower shareholders passed the legislature, but was vetoed by the governor.[58] Maryland, among other states, considered shareholder consent legislation in 2015.[59] Professor Jamie Raskin, who is a member of the Maryland Legislature, introduced a bill to give shareholders the right to consent to corporate political spending. He wrote about why he took this legislative approach of shareholder consent in the *Washington Post:* "[w]hat unites shareholders invested in McDonald's or General Motors ... is not our political beliefs but our financial investments. If we share any political belief at all, it is probably this one: No corporation speaks for us politically, and no corporation should purport to do so and spend our money on political candidates without our knowledge and our consent.... My legislation seeks to secure that right [of consent] for the shareholders of Maryland corporations."[60] States can also change their laws to implement more internal controls within the corporate structure. In 2010, Iowa repealed its corporate independent expenditure ban and passed a law requiring corporations to get the board of directors to approve any independent expenditures.[61]

---

57. *See* S.B. 570, 2010 Leg., 427th Sess. (Md. 2010); S.B. 101, 2011 Leg., 234th Sess. (N.Y. 2011); A.B. 919, 2009 Leg. (Cal. 2009); Pa. H.B. 1002, 2011 Leg. (Pa. 2011); H.P. 1120, 2011 Leg., 125th Sess. (Me. 2011); Peter Hardin, *WI Senate OKs Shareholder Consent Bill*, GAVEL GRAB, (Apr. 14, 2010), http://www.gavelgrab.org/?p=9793.

58. Mark Pazniokas, *Common Cause Slams Malloy Veto of Campaign Finance Bill*, CT MIRROR, http://ctmirror.org/2012/06/15/common-cause-slams-malloy-veto-campaign-finance-bill/ (June 15, 2012) (discussing the governor's veto of H.B. 5556 in 2012).

59. S.B. 153, 2015 Leg., 432nd Sess, (Md. 2015); Jamie B. Raskin, *A Shareholder Solution to 'Citizens United'*, WASH. POST, Oct. 3, 2014, *available at* http://www. washingtonpost.com/opinions/a-shareholder-solution-to-citizens-united/2014/10/03/5e07c3ee-48be-11e4-b72e-d60a9229cc10_story.html; *see also* Liz Essley Whyte, *States consider requiring shareholder approval for political gifts*, CTR. FOR PUB. INTEGRITY, (Feb. 17, 2015), http://www.publicintegrity.org/2015/02/17/16757/states-consider-requiring-shareholder-approval-political-gifts ("State legislators in Maine, Maryland, New York and New Jersey have introduced bills that demand that a majority of shareholders approve corporate gifts to political committees or candidates.").

60. Jamie B. Raskin, *A Shareholder Solution to* Citizens United, WASH. POST (Oct. 3, 2014), https://www.washingtonpost.com/opinions/a-shareholder-solution-to-citizens-united/2014/10/03/5e07c3ee-48be-11e4-b72e-d60a9229cc10_story.html.

61. IA Stat. §68A.404(2); Iowa Right to Life Comm., Inc. v. Tooker, 717 F.3d 576, 605 (8th Cir. 2013), *cert. denied* No. 13-407 (Apr. 7 2014) (Eighth Circuit holding "because [Iowa Right to Life Committee, Inc.] fails to show that the board-authorization requirement treats corporations differently from other entities, Iowa Code subsections 68A.404(2)(a) and (b) are constitutional under the Equal Protection Clause....").

With this law, Iowa joined Louisiana and Missouri, which require board approval of corporate political expenditures.[62]

Some congressional fixes to the other issues raised in this book could be comparatively easy to fix, but for the corporate lobbying and campaign funding standing in their way. So these fixes are politically difficult, but not conceptually complex. For example, closing the "Halliburton loophole" would require Congress to regulate fracking chemicals under already existing environmental protection laws like the Clean Water Act. To address the jurisdictional approaches in *Kiobel* and *Daimler*, Congress could clarify under what circumstances it would be appropriate for U.S. Courts to hear "foreign cubed" cases. Congress could also clarify that corporations can be sued under the Alien Tort Statute, and other laws that provide human rights protections. The holding in *Hobby Lobby* could be undone if Congress specified explicitly that corporations are not covered by Religious Freedom Restoration Act of 1993 (RFRA).

Congressional deadlock, however, does not serve as an insurmountable barrier to reform at the federal level. In terms of corporate political spending and the dark money problem, multiple federal agencies have jurisdiction and therefore could implement significant reforms. Again corporate money goes dark by being funneled through opaque nonprofits before the money is spent in elections. The Federal Election Commission (FEC) has jurisdiction over political ads in federal elections. When the nonprofit reports to the FEC, under the current rules, only the donors of earmarked funds are reportable. Earmarked means the donor said what candidate or ad campaign should be supported with the donor's money. This allows for Alice in Wonderland FEC filings that claim millions have been spent in a federal election, but no one in particular was the source of the funds. The FEC should adopt new rules that require reporting of all funds spent in federal elections, not just the earmarked ones.

The Federal Communications Commission (FCC) has jurisdiction if the dark money is used to buy broadcast ads on television or radio. The Internal Revenue Service (IRS) has jurisdiction over the nonprofit intermediaries. And the SEC has jurisdiction over publicly traded corporations that can be the original source of the dark money. All of these regulators could take action to address the problem of dark money. In addition, there is the perennial problem of pay-to-play corruption where government contractors and lobbyists try to get private ben-

62. See La. Rev. Stat. Ann. § 18:1505.2(F) (also allowing officers of the corporation to make such contributions if empowered to do so by the board of directors); Mo. Ann. Stat. § 130.029.

efits from the government through campaign contributions, gifts, and bribes. So far, only two agencies have taken any action to help either of these problems.

In 2010, the SEC promulgated a new anti-pay-to-play rule that applies to the investment advisers to public pension funds.[63] SEC Rule 206(4)-5 prevents investment advisers from exchanging large contributions for the ability to manage a public pension fund's investments. Under Rule 206(4)-5, the investor advisers can choose to be big fundraisers for municipal and state candidates or they can advise public pension funds, but they cannot do both simultaneously.[64] The estimated size of the public pension fund market is roughly $4.6 trillion.[65] According to the Census Bureau, "[i]n 2010, the largest share of all state government cash and security holdings was in public-employee retirement trust funds …"[66] Fees paid by public pension funds generate lucrative business for investment advisers.[67]

Explaining why a rule was needed to curb pay-to-play for public pensions, Andrew J. Donohue, Director of the SEC's Division of Investment Management, explained, "[p]ay-to-play serves the interests of advisers to public pension plans rather than the interests of the millions of pension plan beneficiaries who rely on their advice. The rule we are proposing today would help ensure that advisory contracts are awarded on professional competence, not political influence."[68] At the time that the Commission's new anti-pay-to-play Rule 206(4)-5 was announced in 2010, then-SEC Chair Mary Schapiro made the following pointed statement articulating the justification for the rule: "An un-

---

63. Ciara Torres-Spelliscy, *Safeguarding Markets from Pernicious Pay to Play: A Model Explaining Why the SEC Regulates Money in Politics*, 12(2) CONN. PUB. INT. L. J. 361 (2012–2013).

64. Political Contributions by Certain Investment Advisors, 17 Fed. Reg. 41,018 (July 14, 2010) (codified at 17 C.F.R. §275.206(4)-5).

65. Towers Watson, *Global Pension Asset Study 2012* (Jan. 2012), http://www.towerswatson.com/assets/pdf/6267/Global-Pensions-Asset-Study-2012.pdf (total pensions in the U.S. have $16.1 trillion in assets and 29% of those U.S. pensions are public for a total of $4.6 trillion in U.S. public pensions).

66. Jeffrey L. Barnett & Phillip M. Vidal, *State and Local Government Finances Summary: 2010*, at 4 (Sept. 2012), http://www2.census.gov/govs/estimate/summary_report.pdf.

67. Robert Reed & Brett Chase, *Sticker Shock: Lofty Fees, Low Returns*, http://www.bettergov.org/sticker_shock_lofty_fees_low_returns/ (Apr. 18, 2012) (reporting that a $30 billion pension fund paid $1.3 billion in investment advisor fees); Mike Alberti, *Private Consultants Rake in Public Pension Fund Fees*, http://www.remappingdebate.org/map-data-tool/private-consultants-rake-public-pension-fund-fees (Apr. 4, 2012) (reporting that, in fiscal year 2011, California Public Employees' Retirement System paid financial advisers $48.7 million, 1/3 the amount it paid its own employees).

68. Curtis C. Verschoor, *We Need to Stop Pay-to-Play Corruption*, STRATEGIC FIN. at 16 (Sept. 2009), http://www.imanet.org/PDFs/Public/SF/2009_09/09_09_ethics.pdf.

spoken, but entrenched and well-understood practice, pay to play can also favor large advisers over smaller competitors, reward political connections rather than management skill, and—as a number of recent enforcement cases have shown—pave the way to outright fraud and corruption.... Pay to play practices are corrupt and corrupting."[69]

The SEC could address the issue of dark money through a new rule. Support for the SEC's improving disclosure of corporate political activity is also high among the general public. According to a 2015 poll, a super majority (88%), including both Republicans and Democrats, wants the SEC to have a transparency rule for corporate political spending.[70] Many members of boards of directors also want an SEC rule. According to the BDO Board Survey conducted in September 2015, "[a]lthough some companies voluntarily disclose corporate political spending voluntarily, a majority (53%) of public company board members believe that the SEC needs to develop mandatory disclosure rules for corporate political contributions."[71]

In 2011, 10 corporate law professors filed a petition with the SEC asking for the Commission to promulgate a new rule requiring transparency for corporate political spending by publicly traded companies. Outgoing SEC Chair Schapiro placed the rule making on the regulatory agenda. By December 2013, the petition had more than 640,000 signatures. But in late 2013, the SEC, under Chair Mary Jo White, removed the rule from its rule making agenda.[72] Support for the rule has continued to grow as an additional 600,000 public comments rolled into the SEC. By the end of 2015, the petition has more than 1.2 million signatories, including institutional investors, state treasurers and members of Congress.[73] This is the greatest number of public comments any SEC

69. Mary L. Schapiro, *Speech by SEC Chairman: Opening Statement at the SEC Open Meeting* (June 30, 2010), http://www.sec.gov/news/speech/2010/spch063010mls.htm.

70. *New Mayday.Us Poll: Voters of Every Political Stripe Agree on the Need for Fundamental Reform to the Campaign Finance System*, MAY DAY PAC (Sept. 25, 2015), http://blog.mayday.us/post/129846704150/new-maydayus-poll-voters-of-every-political (Polling was conducted by Public Policy Polling).

71. *2015 Board Survey*, BDO (Oct. 2015), https://www.bdo.com/insights/assurance/client-advisories/2015-board-survey#sthash.TiOcNaKP.dpuf.

72. Gretchen Goldman & Christina Carlson, *Tricks of the Trade: How Companies Anonymously Influence Climate Policy Through Their Business and Trade Associations*, CTR. FOR SCIENCE & DEMOCRACY AT THE UNION OF CONCERNED SCIENTISTS 9 (Jan. 2014), http://www.ucsusa.org/sites/default/files/legacy/assets/documents/center-for-science-and-democracy/tricks-of-the-trade.pdf.

73. Jennifer Taub, *Still Too Big To Fail: Opportunities for Regulatory Action Seven Years after the Bear Stearns Rescue*, CORPORATE REFORM COALITION 23 (May 7, 2015),

petition has ever received in the history of the Commission. But still the SEC has failed to act.[74]

The SEC can be particularly slow-moving in responding to outside pressure to act. For example, in 2002 while "[t]he EU is requiring sustainability reporting,"[75] such reporting has lagged behind in the United States. In response, the Rose Foundation for Communities and the Environment, along with other institutional investors, including brokerage firms representing combined assets of more than $13 billion, and 28 charitable foundations representing well over $3 billion in combined assets, asked the SEC for a new rule.[76] However, the SEC did not promulgate a new environmental reporting rule. Rather, eight years later, the SEC issued guidance on how to interpret pre-existing rules for reporting environmental liabilities.[77]

The IRS has jurisdiction over the tax exempt 501(c)(4)s and 501(c)(6)s that are being used to funnel dark money in politics. As FEC Chair Ann Ravel warned, "[m]ore and more money is undisclosed even beyond the dark money we know about because it's going through Super PACs. The really dark money is going through other [nonprofit] entities."[78] Perhaps "dark money" doesn't quite capture this phenomenon; call it blackhole money because the public doesn't even know that it is being spent because it never shows up on any public report. This could be remedied by up-to-date rules at the IRS over the appropriate use of nonprofits for political spending. In 2014, the IRS started a rule-making that could have clarified exactly what counts for tax purposes as "candidate-related political activity."[79] After being roundly criticized in more than 100,000 public comments, the IRS decided to scrap the rule and go back to the drawing board. The IRS showed no sign that they will fix the rules for nonprofits that facilitate dark money, or blackhole money, in time for the 2016 election.

---

http://www.citizen.org/documents/still-too-big-to-fail-crc-report.pdf.

74. Lisa Gilbert, *Next SEC Commissioners Should Support Political Spending Disclosure Rule*, Huff. Post (Oct. 21, 2015), http://www.huffingtonpost.com/lisa-gilbert/next-sec-commissioners-sh_b_8343250.html.

75. Interview with Timothy Smith, Walden Asset Management (Aug. 7, 2015).

76. Rose Foundation for Communities and the Environment, *Request for Rulemaking for Clarification of Material Disclosures With Respect to Financially Significant Environmental Liabilities and Compliance with Existing Material Financial Disclosures*, Revised Petition SEC File No. 4-463 (Sept. 20, 2002), https://www.sec.gov/rules/petitions/petn4-463.htm.

77. SEC, *Commission Guidance Regarding Disclosure Related to Climate Change* (Feb. 8, 2010), https://www.sec.gov/rules/interp/2010/33-9106.pdf.

78. Interview with Ann Ravel, Chair, Federal Election Commission (Nov. 3, 2015).

79. IRS REG-134417-13 (2014).

While reform of the FEC is beyond the scope of this book, suffice it to say that the federal government needs a strong and functioning agency to enforce its campaign finance laws and the current FEC is failing in that charge. The issue is structural and ideological. The FEC is made up of three Democratic appointees and three Republican appointees, but the Commission need four votes to act on anything. The two factions can rarely agree, as the Republican Commissioners nearly always vote against enforcement of the laws.[80] Present FEC Chair Ann Ravel stated, "[a]t the moment, the really serious problem is the deadlock because it is incapacitating the agency completely on every possible issue you can imagine—at a level that is actually shocking."[81] The result of the 3-3 ties is that enforcement actions are dropped even after individuals have admitted to breaking the rules, and ties also mean that individuals who have asked for advisory opinions get no guidance from the agency on the meaning of the law.[82] A 3-3 tie at the FEC is how money from a foreign pornographer got into an election in Los Angeles without any federal legal consequences.

Another structural problem at the FEC is very high level regulatory capture. Congress controls the FEC's budget, but the FEC is supposed to regulate members of Congress running for reelection. Moreover, the Senate approves who is seated as Commissioners. Former FEC Chair Trevor Potter asserted "[w]e've seen [regulatory capture] at the FEC. There has been more than 30 years of tension over the controversial relationship between the regulated entities and the appointment of the Commissioners. The members of Congress are all regulated entities and they belong to political parties which are regulated entities and it's those two groups that select FEC Commissioners."[83]

Further hampering the functionality of the FEC is that the agency does not have random audit power over the candidates that file campaign finance reports. The FEC lost its random audit power roughly four years into its existence because Congress did not like being audited.[84] This basically put the

---

80. Potter interview *supra* note 47 ("When Senator McConnell lost his Supreme Court case challenging McCain-Feingold, his fallback position was to appoint FEC Commissioners who would not enforce the law, which is essentially where we are now.").

81. Ravel interview *supra* note 78.

82. Fred Wertheimer & Don Simon, *The FEC: The Failure to Enforce Commission*, AMERICAN CONSTITUTION SOCIETY (Jan. 2013), https://www.acslaw.org/sites/default/files/Wertheimer_and_Simon_-_The_Failure_to_Enforce_Commission.pdf ("If the FEC, for example, votes 3 to 3 on the question of whether to pursue an enforcement matter, the investigation is dropped. If the FEC votes 3 to 3 on issuing an advisory opinion, the individual or group requesting the opinion gets no advice.").

83. Potter interview *supra* note 47.

84. Kenneth A. Gross, *The Enforcement of Campaign Finance Rules: A System in Search*

Congress on the honor system not to break the campaign finance laws.[85] This enforcement system, as this book has demonstrated, is replete with failures. Adding a seventh Commissioner would go a long way toward improving the functionality of the agency, but other fixes would also be needed to make it effective like restoring its audit power and appointing Commissioners who believe in enforcing the law.

Given the overlapping jurisdiction over dark money, which is shared by the FEC, SEC, IRS and FCC, in five years there has been an astonishing lack of regulatory action to address the issue. In addition to the SEC's new anti-pay-to-play rule, one of the only other positive regulatory changes from the Executive Branch was a relatively minor one. The FCC decided to place what is known as the "political file" online for the first time. This allows the public to see political ad buys at broadcasters across the country in one place on the web. Previously, members of the public would have to drive station to station to get this information, which was stored in paper records.[86]

C. Changes in the Jurisprudence

1. Judicial Objections to *Citizens United*

All of the reforms suggested in this chapter so far in the states, in Congress, and in the Executive Branch, are limited in scope because of *Citizens United* and other campaign finance decisions from the Supreme Court. Another approach to reform is to convince the Court that it took a mistaken path when it deregulated many aspects of campaign finance reform.

---

of Reform, 9 YALE L. & POL'Y REV. 279, 300 n.50 (1991) ("In approving the FEC's Fiscal Year 1979 budget request, the House Administration Committee conditioned the approval with a proviso that none of the money could be used to finance random audits. Although the full House upheld the Committee position on a voice vote, it dropped the anti-audit provision in conference with the Senate. After this episode, the FEC dropped the random audit program in a partyline vote on a Republican proposal to continue random audits. Campaign Practices Reports, Apr. 17, 1978, at 1.").

85. *No Bark, No Bite, No Point: The Case for Closing the Federal Election Commission and Establishing a New System for Enforcing the Nation's Campaign Finance Laws*, PROJECT FEC 72-73 (2002), http://www.democracy21.org/uploads/%7BB4BE5C24-65EA-4910-974C-759644EC0901%7D.pdf. ("As Brooks Jackson noted in 1990, 'In effect, Congress put itself on the honor system. The FEC may now audit candidates only when gross discrepancies show up on the face of their reports, but even that requires a four-vote majority decision by the commissioners. In practice, candidates are now audited hardly at all.' ").

86. Interview with Craig Aaron, President, Free Press (July 27, 2015).

One of the ways to reverse *Citizens United* is for the Supreme Court to reverse itself in a future case. The Justices don't have to look far for explanations of what is wrong with the decision. They can turn to their fellow jurists. While disagreement with *Citizens United* has come from the President to average Americans, some of the most trenchant critiques of *Citizens United* have come from sitting and retired judges, who strongly disagree with the conclusions of law reached by the five-person majority on the U.S. Supreme Court.

Judge Richard Posner of the Seventh Circuit Court of Appeals once characterized *Citizens United* as "naïve."[87] Judge Posner, who teaches at the University of Chicago Law School, also accused the Roberts Court of ruining the political system stating: "[o]ur political system is pervasively corrupt due to our Supreme Court taking away campaign-contribution restrictions on the basis of the First Amendment."[88] And a group of retired federal and state judges argued similarly about *Citizens United* that,

> [o]ne need not be a legal scholar to know that the election process should not be equated to money, and money to speech. Not when wealthy individuals and corporations can secretly make contributions of billions of dollars to defeat or elect a candidate, through deceptively named super PACs. This type of clandestine influence peddling destroys both the appearance and the realty of the fair election. The source of funding has a direct bearing on the credibility of the message. Of course, we must adhere to the present edict, but we urge its renunciation.[89]

---

87. Richard Posner, *Unlimited Campaign Spending—A Good Thing?*, BECKNER-POSNER BLOG (Apr. 8, 2012), http://www.becker-posner-blog.com/2012/04/unlimited-campaign-spendinga-good-thing-posner.html ("But the Court, rather naively as it seems to most observers, reasoned in *the Citizens United* case that the risk of corruption would be slight if the donor was not contributing to a candidate or a political party, but merely expressing his political preferences through an independent organization such as a super PAC—an organization neither controlled by nor even coordinating with a candidate or political party.").

88. James Warren, *Richard Posner Bashes Supreme Court's* Citizens United *Ruling*, THE DAILY BEAST (July 14, 2012), http://www.thedailybeast.com/articles/2012/07/14/richard-posner-bashes-supreme-court-s-citizens-united-ruling.html (quoting Judge Posner).

89. Robert K. Young, *Full Disclosure of Super PAC Donations Needed*, THE MORNING CALL (Dec. 4, 2012), http://articles.mcall.com/2012-12-04/opinion/mc-citizens-united-superpacs-judge-young-yv-1205-20121204_1_super-pac-donations-full-disclosure-fair-election (signatories included Judges Maxwell. E. Davison and Thomas A. Wallitsch (Lehigh County); Elizabeth Ehrlich, Forrest Schaeffer Jr., Calvin E. Smith and Albert A. Stallone (Berks County); Robert Freedberg (Northampton County); John P. Lavelle (Carbon County); Leonard Sokolove (Bucks County); Edward N. Cahn (U.S. District Court for the Eastern Pennsylvania)).

The Chief Justice of the Delaware Supreme Court Leo Strine has also expressed withering rebukes of *Citizens United,* including two entire law reviews on the matter.[90] In shorter pieces he has said, "[I] see no basis to contend that business corporations were thought to possess the same speech rights as human beings and that society could not restrict their ability to participate in the political process[.]"[91]

But one of the most damning critiques of *Citizens United* came from a Justice on the Montana Supreme Court in 2011. In dissent in a case called *Western Tradition Partnership,* Justice James Nelson thoroughly rebuked the Supreme Court's decision. Montana was one of the 24 states whose laws were affected by *Citizens United.* Montana was the lone holdout who took the time and energy to defend its corporate ban in court. Then-Attorney General (now Governor) Bullock argued in court that Montana's ban on corporate spending was justified given the state's unique history, including the negative impact of the so-called Copper Kings, especially the notorious W.A. Clark (who was discussed in Chapter 3).

After Clark caused a national embarrassment by buying a U.S. Senate seat, Montana adopted the Corrupt Practices Act of 1912, which provided that "[a] corporation may not make a contribution or an expenditure in connection with a candidate or a political committee that supports or opposes a candidate or a political party."[92] This law was challenged by Western Tradition Partnership, citing *Citizens United.* In December 2011, the Montana Supreme Court rendered its surprising verdict that Montana could keep its corporate ban despite *Citizens United.* This decision would later be overturned by the U.S. Supreme Court.

The Montana Supreme Court wasn't unanimous in upholding the Montana campaign finance law. Of the two dissents, Justice Nelson noted that respect for the rule of law required Montana to give up its century-old law against corruption.[93] He additionally excoriated the U.S. Supreme Court for its *Citizens*

---

90. Leo E. Strine, Jr. & Nicholas Walter, *Conservative Collision Course?: The Tension Between Conservative Corporate Law Theory and* Citizens United, 100 CORNELL L. REV. 335, 386 (2015); Leo Strine & Nicholas Walter, *Originalist or Original: The Difficulties of Reconciling* Citizens United *with Corporate Law History* (Feb. 13, 2015), http://ssrn.com/abstract=2564708.

91. Leo Strine & Nicholas Walter, *The Difficulties of Reconciling* Citizens United *with Corporate Law History,* HARV. L. SCH. FORUM ON CORP. GOV. & FIN. REG. (Feb. 27, 2015), http://corpgov.law.harvard.edu/2015/02/27/the-difficulties-of-reconciling-citizens-united-with-corporate-law-history/.

92. Mont. Code Ann. §13-35-227(1) (1912).

93. Western Tradition Partnership v. Bullock 271 P.3d 1 (Mont. 2011) (Nelson, J., dissenting) ("Whether we agree with the Supreme Court's interpretation of the First Amend-

United decision. These critiques should be considered by future Supreme Court Justices considering regulation of corporate money in politics. Justice Nelson's dissent included the following damning passages:

> the notion that corporations are disadvantaged in the political realm is unbelievable. Indeed, it has astounded most Americans. The truth is that corporations wield inordinate power in Congress and in state legislatures. It is hard to tell where government ends and corporate America begins; the transition is seamless and overlapping. In my view, *Citizens United* has turned the First Amendment's 'open marketplace' of ideas into an auction house for Friedmanian corporatists. Freedom of speech is now synonymous with freedom to spend. Speech equals money; money equals democracy. This decidedly was not the view of the constitutional founders, who favored the preeminence of individual interests over those of big business.[94]

Justice Nelson lamented, "I am deeply frustrated, as are many Americans, with the reach of *Citizens United*. The First Amendment has now been elevated to a vaunted and isolated position so as to endow corporations with extravagant rights of political speech and, with those rights, the exaggerated power to influence voters and elections."[95] Justice Nelson expressed his annoyance with the Roberts Supreme Court for its support for corporate influence in politics and its lack of concern with battling political corruption.[96]

Justice Nelson worried in particular about how *Citizens United* could ruin the integrity of judicial elections in Montana.[97] He has also predicted, "The U.S. Chamber of Commerce could easily dump millions into our judicial elections and could change the make up of the Montana Supreme Court."[98] And Justice Nelson was concerned that more generally, voters would be disempowered by

---

ment is irrelevant. In accordance with our federal system of government, our obligations here are to acknowledge that the Supreme Court's interpretation of the United States Constitution is, for better or for worse, binding on this Court and on the officers of this state....").

94. *Id.*, 271 P.3d at 34, 363 Mont. at 273 (Nelson, J., dissenting) (internal citations omitted).

95. *Id.* at 271 (Nelson, J., dissenting).

96. *Id.* at 275 (Nelson, J., dissenting) ("[i]t should be noted that Montana's Corrupt Practices Act was adopted in 1912 at a time when the country's focus was on preventing political corruption, not on protecting corporate influence. Due to intervening changes in the composition and philosophy of the Supreme Court, that focus has now flip-flopped.").

97. *Id.* at 272 (Nelson, J., dissenting).

98. Interview with Retired Montana Supreme Court Justice James Nelson (Aug. 4, 2015).

allowing corporate political spending to have free reign: "It is utter nonsense to think that ordinary citizens or candidates can spend enough to place their experience, wisdom, and views before the voters and keep pace with the virtually unlimited spending capability of corporations to place corporate views before the electorate." He proceeded, "[i]n spending ability, bigger really is better; and with campaign advertising and attack ads, quantity counts. In the end, candidates and the public will become mere bystanders in elections."[99]

Justice Nelson also critiqued the ever-expanding theory of corporate personhood in the Supreme Court's jurisprudence. He wrote that corporations are not persons, "and it is an affront to the inviolable dignity of our species that courts have created a legal fiction that forces people—human beings—to share fundamental, natural rights with soulless creations of government. Worse still, while corporations and human beings share many of the same rights under the law, they clearly are not bound equally to the same codes of good conduct, decency, and morality, and they are not held equally accountable for their sins. Indeed, it is truly ironic that the death penalty and hell are reserved only to natural persons."[100]

Part of what was remarkable about Justice Nelson's dissent is that it was written while he was still on the bench. Sitting Supreme Court Justices have also voiced their concerns about the impact of *Citizens United*. Writing a rare dissent from summary reversal in *Western Tradition Partnership* (which changed its name to *American Tradition Partnership*), Justices Ginsburg and Breyer wrote, "Montana's experience, and experience elsewhere since this Court's decision in *Citizens United* ... make it exceedingly difficult to maintain that independent expenditures by corporations 'do not give rise to corruption or the appearance of corruption.'"[101] Other sitting judges have also had to hold their noses while ruling in favor of *Citizens United*. Federal District Judge Paul Crotty, when ruling to invalidate a restriction on campaign spending by independent PACs, complained: "[o]ne thing is certain: large political donations do not inspire confidence that the government in a representative democracy will do the right thing."[102] And Judge Crotty concluded that,

---

99. Western Tradition Partnership, Inc., 271 P.3d at 35, 363 Mont. at 274 (Nelson, J., dissenting).

100. *Id.*, 271 P.3d at 36, 363 Mont. at 276 (Nelson, J., dissenting) (internal citations omitted).

101. Am. Tradition P'ship, Inc. v. Bullock, No. 11A762 (statement of Ginsburg, J. & Breyer, J.), http://big.assets.huffingtonpost.com/11A762.pdf (internal citations omitted) (Feb. 17, 2012).

102. New York Progress & Protection PAC v. Walsh, 13 Civ. 6769 (PAC) (Apr. 24, 2014) (Crotty, J.), http://sdnyblog.com/wp-content/uploads/2014/04/13-Civ.-06769-2014.04.24-Opinion.pdf.

the voices of 'we the people' are too often drowned out by the few who have great resources. And when the fundraising cycle slows (it never stops), lobbyists take over in a continuing attempt to gain influence over and access to elected officials. This is not a left or right, liberal or conservative analysis, but all the points on the political spectrum are increasingly involved in shaping this country's political agenda. In today's never ending cycle of campaigning and lobbying; lobbying and campaigning, elected officials know where their money is coming from and that it must keep coming if they are to stay in office. Ordinary citizens recognize this; they know what is going on; they know they are not being included. It breeds cynicism and distrust.[103]

But because so many of the cases discussed in this book have been Supreme Court cases, only the Supreme Court itself, or a constitutional amendment, can undo the trends of granting corporations more citizenship rights and fewer responsibilities. Unless there is some unforeseen crisis at the Court, the current justices are unlikely to reverse course. The vacancy left by the death of Justice Scalia is pregnant with the possibility of change. Much depends on who fills this vacancy. As many of the Justices are age 78 or older,[104] the personalities on the Supreme Court are likely to change during the next administration.

2. The Comity Clause and Other Textual Pegs

With a new Supreme Court there is a new opportunity to rethink the scope of rights and responsibilities that should attach to corporations. And an interesting place for a new Court to start is to rediscover the Supreme Court's own jurisprudence on the Comity Clause, which has always treated corporations and human beings as being utterly distinct (as discussed in Chapter 2). As a reminder, the Court has held repeatedly, as it did in *Grosjean*: "[a] corporation, we have held, is not a 'citizen' within the meaning of the privileges and immunities clause."[105] Applying the logic of these Comity Clause cases would be a good place to start to bring back a sense of proportion to corpo-

---

103. *Id.*

104. Terence P. Jeffrey, *75: Average Age of Current Justices Before Next Presidential Term Ends*, CNS News (June 17, 2015), http://cnsnews.com/commentary/terence-p-jeffrey/75-average-age-current-justices-next-presidential-term-ends.

105. Grosjean v. American Press Co., 297 U.S. 233, 244 (1936) (citing Covington & L. Turnpike Road Co. v. Sandford, 164 U.S. 578, 592, 17 S. Ct. 198, 41 L. Ed. 560; Smyth v. Ames, 169 U.S. 466, 522, 18 S. Ct. 418, 42 L. Ed. 819)).

rate rights. If a new Supreme Court reconsiders the approach in the Comity Clause cases, they may reach a different conclusion than the ones they reached in *Citizens United* and *Hobby Lobby*. There may be fertile ground for other approaches as well. Justice Nelson suggested perhaps the Guarantee Clause,[106] which ensures a republican form of government, may prove a more fruitful ground for a justification for regulating money in politics, instead of the current approach which narrowly focuses solely on fighting corruption.[107] Another starting point for a refreshed jurisprudence would be deeper consideration of electoral integrity as a compelling state interest, a viewpoint offered by Justice Stephen Breyer:

> To focus upon the First Amendment's relation to the Constitution's democratic objective is helpful because the campaign laws seek to further a similar objective. They seek to democratize the influence that money can bring to bear upon the electoral process, thereby building public confidence in that process, broadening the base of a candidate's meaningful financial support, and encouraging greater public participation. Ultimately, they seek thereby to maintain the integrity of the political process ...[108]

The Supreme Court could also clarify that a lower level of scrutiny is appropriate in the context of the regulation of corporate commercial speech. Finally, the Supreme Court needs to reconsider the jurisdictional limits on holding corporate actors accountable for human rights violations if they conduct significant business in the United States.

D. A Constitutional Amendment

Because Citizens United was decided on constitutional grounds (not statutory grounds), this means there are only two ways to get rid of it. Either the Supreme Court itself can overrule the decision in a later case or the people must amend the Constitution to negate the case using the process provided in

---

106. U.S. Const. Art. IV, Section 4.

107. Nelson interview *supra* note 98 ("The Supreme Court almost interpreted the First Amendment as being absolute. It is not absolute. No constitutional right is absolute. They could have balanced it against the right to vote, which is a fundamental right. They could have balanced it against the obligation that states have to guarantee free and fair and open elections.").

108. STEPHEN BREYER, ACTIVE LIBERTY INTERPRETING OUR DEMOCRATIC CONSTITUTION 47 (2005).

Article V of the U.S. Constitution. Addressing the limits of the logic of *Citizens United*, Second Circuit Judge Calabresi, the former Dean of Yale Law School, anticipating that *Citizens United* might be overturned, wrote:

> The ability to express one's feelings with all the intensity that one has—and to be heard—is a central element of the right to speak freely. It is, I believe, something that is so fundamental that sooner or later it is going to be recognized. Whether this will happen through a constitutional amendment or through changes in Supreme Court doctrine, I do not know. But it will happen.[109]

Six years have passed and the slim 5–4 majority that decided *Citizens United* has shown no appetite to reverse it.[110] The late Justice Scalia was part of that five person majority. If he is replaced by a more progressive jurist, the majority could shift on campaign finance cases.

In his book Six Amendments, retired Justice John Paul Stevens argues that the Constitution should be amended to undo *Citizens United* because "it is unwise to allow persons who are not qualified to vote—whether they be corporations or nonresident individuals—to have a potentially greater power to affect the outcome of elections than eligible voters have."[111] In 2015, a *Bloomberg Politics* national poll showed that 78 percent of those polled believed *Citizens United* should be overturned.[112] So far, 16 states have voted in favor of resolutions calling for an amendment. In Montana, the vote in favor of a constitutional amendment was 75 percent to 25 percent.[113] And the vote was nearly identical and lopsided in Colorado.[114]

---

109. Ognibene v. Parkes, 671 F. 3d 174, 201 (2d Cir. 2011) (Calabresi, J., concurring).

110. Interview with Warren Langley, Former President of the Pacific Stock Exchange (July 14, 2015) ("I think the only way reverse *Citizens United* is a constitutional amendment because it is rare for the Supreme Court to change its mind.").

111. John Paul Stevens, Six Amendments How and Why We Should Change the Constitution 59 (2014).

112. Greg Stohr, *Bloomberg Poll: Americans Want Supreme Court to Turn Off Political Spending Spigot*, Bloomberg (Sept. 28, 2015), http://www.bloomberg.com/politics/articles/2015-09-28/bloomberg-poll-americans-want-supreme-court-to-turn-off-political-spending-spigot.

113. Montana Corporate Contributions Initiative, I-166 (2012), http://ballotpedia.org/Montana_Corporate_Contributions_Initiative,_I-166_(2012).

114. *Money, Elections and Citizens United: Campaign Finance Reform For Colorado*, U. Denver Strategic Issues Panel on Campaign Finance 14 (2013), http://www.du.edu/issues/media/documents/CampaignFinanceReportFinal.pdf ("In 2012, voters overwhelmingly approved Amendment 65, which asked Colorado's federal legislative delegation to support an amendment to the U.S. Constitution ... the fact that Amendment 65 garnered

Several bills have been introduced in Congress to reverse *Citizens United* including Sen. Tom Udall's S.J. Res. 19 to amend the Constitution to allow Congress and the 50 states to limit contributions and expenditures. A constitutional amendment to address *Citizens United* would conform with previous pro-democratic amendments to the Constitution. As Yale Professor John Hart Ely once explained, "[e]xtension of the franchise to groups previously excluded has therefore been the dominant theme of our constitutional development since the Fourteenth Amendment[.]"[115]

E. Conclusions

The English word democracy comes from the Greek word *demokratia*. Its roots are *demos* "common people" and *kratos* "rule." Accordingly, democracy at its most basic and fundamental level, must mean rule by actual people.[116] But just because corporations shouldn't be granted citizenship rights, doesn't mean they cannot, in the language of corporate social responsibility, [117] be better and more responsible citizens. They can improve their relationship with human rights and the environment.[118] As this book has demonstrated, these two objectives often go together, hand in glove.[119]

History also shows that size matters. We've gone from "too big to fail" to "too big to jail" to "too big to for general jurisdiction." We cannot reach the point where there are firms that are "too big to regulate." And gigantism matters a great deal if real citizens are expected to compete with corporations for the attention of elected officials in policy making, or for the attention of their

---

support from nearly three-fourths of those voting shows a high level of interest in the topic among Colorado citizens.").

115. John Hart Ely, Democracy and Distrust: A Theory of Judicial Review 99 (1980).

116. Interview with Ben Cohen, CEO, Ben & Jerry's (Nov. 4, 2015) ("[e]veryone except the Supreme Court understands that a person is a living breathing being and a corporation is just a legal fiction.").

117. Interview with Phil Radford, Former Executive Director of Greenpeace (Aug. 5, 2015) ("[t]o be a good corporate citizen, ... really look at the triple bottom line where you evaluate yourself on profit, your impact on your community, and the environment.").

118. Minow interview *supra* note 3 ("Companies that are acting like ostriches on the environment are not good long term investments.").

119. Schwarz interview *supra* note 14 ("a good corporate citizen ought to have a culture not just of focusing on short term earnings. Rather they should look at long term value. They need to increase their conception of duties owed to people and the environment.").

fellow citizens during elections.[120] Protecting the ideal of one-person-one-vote requires mitigating the power of big money in politics.

There is still hope that we are not so far gone that we cannot restore real citizens back to their proper place at the center of American democracy. Most of the mistakes that have been made to get us here have been legal mistakes made by just a few wrong-headed jurists. These mistakes now have powerful constituencies to defend them, but there are also powerful forces resisting the slide toward too much power pooling in too few hands.

120. *Liggett*, 288 U.S. at 564-65 (Brandeis, J., dissenting in part).

Index